MW00744615

Creative
Teaching in
Health

DONALD A. READ ■ WALTER H. GREENE

WORCESTER STATE COLLEGE   TEMPLE UNIVERSITY

Creative Teaching in Health

SECOND EDITION

Macmillan Publishing Co., Inc.
NEW YORK

Collier Macmillan Publishers
LONDON

Copyright © 1975, Macmillan Publishing Co., Inc.

Printed in the United States of America

All rights reserved. No part of this book may be reproduced or transmitted in any form or by any means, electronic or mechanical, including photocopying, recording, or any information storage and retrieval system, without permission in writing from the Publisher.

Earlier edition copyright © 1971 by Macmillan Publishing Co., Inc.

Macmillan Publishing Co., Inc.
866 Third Avenue, New York, New York 10022

Collier-Macmillan Canada, Ltd.

Library of Congress Cataloging in Publication Data

Read, Donald A.
  Creative teaching in health.

  Bibliography: p.
  1. Health education. I. Greene, Walter H., joint author. II. Title. [DNLM: 1. Health education. 2. Teaching. QT200 R282c]
RA440.R4   1975   613'.07   73-20873
ISBN 0-02-398710-3

Printing: 3 4 5 6 7 8   Year: 6 7 8 9 0

Preface

This second edition of *Creative Teaching in Health* represents a considerable amount of thinking and rethinking, brainstorming, and examination of the changes taking place in the field of education, together with the critically constructive comments of fellow colleagues. Also represented in this edition are the comments of very special students in regard to specific aspects of the first edition. In short, much has transpired during the past few years, and this edition seeks to reflect the more useful and enduring changes while at the same time minimizing the change-for-change-sake philosophy that seems so prevalent in today's world.

Within the field of health education, as in other subject areas, there is a growing realization that if teachers are to effectively reach young people they must be something more than knowledgeable professionals with a sense of organization and list of behavioral objectives. On every teaching staff, whether it be the elementary, secondary, or college campus, one is able to find those special individuals who seem to have a knack for making the most of the available material and human resources. When these teachers enter a classroom, one can almost "feel" the excitement. The classroom literally comes alive. For the authors, a certain amount of "creativity" and "humanism" are the most important ingredients responsible for this "aliveness." And, because of the popularity and importance of this nebulous concept, we felt very strongly that there was a need for a book on creative teaching as it applies to health education.

When we selected creativity as a point of reference for an examination of the teaching process, we found that simplified views no longer applied. Teaching becomes a highly complex task involving an interaction of content, technique, learner, teacher, and environment, each of which possesses qualities that are constantly changing and rechanging. These factors render every situation unique to some degree; the teaching process thus becomes a kaleidoscope of changing patterns rather than a fixed set of rules, and creativity becomes essential to good performance. The purpose of this book, as we see it, is to stimulate the thinking of both present and/or future health teachers on the role of the creative element in effective teaching. It is hoped that this book will contribute to the development of the new and vital approach in health education that seems to be slowly emerging. To this end we have sought to provide the stimulus for developing creative and ever exciting ways of teaching.

If it can be said that this book has one central focus, it is the role and responsibilities of the classroom teacher as a major force in the creative teaching-learning environment. The emphasis is on creativity as it relates to such things as gaining insights into the needs and interests of students, the self-that-relates-to-others, use of behavioral objectives, creative use of the teaching-learning environment, the development of teaching techniques, and the evaluation of instructional outcomes. Important features include the application of the taxonomies of both the cognitive and affective domains in the construction of objectives and the presentation of suggested concepts for use within the more critical areas of the health education curriculum. This is perhaps the first time the affective domain is discussed with any degree of thoroughness in a text of this type.

In the organization of this volume we have sought to provide a framework for the logical examination of new ideas and developments in health education. Part I examines the status of and trends in health education today and includes a discussion of some of the basic prerequisites for effective teaching. The teacher's major duties and responsibilities in setting the stage for teaching are examined in Part II. Part III discusses the nature and the potentiality of creativity in the classroom. A new chapter focusing on the affect (feeling) in the classroom has been added to this section. Part IV provides examples of creative teaching as applied to certain priority topics at the elementary/secondary levels. It should be noted here that we draw no strong distinctions between elementary and secondary teaching. This is because we believe that health education should be geared to the student, not the class level. Second, it should be viewed as a free-flowing, ongoing process, maturing with the student. Part V explores the possibilities of creative evaluation and the teacher's continuing growth.

Creative Teaching in Health includes a good deal of background information on crucial health problems and provides curriculum recommendations in the form of priority concepts. However, these are included to stimulate the reader's critical processes, rather than to provide a curriculum model. Final decisions on matters of curriculum emphasis, contents, and so forth can utimately only be made on the basis of one's own unique teaching-learning situation. This well-accepted principle, although presented repeatedly throughout this text, merits additional emphasis here. Once the basic curriculum decisions have been made, the teacher faces the challenging task of selecting specific facts, examples, materials, and techniques in the proper combination to reach a specific group of students. At this point the element of creativity is essential to quality teaching; this is the element we hope to develop.

D. A. R.
Amherst, Massachusetts

W. H. G.
Hatboro, Pennsylvania

Contents

PART **III** Creativity in the Classroom

Creative
Teaching in
Health

PART

Gaining Insights

A man's mind, stretched by a new idea, can
never go back to its original dimension.

OLIVER WENDELL HOLMES

1 ■ NEW IDEAS AND SUGGESTED TRENDS IN HEALTH EDUCATION

It is not enough today to consider the student as a human vacuum into which a teacher can pour all the accumulated wisdom of good health. For one, the practice of merely teaching unrelated facts of doubtful relevance is receiving severe criticism today. Essential background must not be omitted, of course, but its purpose should be considered carefully so that the information being dealt with in the classroom is of concern *to the student*. When the curriculum is unrelated to student concerns, it becomes what Mario Fantini and Gerald Weinstein, in *The Disadvantaged*, call "the irrelevant curriculum." [1]

A second consideration must be given to the students themselves. Mere translation of knowledge by an adult does not necessarily make him an adequate teacher in the eyes of his pupils. The students have been raised in a society that considers them free individuals, and teachers whose presentations are dry will soon realize that their students are obviously bored, restless, or absent frequently.

Two of the primary responsibilities of the health educator are to reach the level of self-awareness in the student and to penetrate beneath the surface of the student, to where he "lives," thus allowing him to become a more *active participant* in his own education. To ensure that this participation becomes an ongoing, worthwhile process that is capable of change and adaptation, the health teacher must not only consider the needs and interests of the students while they are in school, but he must also help to prepare them to be capable of identifying and satisfying those needs that may arise in the future. In addition the health teacher should

---

[1] Mario D. Fantini and Gerald Weinstein, *The Disadvantaged: Challenge to Education* (New York: Harper & Row, 1968).

3

be prepared to guide the student to concentrate on his own sense of the disparity between what he is learning in school, what he values in his own life, and how he acts.

The health teacher should also recognize that good health may mean different things to different people. The student, the parent, the office worker, the man in the ghetto, the man living in a rural setting—all have diverse ways of life that may require varying ways of dealing with their health. Health teachers can no longer afford to ignore these basic differences. Health education, if it is to be truly effective, *must be considered in terms of the individual*. As Borton states in the preface to his book *Reach, Touch and Teach*, "I believe that what a student learns in school, and what he eventually becomes are significantly influenced by how he feels about himself and the world outside." [2]

WHAT IS HEALTH?

Until fairly recently, health was defined negatively as the absence of disease: as long as an individual was not sick (or disabled) he was thought to be healthy. Health is now coming into being as an entity in its own right, rather than as the absence of the more easily definable entity of disease.

In 1947 the World Health Organization defined health as "a state of complete physical, mental and social well being and not merely the absence of disease or infirmity"; [3] it further stated that "the enjoyment of the highest attainable standard of health is one of the fundamental rights of every human being without distinction of race, religion, political beliefs, or economic or social condition." [4]

The emphasis has been reversed, and illness is now the absence of health. But still, the question remains, "What is health?" As a state of complete physical well-being, it is fairly easy to define and understand. However, once health is moved into the realm of mental and social well-being, its determinants are no longer as easily distinguishable or self-contained. Assessing and defining the health status of the individual become infinitely more complex as man is viewed in terms of his entire environmental milieu. We can no longer look at the individual alone and assess his health status or health problems with any great degree of accuracy. In an attempt to deal with the many facets of the health-illness continuum, we can view health as a process or consequence of behavior rather than as a fixed attribute of an individual: [5] it is the ability of an individual to interact effectively—physically, psychologically, and socially

[2] Terry Borton, *Reach, Touch and Teach* (New York: McGraw-Hill, 1970).

[3] "Constitution of the World Health Organization," *Chronicle of the WHO*, 1947, p. 3.

[4] Ibid.

[5] Robert N. Wilson, *The Sociology of Health* (New York: Random House, 1970), p. 8.

—with other individuals, groups, society, and with the environment in which that individual and society function. Dunn defines optimal health, or "high-level wellness," as "an integrated method of functioning which is oriented toward maximizing the potential of which the individual is capable. It requires that the individual maintain a continuum of balance and purposeful direction within the environment where he is functioning." [6] Thus health is not a fixed status or level, but rather a direction in progress toward an ever higher potential of functioning. Health is wholeness, unfolding;[7] it is fitness for survival and self-renewal, creative adjustment and fulfillment.[8]

If the health of the individual is determined to a great extent by the total environment in which he functions, then individual and community health are mutually dependent and one may not be assessed at the exclusion of the other. If health is to be considered in its broadest sense, it must be considered within the framework of all the external forces that affect man and his way of life. "Only in the thorough embeddedness of man-in-community, the human population moving through family, school, work, and neighborhood can such exploration (of the multicausal nature of illness) be carried out." [9]

WHAT IS HEALTH EDUCATION?

The second use of the word considers health as a subject that may be pursued and taught, in contrast to a general state of well-being of mind and body. Students attend health education classes in order to learn various concepts of a healthy state of being. In this sense, the term *health education* is more common than *health*; it is defined as "the process of providing or utilizing experiences for favorably influencing understandings, attitudes, and practices relating to individual, family, and community health." [10]

Various health and educational groups have adopted resolutions or have issued statements concerning health education in the schools. Two of the more noteworthy groups, the American Medical Association and the National Education Association, have made very positive statements concerning the need for health education. In June of 1960 the House of Delegates of the American Medical Association adopted a resolution supporting school and college health instruction. It was as follows:

[6] Halbert Dunn, *High-Level Wellness* (Arlington, Va.: R. W. Bearry, Ltd., 1961), pp. 4–5.

[7] Nancy Milio, 9226 *Kercheval Street: The Storefront That Did Not Burn* (Ann Arbor: University of Michigan Press, 1970), Prologue.

[8] H. S. Hoyman, "An Editorial: Health and a Living Faith," *Journal of School Health*, Vol. XI (June 1970), p. 279.

[9] Wilson, op. cit., p. 58.

[10] Joint Committee on Health Education Terminology, "Health Education Terminology," *Journal of Health, Physical Education and Recreation*, Vol. 33, No. 28 (November 1962).

Resolved, that the American Medical Association reaffirm its long standing and fundamental belief that health education should be an integral and basic part of school and college curriculums and that state and local medical societies be encouraged to work with the appropriate health and education officials and agencies in their communities to achieve this end.

The National Education Association in its project for instruction, *Schools for the 60's*, stated in 1963,

The content of health instruction belongs in the school curriculum because such knowledge is necessary, is most efficiently learned in schools, and no other public agency provides such instruction.

These two organizations have also prepared a statement that defines what health education is and is not. This statement focuses essentially on health education as an academic field and subject.

HEALTH EDUCATION IS:

education for health; education for healthful living of the individual, family, and community.

an academic field and subject. All of its content and objectives are intellectual and academic in nature. Its content must have meaning and purpose to the students now as well as in the future.

a relatively new discipline. The natural (biological), the behavioral, and the health sciences provide its foundation.

a combination of facts, principles, and concepts pertaining to healthful living. These constitute its body of knowledge.

a body of knowledge identified, organized, synthesized, and utilized in appropriate courses and experiences and sequentially arranged to form the discipline.

derived from sociology, psychology, educational psychology, and the behavioral sciences—its purpose is to change health behavior favorably.

HEALTH EDUCATION IS NOT:

hygiene of yesteryear. It is not "blood and bone" hygiene, nor is it physiological hygiene.

anatomy or physiology or both of these combined. These fields serve as its foundation, but do not contribute the major concepts of its body of knowledge. They are necessary as background to understand health concepts applied to living.

a pure science, but an applied science. It is an applied science concerned with man's understanding of himself in relation to health matters in a changing society.

physical education. Health education and physical education are separate and distinct fields. They have similar goals and are closely related, but their activities are completely different.

physical fitness. It contributes to the total fitness of man. It is not synonymous with muscle fitness.

driver education. Health education is related to driver education through its safety area.

HEALTH EDUCATION IS:

a needed approach to bridge the gap between scientific health discoveries and man's application of these discoveries in daily life.

an integral part of the curriculum at every level. It is an essential element in the general education of all students.

the education component of a school, college, or university health program.

a contribution to the well-educated individual by providing meaningful health experiences which can change health behavior.

best achieved by developing the rational powers of man (critical thinking). This enables him to make wise decisions and solve personal, family, and community health problems.

based upon and improved by basic and applied research.

best conducted by professionally prepared health educators from accredited colleges and universities.

HEALTH EDUCATION IS NOT:

a requirement course organized to deal with legal provisions of alcohol, narcotics, and fire prevention. These are essential problems that should be incorporated with other basic problems to provide a structure course or program.

rainy-day or incidental instruction. Health education must be carefully planned and incorporated in the curriculum. It must be taught in a wholesome learning environment in which pupil activities can be carried out, particularly through problem-solving situations, under the guidance of professionally prepared health educators.

only instruction on grooming practices, such as tooth brushing and combing the hair.[11]

Other authoritative groups—such as the American Association of Health, Physical Education and Recreation; the American Dental Association; American School Health Association; American Public Health Association; and the American College Health Association—have adopted strong resolutions calling for a strengthening of health instruction in schools and colleges across the nation.

A NEED FOR IMPROVEMENT

It goes without saying that the health profession has come a long way from the days when Horace Mann, in 1842, urged educators to include health

[11]Joint Committee on Health Problems in Education of the National Education Association and the American Medical Association, *Why Health Education?* (Washington D.C.: The Associations, 1965), pp. 1–2.

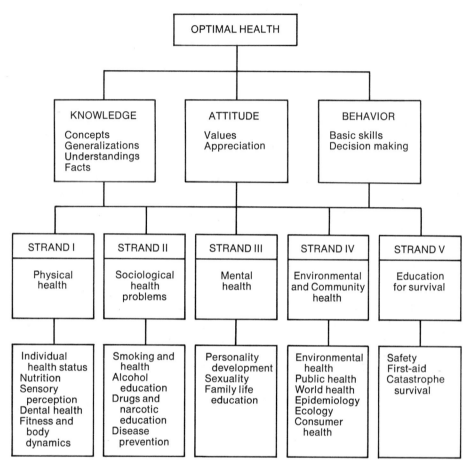

Figure 1–1. *Outline of New York State school health education program.* Source: *Pearl E. Britton and John Sinacore, "Critical Health Problems Legislation,"* Journal of Health, Physical Education and Recreation *(March 1968), p. 12. Reprinted by permission of the Joint Committee on Health Problems in Education of the National Education Association and the American Medical Association, Washington, D.C., and Chicago.*

teaching in the public schools. But there is no doubt that still more improvement is needed in school health instruction on a broad scale.

A nationwide examination by the School Health Education Study Advisory Committee of large, medium, and small school districts in the United States revealed some glaring weaknesses in health education.[13] The study focused on where health education is taught, how it is organized, and who teaches it. Some of the problems that were found to exist were the following:

[13] School Health Education Study Advisory Committee, *Health Education: A Conceptual Approach to Curriculum Design* (St. Paul, Minn.: 3M Education Press, 1967).

1. An unawareness on the part of the general public of the important role of the school in the development of proper health attitudes and skills.
2. Lack of effective communication between schools and medical organizations.
3. Poor and inadequate preparation of teachers in health education.
4. A lack of sincere interest by administrators and curriculum supervisors of the need for health instruction and/or a tendency to regard health education and physical education as one and the same.
5. Little or no working relationship between public and related health agencies and school health personnel.
6. A tendency for people responsible for curriculum planning to give health education low priority.

Along with these findings, the School Health Education Study Advisory Committee found that the content area of the curriculum was repetitious and that specific areas such as venereal disease, consumer awareness, and sex education were completely neglected in the health classes across the nation.

Roger F. Aubrey, in an article entitled "Health Education: Neglected Child of the Schools," stated that, with few exceptions, health education in the public schools had both low status and esteem in the eyes of most teachers, students, and administrators. Some of the factors that he felt led to the lack of success include:

1. *Inadequate training of teachers during college preparation*
   A. Failure of colleges to stress importance and worth of this area.
   B. Failure of colleges to introduce future teachers to useful materials, units, lessons, and concepts.
   C. Failure of colleges to train teachers in principles of group dynamics, attitude formation and value clarification.

2. *Lack of enforcement of mandatory state regulations concerning the teaching of health*
   A. Lack of funds and personnel to visit and monitor separate school districts.
   B. Inadequate numbers of state department of education personnel to train teachers and supply materials to individual districts and schools.
   C. Antiquated and unrealistic expectations of state legislators and state department of education officials.
   D. Low priority of health education among school administrators, the general public, and state officials.
   E. Lack of local, state, and federal monies for staff and materials.

3. *Resistance and apathy of teachers*
   A. Demands of other disciplines preempt the time and energy of teachers for health.

B. Lack of central coordination forces teachers to seek out their own programs and materials and reduces incentive by failing to have a central person to reward and encourage them.

C. Health is not a high priority item because in colleges and in public schools, professors and school administrators fail to place a premium on this area.

D. In health areas of sex, drugs, mental health, and so on, the teacher is usually ill at ease and unprepared to deal with the emotions, feelings, attitudes, and values of students.

E. Little real attempt has been made at integrating health with other disciplines, therefore forcing teachers to teach health separately and isolated from the security and interest of other disciplines.

4. *Indifference and low priority of health among school administrators*

A. No *enforced* state regulations in this area.

B. Lack of state or federal funding for this discipline.

C. Lack of staff interest and enthusiasm.

D. Difficulty in adjusting master schedule to arrange for course scheduling.

E. Fear of parental response in areas of sex, drugs, and so on.

F. Few outside pressure groups demanding the inclusion of a total health program.

5. *Difficulties in building student interest and involvement*

A. Poorly prepared materials, units, and lessons.

B. Inappropriate programs and techniques.

C. Lack of relatedness to one's own life situation and encounters.

D. Lack of teacher training, experience, and enthusiam for health.

E. Classes too large and inadequately matched for in-depth exploration of certain topics.

F. Too great an emphasis on content and not enough on process.

G. Too many "one-shot" approaches with a lack of follow-up and assessment.

6. *Parental resistance and indifference*

A. Parents' own school experiences in areas of health unsatisfactory and unrewarding.

B. Fear of many parents of evoking premature curiosity of students in such areas as sex and drugs.

C. Desire of many parents to handle certain areas in home training of their children.

D. Lack of interest and awareness of parents in many vital areas of health.

E. Failure of school to inform and reach out to parents with new and continuing health programs.

F. Failure of school to train and utilize parents and community figures in health programs.[14]

[14] Roger F. Aubrey, "Health Education: Neglected Child of the Schools," *The Journal of School Health* (May 1972), pp. 285–288.

It is heartening to note that the author of the above-mentioned article also spent the time to present suggestions for changes in present practices. These included the transfer of health education from the department of physical education to a dual program embracing guidance and health education, use of the various principles of group dynamics in school health classes, inclusion of parents in planning and implementing health programs, concentration of health programs at selected grade levels, and use of community resources in school health programs.

THE ELEMENTARY TEACHER AS HEALTH EDUCATOR

One of the primary figures in health instruction is the elementary teacher, yet those preparing for this profession receive little, if any, actual health education training. In most cases elementary education majors receive most of their training in the area of methods and materials, with a little health added.

This unfortunate lack of training for prospective elementary teachers prompted the American Association of Health, Physical Education and Recreation to form a committee to focus on the need for improvements in an elementary program of health education. Three noteworthy statements by the committee that have relevance to the discussion here are given.

1. There is a need for more and better (high quality) preparation in health education for prospective elementary school teachers. Too many teacher education programs provide, at best, minimal experiences in health education, so that teachers frequently do not understand or appreciate the relationship between well-being and the teaching-learning process.
2. Public and private colleges and universities with teacher preparation programs should establish reasonable requirements in the area of health concept or health-related knowledge courses for all elementary school teacher candidates.
3. . . . . Administrative support of health instruction programs needs to be encouraged. Teacher preparation courses in health education especially should gear efforts to students as potential administrators/ teachers. Tomorrow's teachers are the administrators of the more distant future, whose support should be cultivated *while they are undergraduates*. Greater support from today's administrators, too, ought to be sought. School boards of education also have to be told and sold the need for health education by America's children to help ensure the well-being of our country.[15]

The great knowledge explosion of the last ten years creates a greater need for teachers who have a commitment to the field of health education.

[15] Evelyn G. Clark et al., "Needed Improvements in Elementary School Health Education Programs," *Journal of Health, Physical Education and Recreation* (February 1967), p. 28.

The profession can no longer merely get by with part-time teachers, resource people, and hand-out material. The struggle to keep abreast of health information even within the profession will require very soon a complete redefinition of the subject matter. Even trained health teachers are finding it more and more difficult to teach health education as an isolated subject. It is obvious that a program of continuous education from kindergarten to twelfth grade will be essential if those interested and involved hope to do the job.

Part of what *is* necessary can be found in the recommendations made by Jessie Helen Haag after she had reviewed the teacher certification requirements for secondary school teachers in the fifty states and the District of Columbia. Her reasons for the choices of the content areas, semester hours, and description of content are given in her article.

I. Provisional certificate
   Academic major—health education.
   An approved program of health education offered in an accredited college or university.
   Three semester hours of methods in health education as a part of the professional or teacher education requirements.
   Six semester hours of student teaching in health education as a part of the professional or teacher education requirements and under the supervision of professors of health education with an academic major in health education and with public school teaching experiences in health education as their major assignment.
   Twenty-four semester hours in an academic *minor*, preferably biology with major emphasis upon human anatomy and physiology.
   Twenty-four semester hours in an academic *minor*, preferably education in Departments of Health and Safety Education, Health Education, Health and Physical Education, or Physical Education. Program consultant is a professor of health education with an academic major in health education and public school teaching experiences in health education as his major assignment.
   (*Omission* of courses in driver education and physical education such as adapted or corrective physical education, kinesiology, physiology of exercise, applied anatomy, athletic training, tests and measurements in health and physical education, organization and administration of health and physical education, school programs in health and physical education, and history and philosophy of health and physical education.)

   Content in Academic Major:

   1. *Current Health Problems* including mental health; skin infections; dental health; eye injuries, defects, and infections; posture; alcoholism; narcotic addiction; misuse of drugs; smoking; health condi-

tions with no known cause and/or treatment such as diabetes; wise consumer of health products and services; quackery.

2. *School Health Program.*

3. *American Red Cross First Aid* and *Medical Self-help.*

4. *Safety Education* including occupational, home, and recreational safety; and man-made and natural disasters.

5. *Community Health* including water purification and pollution, water-borne diseases, sewage treatment and diseases resulting from inadequate sewage disposal, vector control, rabies and rodent-borne diseases, food-meat-milk inspection, air pollution, radiation control, sanitation in food establishments, refuse disposal, and the agencies promoting community health; United States Public Health Service, state and local health departments, and numerous non-official health agencies.

6. *Nutrition in Health Education* including the science of nutrition, wise selection and use of foods, obesity, weight control, food faddism, food fallacies, and controversial nutrition topics.

7. *Disease Prevention* including the causative agent of each disease, occurrence, reservoir and source of infection, methods of transmission of the causative agent, incubation period, period of communicability, susceptibility, and many methods of control of the sixty most common diseases occurring to man.

8. *Family Life Education* including problems associated with the secondary school student's sex adjustment during his growth and development. Problems range from simple matters of personal health to the complicated physical, social, psychological and moral factors promoting a successful marriage and family relations.

II. Professional certificate (teacher of health education in secondary schools with provisional certificate and at least three years of teaching experiences, graduate student in health education with teaching experiences in health education, and a 5th-year prepared teacher with appropriate teaching experiences.)

Academic major—health education.

An approved program of graduate study in health education offered in an accredited college or university.

Of the thirty-six semester hours, twenty-four semester hours of graduate study in health education in Departments of Health and Safety Education, Health Education, Health and Physical Education, or Physical Education. Program consultant is a professor of health education with an academic major in health education and public school teaching experiences in health education as his major assignment.

Content in Academic Major:

Twenty-four semester hours of graduate study in health education. Nine semester hours from

Consumer Health including consumer protection agencies, health misconceptions, health insurance plans, and health careers.

Mental Health.

Misuse of Alcohol, Tobacco, Narcotics, and other Stimulants, and *Depressants.*

Supervision of Health Education.

Three semester hours from *Safety Education, Family Life Education,* or *Community Health.*

Three semester hours from *International Health, Adult Health Problems,* or *Disease Prevention.*

Three semester hours in *Research in Health Education.*

Six semester hours in a *thesis* or *project* in health *education.* Project must be acceptable to the Graduate School.[16]

THE ROLE OF THE SCHOOL NURSE

Unlike the band-aid image of the past, the school nurse today has wide-ranging responsibilities. Dorothy Tipple, in her speech "Overview of School Nursing Today," described representative school nurse responsibilities as follows:

1. To conduct periodic examinations and screening procedures to determine health status of students, with these, plan to constitute an integral part of the curriculum in health education.
2. Counseling with students and parents to interpret health problems, to assist parents in utilizing professional resources, and to interpret professional recommendations.
3. To confer with teachers and other school personnel to share and interpret students' health problems and to develop plans for modification of the program.
4. To assist teachers in planning, coordinating and evaluating health education activities, serving as a consultant in health instruction, evaluating health instruction materials.
5. Assist in planning and maintaining a safe and healthful school environment including the establishing and implementation of emergency care procedures.
6. Conferring with representatives of community agencies in matters pertaining to family and community health.
7. Providing in-service health education for teachers and other school staff.
8. Evaluating the outcomes of the school health programs.[17]

[16] Jessie Helen Haag, "Certification Requirements for the Teacher of Health Education in the Secondary Schools," *Journal of School Health,* September 1968, pp. 439–441.

[17] "New Dimensions in School Nursing Leadership." *Proceedings of the Conference on New Dimensions in School Nursing Leadership.* Sponsored by the National Council for School Nurses, School Health Division of the American Association of Health, Physical Education and Recreation, August 3–5, 1968, NEA Center, Washington, D.C., 1969.

RECENT TRENDS

A lot has been happening since the first edition of this book was published. Such things as implementation of new and exciting programs, both at the local and state levels, improvement of and broadening of topics being taught in health education, and the implementation of competency-based programs and discussion of accountability in school health—all indicate a new push for more and better health education programs. In the classroom and in various articles in professional journals one is seeing terms like "values clarification," "humanistic education," "affective education," "behavior modification," "sensitivity" and "dealing with feelings."

Although it is impossible to view, in depth, all of these new innovative programs and teaching strategies, we can touch on some—as reported on by Richard K. Means—so that we can get a feel for what is happening.

What some cities are doing. A number of cities and local school districts have initiated innovative programs in health education, many stimulated by the nationwide School Health Education Study. The following should help to illustrate the diversity and progress of some selected programs.

Ellensberg, Washington, aided by a federal grant, implemented a K–12 Health curriculum.

Kansas City, Kansas, Springfield, Oregon, and San Mateo County, California, are conducting health and family life pilot programs.

North St. Paul, Minnesota, without federal funds, is nevertheless introducing health education courses at certain grade levels.

Verona, New Jersey, population 13,000, which ran a pilot program last year, has now instigated a K–12 family life program.

In 1966 the San Francisco Unified School District decided to develop a curriculum of family life education to meet the growing needs for such instruction in its elementary and secondary schools. At the same time, a revision of the course of study in Health Education was undertaken, the intent being to combine the two overlapping fields under the title health and family life education . . . some 600 teachers and public health staff people attended in-service training courses and worked on curriculum committees.

School officials in Atlanta, Georgia, have launched a program to strengthen their high school health education curriculum by taking students into local hospitals where first-hand experiences with health problems personalize the theoretical knowledge acquired in the classroom.

In New Brunswick, New Jersey, school and city health officials, local medical groups, and representatives from two area colleges organized a learning center which serves to pump new ideas into the local schools' health education programs.

Five unified school districts in Los Angeles County are cooperating in a program to upgrade instruction in disease prevention, stimulants and depressants, nutrition, consumer health, safety and first aid, environmental health, mental and social health, growth and development, sex education and family life education for grades K–12.

In Highland Park, Illinois, health and sex education are available to the whole community. Modern programs of instruction in these subjects, including in-service training for teachers, have been initiated in the local grade and high schools and community health and civic organizations have combined to provide similar classes for adults.

These are but a few concrete examples of the many recent programs initiated to improve health instruction in schools at the local level. A number of other communities have instigated similar programs.

What's happening at the state level? Significant developments aimed at the improvement of health education likewise have taken place at the state level. The following are but several illustrations.

Recently, the Connecticut State Department of Education, eager to prepare guidelines and extend other forms of assistance to help local school districts strengthen their health education curriculums, conducted a survey of 5,000 elementary and secondary school students to determine what their health interests, concerns, and problems were. Many of the high school seniors agreed that the schools should provide extensive health education programs, extending from preschool through all grades.

In Ohio the State Planning Committee for Health Education sponsors year-long workshops and other activities to actively promote the formation of local health committees.

Eighth-grade pupils in the Unorganized Territory Schools of Maine are now receiving regular instruction in health education through an educational television hookup.

The New York State Department of Education has been replacing its health syllabus for grades K–12 with new health curriculum guides which utilize what officials on this revamping project call the five-strand approach.

Idaho is committed to a broad health education program; a few districts are undertaking pilot programs and plans are under way to offer teachers additional in-service training.

Florida has a federally financed project underway in five counties, the chief purpose of which is to evaluate health education curriculum and instructional material, including some SHES material.

A number of other states currently have projects completed or under way on school health education. These include Alabama, California, Illinois, Indiana, Louisiana, Michigan, Minnesota, Oregon, South Carolina, Texas, and Washington.[18]

Other states that have programs under way or in the planning stages include Illinois, Tennessee, Alabama, California, Michigan, Indiana, Loui-

[18] Richard K. Means, "Progress and Promise," *School Health Review* (September–October 1972), pp. 23–24.

siana, Michigan, Minnesota, Oregon, South Carolina, Texas, and Washington.

Figure 1–1 provides an excellent view of the outline and scope of the curriculum now in effect in New York State. Fig. 1–2 shows health instruction requirements by states.

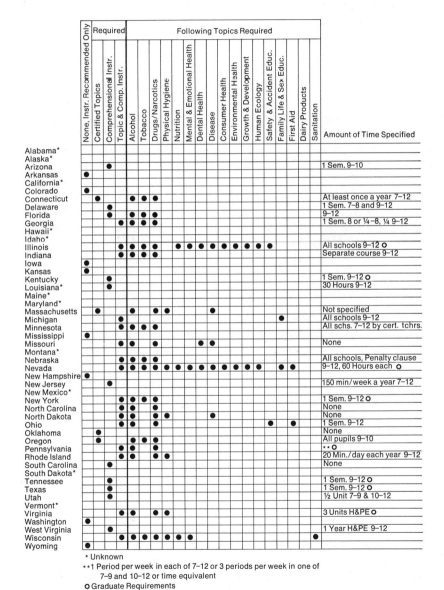

	Required			Following Topics Required																	
None, Instr. Recommended Only	Certified Topics	Comprehensive Instr.	Topic & Comp. Instr.	Alcohol	Tobacco	Drugs/Narcotics	Physical Hygiene	Nutrition	Mental & Emotional Health	Dental Health	Disease	Consumer Health	Environmental Health	Growth & Development	Human Ecology	Safety & Accident Educ.	Family Life & Sex Educ.	First Aid	Dairy Products	Sanitation	Amount of Time Specified

State	None	Cert.	Comp.	T&C	Alc	Tob	Drug	PhyH	Nutr	MEH	Dent	Dis	Cons	Env	G&D	HumE	Safe	FL&S	FA	Dairy	San	Amount of Time Specified
Alabama*																						
Alaska*																						
Arizona			●																			1 Sem. 9–10
Arkansas	●																					
California*																						
Colorado	●																					
Connecticut		●			●	●	●															At least once a year 7–12
Delaware			●		●	●	●	●														1 Sem. 7–8 and 9–12
Florida			●		●	●	●	●														9–12
Georgia				●	●	●	●	●														1 Sem. 8 or ¼–8, ¼ 9–12
Hawaii*																						
Idaho*																						
Illinois				●	●	●	●	●	●	●	●	●	●	●	●	●	●					All schools 9–12 o
Indiana				●	●	●	●	●														Separate course 9–12
Iowa	●																					
Kansas	●																					
Kentucky			●																			1 Sem. 9–12 o
Louisiana*			●																			30 Hours 9–12
Maine*																						
Maryland*																						
Massachusetts		●			●		●	●					●									Not specified
Michigan			●														●					All schools 9–12
Minnesota			●		●	●	●	●														All schs. 7–12 by cert. tchrs.
Mississippi	●																					
Missouri					●	●		●				●	●									None
Montana*																						
Nebraska			●		●	●	●	●														All schools, Penalty clause
Nevada			●		●	●	●	●	●	●	●	●	●	●	●	●			●	●		9–12, 60 Hours each o
New Hampshire	●																					
New Jersey			●																			150 min/week a year 7–12
New Mexico*																						
New York			●		●	●	●	●														1 Sem. 9–12 o
North Carolina			●		●	●		●														None
North Dakota			●		●	●		●	●						●							None
Ohio			●		●	●		●									●		●			1 Sem. 9–12
Oklahoma		●																				None
Oregon			●		●	●	●	●														All pupils 9–10
Pennsylvania			●		●	●		●														**o
Rhode Island			●		●	●		●	●													20 Min./day each year 9–12
South Carolina		●																				None
South Dakota*																						
Tennessee		●																				1 Sem. 9–12 o
Texas		●																				1 Sem. 9–12 o
Utah		●																				½ Unit 7–9 & 10–12
Vermont*																						
Virginia			●		●	●		●	●													3 Units H&PE o
Washington	●																					
West Virginia		●																				1 Year H&PE 9–12
Wisconsin					●	●	●	●	●	●	●										●	
Wyoming	●																					

* Unknown
**1 Period per week in each of 7–12 or 3 periods per week in one of 7–9 and 10–12 or time equivalent
o Graduate Requirements

Figure 1–2. *Health instruction requirements by state.*
Source: *Terrence M. Leigh, "National Profile of Health Instruction,"* School Health Review *(May–June 1973), p. 39.*

ACCOUNTABILITY. In the area of accountability, the Joint Committee on Health Problems in Education of the NEA and the AMA in February of 1971 adopted this resolution:

ACCOUNTABILITY IN SCHOOL HEALTH

Whereas, School board members and the community at large are very much concerned with the effective use of tax moneys, and

Whereas, School health personnel have been screening students to identify problems and to encourage correction, and

Whereas, There has been a failure to relate these improved conditions to behavioral changes in such items as academic performance, verbal efficiency, and social adjustments, and

Whereas, Health teaching has been limited to evaluating knowledge and attitudes, and

Whereas, Teachers are being asked to account for their instructional efforts in terms of preconceived goals, specific pupil performances, and other behavioral changes, therefore be it.

Resolved, That the total school health program be directed to give more attention to student behavioral change through such evaluations as parent, teacher, peer interviews and case studies, and review of school records, and be it further

Resolved, That school health personnel develop accountability systems that will establish a more sophisticated measurement of health practices.[19]

THE STUDENT, THE TEACHER, AND HEALTH

Although students constitute the majority group, they are at the bottom of the role hierarchy, and they are the only members of the system who have no real choice about being there. Moreover, while students are the school's "clients," and the major school decisions are made on the grounds of "the good of the student," they have little say in such matters as curriculum development, choosing texts, classroom environment, etc.

An entire literature, mainly evocative rather than grounded in empirical research, is growing up around the theme that students are being exploited by the very institution that was designed to serve them. Farber, in *The Student as Nigger*, claims "coercion" and "exploitation" of students by the authoritarian educational "establishment" and calls for liberation via protest sit-ins, etc.[20]

In *How Children Fail* and *How Children Learn*, Holt's basic complaint is that playing the student role calls for a kind of playacting in which the players' energies are spent on figuring out the "correct" answer the teacher wants, in order to avoid embarrassment, rather than on mastering

---

[19] "Accountability in School Health," *School Health Review* (April 1971), p. 27.

[20] Jerry Farber, *The Student as Nigger* (North Hollywood, Calif.: Contact Books, 1969).

skills and understanding ideas.[21] Kozol attacks racism and brutality in the school, in *Death at an Early Age*,[22] Kaufman provides us with a depressing account of the mountain of trivia one deals with in education in *Up the Down Staircase*.[23]

But many also see the bright side and are dedicated to the concept of educational reform. More and more educators are finding that a child's best teacher is often a combination of his own curiosity and physical and mental ability freed to explore his individual interests at his own speed. This, after all, is the way children first begin to talk and to walk.

When the teacher is dealing with the subject of health it seems natural to allow each student the opportunity to explore topics he feels are important for his own living experiences. In short, he makes the knowledge gleaned fit him personally. Good teachers recognize this unique personal characteristic of health and use it to great advantage.

Frequently teachers neglect to recognize this marvelous opportunity to present health in terms of personal needs and they interject their own value systems into their teaching. Examples of the "good" and the "bad" in teaching health can be given here. The teacher who discusses the negative aspects of smoking with his class of senior high school students can be certain that there are a good number of smokers present. This teacher offers no alternatives to his students but one, stop smoking. Students cannot identify with the subject when it is presented in this way. The smoker has heard this story a thousand times and is unconcerned. His father smokes and feels just fine. Besides, he cannot worry about what may happen when a person is forty-five years old or more. (That's almost a quarter of a century away!) The teacher who harangues his students with facts and figures, who places his own values ahead of objectivity, loses sight of the very personal nature of the subject matter. The effective teacher is the one who keeps his values to himself. He allows all sides to be heard, the nonsmokers, the smokers, the experimenters, the undecided. He attempts to let the pupils seek alternatives. He also helps the students develop, identify, and review their own values. He places the needs of the students ahead of facts and statistics. Such a teacher recognizes that young people do not smoke out of a desire for self-destruction, but out of a very basic need for acceptance, identity, or adult responsibility. He is the teacher who ultimately receives satisfaction in teaching health. He realizes that health education is more than presenting the most obvious point of view and that in order to achieve a margin of success, he must be willing to

[21] John Holt, *How Children Fail* (New York: Dell, 1970); *How Children Learn* (New York: Dell, 1970).

[22] Jonathan Kozol, *Death at an Early Age: The Destruction of the Hearts and Minds of Negro Children in the Boston Public Schools* (Boston: Houghton Mifflin, 1967.

[23] Bel Kaufman, *Up the Down Staircase* (Englewood Cliffs, N.J.: Prentice-Hall, 1964).

sacrifice the obvious for an often frustrating search for realistic alternatives.

To be a teacher of health today requires more than an accurate knowledge of subject matter. It requires sensitivity to the very personal nature of the subject; an awareness of individual needs, beliefs, and prejudices; and an understanding of the multifarious aspects of the subject.

The question now becomes one of discovering what will influence each student to gain knowledge that will build healthful attitudes and behaviors. We cannot accept the dictum that "some will get it and some will not." By its very structure, health can hold a vital fascination for every student. All it takes is the wise and interested teacher to elicit this interest.

When one examines life patterns he will find that each student has specific individual needs as well as certain universal physiological and psychological ones. Maslow, for example, offers a thorough analysis of basic psychological and physiological needs, which seems especially appropriate to the study of the needs of young people.[24] These he classifies as (1) *physical needs* (food, water, and so on); (2) *safety needs* (freedom from threat, sense of physical security); (3) *belonging and love needs* (need for affection); and (4) *esteem needs* (need for respect as an individual). Maslow believes that there is a hierarchy of needs, and that once a person is able to cope with the lower needs as they arise, he will eventually be able to achieve *self-actualization,* which according to Maslow is the highest need classification and which he defines as the need to become what one is capable of becoming.

We have been able to help young people in health achieve relative degrees of success in meeting lower needs. What now must be done is to help these students achieve a degree of self-actualization. If a student is able to achieve a state of well-being that enables him to function "normally," he will be relatively free to satisfy his higher needs. These higher needs are necessarily more complex than the lower; they become highly individual as one seeks their meanings. (See Chapter 2.)

The very close relationship between the existing educational needs of students and adult interpretations of student needs is illustrated by the "Ten Imperative Needs of Youth," formulated by the Educational Policies Commission of the National Education Association.

1. All youth need to develop and maintain good health and physical fitness.
2. All youth need to understand the significance of the family for the individual and society and the conditions conducive to the successful family life.
3. All youth need to know how to purchase and use goods and services intelligently, understanding both the values received by the consumer and the economic consequences of their acts.

[24] Abraham H. Maslow, *Motivation and Personality* (New York: Harper, 1954), pp. 80–106.

4. All youth need to understand the methods of science, the influence of science on human life, and the main scientific facts concerning the nature of the world and of man.
5. All youth need to be able to use their leisure time well and to budget it wisely, balancing activities that yield satisfactions to the individual with those that are socially useful.
6. All youth need to develop respect for other persons, to grow in their insight into ethical values and principles, and to be able to live and work cooperatively with others.
7. All youth need to grow in their ability to think rationally, to express their thoughts clearly, and to read and listen with understanding.
8. All youth need to develop salable skills and those understandings and attitudes that make the worker an intelligent and productive participant in economic life.
9. All youth need to understand the rights and duties of the citizen of a democratic society, and to be diligent and competent in the performance of their obligations as members of the community and citizens of the state and nation.
10. All youth need opportunities to develop their capacities to appreciate beauty in literature, art, music, and nature.[25]

THE TEACHER AS EDUCATOR. Henry Adams is credited with saying that no man can be a teacher for ten years and remain fit for anything else, and certainly the teacher's position in the modern school is a strangely inconsistent one. On the one hand, the teacher is in sole command of his classroom; on the other hand, he lacks the salary, prestige, and decision-making power at the level of the school as a whole which are commonly associated with a professional role.

Yet the often long hours, often poor teaching environment, and lack of administrative support are balanced by the excitement of a student who yells "Look, I can do it!"

Mahan, in "The Teacher as Provocative Adventurer," suggests that the teacher's role is threefold:

(a) To bring about an encounter with each pupil which shakes his usual mode of perceiving persons and things. This should begin some breakdown in the established perceptual defenses related to school, confront the pupil with the teacher as a person who engages in "evocative" behavior that demands an idiosyncratic response and provides the basis for psychological identification and "referent power.". . .
(b) To provide a dialogue between pupil and teacher which challenges each individual's view of himself and creates an atmosphere for the development of a sense of "commitment."

[25] Educational Policies Commission, *Education for All American Youth* (Washington, D.C.: National Education Association, 1944), pp. 225–226.

(c) To enlarge the pupil's perception of himself in relation to the world through the use of curricular materials which are relevant, because of teacher modification of the materials, to the pupil's cognitive map.[26]

To accomplish this the teacher must adopt a point of view that focuses on behavior and behavior change. He must engage in a process that can be best described as "creative diagnosis"—a continual quest for understanding of the youngster which is built on a sequential development of hypotheses. To do this the teacher behavior must take on the qualities described by Bruner in *Towards a Theory of Instruction:*

a. *Detachment and Commitment.* The teacher must be able to stand back and look at behavior, pupil and teacher behavior, and do so without a sense of undue pressure or anxiety. There must be a feeling of freedom to experiment within a context of deep concern to understand—and the school structure must be modified to ensure this freedom from pressure to engage in the usual and safe.
b. *Passion and Decorum.* The teacher must develop a sense of personal security so that intuitions and impulses can be accepted and utilized—and then incorporated into a more logical framework.
c. *Freedom to Be Dominated by the Object.* The teacher must be able to submerge himself, his needs, his values and see the pupil as he exists and acts.
d. *The Internal Drama.* Out of his interactions with pupils the teacher should become more and more aware of himself, his contradictions, his own "incarnation of dissonance," and in the crucible of this experience broaden and deepen his sensitivity to others.[27]

In concluding this section it would be worthwhile for each of us—future as well as present teachers—to ask ourselves to consider some questions proposed by Purkey:

SELF CONCEPT AND SCHOOL ACHIEVEMENT

☐ Am I projecting an image that tells the student that I am here to build, rather than to destroy, him as a person?

☐ Do I let the student know that I am aware of and interested in him as a unique person?

☐ Do I convey my expectations and confidence that the student can accomplish work, can learn, and is competent?

☐ Do I provide well-defined standards of values, demands for competence, and guidance toward solutions to problems?

☐ When working with parents, do I enhance the academic expectations and evaluations which they hold of their children's ability?

[26] Thomas W. Mahan, Jr., "The Teacher as Provocative Adventurer," *Teachers College Record,* 1966–67, pp. 330–337.

[27] Jerome Bruner, *Towards a Theory of Instruction* (Cambridge, Mass.: Harvard University Press, 1966.)

☐ By my behavior, do I serve as a model of authenticity for the student?
☐ Do I take every opportunity to establish a high degree of private or semi-private communication with my students? [28]

HEALTH AS SUBJECT MATTER. The variety and complexity of subject matter receiving attention in health education today add to the difficulties of defining health as a field of study. One must now decide what to teach out of the many areas comprising the entire field of health. The health teacher will need to ask for what purposes he elects to choose specific areas of the subject matter and whether these are in accord with the needs and interests of the students. Moreover, if health is to become a dynamic study in a rapidly changing world, the teacher must incorporate the findings of the new behavioral sciences, as well as those of the medical, social, and physical sciences.

To be effective, the health teacher needs to keep abreast of current information. Consequently, it is becoming increasingly difficult to expect part-time health teachers to handle a full-time subject.

SUMMARY

If we are ever to help young people travel the road to a more meaningful and rewarding life, we must start by establishing a firm foundation of health knowledge, attitudes, and practices. Without this, the individual will lack the ability to reach his full potential or enjoy his achievements.

Health as a subject has become too complex for the average teacher. A certain amount of concentrated training and specialization prior to teaching has become necessary. Moreover, various states are now seeking more qualified teachers to conduct efficient programs. If this is any indication of things to come, then colleges and universities across the nation will need to reevaluate their own teacher preparation programs. The enlightened people who leave these programs will become the future citizens who will place a higher value on the need for a productive, creative, and meaningful program of health education for all youth.

To accomplish the task before us, many questions must be considered. What should the health curriculum be? How should it be taught? What are the needs and interests of students and of society? Finally, what is the educator's responsibility in general and the health teacher's in particular?

REFERENCES

Brennecke, John, and Robert G. Amick. *The Struggle for Significance.* Beverly Hills, Calif.: Glencoe Press, 1971.

[28] William W. Purkey, *Self Concept and School Achievement* (Englewood Cliffs, N.J.: Prentice-Hall, 1970), pp. 49–50.

Brown, George Isaac. *Human Teaching for Human Learning.* New York: The Viking Press, Inc., 1971.

Borton, Terry. *Reach, Touch and Teach.* New York: McGraw-Hill Book Company, 1970.

Bruner, Jerome. *The Process of Education.* Cambridge, Mass.: Harvard University Press, 1960.

————. *Towards a Theory of Instruction.* Cambridge, Mass.: Harvard University Press, 1966.

Gregory, Thomas B. *Encounters with Teaching.* Englewood Cliffs, N.J.: Prentice-Hall, Inc., 1972.

Hill, Patricia. "Health Education Needs of Preschool and School Age Children and Youth," *School Health Review* (September–October 1972).

Lifton, Walter M. *Working with Groups.* New York: John Wiley & Sons, Inc., 1961.

Lussier, Richard R. "Health Education and Student Needs," *The Journal of School Health* (December 1972).

Moustakas, Clark. *Teaching As Learning.* New York: Ballantine Books, Inc., 1972.

Naranjo, Claudio. *I and Thou, Here and Now.* Esalen paper No. 2 Big Sur, Calif.: Esalen Institute.

Nyquist, Edwald B. "Imperative-Redesign for Health Education with Particular Reference to the Program in the State of New York," *The Journal of School Health* (January 1972).

Read, Donald A. *The Concept of Health,* 2nd ed. Boston: Holbrook Press, 1973.

———— (ed.). *New Directions in Health Education.* New York: Macmillan Publishing Co., Inc., 1971.

"The Significance of Professional Preparation in Health Education," *School Health Review* (September–October 1972).

Torrance, E. Paul. *Guiding Creative Talent.* Englewood Cliffs, N.J.: Prentice-Hall, Inc., 1962.

Tumin, Melvin. "Teaching in America," *Saturday Review* (October 21, 1967).

2 ■ BECOMING AN EFFECTIVE TEACHER

Young people, as never before, have remarkable opportunities for living and learning in an environment marked by change "so profound and far-reaching that the mind can hardly grasp all the implications." [1] The speed of change has been accelerated by, among other things, an explosion of knowledge, mobility, and mass communication. These changes have also had tremendous implications in terms of man's health. The unveiling of the DNA molecule will have a profound and lasting impact because of its potential for manipulating nature in ways that we cannot now even imagine. The frontiers of medical science are expanding rapidly, and the pioneers are pushing their explorations into areas unthought of before. Heart, kidney, and other organ transplants are only the beginning. New drugs are being produced for cure and prevention and may one day unlock the mysteries of the human mind.

However, the very changes that have caused the miracles of discovery have also produced some ominous side effects. Rapid transportation has increased the likelihood of the spread of certain communicable diseases. An example of this occurred during the Hong Kong flu epidemic of 1968. Mass communication bombards man with a constant flood of exaggerated claims for products. Mobility has led to personal instability and isolation because it tends to prevent people from attaining a lasting relationship and identification with others. [2] The thalidomide tragedy of a few years back presents a picture of the complications that can arise out of too rapid a change. Man is sometimes unable to overtake, let alone understand, what he has produced.

[1] John W. Gardner, *Self-Renewal* (New York: Harper & Row, 1965), p. xi.
[2] See Ernst van den Haag and Ralph Ross, *Fabric of Society* (New York: Harcourt, 1957), pp. 138–166.

THE ROLE OF THE HEALTH EDUCATOR

How does the health educator fit into this kaleidoscopic pattern? Should he attempt to reshape information to fit the needs of his students? Should he simply serve as a catalyst between the information to be learned and the learner? Or should he establish conditions of inquiry and free the mind of the student to explore, to feel, and to discover? The fact is that good teaching may require some of all these methods, plus a little more.

With the rapid increase in knowledge has come a new and more challenging role for the teacher. Times change and we must be prepared to change with them. Today we must not only have an understanding of subject matter, but also an understanding of and "sensitivity" to the students.

As Clark Moustakas states in *Teaching as Learning:*

> The educational situation which most effectively promotes learning is one in which (a) the uniqueness of the learner is deeply respected and treasured and (b) the person is free to explore the relationships, ideas, materials, and resources available to him in light of his own particular interests, potentialities, and experiences.[3]

UNDERSTANDING THE PUPIL

All individuals are different, and because of these differences teachers must consider two important facts. First, teachers must understand and recognize the differences. Second, they must use the results of their observations as a basis for curriculum planning and creative teaching.

In health the teacher will want to have some understanding of the growth, development, needs, and interests of the pupils with whom he is working.

IDENTIFYING THE NEEDS AND INTERESTS OF STUDENTS

There are various ways of identifying the needs and interests of students. These include review of literature, health knowledge tests, student interest scales, and the like. In the following pages we will look at some practical methods of determining needs and interests.

Review of Literature

There is a wealth of literature, including research, that has delved into the needs and interests of students at all ages. The Connecticut State Board of Education taped the interests of over 5,000 young people.[4] They found that the students would like to see the following health areas taught at the secondary level:

[3] Clark Moustakas, *Teaching as Learning* (New York: Ballantine, 1972), p. 76.
[4] Ruth Byler, Gertrude Lewis, and Ruth Totman, *Teach Us What We Want to Know* (Hartford: Connecticut State Board of Education, 1969).

Sex Education	Understanding Self and Others
Drugs, Drinking, Smoking	Community Health
Food, Nutrition, Diet	Grooming
Personal Hygiene	Health Maintenance
Disease	Family Life
First Aid and Safety	Birth Control and Birth Defects

Drawing on their own classroom experiences and the consensus of psychological literature, Weinstein and Fantini defined three broad areas of student concerns: "relationship" (connectedness), "self-identity," and "control." By relationship they meant the student's sense of the relation between himself and other people and the world. By self-identity they meant the student's sense of himself. By control they meant the student's sense of his ability to make himself felt in his world.[5]

The Use of Measuring Devices

One effective means of indicating areas needing emphasis in the instructional program is to administer a test at the beginning of the first class. There are a number of tests available for this purpose, but those teachers who are interested in using one or more of these tests should be aware of some obvious shortcomings. One important factor is the impossibility of keeping these tests up to date. Some tests available for use by health educators date back as far as 1957. One that is fairly up to date is the Fast-Tyson Health Knowledge Test that was developed primarily as a diagnostic instrument to assist health teachers and/or administrators in improving instruction and curriculum patterns.[6]

A second factor is the inability of the tests to consider certain specific problems applicable only to a particular geographical area or socioeconomic level.

Others in the educational field also caution us against the uncritical use of standardized tests.

Over the years, it is neither the publisher nor the critic who most effectively determines the quality of tests; rather it is the test user. . . . There is no Good Housekeeping seal of approval in the field of test publication; there is no substitute for professionally competent and conscientious judgment on the part of the test user. Test publishers have important professional obligations; test users have parallel responsibilities.[7]

In many cases it would seem worthwhile for the teacher to consider some of the principles covered in Chapter 19, "Teacher-Student Evaluation

[5] Gerald Weinstein and Mario Fantini, A Model for Developing Relevant Curriculum (New York: Ford Foundation Publication, Praeger, 1970).

[6] The Fast-Tyson Health Knowledge Test (1971), Dr. C. G. Fast, Northeast Missouri State College, Kirksville, Missouri 63501.

[7] Alexander G. Vesman, "The Obligations of the Test User," Proceedings, 1955 Invitational Conference on Testing Problems (Princeton, N.J.: Educational Testing Service, 1956), p. 61.

and Professional Growth," and begin to develop the ability to construct his own health knowledge test. In this way the teacher can develop a timely and relevant instrument suited to the needs of his students and also perfect his skills in test construction.

Teacher Observation

As a source of information and as a means of getting to know each student, teacher observation, both formal and informal, is one of the best ways of accomplishing these goals. An alert teacher, properly trained, can often find clues to student needs and interests by observing the appearance and general behavior of the student. Observation should also be made of such specific things as peer relationships, behavior on the playground and in the classroom, type of questions the student asks, and learning ability.[8]

It is also important that the teacher not limit his observation to the pupil. Many times the teacher can understand a pupil's problems better after talking with the parents. By using the information gleaned through these observations, the teacher is often able to become more sensitive to the needs and interests of individual students.

This may all be well and good but the prospective teacher may ask, "What is it I am supposed to be observing?" and "Where and how does one look?"

In health education, as in other subjects, the major areas of concern— and those we should be observing and learning from the most—are the physical, social, and emotional aspects of the student.

Among the qualties that one should be observing under the physical aspects of the student are the following:

- *Normal vs. deviant physical development.* One needs to recognize changes in growth that are basically due to *normal* physical development as opposed to those that may be due to faulty eating habits, hormone production, birth defects, illness, accidents, or lack of proper exercise.
- *Motor development.* Motor development is the ability of the individual to control his body. Motor development includes eye coordination, leg and foot coordination, arm and hand coordination, walking posture, such skills as running, jumping, lifting, climbing, writing, and manipulatory and repetitive activities. Teachers can observe a student's ability to control his body both inside the classroom and during recess.
- *Sexual development.* An accurate knowledge of sexual adjustment can help meet the needs and interests of young people. Observation of the everyday behavior of the pupils indicates the readiness of the student to learn new material in sex education.

[8] An excellent book on observation is George M. Wheatley, M.D., and Grace T. Hallock, *Health Observation of School Children*, 3rd ed. (New York: McGraw-Hill, 1965).

- *Personal appearance.* Teachers should be constantly alert to the physical appearance of the student. They should be alert to respiratory or skin disease and other conditions which may warrant inclusion of specific subject matter. For example, the teacher may note an increase in symptoms of the common cold during the month of November. This could possibly indicate a need to shift the curriculum in order to present the discussion on communicable disease earlier in the year rather than in the month of January.[9]

Among the social and emotional conditions that a teacher may want to note as he observes his students or that may be brought to his attention are the following:

- *Check for physical problems.* A student who does not hear or see well, for instance, might well become an isolate, have difficulty in reading or reading from the blackboard. General school checkups do not uncover many vision and hearing problems, so if you suspect these might be involved, push for a follow-up.
- *Think about other physical problems* that could be present, such as strong body odor, acne, embarrassing fat or boniness, poor co-ordination, weakness, or disfiguration. All of these, or any one of them, could play a major role in one's emotional makeup. A school nurse should look into any of these and begin a program to improve the situation. You might inquire of the physical education teacher about a student's problems. Certainly the student's medical record should be checked, but in fact a counselor might be the person to elicit some real or imagined worry or embarrassment about a physical problem.
- *Observe the student* to see if he can be described in one of the following ways, which may suggest directions you may take to help the student:
1. Is he a shy student who takes refuge in just one companion?
2. Is he an overaggressive student who is always bullying others?
3. Does he have some markedly strong interest that brands him as different? Is he a bookworm when everyone else is playing basketball, for instance?
4. Does he have a trait which makes him somehow different from community norms such as being a member of a family that moves frequently so that he never lives in any one place for long; membership in a minority group; family reputation; clothing which is inappropriate, poor, or otherwise noticeable? Try to see if any of these traits affect his relationship with his peers.

[9] See Stephen M. Schneeweiss and Ralph Jones, "Time Linked Health Problems: The Monthly Health Special Calendar Approach for Use in Grades K–6," *The Journal of School Health,* Vol. XXXVIII, No. 8 (October 1968), pp. 524–27.

5. Does he—or did he for a while—try to make friends but not seem to know how?
6. Has he become a group scapegoat?
7. Is he a thoroughly "colorless child who asks nothing and receives nothing?" [10]
8. Does he have heavy responsibilities at home that do not permit him time to be with other children?
9. Does he lack certain initial skills that most children at your school use in games?

- *Set in motion any medical assistance,* parent discussions, or referrals you see appropriate after observation.
- Keep in mind that there is occasionally an individual, even though seeming to be a "little odd," who really is quite happy.
- If the student seems to be in a fantasy world of daydreams most of the time, or is extremely anxious about peer contacts, it would be wise to press for a counselor or other guidance worker to see him.
- Some students act out certain types of behavior because other students are threatening them with injury or blackmail. You may need to turn detective in order to discover this, so that such a situation can be rectified.
- Students who are going through physical changes related to puberty or are thinking about sexual issues may be preoccupied with them and need to discuss them. Depending on the philosophy of your community, you may wish to discuss such changes in a health unit.

The teacher's efforts will probably have to be twofold: to help the student to become involved and to encourage the group to be accepting. Another way to assess the behavior of a student is to discover who is having the problem behavior: is it the student who stays alone for example, or is it his peer group, which for some reason is rejecting him, or is it you who are modeling rejecting behavior?

Wheatley and Hallock, in *Health Observation of School Children,*[11] have compiled a list of some common indications of maladjustment in schoolchildren which the teacher can use as a guide in observation. They are too numerous to list, but the source is highly recommended by the authors.

Another important factor in gaining impressions of the social and emotional problems of young people is understanding them in terms of their needs. All students have basic needs.[12] For this reason it seems im-

[10] Carl R. Rogers, *Freedom to Learn* (Columbus, Ohio: Merrill, 1969).
[11] Wheatley and Hallock, op. cit.
[12] See John E. Horrocks, *The Psychology of Adolescence* (Boston: Houghton Mifflin, 1962), pp. 502–19, for a discussion of psychological needs during adolescence.

portant that a teacher have some understanding of these needs, not only to enhance communication between himself and the student, but to plan class objectives and select subject matter. With an eye to helping students meet their needs, an instructor can promote positive health attitudes at the same time.

Looking at Basic Needs

Maslow [13] offers a thorough analysis of basic needs, which seems especially appropriate to a study of the needs of school-age children. He proposes the concept of "hierarchies of prepotency" in which needs develop in a hierarchical sequence from the lowest survival needs to the highest achievement of need-oriented goals. This transition is accomplished by what he terms *prepotency* of need fulfillment. A need that has been satisfied is no longer a need; therefore, the satisfaction of one need releases the individual to try to satisfy other needs. This hierarchy, from lowest to highest, includes *physical needs*, such as hunger and thirst; *safety needs*, such as protection from injury and fostering of a sense of security; *belongingness and love needs*, such as the need for affection, love, and a feeling of belonging; and *esteem needs*, which includes one's desire for self-respect.

According to Maslow, once the lower needs have been gratified, the individual is capable of becoming "actualized in what he is potentially." In other words, he will be free to achieve *self-actualization*.

The student's behavior is affected by his needs, as well as by his environment, parents, peer group, and pressure for achievement in school and in life. If the teacher understands the effect of such influences upon the student, his teaching will become that much more effective and meaningful to the student. Let us look more closely at Maslow's needs to gain understandings of why students are as they are.

The *physical needs* include the need to maintain internal equilibrium. This need of the organism to maintain a constant state of functional balance is called homeostasis. Claude Bernard was the first man to draw scientific attention to the fact that one of the most characteristic features of all living beings is their ability to maintain the constancy of their internal milieu, despite changes in the surroundings. Bernard was, appropriately, the father of modern physiology.

Walter B. Cannon subsequently called this power to maintain constancy in living organisms homeostasis (a word derived from Greek which means "staying the same").[14] Just as the automatic shift in an automobile works to put the car into another, more efficient gear when it reaches a certain speed, so the human body also has many automatic-control mechanisms which enable it to cope with some challenge or body need.

---

[13] A. H. Maslow, *Motivation and Personality* (New York: Harper & Row, 1954), p. 80.

[14] W. B. Cannon, *The Wisdom of the Body* (New York: Norton, 1932).

Put an "X" after item when there seems to be an abnormality of defect		TEACHER'S OBSERVATIONS	Circle "X" when defect has been corrected or pupil is under medical care
General	Appearance		
	Tires easily		
	Posture		
	Muscular coordination		
Eyes	Eyelids		
	Crossed eyes		
	Squint		
	Frequent headaches		
Ears	Discharge		
	Earache		
	Does not hear well		
	Turning his head		
	Cupping his ears		
Nose, Throat, Mouth	Frequent colds		
	Mouth breathing		
	Frequent sore throat		
Behavior	Speech defect		
	Emotional disturbance		
	Nervousness-restlessness		
	Twitching movements		
	Shyness		
	Over-aggressiveness		
	Nail biting		
	Excessive use of lavatory		
	Very shy		
	Aggressive		
Hygiene	Personal hygiene		
	Food habits		
Other	Obvious orthopedic defects		
	Obvious dental defects		
	Obvious posture problems		

Days absent due to illness	

Figure 2–1. *Example of a form used by the teacher in recording observations.*

Figure 2–2. *A bodily need achieving homeostasis.*

Cannon cited a number of factors that are influenced by homeostasis. These include the content levels of water in the blood and the amount of salt, sugar, protein, fat, calcium, and oxygen in the body. Also significant are the constant hydrogen-ion level and the constant temperature of the blood.

An example of a bodily need achieving homeostasis may be represented as shown in Figure 2–2.

Safety needs are almost as important as are physiological needs, especially at an early age. These safety needs include freedom from injury and threatening situations, as well as a feeling of security from life's major hazards. The teacher can help the student to achieve these needs through the promotion of safety education. One way to get information on what to teach is to observe the leading causes of deaths resulting from accidents at different age levels. (See Table 2–1.)

Belongingness and *love needs* emerge after the safety needs have been gratified. The family and the school are ideally suited to the fulfillment of these needs. The teacher can help the student toward achieving

TABLE 2-1 DEATHS FROM HOME ACCIDENTS, BY TYPE AND AGE, UNITED STATES, 1971

TYPE OF ACCIDENT	ALL AGES	0–4	5–14	15–24	25–44	45–64	65–74	75 AND OVER
Total	27,500	4,100	1,400	2,400	3,000	4,400	3,200	9,000
Falls	10,000	300	120	80	360	1,100	1,600	6,500
Fires and flames	5,700	900	500	300	700	1,400	900	1,000
Poisoning by solids and liquids	3,000	250	60	1,000	950	500	100	140
Inhalation and ingestion of food or other object	2,400	900	100	120	250	400	180	450
Firearms	1,200	80	300	300	250	190	50	30
Poisoning by gases and vapors	1,200	60	50	300	250	300	110	130
Mechanical suffocation	1,000	600	170	60	50	50	40	30
Other	3,000	1,010	100	240	250	460	220	720

SOURCE: Estimates by National Safety Council, based on data from National Center for Health Statistics and state health departments.

these needs by covering the role of the individual in healthy interpersonal relationships. The teacher can also promote this need for belongingness through the development of an environment that recognizes the student as an individual.

Esteem needs are represented by one's desire for a "stable, firmly based, usually high evaluation" of himself. The student needs a feeling of self-respect. He needs the feeling of accomplishment to feel adequate. Many small children begin elementary school with high hopes and enthusiasm, only to become frustrated and unhappy because they cannot do what is expected of them. Soon they cannot even complete tasks set by themselves because they see themselves as failures. A teacher can help every student to achieve some measure of success by praising all sincere efforts, however meager. The student's ability to fulfill these esteem needs will allow him to become a useful and mentally healthy member of the class. It is hoped that the self-confidence gained in good classroom situations will enable him to participate as a responsible adult.

The *need for self-actualization*, according to Maslow, is the highest of all the need groups. Under Maslow's hierarchical sequence, once the individual is able to satisfy the lower needs, which may vary from individual to individual, he is able to pursue goals outside of providing for the physical self. This will ultimately enable him to attain self-actualization. It is a moot question whether one can ever achieve complete self-actualization. Like good health, a person works toward it, satisfying other commitments and overcoming other obstacles as he does what he feels he is capable of doing under the circumstances. If an individual has a talent or interest in his life and pursues it, he has "actualized" more of his potential than one who has never bothered to develop any interest or discover what talents lie within him.

In its instructional aspects, health education must stress the fact that the physical self and the psychological self do not constitute a duality, but are unitary in their operation. What affects one affects the other in health and sickness. If the student is not able to satisfy certain lower needs, then these more basic needs will thwart his positive efforts toward self-actualization.

Teaching creatively can help to achieve this goal. Inlow describes a classroom climate where creativity can develop as one in which good mental health is promoted as a prime goal.[15] The author points out that mental health and creativity lie along the same affective dimensions; both seek psychic fulfillment and self-actualization. Thus, Inlow contends, a classroom climate that produces good mental health is one that also nurtures creative productiveness.

[15] Gail M. Inlow, *The Emergent in Curriculum* (New York: McGraw-Hill, 1966), chap. 5.

Questionnaires as a Source of Information

Another way to discover the needs and interests of pupils is by simply asking them. This can be done in a number of ways. One is the preparation of a questionnaire in which the teacher determines what he wants to know and then designs questions that will get the information. For example, a teacher in a senior high school wanted to learn what areas of drug education most interested his students. To find out, he designed the following questionnaire;

I would like to find out some of the areas which you are interested in learning about in drug education (for example, alcohol, smoking, marijuana, LSD, and so on). For this reason I am asking you to rank the areas I have listed, using the system set up below. At the end is a space for any additional comments you may have.

1. very interested in learning about.
2. interested.
3. not so interested.
4. not interested at all.

_____ Effects of alcohol on
     the body
_____ Social problems of alcohol
_____ Alcohol and personality
_____ Alcohol dependence
_____ Why people drink
_____ Opiate drugs
_____ Depressant drugs
_____ Glue sniffing, etc.
_____ Stimulant drugs
_____ Hallucinogenic drugs

_____ Why people smoke
_____ Smoking and health
_____ Psychological aspects of
     smoking
_____ Social aspects of smoking
_____ How to quit smoking
_____ Legal aspects of drug use
_____ Social aspects of drugs use
_____ Psychological aspects of drug
     use
_____ Positive use of drugs

Additional areas not covered (please list)

_____
_____
_____

Comments:

_____
_____
_____

This questionnaire is obviously limited, and only a few of the many subject areas in drug education are listed.

Questionnaires such as these are rarely effective at lower grade levels. One reason for this is that students in early elementary grades have no reference point from which to base their answers. As they move higher in the grades, they acquire some foundation with which to recognize areas of growing interest.

A way to tap the interests of pupils, especially at the elementary level, is to have them respond to a questionnaire such as "Things That I Do Which Are Unhealthy." An extension of this device is to use an open-ended questionnaire, which allows the students to elaborate their answers. Shown here is an example of this.

The foods I like to eat in the morning are_____.
I brush my teeth_____.
Before eating I_____.
When it is cold out_____.
Smoking_____.
When I ride in a car_____.

Another way to get at students needs is to have a panel discussion. For example, you could have a topic related to getting along with others which might help a group of students to be alert to their needs and those of others. The panel may be composed of students who are two or three years older if students in the class are self-conscious. Some topics include:

- Is there any relationship between being popular and being self-confident?
- What are some situations in which people feel awkward? What are some things they can do to help overcome these feelings?
- When do you feel lonely? How do you deal with it?
- What are some of the advantages of belonging to a group? What are some of the disadvantages?

Yet another way of finding out what students want is to select a spot in the room where you can hang a large piece of cardboard, or other material, which students will be able to write on. At the top of this board write "STUDENT WANT ADS." Here students will be allowed to place personal ads for things they want to know. This should be kept up during the entire course so that new ads can be placed from time to time.

Gaining Information from Others in the School Environment

Teachers, school nurses, guidance counselors, school custodians, cafeteria personnel, the principal, and, when possible, the school doctor and dentist can all provide help to those teachers who wish to learn about their students. From these people can be gained the following information.

1. Health histories.
2. Personality ratings and descriptions.
3. Anecdotal reports.

4. Pupil's personal goals.
5. Prevalent health problems in and around the school.
6. Test data.
7. Levels of achievement.
8. Prevalent dental problems.
9. Accident problems in and around the school.
10. Major causes of absences.
11. School environment.

These people can also be invaluable in assisting the health teacher in planning and preparing the classroom curriculum, as well as providing an excellent source of guest speakers.

With those people who are directly associated with the school environment are also a number of sources of information outside the school. The local health department, hospital, police department, and newspapers are all sources for discovering local health conditions and problems. In fact, this is only a partial list and it can certainly be augmented by the interested and resourceful teacher. Every situation is unique in what it has to offer. The teacher's responsibility is to seek each opportunity out and take advantage of it.

PUTTING KNOWLEDGE TO WORK
Vital information the teacher should have concerning students usually involves two important questions:

1. How much should the teacher know about each pupil?
2. How can the teacher put this information to work for him?

Information a Health Education Teacher Should Know About Each Pupil
A. Vital statistics (from student).
  1. Name.
  2. Age.
  3. Sex.
  4. Grade.
B. Family sketch (from school records, personal interviews, school counselor).
  1. Father's occupation.
  2. Mother's occupation.
  3. Number of brothers and sisters, age of each.
  4. Grandparents in home.
  5. Environmental surroundings.
  6. Pets.

C. Health evaluation (from school doctor, nurse, dentist, health records).
   1. Diseases contracted, if any.
   2. Mental or physical factors (defects?).
   3. Social-emotional adjustment.
D. Academic evaluation (from prior teacher and personal records).
   1. Standard test results.
   2. Reading level.
   3. Previous health tests.
E. Future aspirations (from guidance counselor or from student).
   1. College.
   2. Skilled or unskilled labor.
   3. Trade school.
F. Recreational interests (from personal profile or observations).
   1. Hobbies.
   2. Athletic interests.
   3. Part-time jobs.
   4. Father's and/or mother's interests.
G. Health interests (from student and interest tests).
   1. What pupil would like to learn.
   2. What pupil would not like to learn.
H. Present health knowledge (from health knowledge tests, observations).

Combined with specific teacher observations, parent–teacher conferences, and other additional information that the teacher may have gathered in the school and community, this information will help the teacher to become more sensitive to the needs and interests of students. By blending the needs of the school, the community, and society at large with the individual needs and interests of student, the teacher should be more readily able to develop a varied and interesting curriculum.

The teacher can put this information to work by

1. Grouping students in class according to interests and levels of knowledge. Grouping, if flexible, can encourage both cooperation and healthy competition.
2. Planning lessons to meet individual needs.
3. Establishing realistic objectives that the students can attain.
4. Helping evaluate the course at the end of the semester or school year.
5. Helping to plan specific class activities.
6. Helping to evaluate individual students.

THE TEACHER IN SEARCH OF HIMSELF

In this chapter we have been discussing ways in which one can become an effective teacher. This can be achieved to some degree through gaining insights into individual students, their individual likes, dislikes, needs, and interests. But what about the teacher? Should he not also know who he is? Jourard, in his book *The Transparent Self*, thinks so.[16] He states, "Alienation from one's real self not only arrests one's growth as a person; it also tends to make a farce out of one's relationships with people." Because a healthy personality (which includes the ability to know one's self) has been found to be so important in teaching, the sole criteria of the ability to teach are no longer a mastery of subject matter and the acquisition of one or two degrees. Today in order to understand students the teacher must first be able to understand himself. This theme is discussed by Combs and Snygg in their book *Individual Behavior*, where they state, "Effective teaching depends upon teacher perceptions. In particular, it depends upon the kinds of perceptions they possess about these things: (1) What people are like, (2) The goals and purposes of education in our society, (3) Effective methods of encouraging learning, and (4) The adequacy of the teacher's own personality." [17]

We have discussed or will discuss the first three to some degree in this book. What we want to do here is to explore briefly the fourth area, which concerns itself with the personality of the teacher. More specifically, Combs and Snygg are concerned with "the teacher's own concept of himself and of his role as a teacher." What does concept of self mean? Very simply, it means the concept an individual has concerning who and what he is. We know that, for example, a person who likes himself has one of the qualities necessary for good mental health. Conversely, one who has a strong dislike of himself has one of the typical symptoms of maladjustment. The way one views oneself influences his behavior. Thus, if a teacher sees himself as a main source of information rather than a resource upon which students can draw, as a stifler of activity rather than a stimulator, then his concept of himself will determine how the class is conducted. Similarly, if the teacher hopes to know as much as he can about each individual in his class, he must be able and willing to let others know him.

How does one achieve a degree of openness with himself and others? Rogers has a number of worthwhile factors to consider:

1. *Rejection of façades:* The ability to reject being what one is not.
2. *Rejection of submissiveness:* The ability to reject being what one ought to be and ought to become.

[16] Sidney M. Jourard, *The Transparent Self* (Princeton, N.J.: Van Nostrand, 1964), p. 25.

[17] Arthur W. Combs and Donald Snygg, *Individual Behavior* (New York: Harper & Row, 1959), pp. 399–400.

3. *Rejection of cultural expectations:* One begins to evaluate the worth of his cultural socialization.
4. *Movement away from trying to please others:* A person begins to do what he feels is most natural to his own actual selves.
5. *Movement toward being a "person" in flux:* One begins to be cognizant of fluid potentialities, not fixed goals.
6. *Movement of completeness of self:* A person needs to realize that he must possess a personality consistent with itself.
7. *Movement toward being open to experience:* One does not blot out thoughts, perceptions, feelings, and memories which may, at times, be unpleasant.
8. *Movement toward acceptance of others:* One is able to accept others.
9. *Ability to trust just his "selves":* There exists the ability to trust and accept one's selves.[18]

To help students discover themselves the teacher must first be able to discover himself. He can begin by becoming aware that various aspects of himself form a composite. Knowledge of what motivates these various aspects and to what extent he can control the motivations provides a valuable key to unlock his inner self.

Combs's approach to this is to encourage the teacher's exploration, involvement, and sensitivity to the individual. He explains:

I have given up asking my students to make coldly factual, detailed observation reports. I now ask them to do what I do myself when I watch a child behaving or a teacher teaching—to get the "feel" of what's going on, to see if they can get inside the skin of the person being observed, to understand how things look from his point of view. I ask them, "What do you think he is trying to do?" "How do you suppose he feels?" "How would you have to feel to behave like that?" "How does he see the other kids?" "What does he feel about the subject?" and so on.[19]

It reminds one of the main character, a teacher, in Harper Lee's *To Kill a Mockingbird:*

"First of all," he said, "if you can learn a simple trick, Scout, you'll get along a lot better with all kinds of folks. You never really understand a person until you consider things from his point of view—"

"Sir?"

"—until you climb into his skin and walk around in it." [20]

[18] Carl Rogers, *On Becoming a Person* (Boston: Houghton Mifflin, 1961), pp. 163–198.

[19] A. W. Combs, *The Professional Education of Teachers: A Perceptual View of Teacher Preparation* (Boston: Allyn & Bacon, 1965), p. 66.

[20] Harper Lee, *To Kill a Mockingbird* (Philadelphia: Lippincott, 1960), p. 36.

SUMMARY

Health education has undergone rapid and drastic change since the turn of the century. Tremendous shifts of interest have occurred, both in the subject and in those being taught. Yet, along with this rapid change, there exist throughout our schools teachers whose outmoded ideas and methods of organization and teaching are woefully inadequate. Moreover, these people are detrimental to the overall growth and development of the students subjected to their influence. These teachers fail to consider the needs, interests, and readiness of students. They push students to learn subject matter that is seemingly unrelated to their previous experiences. Often these teachers scold students because they cannot learn or are not interested in learning. They view students not as individuals but as components of a group.

This dismal picture of course does not pertain to the majority of teachers. More and more teachers are learning to utilize the individual differences of students in constructing their curricula. Rather than being the sole judge of what will be learned, instructors are gaining knowledge of growth and development, student readiness, interests, and needs. The advantages in this type of planning for a teaching–learning situation are endless. Most important, such a situation involves the teacher in the act of becoming a more "tuned-in" participant in the classroom environment.

This pupil-centered approach is not without its critics. There are those who feel that information based on situdent interest often has little or no scientific support through research. Obviously there must be a healthy balance between the pupil-centered approach and the teacher- and subject-matter-centered approaches to curriculum planning and teaching.

REFERENCES

Alschuler, Alfred (ed.). "New Directions in Psychological Education," *Educational Opportunities Forum*. New York State Department of Education, Albany, N.Y., June 1969.

Association for Supervision and Curriculum Development. *Perceiving, Behaving, Becoming: A New Focus in Education*. Yearbook. Washington, D.C.: National Education Association, 1962.

Bessell, Harold. "The Content Is the Medium: The Confidence Is the Message," *Psychology Today* (January 1968), pp. 32–35.

Borton, Terry. "What Turns Kids On?" *Saturday Review* (April 15, 1967), pp. 72–74.

Bettelheim, Bruno. *Love Is Not Enough*. New York: The Free Press, 1950.

"Bionics." *Journal of Creative Behavior* (Winter 1967), pp. 52–57.

Bugental, J. F. T. *The Search for Authenticity*. New York: Holt, Rinehart and Winston, Inc., 1965.

Jones, Richard M. *Fantasy and Feeling in Education*. New York: New York University Press, 1968.

Lederman, Janet. *Anger and the Rocking Chair.* New York: McGraw-Hill Book Company, 1969.

Leonard, George. *Education and Ecstasy.* New York: The Delacorte Press, 1968.

Lynd, Albert. *Quackery in the Public Schools,* Boston: Little, Brown and Company, 1953.

Mead, Margaret. *Culture and Commitment.* Garden City, N.Y.: Doubleday & Company, Inc., 1970.

Parker, J. Cecil, and Louis J. Rubin. *Process as Content: Curriculum Design and the Application of Knowledge.* Skokie, Ill.: Rand McNally & Co., 1966.

Rogers, Carl R. *Freedom to Learn.* Columbus, Ohio: Charles E. Merrill Publishers, 1969.

Rosenthal, Robert. "Self-Fulfilling Prophecy," *Psychology Today* (1968), pp. 46–51.

———, and Lenore Jacobson. *Pygmalion in the Classroom, Teacher Expectation and Pupils' Intellectual Development.* New York: Holt, Rinehart and Winston, Inc., 1968.

Silberman, Charles E. *Crisis in the Classroom: The Remaking of American Education.* New York: Random House, Inc., 1970.

PART II

Setting the Stage for Teaching

Man thinking; him Nature solicits with all her
placid, all her monitory pictures; him the
past instructs; him the future invites. Is not
indeed every man a student, and do not all
things exist for the student's behoof? And,
finally, is not the true scholar the only true
master? But the old oracle said, "All things have
two handles: beware of the wrong one."

EMERSON

3 ■ THE ART OF PLANNING

Walking into a classroom at any level without having first planned the day's objectives is like beginning an automobile trip with an empty gas tank. Like any task undertaken, teaching needs preparation. Unfortunately, this is not as easily accomplished as one may think. Research has indicated that basic to creative planning is the individual's ability to attain a full mastery of his subject, to be curious, open-minded, objective, and indifferent to conformity and to have an eagerness to experiment with new ideas. This person must also be willing to work long hours on demanding work.

One can see that the process of planning for creative teaching can become laborious. Ghiselin stated, "The sheer labor of preparing technically for creative work, consciously acquiring the requisite knowledge of a medium and skill in its use, is extensive and arduous enough to repel many from achievement." [1] Unfortunately, this is true too often.

What are the basic ingredients of creative teacher planning? Probably they can be reduced to those listed below.

What the teacher expects the pupils to learn	Concept formation Behavioral objectives Selection of content
How the teacher hopes to influence this learning	Organization of subject matter Creative teaching Creative use of instructional media Teaching methods and techniques Creative teaching applied

---

[1] Brewster Ghiselin, *The Creative Process* (New York: Mentor Books, 1955), p. 28.

This chapter and the chapters that follow will be devoted to the preceding ingredients as they concern teacher planning. The present chapter will be concerned primarily with the objectives and content necessary to achieve these objectives in health education.

TEACHING AND LEARNING THROUGH CONCEPTS

Not only must a teacher know *how* to teach, but he must know what *ends* he hopes to achieve in his instruction. Problem solving is not the current method; concept formation is. According to Woodruff, a concept "is a relatively complete and meaningful idea in the mind of a person. It is an understanding of something." [2] To build concepts efficiently one must give the student the opportunity to learn specifics and then encourage the student to build the desired concepts or generalizations himself by inference from the data. One of the major roles of the teacher is to help the student to form meaningful and useful concepts.

How to Teach Concept Formation

Many concepts are developed without specific teaching. For example, young children form concepts by seeing certain qualities and relationships repeatedly in a number of successive experiences. In the course of several trials a child is able to develop a concept of *dog*, as distinguished from *man*. He may also see a dog, touch one, and develop positive and/or negative attitudes toward certain dogs. Finally he may own and name his dog.

Unfortunately, however, many students are just as likely to form incorrect concepts. To avoid this the student must be encouraged to organize facts, symbols, and isolated experiences around a concept or conceptual scheme.

To help you gain insight into the conceptual approach, we provide here an excerpt from the School Health Education Study.[3]

The conceptual framework. Broadly the conceptual framework for the health education curriculum comprises three categorizations. These are presented in a hierarchy as follows:

Three broad *key concepts*—the highest conceptual level representing the unifying threads of the curriculum that characterize the processes underlying health.

[2] Asahel D. Woodruff, *The Nature and Elements of the Cognitive Approach to Instruction* (Salt Lake City: University of Utah, May 28, 1964). (Unpublished material.)

[3] From R. K. Means, *The Conceptual Approach in Structuring the Health Education Curriculum* (Washington, D.C.: National Conference for School Health Education Curriculum Development, February 10, 1967); adapted from School Health Education Study, *Health Education: A Conceptual Approach to Curriculum Design* (St. Paul, Minn.: 3M Education Press, 1967), pp. 15–26.

Ten *concepts*—the major organizing elements of the curriculum reflecting the scope of health education.

Thirty-one *subconcepts*—the lowest conceptual level involving the supporting ideas, viewed in three dimensions, that serve as guides in selecting and ordering the subject matter in health education.

The Key Concepts. The three key concepts, or processes affecting health behavior, represent the highest conceptual level of the framework and serve as the unifying threads of the curriculum. Each of the concepts characterizes a process in the life cycle that is typical of *every* individual, regardless of sex, occupation, economic level, or social status. These include the following:

Growing and developing: A dynamic life process by which the individual is in some ways like all other individuals, in some ways like some other individuals, and in some ways like no other individual.

Interacting: An ongoing process in which the individual is affected by and in turn affects certain biological, social, psychological, economic, cultural, and physical forces in the environment.

Decision making: A process unique to man of consciously deciding to take or not take an action, or of choosing one alternative rather than another.

These three key concepts illuminate the overall concept of health and hence form a framework for health education. They represent a dynamic interrelationship which can be illustrated by the following example related to the use, nonuse, or misuse of alcoholic beverages as the context:

In the *growing and developing* process that is living, the individual, during childhood, comes in contact with—*interacts* with—the phenomenon of alcoholic beverages—or, more specifically, with people who use them. At some point in the life of each individual, probably in the mid-teens, *interaction* leads to the necessity of making a *decision* about use or continued non-use of alcoholic beverages. If the *decision* is to try drinking, then other *interactions* take place—with the beverage itself, with others who drink, with those who do not, with society and the adult world and, in some way, with the individual's own self-concept and conscience. *Growing and developing* continues, of course, with this new element included. If one's reactions—physical, emotional, and social —to the beverage are basically more pleasant than painful, the individual may continue *growing and developing* as one who uses alcoholic beverages. If the balance becomes more painful than pleasant, the "tester" may *decide* to go back to abstinence. If the *decision* is to maintain abstinence, when drinking is a possibility, then still other *interactions* take place.

The Concepts. Whereas the three key concepts represent the unifying threads of the curriculum that characterize the processes underlying health, the ten concepts serve as the major organizing elements of the curriculum reflecting the scope of health education. According to several authorities, a conceptual statement is a complete description and not merely a definition, topic, or premise. It specifies clearly what the student is expected to know when the learning experience is over. The traditional topical areas were utilized as "checks" in the development of the conceptual statements.

The Subconcepts. Within the heretofore described framework, a third level of differentiation was made. Each concept is represented by substantive elements termed subconcepts. These provide the supporting ideas, viewed in three dimensions, that serve as guides in selecting and ordering the subject matter of health education. The physical, mental, and social dimensions of each subconcept are identified to assure that the teaching–learning situation would provide recognition of the total individual.

BEHAVIORAL OBJECTIVES

Defined

"A behavioral objective is a goal for, or desired outcome of, learning which is expressed in terms of observable behavior or performance of the learner." [4]

Before the teacher plans a lesson to be presented to the class, he should have in mind what the students should be able to do or say at the end of the lesson. This is because behavioral objectives "become the criteria by which materials are selected, content is outlined, instructional procedures are developed and tests and examinations are prepared." [5]

In terms of the student, the resulting behaviors to be observed at the end of the lesson are either new behaviors or extensions of existing behaviors (see Figure 3–1).

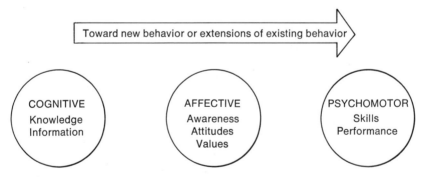

Figure 3–1. *Observation of behaviors.*

[4] Earl J. Montague and John J. Koran, Jr., "Behavioral Objectives and Instructional Design: An Elaboration," *TST Forum, The Science Teacher* 36:10 (March 1969).

[5] Ralph W. Tyler, *Basic Principles of Curriculum and Instruction* (Chicago: University of Chicago Press, 1950), p. 3.

Some Functions of Behavioral Objectives

Behavioral objectives can serve several functions including:

1. to identify the expected learner outcomes for a given lesson or unit of study.
2. to provide a basis for the selection and organization of materials and experiences for effective learning.
3. to provide a basis for the type of cognitive and affective experiences that will be presented to the student.
4. to provide a systematic means for devising ways of evaluating student performance.

Writing Behavioral Objectives

When writing a behavioral objective, one must use a specialized verb limited to few interpretations. Such a verb, which precisely describes the desired behavior, gives the teacher a reference point from which he can judge whether the learner has demonstrated the desired behavior. Some examples of these verbs, which correspond with objectives designed to measure thinking (and open to fewer interpretations), are

to write	to recite
to describe	to identify
to list	to predict
to compare	to measure
to state	to contrast
to demonstrate	to solve
to select	to infer

Examples: The student should be able to

- List the various physiological/psychological effects of marijuana on the body.
- Identify the problems prevailing concerning the legal aspects of marijuana use in the U.S.
- Describe how and why a Caesarean section is performed.

Those verbs that are open to interpretation and unacceptable for writing behavioral objectives include:

to know	to have faith in
to enjoy	to learn
to appreciate	to fully appreciate
to believe	

If you are worried that the ABC's of writing behavioral objectives described above are an oversimplified analysis of educational objectives, you

·may be quite right. But the authors must assume that the reader will continue to read and research and, most important, that he will practice writing behavioral objectives. A good resource book on behavioral objectives is Mager's *Preparing Instructional Objectives*.[6]

Finally, it should be recognized that writing behavioral objectives is not an end in itself. It is merely a means to an end. Objectives offer a blueprint for some kind of instruction. Although it is desirable to be able to describe, measure, and replicate behavior, the end product may be effective and efficient student learning or "positive" changes in attitudes and behavior. The behavioral objectives, then, are merely indices of a particular kind of learning.

Expressing Behavioral Objectives in the Different Domains

In 1948 the American Psychological Association conceived an idea by which educational objectives could be classified in such a way as to be useful and still general enough to be applicable to most areas of education. After eight years of individual and group work, the committee published the *Taxonomy of Educational Objectives, Handbook I: Cognitive Domain*. The association saw a natural organization for all types of good objectives, classifying them into three broad categories, or *domains*. In the first, the *cognitive domain*, the objective is achieved through a progressive sequence of levels. The full sequence begins with knowledge and ends with evaluation [7] and can best be elucidated by questions.

Knowledge: What food nutrients do all of us need? In what foods may they be found?

Comprehension: Can you explain in your own words why we need vitamins and minerals? What problems may arise if the soil in which food plants are raised is not fertilized?

Application: How can we use what we have learned to improve our eating habits? How can we check to be sure we have a balanced diet?

Analysis: What is meant by the statement that this cereal contains one-half of the minimum daily requirements? Who can analyze this menu to find out if essential nutrients are included?

Synthesis: Who can organize what we have learned about vital nutrients into a set rule for good eating habits? What soil conditions are necessary to produce vegetables that contain vitamins and minerals?

Evaluation: Are the claims in this advertisement consistent with what we have learned about vitamins? Which of the three dinner menus on the chalkboard is best in terms of our criteria for balanced meals? [8]

[6] Robert F. Mager, *Preparing Instructional Objectives* (Palo Alto, Calif.: Fearon, 1962).

[7] Benjamin S. Bloom (ed.), *Taxonomy of Educational Objectives* (New York: David McKay, 1956).

[8] John U. Michaelis et al., *New Designs for the Elementary School Curriculum* (New York: McGraw-Hill, 1967), p. 294.

The cognitive domain may be described as including such behavior as remembering, reasoning, problem solving, concept formation, and to a limited extent, creative thinking. Objectives that emphasize remembering or reproducing something that has presumably been learned are included in this. Also included are objectives that involve solving some intellective task for which the individual has to determine the essential problem. He must then reorder given material or combine it with ideas, methods, or procedures previously learned. Cognitive objectives vary from simple recall of material learned to highly original and creative ways of combining and synthesizing new ideas and materials.

Concepts, reasoning, generalizations, and scientific knowledge constitute the basis for sound health practices. Specific objectives in the cognitive domain are for the student to be able to

- Identify the principal components of the WHO definition of health.
- List five of the contributions of physical exercise to one's physical health.
- Define the term *frustration*.
- List man's basic needs as given by Maslow (see Chapter 2).
- Describe the process necessary in order to analyze critically and evaluate health advertising and publicity.

The *affective domain* is an active extension of the various subcategories of the cognitive domain. The two domains are compared in the original source, Volume II of the *Taxonomy*.[9]

Cognitive	Affective
1. The cognitive continuum begins with the student's recall and recognition of *Knowledge*,	1. The affective continuum begins with the student's merely *Receiving* stimuli and passively attending to it. It extends through his more actively attending to it,
2. it extends through his *Comprehension* of the knowledge,	2. his *Responding* to stimuli on request, willingly responding to these stimuli, and taking satisfaction in this responding,
3. his skill in *Application* of the knowledge that he comprehends,	3. his *Valuing* the phenomenon or activity so that he voluntarily responds and seeks out ways to respond,

---

[9] David R. Krathwohl et al., *Taxonomy of Educational Objectives, Handbook II: Affective Domain* (New York: McKay, 1964), pp. 49–50.

COGNITIVE	AFFECTIVE
4. his skill in *Analysis* of situations involving this knowledge, his skill in *Synthesis* of this knowledge into new organizations,	4. his *Conceptualization* of each value responded to,
5. his skill in *Evaluation* in that area of knowledge to judge the value of material and methods for given purposes.	5. his *Organization* of these values into systems and finally organizing the value complex into a single whole, a *Characterization* of the individual.

The comparisons given are seldom so easily dichotomized within a given objective and its intended results, but they illustrate how one continuing domain gives rise to another.

One can see that the affective domain refers to value, attitude, feeling, and appreciation objectives. This is a particularly difficult area to represent in terms of behavioral objectives because the observable behaviors are open to many interpretations, and the teacher makes inferences to decide whether the learning has taken place. See Eiss and Harbeck, *Behavioral Objectives in the Affective Domain.*[10]

An example of a *receiving objective* is:
> After a series of lessons on reproduction in animals in the classroom, the child voluntarily goes to the cages and looks at the animals.

A *responding objective* is:
> When live animals are being kept in the room, the child feeds the animals and cleans their cages and appears satisfied with the clean cages.

A *valuing objective* is:
> During discussions in the health class about physical exercise, the student asks many questions and often states a preference for specific explanations.

Objectives that seek to identify behavior that is organizing in nature are those that describe student attempts to conceptualize a value and organize a value system. Two objectives in this area are:

1. Provided with the time and materials, the student will select a health topic to explore and participate in research on his own initiative in areas that interest him.
2. Following a series of lessons on pollution, the student identifies a local industry contributing to pollution and formulates a suggested course of action to convince the industry to take precautions against pollution.

---

[10] Albert F. Heiss and Mary Harbeck, *Behavioral Objectives in the Affective Domain* (Washington, D.C.: National Science Teachers Association, 1969).

What is important to note about affective objectives is that they do not include a clear-cut criterion level for performance. This is because affective objectives are themselves value-laden. They vary greatly with the individual, the subject area, the school, and the social situation. Consequently, *these objectives should be thought of as open-ended in nature.*

Psychomotor learning refers to the ability to coordinate muscular movement with sensory perception. It involves simple motor skills like typing and focusing a microscope, as well as skills such as talking and writing. See DeCecco, *The Psychology of Learning and Instruction: Educational Psychology.*[11] Thus far, however, psychomotor objectives have not had wide application within health education.

In a somewhat unique proposal, the School Health Education Study includes an *action* domain to indicate aspects of health behaviors that are applied to actual life.[12] Although presented as an autonomous category, the action domain is similar to the top level of the affective domain wherein internalized values serve to regulate real life behavior.

The behavior of the students cannot always be measured in terms of how they translate and use information, because some behavior is nonobservable and some cannot be measured until the students are in life situations outside the college. Thus, a student can be exposed to a body of information (cognitive), realize and place its implication within his individual character (affective), and also show that the values inherent in the information can be expressed in actual behavior (action).

In concluding this section on behavioral objectives it should be said that a sensitivity to the distinctly different ways in which learning may be expressed permits the teacher to develop behavioral objectives that sample a wide range of learning outcomes. It also guides the teacher to design instruction so that student intellectual development takes place in each of these areas. Figure 3–2 shows an effective way to think of the relationship between these three types of learning.

SELECTION OF CONTENT

The next logical step in curriculum development is moving from stated objectives to the selection of subject matter. This is really the heart of the curriculum. A teacher or curriculum planner may spend months on this phase of preparation. A brief list of guidelines to observe in the selection of subject matter follows:

1. Objectives of the course should be observed.
2. Representative content should be chosen.

[11] John P. DeCecco, *The Psychology of Learning and Instruction: Educational Psychology* (Englewood Cliffs, N.J.: Prentice-Hall, Inc., 1968).
[12] School Health Education Study, *Health Education: A Conceptual Approach to Curriculum Design* (St. Paul, Minn.: 3M Education Press, 1967).

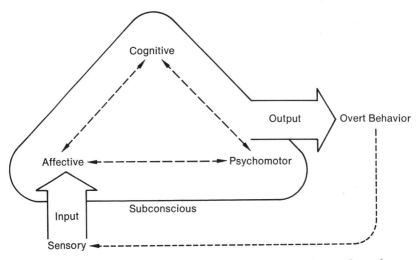

Figure 3–2. *Relationships between the cognitive, affective, and psychomotor areas of learning.*

Source: *Albert J. Eiss and Mary Blatt Harbeck,* Behavioral Objectives in the Affective Domain. *Washington, D.C.: National Science Teachers Association, 1969.*

3. Content selected should be organized according to the logical development of the subject matter.
4. The content selected should be suitable to the students' interests and activities.
5. The content should be flexible.
6. The teacher must be aware of the degree of the students' readiness to learn new material.
7. Time allotment must be considered.

Further development of each guideline seems necessary at this point.

OBJECTIVES OF THE COURSE SHOULD BE OBSERVED. As was mentioned, basic to the entire success of the curriculum is the teacher's ability to formulate the expected outcomes of his class or subject. In establishing and using course objectives the teacher should always keep in mind that objectives represent what he hopes his students will learn or achieve, not merely what they will do in the process of learning. Thus, for example, one of the objectives of a fourth-grade lesson plan in health is not to see a film on nutrition, but to learn the relationship between vitamins and good health. Viewing the film is an activity.

While using objectives as a basis for selection of subject matter, it should be remembered that the teacher's objectives should not be confused with behavioral objectives. Burton, in his text on learning, discussed this point by stating,

The teacher's objectives and the pupil's objectives in any learning situation are not similar in form, but they are intimately related. The teacher's objectives are the desirable educational outcomes . . . which he hopes the pupil will achieve. The pupil's objectives are the immediate results which he sees and desires and which will result from his activity in solving the question in which he is interested. The teacher hopes so to guide the learning experience that desirable educational results (the teacher's objectives) will be achieved while the pupil is achieving his objectives. Failure to realize the difference and relation between teacher's and learner's objectives has caused not only much ineffective and useless teaching but has developed detrimental attitudes and practices and much pupil antagonism toward education. In many schools the pupil does not know or care what the teacher's objectives are. Worse, the teacher too often does not know or care what the pupil's objectives are. Because of this, teachers often cover the ground, go through the motions, and think that they have achieved their objectives when, in fact, they have achieved no educative results. The pupil has realized neither objectives of his own, nor those of the teacher.[13]

Another pitfall can occur when a teacher, intent upon fulfilling his educational goals, brushes aside a relationship seen and offered by a creative student. If the relationship is irrelevant, the teacher must attempt to show the student his error in a positive and helpful fashion. If the relationship does not fit into the well-organized pattern of the subject matter yet is actually a fresh insight, the teacher must vary his objectives to include the new relationship. The teacher should feel encouraged that his classroom atmosphere elicited such a response.

REPRESENTATIVE CONTENT SHOULD BE CHOSEN. The subject area of health is broad and in a constant state of flux because of new findings and advances in research. Selecting subject matter representative of content in a particular health curriculum is an awesome task at best. In order to be representative, the teacher is sometimes forced to select only major concepts, ideas, and skills for the student to use in gaining greater insights. Phenix illustrated this when he said,

from the large resources of material in any given discipline, those items should be chosen that are particularly representative of the fields as a whole. The only effective solution to the surfeit of knowledge is a drastic process of simplification. This aim can be achieved by discovering for each discipline those seminal or key ideas that provide clues to the entire discipline. If the content of instruction is carefully chosen and organized so as to emphasize these characteristic features of the disciplines, a relatively small volume of knowledge may suffice to yield effective understanding of a far larger body of material.[14]

Borrowing a concept from the School Health Education Study that the "use of substances that modify mood and behavior arises from a variety

13 William H. Burton, The Guidance of Learning Activities (New York: Appleton-Century-Crofts, 1962), p. 54.

14 Philip H. Phenix, Realms of Meaning (New York: McGraw-Hill, 1964), p. 11.

of motivations," one could say that in order to search for representative content to cover the drug area, the teacher may have to limit himself to those substances that are now in common use by young people. These would include alcohol, tobacco, certain selected stimulants and depressants, and psychedelic drugs. By discussing a representative few within these major groups, the teacher can elicit from the students such discoveries as the relationship between these substances and health, how drugs modify mood and behavior, how they influence the individual psychologically, and most important, relationships between these substances and an individual's needs.

In contrast to the traditional K–12 health program, which deals specifically with "subject matter areas" (i.e., drugs, human sexuality, communicable disease, physical fitness), Project Quest has organized their course of study around student behaviors. Here, for example, the five Goals are the major organizing elements in the curriculum, and each of the Goals calls for a student behavior, i.e. *Cares for the Human Body, Develops A Mature Personality*, etc. This approach, they feel, "puts the student at the center of the curriculum." (See Figure 3–3).

THE CURRICULUM SHOULD BE ORGANIZED ACCORDING TO THE LOGICAL DEVELOPMENT OF THE SUBJECT MATTER. Each learning experience should be built on the previous learning experience of the student; each new learning experience should develop a basis for performance required in subsequent learning experiences. In other words, the teacher should know where he and his class have been and where they are going. This continuity is especially important, in the case of building attitudes and behavior. Both take time and gradual development.

It should be explained here that a learning experience is not confined merely to subject content. It "refers to the interaction between the learner and the external conditions in the environment to which he can react." [15] This does not mean that each student will necessarily assimilate all that the teacher provides. No matter what content is presented or who presents it, the student is ultimately the one who is the determiner of what the experience will involve.

Maintaining continuity in curriculum planning also implies that learning experiences proceed from the concrete to the abstract, and from tasks requiring simple thought processes to those requiring abstract and formal reasoning. The following situation shows an example of this continuity: A teacher wanted to present a unit on growth and reproduction. In doing this she decided first to discuss early sexual development, starting from birth to adolescence. Next she covered the reproductive organs of the male and female, including a discussion of their functions. She felt it appropriate to bring up some normal sexual outlets of young people (masturbation, nocturnal emissions, and so on). She ended the unit by

[15] Tyler, op. cit., p. 41.

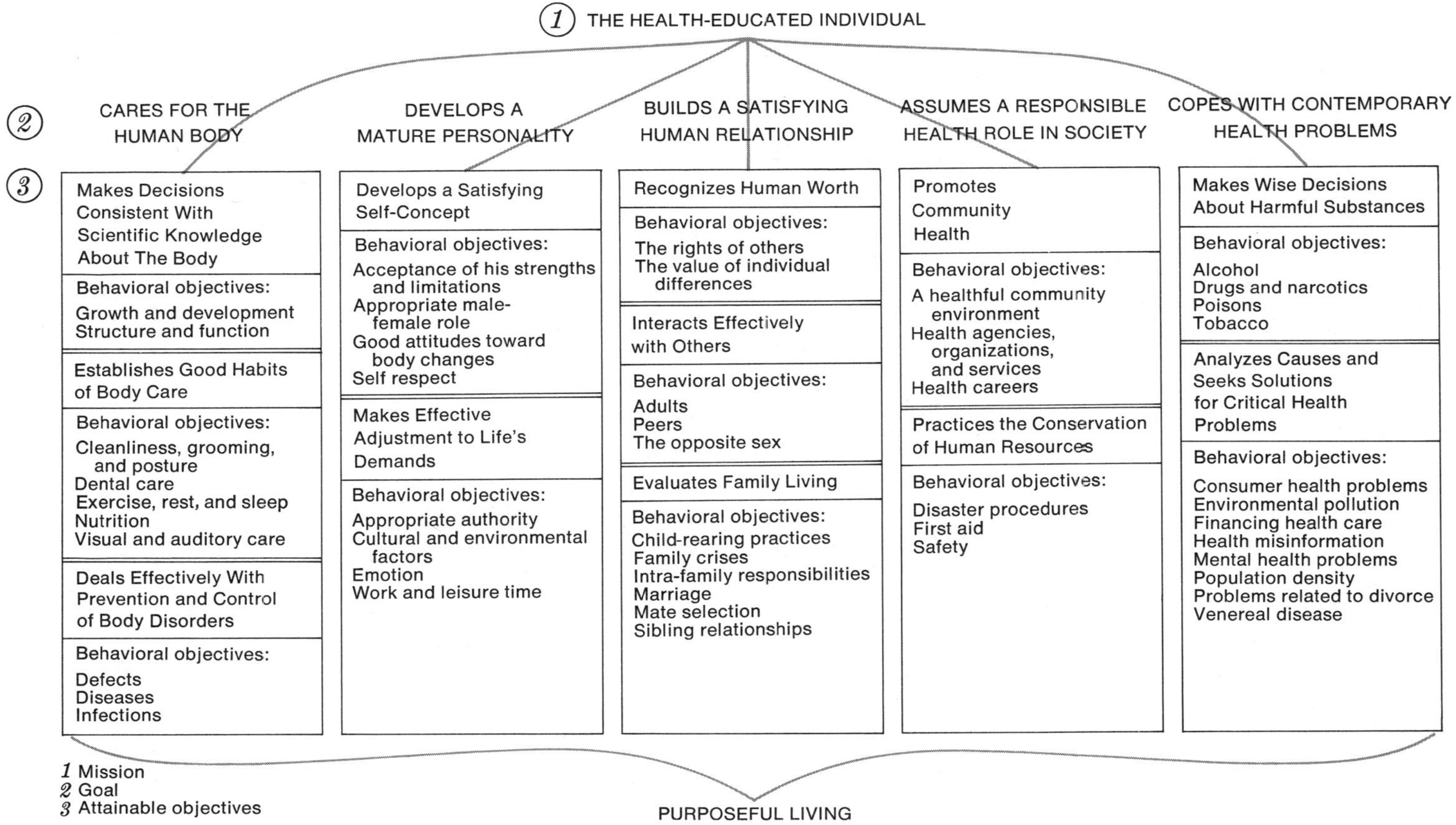

Figure 3–3. *Project Quest.*

Source: Project Quest: Health Instructional Guide. *Los Angeles County Superintendent of Schools, Los Angeles, California, 1968.*

discussing ovulation, menstruation, fertilization, conception, pregnancy, and birth. The unit had completed a cycle and ended where it had begun. In this way the students were exposed to a pattern of the normal developmental stages that take place in growth and reproduction.

THE CONTENT SELECTED SHOULD BE SUITABLE TO THE STUDENTS' INTERESTS AND ACTIVITIES.   Clark and Starr believe that a course can be organized in one of two ways: (1) "according to the logical development of the subject matter or (2) according to the psychological development of the pupils." [16] At the secondary school level, they feel that courses should be organized psychologically (around the student rather than around the subject matter).

In arranging the course content around the interests and activities of the students, suggested guidelines can be considered.

1. Teachers must keep themselves "tuned in" to the needs, interests, and activities of their students.
2. Because all pupils are not alike, the teacher must be prepared to provide alternate learning experiences for each topic.
3. The teacher must have a personal rapport with his students.
4. The teacher must be open to content suggestions from his students.

An excellent example of one teacher who had a tuned-in ear can be found in *Teacher* by Sylvia Ashton-Warner.[17] By knowing and planning for the needs and interests of the small Maori children, she could evoke originality, achieve educational goals, and at the same time keep a relative amount of order amid chaos. Mrs. Ashton-Warner discovered very quickly that the children refused to become interested in the activities of Dick and Jane in the basic reader. Reversing her methodology of using the basic book first, she encouraged them to compose their own "books." These frequently contained stories about skeletons, kissing, witches, getting drunk, and fights with mommy and daddy. The children, needing other words to connect and make their stories complete, gradually learned most of the vocabulary included in the Dick and Jane series. Her methods can be applied in health as well. If a teacher in a health class senses the class before him is exceedingly restless during a unit on nutrition, could it not possibly signal that there is no need for such stress on that particular aspect of health *at that time?* When, instead, the class becomes alert and inquisitive during the discussion of drugs, would this not be a good time to extend those discussions? A teacher can learn much of the needs of his class through their questions and reactions and can make new plans for each class, if necessary, in order to help the students discover *for themselves* the important issues in health.

[16] Leonard H. Clark and Irving S. Starr, *Secondary School Teaching Methods* (New York: Macmillan Co., Inc., 1967), p. 102.
[17] Sylvia Ashton-Warner, *Teacher* (New York: Bantam Books, 1964).

One relatively simple way to tap the interests of students is to ask them to list some questions they would like to have answered during class. This has been done quite effectively in many schools. An example can be seen in these questions that fifth- and sixth-grade children ask about drugs.[18]

1. What does LSD stand for?
2. Where do drugs that people use come from?
3. Do people who sell drugs use them?
4. What is the most popular drug that people use?
5. Is LSD ever helpful to man?
6. Can LSD kill people under age 12?
7. How does glue sniffing make you high?
8. Is marijuana as dangerous as LSD?
9. Why do people take drugs?
10. How were drugs invented?
11. Are drugs harmful to animals?
12. What good are drugs?

An important factor to keep in mind is that the teacher must instruct in a manner that will enable his students to use their information, not merely remember it. If the knowledge presented is appealing and the pupils can be properly motivated, the class will develop the proper attitudes through practical application of the information.

THE CONTENT SHOULD ALLOW FOR FLEXIBILITY. Although the curriculum cannot always be changed at will, it should not succumb to inflexibility. The teacher should always plan for unforeseen developments that can and will appear from time to time. Plans often need to consider schedule changes; world, national, or local events; visiting lecturers; and so on.

THE TEACHER SHOULD BE AWARE OF THE READINESS OF THE STUDENTS TO LEARN NEW MATERIAL. The term *readiness* is also an important consideration in teacher planning. When is the best time to introduce a new learning experience to students? The wise teacher will be careful to appraise the level of readiness of each pupil for new material and consider how and when he can take the next step.

These individual readiness levels become less and less defined as pupils get older. The first grade teacher has a much wider range of readiness levels in her class than does the senior high school instructor. Elementary teachers generally realize that it is necessary to keep pupils' physical and mental developments and capacities in mind, whereas secondary and college teachers look for more subtle readiness cues. Introducing a unit on sex education before the teacher knows the background and prejudices of students (and their parents) can prove disastrous. The ability to judge

---

[18] Questions were compiled from over 100 fifth- and sixth-grade students at Crocker Farm Elementary School in Amherst, Mass., 1969.

when a class is "ready" should not be taken for granted, but can be developed by observant, sensitive teachers.

Time allotment must be considered. One of the main criteria to be considered in the selection of subject matter is time. All good teachers ask from time to time, "How am I going to fit it all in?" Even when one is able to determine the amount of time available for teaching a given subject, the teacher is plagued with such things as unscheduled days out of school, special school activities that remove various students from the classroom, and so on. To overcome this the teacher should do his planning, keeping in mind the possibility of unexpected interruptions throughout the year. If he makes a few of his lesson plans elastic enough, he can expand or shorten certain phases of his plan at will.

An example of the amount of time that certain subjects may take is shown in the curriculum bulletin of the Cincinnati Public Schools

Units of Work Arranged by Grades

	APPROXIMATE NUMBER OF CLASS PERIODS
Grade 10	
I. Personal hygiene	9
II. Driver education	36
(one semester)	45
III. Physical growth and development	9
IV. Social and emotional growth	9
V. Nutrition	9
VI. Social hygiene	9
VII. Use of drugs, cosmetics, and health appliances	5
VIII. School and community health resources	4
(one semester)	45
Grade 12	
I. First aid	25
II. Family health and home nursing	20
(one semester)	45
III. Mental hygiene	15
IV. Marriage and family living	25
V. Recreation and body mechanics	5
VI. Driver training (optional)	
(one semester)	45

SOURCE: *Health and Safety: Senior High Schools,* Curriculum Bulletin 233, Cincinnati Public Schools, Cincinnati, Ohio.

SOURCES OF INFORMATION IN CHOOSING CONTENT

There are many sources of information that can be used in determining course content. In fact, it should be emphasized that *as many sources as possible should be used* to eliminate bias, errors, and misconceptions that creep into curriculum guides as well as daily lessons and must be eliminated by careful use of current materials. Many and varied sources also offer the teacher a choice of those topics that will help most to achieve the particular objective of the curriculum. Through the use of many resources, one is also able to recognize those areas and subjects that overlap and those that possibly need more exposure.

Textbooks, journals, vital statistics, curriculum research, courses of study, surveys, school health examinations and records, school personnel, special television programs, pupil interest inventories, and health knowledge tests provide excellent sources of information for curriculum development. These cannot be chosen at random. Three suggested criteria follow:

THE CONTENT CHOSEN SHOULD BE BASED ON THE LATEST FINDINGS AND RESEARCH. Such periodicals as the *Journal of School Health* and the *Journal of Health, Physical Education and Recreation* will, from time to time, present articles and current research findings relevant to health education. These journals also present new and innovative ideas for teaching in health.

The teacher can conduct research within the school in which he is teaching. Information can be gathered from such sources as the school physician, nurse, principal, cafeteria personnel, and physical education teacher on such subjects as school accidents, sickness, nutrition, and absences from school. The teacher can independently construct interest inventories and administer health knowledge tests within the classroom.

COURSES OF STUDY AND CURRICULUM GUIDES SHOULD BE CONSULTED. These aids not only are valuable in helping the teacher to determine what content should be covered but also help to decide the sequence of topics. Many courses of study and curriculum guides outline in great detail suggested topics and sequences. An example is the May 1967, issue of the *Journal of School Health*, which devoted its entire issue to a suggested program of sex education for grades K through 12. One outline for grade 7 on "The Family" was as follows:

A. Teachable Material
   1. Family structures
      a. the "typical" family in the United States
         (1) monogamous marriage
         (2) household consists of only mother, father, children
      b. other kinds of families in our culture, e.g.:
         (1) the one-parent family
         (2) families in which persons of several generations live as a single family unit within the same household

(3) families in which children live with someone other than either one or both of their parents

(4) families in which there are no children

2. Why did the family, as such, develop?
   a. influence of ancient civilization
   b. current environmental influences
3. How have families in the United States developed and changed over the years?
   a. ways in which they have changed
   b. forces influencing these changes
4. The purposes and functions of the family
   a. the importance of the family to the mother
   b. the importance of the family to the father; what is the role of the father in family living?
   c. the importance of the family to the children
   d. the importance of the family to the community
5. Making adjustments within the typical family unit
6. Different families have different approaches to family living.
   a. approach to health; the health status, attitudes and practices of each family member influence the lives of all family members
   b. approach to discipline
      (1) parental controls
      (2) developing one's own controls—self-discipline and responsibility
   c. ways of expressing love and concern
   d. religious attitudes and customs [19]

A second example is the *Health Instruction Guide* for the North Dakota schools, which outlines the relative emphasis that should be placed on health knowledge, attitudes, practices, and skills by grade levels for the major health areas.

TEXTBOOKS SHOULD BE USED. Just as courses of study and curriculum guides can be useful in curriculum development, so can textbooks help in the selection of content. They can afford the beginning teacher the opportunity to observe the sequence in which the content can be placed. Before relying too heavily on any one textbook, though, the teacher will do well to consider that

1. The sequence in which the material has been placed in a given text may not necessarily be the best order for a particular class.
2. All chapters should not be considered as having equal importance.
3. Some of the material presented may be out of date.

[19] American School Health Association, *Journal of School Health*, Kent, Ohio (May 1967), pp. 59–60.

			GRADE				JR.*	SR.*
	1	2	3	4	5	6	HIGH	
Community Health				xx	xx	xx	xx	xx
Consumer Health				x	xx	xx	xx	xxx
Disease Control				xxx	xx	xx	xx	x
Family Living	x	x	xx	xx	xx	xxx	xx	xxx
Mental Health	x	x	x	xx	xx	xx	xxx[2]	xx
Personal Health [1]	xx	xx	xx	xx	xx	xxx	xx	x
Safety and Accident Prevention	xx	xx	xx	xx	xxx	xx	xxx	xx[3]

source: *Health Instruction Guide*, North Dakota Schools, Department of Public Instruction, Bismarck, N.D., 1965, p. 6.

Note: xxx = Major emphasis on this area at this grade level.
　　 xx = Moderate emphasis on this area at this level
　　　x = Some attention, particularly to attitudes and practices rather than to knowledge
　Blank = No attention to this area at this grade level
　　　* = One semester or the equivalent at each level
　　　1 = Including community health and disease control in grades 1–3
　　　2 = Preferably late junior high school
　　　3 = First Aid

SUMMARY

Certainly not all the important factors that are involved and worth considering in effective planning of the curriculum have been covered here. Unexpected problems will always arise. It is sufficient to say that if the teacher is creative enough and competent in the area of health knowledge, then the problems that do arise will be minor in their effect on the overall program. Stress is mainly placed on the importance of good teacher planning. Objectives should be designated before the organization of subject matter and the organization of subject matter should be used to reach these stated objectives.

It must be stressed again that no single source of information can be considered adequate in providing information relevant to course content. Each and every source available to the teacher or curriculum committee should be given consideration in planning any comprehensive curriculum. How the resulting learning experiences will be absorbed by the students will be examined in the next chapter.

REFERENCES

Anderson, Ronald D. "Has the Objective Been Attained? Evaluation in Elementary School Science (Part II)," *Science and Children* 5:33–36 (October 1967).

Ashton-Warner, Sylvia. *Teacher*. New York: Bantam Books, Inc., 1964.

Bloom, Benjamin S. (ed.). *Taxonomy of Educational Objectives. Handbook I: Cognitive Domain*. New York: Longmans, Green and Co., 1956.

DeCecco, John P. *The Psychology of Learning and Instruction: Educational Psychology*. Englewood Cliffs, N.J.: Prentice-Hall, Inc., 1968.

Eiss, Albert F., and Mary Harbeck. *Behavioral Objectives in the Affective Domain*. Washington, D.C.: National Science Teachers Association, 1969.

Gronlund, Norman E. *Stating Behavioral Objectives for Classroom Instruction*. New York: Macmillan Publishing Co., Inc., 1970.

————. *Preparing Criterion-Referenced Tests for Classroom Instruction*. New York: Macmillan Publishing Co., Inc., 1973.

Koran, John J., Earl J. Montague, and Gene E. Hall. "How to . . . Use Behavioral Objectives." *National Science Teachers Association*, 1969.

Krathwohl, David R., et al. *Taxonomy of Educational Objectives. Handbook II: Affective Domain*. New York: David McKay Company, Inc., 1964.

Mager, Robert F. *Preparing Instructional Objectives*. Palo Alto, Calif.: Fearon Publishing, 1962.

Montague, Earl J., and David P. Butts. "Behavioral Objectives." *The Science Teacher*, 35:33–35; March 1968.

Popham, W. James, and Eva I. Baker. *Establishing Instructional Goals*. Englewood Cliffs, N.J.: Prentice-Hall, Inc., 1970.

4 ■ ORGANIZATION OF SUBJECT MATTER

After objectives and the selection of content, the next logical step in the planning process is that of organizing subject matter, teaching techniques, and teaching devices, as well as creating an environment in which effective teaching and learning situations will be possible. As previously stated, prior to this point in teacher planning, most teachers will designate specific course objectives and select and arrange the course content in order to meet these objectives. From this point the teacher will begin to sketch in lightly the work that will be covered in a semester or quarter and then proceed to plan the major units of work around which the daily and weekly lesson plans will revolve.

The vast explosion of knowledge in health, as well as in other subjects, presents a tremendous challenge to elementary and secondary teachers, principals, and supervisors to select and organize tentative learning experiences of young people—experiences that will be adequate and effective for living healthfully. (See Chapter 2.) Educators generally agree that unit planning in teaching is one of the best ways to provide for learning experiences on a sufficiently broad base.

In order to help the reader decide what constitutes a good unit, several definitions are cited. One group of authors states, "A unit, or a unit of work, can be defined as purposeful learning experience focused upon some socially significant understanding which will modify the behavior of the learner and enable him to adjust to a life situation more effectively." [1]

---

[1] Lavone A. Hanna, Gladys L. Potter, and Neva Hagaman, *Unit Teaching in the Elementary School* (New York: Holt, 1955), p. 101.

Adams writes that, "The unit of work consists of unified coordinated elements, each of which is a part of the functional whole. Each of these major elements is an organized aspect of the total unit." [2]

Burton gives the following definition of a unit: "A unit is any combination of subject-matter content and outcomes and thought processes into learning experiences suited to the maturity and needs (personal and social) of the learners, all combined into a whole with internal integrity determined by immediate and ultimate goals." [3]

The unit has been defined by the *Dictionary of Education* as, "An organization of various activities, experiences, and types of learning around a central problem, or purpose, developed cooperatively by a group of pupils under teacher leadership; involves planning, execution of plans and evaluation of results." [4]

Thus it can be noted that the modern notion of the unit is based upon a Gestalt type of psychology, in which figure–field relationships are important. Such relationships mean the association of one element or item with another and organization around one central theme. The unit of work is organized on a psychological basis—what is meaningful to the students.

To observe more closely the internal aspects of the unit, it would be helpful to cite the six essential elements of the unit as given by Blount and Klausmeier.

FRAMEWORK FOR A TEACHING–LEARNING UNIT [5]

I. *Introductory Statement*
   A. State the age, grade level, and ability grouping, if any, for which the unit is planned.
   B. Estimate the length of time that is needed for the unit.
   C. Indicate briefly the over-all plan into which this unit fits.

II. *Outline of Objectives*
   A. State the specific concepts, facts, and generalizations that students will acquire.
   B. List the specific skills that students will develop.
   C. List the specific attitudes that students will develop.

---

[2] Fay Adams, *Educating America's Children*, 2nd ed. (New York: Ronald, 1954), p. 140.

[3] William H. Burton, *The Guidance of Learning Activities*, 3rd ed. (New York: Appleton-Century-Crofts, 1962), p. 329.

[4] Carter V. Good (ed.), *Dictionary of Education* (New York: McGraw-Hill, 1959), p. 387.

[5] Framework for a Teaching–Learning Unit" from *Teaching in the Secondary School*, 3rd edition, by Blount and Klausmeier, pp. 200–201. Copyright © 1953 by Harper & Row, Incorporated. Copyright © 1958 by Herbert J. Klausmeier. Copyright © 1968 by Nathan S. Blount and Herbert J. Klausmeier. Reprinted by permission of Harper & Row, Publishers.

III. *Content Outline*
   A. Outline the major subject-matter content, and/or
   B. Outline the problems to be solved, and/or
   C. Outline a series of projects to be completed.

IV. *Learning Activities*
   A. Initiatory activities
      1. Outline a series of activities that will get the students off to a successful beginning; using your ideas as to how to initiate a good teaching–learning situation, indicate the sequence of these activities.
      2. Indicate the approximate amount of time required for initiating the unit.
   B. Developmental activities
      1. Outline the activities in which the students will engage to acquire concepts, skills, and attitudes; indicate the successive steps students go through in learning a concept or skill in the order in which you think these best learned.
   C. Culminating activities
      1. Outline a summarizing activity or group of activities that each student can contribute to, that the whole group will direct its effort toward during the major part of the learning period, that will best satisfy each student's need for approval from classmates and others, and that will promote good attitudes toward classmates, teacher, school, and subject matter.
      2. Indicate the time needed for this phase, allowing for appropriate student participation.

V. *Materials and Resources*
   A. Locate reading materials, audio-visual materials, and demonstration and experimentation materials that are needed to make the activities worthwhile.
   B. Locate and list facilities that will be used in the school (outside the classroom) and in the community.
   C. Devise procedures for bringing people from the community to the classroom and for taking the students into the community.
   D. Outline the procedures you will use when it is necessary for students to contact persons or to secure materials outside the classroom.

VI. *Evaluation Procedures*
   A. Outline the procedures you will employ to determine where students are when the unit starts.
   B. Outline the methods you will use in assisting students to measure their own progress as the unit develops.
   C. Outline the procedures you will use to measure student growth in concepts, facts, skills, and attitudes when the unit ends.

THE UNIT AS IT RELATES TO THE NATURAL
EDUCATIVE EXPERIENCE

Other writers, in outlining what they feel are essential elements of the unit, have agreed with those proposed by Blount and Klausmeier. As you read over the elements again, you will note that there is nothing arbitrary in the organization of a unit. Each element is considered in an organized fashion, which is based on what we now know about the natural learning process. This can be illustrated by using the sequence of steps in the learning process developed by Woodruff (see Table 4-1) and comparing them with the elements of a teaching–learning unit proposed by Blount and Klausmeier.

The *introductory statement* and rationale are important to the teacher and the pupil at the beginning of a unit, as it will define vital guidelines necessary for integration or coordination of the unit with others and can provide a tentative time table to which he can refer while making daily plans. At the same time, *outlining objectives* will prove necessary for the justification of teaching the unit. Having these written goals speeds the preparation of activities and project planning. In addition, the students can better define their personal goals if the teacher has clearly defined his objectives. Not knowing to what end a lesson is progressing (or for what reasons it has been given) can result in students' acquiring negative attitudes toward all formal education. Ironically enough, this happens even in cases where a teacher is given suggested objectives in a thoughtfully prepared curriculum guide. If the objectives are not studied carefully (whether a teacher or curriculum committee has prepared them), the purposes for which the unit is taught are nebulous, resulting in an educational setback rather than an intellectual and social gain. Unfortunately, the educational uncertainties experienced by the pupils in such a unit as the one described makes it more difficult for Step 1 to occur.

Normally, when Step 1 does occur, "Motivation within the learner makes him receptive to stimulation," the teacher can maintain the students' levels of stimulation, or raise them, if he has carefully planned appropriate *learning activities*. (Item IV, p. 67.) These should be timed so that interest is not lost before "a goal becomes related to the motivation" (Step 2). As the motivating activities present problems that the students cannot immediately solve, the necessary tension arises, which Step 3 describes. The elements of *content outline*, item III, and *learning activities*, item IV, are important to the learners involved in Step 4. Teacher guidance is important at this point, as many vital skills in communication, deductive and inductive reasoning, research methods, and so on, are utilized during this stage. Again, objectives must be clarified so that students will gain the benefits of the knowledge discovered.

The results of Steps 5 and 6 become good indicators of the *evaluation procedures* which the teacher outlined before beginning the unit. They also are an indication of whether the subheadings under *materials* and *resources*

TABLE 4-1 SEQUENTIAL STEPS IN LEARNING

1	2	3	4	5	6
Motivation within the learner makes him receptive to stimulation.	A goal becomes related to the motivation. A. The goal is not at once attainable. B. A barrier exists.	Tension arises. A. Energy is released within the learner; he is ready to act. B. The barrier prevents an appropriate discharge of the energy and creates tension.	Learner seeks an appropriate line of action to reach goal. A. In every situation there are a number of possible ways of acting. B. The selection of one of those ways of acting will involve elements of chance and/or analysis. C. When the selection is made, action toward the goal is attempted. D. If the selected line of action is inappropriate steps A, B, and C will be repeated until an appropriate action occurs. E. When an appropriate action occurs, it will involve: 1. Some degree of success in terms of the goal. 2. A sense of satisfaction and a reduction of tension to the extent that the motive is satisfied.	Learner fixes the appropriate line of action. A. Skills are acquired by drill or practice. B. Concepts are developed by becoming familiar with the referent. C. Memorization is accomplished through meaningful repetition. D. Tastes and preferences are established by the satisfyingness or annoyingness of the experience. E. Ability to solve problems is a product of A and B above. Speed of Learning Varies A. May be relatively sudden. B. May be very slow. C. Depends on: 1. Nature of the problem. 2. Degree of motivation. 3. Capacity of the learner.	Inappropriate behaviors are dropped. A. Yielding no satisfaction, they lose attractiveness.

SOURCE: Copyright 1948; renewed 1974 by David McKay Co. Inc. From the book, *The Psychology of Teaching* by A. B. Woodruff. Published by David McKay Co. Inc. Used with the permission of the publishers.

were adequate. *Culminating activities* should further enable both students and teacher to evaluate the success of the learning experience.

TYPES OF LESSON PLANS

In many schools today the unit is the typical way of organizing a learning situation. If one were to read any number of educational texts, he would find many of the authors talking in terms of resource units, teaching units, descriptive units, appreciation units, process units, and other special-purpose units. The reader should not let this terminology overpower him. These titular variations are due to differences in the students, teachers, educational philosophy, curriculum, cultural environment, and part of the country in which the schools are located. For our purposes, we will examine those types of units which may assist teachers and others in planning and teaching.

The Resource Unit

Klohr has defined the resource unit as "a carefully planned series of suggestions centered in some broad problem, topic, or area of experience and organized to serve as a source of ideas, materials, and procedures to help a teacher in preplanning a learning unit." [6] This resource unit is quite often prepared by a group of teachers to be used with any group of children of appropriate age and grade levels. Some units may be prepared by a group of teachers in cooperation with curriculum consultants. These units usually contain a wealth of material, ideas, and suggestions from which a teacher may select when working with a given group of pupils. They may become part of a course of study or be published so that other schools and school systems can use them as a source of reference.

Krug suggests that the format for a resource unit include the following parts:

    I. Significance of the topic or area
   II. Inventory of possible objectives
  III. Content outline (expository outline, list of questions or problems or both)
  IV. Suggested activities
     A. Introductory
     B. Developmental
     C. Culminating
   V. Bibliographies and lists of materials
  VI. Suggested evaluation procedures [7]

[6] J. Galen Saylor and William M. Alexander, *Curriculum Planning for Better Teaching and Learning* (New York: Holt, 1964), p. 403.

[7] Edward A. Krug, *Curriculum Planning*, rev. ed. (New York: Harper & Row, 1957), p. 236.

To examine what constitutes each part, it will be necessary to examine them individually. You will notice that the areas are similar to the elements of a unit suggested by Blount and Klausmeier.

SIGNIFICANCE. The importance of the unit for the students is pointed out here, as well as its sequential place in the structure of other subject fields involved. An example that can be used in illustrating this and the other steps in a resource unit can be given in a fifth-grade unit on family life or sex education.

The importance of sex education: The American School Health Association states that "As long as there is growth and change in the individual and the community, there is need for sex education which will prepare one to accept these changes with equanimity and contribute to one's salutary interaction in a heterosexual society.

"Although sex education begins in the home and is the parents' privilege and responsibility, schools have some obligation to make room in their curricula for those courses of study which will strengthen character and contribute to development toward well balanced responsible citizenship." [8]

OBJECTIVES. Objectives should relate to the specific unit being planned and not to the whole range of objectives for the subject field or fields involved. Usually a few of the most significant objectives for a given unit are adequate and much more effective and usable in carrying out a unit than a long list of goals. This list of objectives should encompass the areas of knowledge, attitudes, and behavior.

Some general objectives that may prove effective in sex education for fifth-grade students are the following:

1. To develop an acceptable scientific vocabulary useful in describing body parts and processes.
2. To develop a knowledge of how reproduction occurs and life begins.
3. To understand that heredity and environment influence growth and development.
4. To develop an awareness that each individual grows and develops uniquely according to a "timetable" which follows a predictable sequence.
5. To be familiar with the changes that take place as the individual advances from childhood to adulthood.
6. To differentiate between the role of the male and female in the conception, birth, and nurture of a human being.
7. To develop an awareness of the importance of the family structure to the individual members. [9]

[8] Committee on Health Guidance in Sex Education, "Growth Patterns and Sex Education," *The Journal of School Health*, Vol. XXXVII, No. 5a (May 1967), p. 1.

[9] *Sex Education: Resource Unit for Grades 5, 6, or 7* (1967). The American Association for Health, Physical Education, and Recreation, 1201 Sixteenth Street, N.W., Washington, D.C., 20036.

CONTENT. The content of a given unit may be indicated in a number of ways. Often it is presented through a series of "Problems for Developing the Unit." If these problems are carefully formulated and take into account the structure of the subject matter, they can be most effective. This method of indicating the content of a unit provides good leads for the use of problem-solving methods and experiences in the classroom.

The following is an illustration of an outline for a family-life-education program used in the Oakland Public Schools for grades K through 12.

I. *The Person*
    Unit A. Stages of Life (Growth and Development)
            1. Infancy and Childhood
            2. Adolescence
            3. Adulthood
            4. Aging
          B. Interpersonal Relations
            1. Needs and Competencies of Individuals
            2. Interaction of Individuals (with each other or in the group)
          C. Health and Safety
            1. Early Sexual Characteristics
            2. Physical Fitness
            3. Mental Fitness
            4. Safety and First Aid
          D. Human Sexuality
            1. Early Sexual Characteristics
            2. Sexual Maturity
            3. Sex in Marriage
            4. Sex Changes in Aging
          E. Preparation for Marriage
            1. Preparation for Marriage and Parenthood
            2. Marriage
            3. Parenthood and the Family Life Cycle

II. *The Family*
          A. Family Membership
            1. Primary Tasks of Families
            2. Similarities and Differences between Families
            3. Changes that Affect the Family
            4. Effect of Residence on Families
          B. Family Relationships
            1. Socialization of Family Members
            2. Developmental Tasks in Marriage and Parenthood
          C. Family Economics and Management of Resources
            1. Essential Factors in Family Management
            2. Procedures and Techniques
            3. Influencing Factors

D. The Family in the Community
   1. Family Responsibility and Obligation to Community
   2. Rights of the Family as Community Members
   3. Privileges of Living in a Community [10]

SUGGESTED ACTIVITIES. Activities are an important aspect of the re-source unit. Many kinds of activities should be included. Above all, the planners should be certain that a balance is attained in the kind of activities suggested. Among those listed should be introductory, developmental, and culminating experiences.

The introductory experiences should provide several ways in which the students can become acquainted with the subject matter. These may include films, filmstrips, and other audio and visual aids, discussions of current events relating to the topic, trips, guest speakers, experiments, observations, and problem solving.

Some suggested activities for a sex-education resource unit are briefly sketched here.

- Collect magazine pictures of boys and girls of approximately the ages of fifth-graders to use in making a bulletin board display illustrating differences in size and body build among children of the same age. Investigate reasons for differences.
- Have male and female guinea pigs in the classroom. If possible breed a black guinea pig with a white one to observe hereditary character-istics in off-spring. Describe observations on birth.
- Discuss reasons for using scientific terminology rather than "pet" family expressions or peer slang in the study of sex education.
- Through a lecture-discussion, start with the basic structural unit, the cell, and "build" a person. Include in the dialogue an analogy between the human body and a building: cell–bricks; tissues—walls; organs—rooms; systems—apartments; and organism—building.
- Have students write brief essays on topics such as "Qualities I Like in Other Boys and Girls My Age," "The Personality of My Best Friend."
- Visit the local health or science museum to view exhibits dealing with body systems and the reproductive process.
- View and discuss films.
- Have a guest speaker (doctor, nurse) talk on some aspect of reproduc-tion.
- Have buzz groups [see Chapter 8 of the present book] on (a) ways of showing love and respect for friends, (b) ways of showing love and respect for members of my family.
- Stage a sociodrama, with students portraying characters exemplifying different rates of growth and development.[11]

[10] Rita M. Hose, "The Interagency-Interdisciplinary Approach to Family Life Education," *California School Health*, Vol. 3, No. 1 (January 1967), pp. 28–29.

[11] Committee on Health Guidance in Sex Education, *Journal of School Health*, op. cit., pp. 35–39; *Sex Education: Resource Unit*, op. cit., pp. 4–5.

Many resource units suggest ways in which a unit may be enriched and brought to a close. Such activities are labeled "culminating" or "concluding" activities. Not every unit must close with such projects: nevertheless, these activities provide excellent means for reviewing, evaluating, and summarizing what has been accomplished through the unit experience and serve as a basis for determining next steps.

- Have a "college bowl" game, with the questions covering what was presented and discovered in the unit.
- Discuss the relative importance of what has been learned in this unit in relation to the development of a healthy personality.
- Have students prepare a report which summarizes how their attitudes have changed (if they have) since they have participated in the unit.
- Have the students prepare a play, assigning roles to the various elements of an organism—cell, tissue, etc. Each could bring up interesting features about himself and his connection or relationship to other features.
- Develop a cartoon-type bibliographical story which contrasts the life cycle of a male with that of a female.
- Develop a "what would I have done" series on film (8 mm), built around growth and development differences in people of all ages.

BIBLIOGRAPHIES AND MATERIALS. It is customary and helpful to include lists of materials and necessary equipment in most resource units. Here may be listed textbooks, supplementary books (fiction, biography, nonfiction), reference books, reproductions of art, films, filmstrips, references for the teacher, and other materials and sources of materials for the unit.

The outline of materials used in our unit on family life includes the following:

FILMS

The Day Life Begins. Carousel Films, 1501 Broadway, New York, N.Y. (23 min.). 10036.

Everyday Courtesy. Churchill Films, 6671 Sunset Blvd., Hollywood, Calif. 90036.

Exploring Growth. Churchill Films, 6671 Sunset Blvd., Hollywood, Calif. 90036.

Growing Up. McGraw-Hill Book Company, Text Film Preview, Library, Distribution Center, Hightstown, N.J. (10 min.). 08520.

Miracle of Reproduction. Sid Davis Productions, 1418 N. Highland Ave., Hollywood 28, Calif. (15 min.). 90036.

Story of Menstruation. Kimberly-Clark Cort., Neenah, Wis. (10 min.). 54956.

It Happens. Pyramid Films, Box 1048, Santa Monica, Calif. 90406 (13 min.).

SOUND FILMSTRIPS

Especially for Boys. Sylvexler Film Productions, 801 Seward Ave., Los Angeles, Calif. 90069.

Human Reproduction. Eye Gate House, Inc., 146–01 Archer Ave., Jamaica, N.Y. 11435.

BOOKS FOR STUDENTS

Anglund, Joan W. *What Color Is Love?* New York: Harcourt, Brace & World, Inc., 1966.

Hobson, Laura. *I'm Going To Have a Baby.* New York: The John Day Company, Inc., 1967.

Johnston, Dorothy. *All About Babies.* Grand Rapids, Mich.: Zonclervan Publishing House, 1962.

PAMPHLETS

Accent on You. Tampax Incorporated, Education Department, New York, N.Y. 10017.

A Boy Today—A Man Tomorrow. Optimist International, 4494 Lindell Blvd, St. Louis, Mo. 63108.

Growing Up and Liking It. Personal Products Corporation, Milltown, N.J. 08850.

Lerrigo, Marion, and Dr. Milton Senn. *A Story About You.* American Medical Association, 535 North Dearborn Ave., Chicago, Ill. 60610.

Very Personally Yours. Kimberly-Clark Corporation, Neenah, Wis. 54956.

World of a Girl. Scott Paper Co., Home Service Center, International Airport, Philadelphia, Pa. 19113.

You're a Young Lady Now. Kimberly-Clark Corporation, Neenah, Wis. 54956.

Talking to Preteenagers About Sex. Public Affairs Committee, 381 Park Ave. South, New York, N.Y. 10016.

TEACHER REFERENCES

Chanter, Albert A. *Sex Education in the Primary School.* Macmillan and Co., Ltd., Little Essex St., London WC2, England, 1966.

Currah, Ann M. *Best Books for Children* (1967). R. R. Bowker Co., 1180 Ave. of America, New York, N.Y. 10036.

Curriculum Guides for Family Life and Sex Education: An Annotated Bibliography (1972). E. C. Brown Foundation, Portland, Oregon. 97204.

Gottlieb, Bernard S. *What a Boy Should Know About Sex.* Indianapolis: The Bobbs-Merrill Co., Inc., 1961. 46206.

————. *What a Girl Should Know About Sex.* Indianapolis: The Bobbs-Merrill Co., Inc., 1961. 46206.

Growth Patterns and Sex Education: A Suggested Program K–12. Vol. XXXVII, No. 5a (May 1967). American School Health Association, Kent, Ohio. 44240.

Family Life Education Bibliography of Selected Books, Pamphlets, Curriculum Guides and Materials Since 1960. California State Department of Education, Bureau of Homemaking Education, 721 Capitol Mall, Room 407, Sacramento, Calif. 95800.

Hook, Andrew J. *Sex Education Curriculum* (1966). Aurora Public School, East Side District 131, Aurora, Ill. 60500.

Mangan, Kenneth. *Social Hygiene Guide—Family Life and Development* (1966). Illinois School for the Deaf, Dept. of Children and Family Services (1966). Jacksonville, Ill. 62650.

Reading Materials on Aspects of Sex Education for Parents and Children (1966). Health Education and Welfare, U.S. Dept. of Health, Education and Welfare Administration Children's Bureau, Washington, D.C. 20000.

Reference List of Resource Materials in Child Development and Family Life for Classroom Use in Elementary School. Contra Costa County schools, 75 Santa Barbara, Pleasant Hill, Calif. 94523.

Reik, Theodor. *What Shall I Tell My Child?* (New York: Crown Publishers, 1966. 10016.

Sex Education Guide for Teachers (1967). Family Life Education Program, Flint Community Schools, Flint, Mich. 48500.

Sex Education and the New Morality (1967). Child Study Association of America, 9 East 89th St., New York, N.Y. 10001.

Sex Education—Resource Unit for Grades 5, 6, or 7 (1967). The American Association for Health, Physical Education, and Recreation, 1201 Sixteenth St., N.W., Washington, D.C.

Special Issue: Human Sexuality and Education, Vol. 3 (January 1967). California School Health Association, 693 Sutter Street; San Francisco, Calif.

What to Tell Your Children About Sex (1964). Child Study Association of America, Pocket Books, Inc., New York, N.Y. 10028.

EVALUATION. Every resource unit should indicate ways of evaluating the outcomes. These suggestions may appear in the section on activities or may be presented as separate items. They should recommend a variety of evaluational measures that are in keeping with the objectives. They may include testing, analysis of written and oral expression, observation of behavior in various activities and situations, and student comments.

THE TEACHING–LEARNING UNIT

Basically, the teaching–learning unit is planned by the teacher for a particular group of students. Blount and Klausmeier list four basic differences between the teaching–learning unit and the resource unit.

1. A teaching–learning unit takes into consideration the achievements, interests, and abilities of specific students.
2. A teaching–learning unit is formulated according to one's idea of the successive steps, the sequence, most effective in learning concepts, skills, and abilities.
3. A teaching–learning unit presents a limited number of concepts, skills, and attitudes; the number is determined by the time available, the

specific objectives of the unit, the manner and sequence in which the concepts will best be learned, and so on.

4. A teaching–learning unit is often in a format suitable for student use.[12]

The teaching unit is what many teachers take with them to class each day. In it are guidelines for the day's teaching, materials to be used, and tentative schedules of time involved in each lesson. While he is in the classroom, the teacher is able to work with the students in planning the activities that will go into the unit. These activities are performed, with the help of the teacher, by motivated students. It should be remembered, though, that at no time does the teacher allow the students to take complete control of the planning. This responsibility can never be completely relinquished by the teacher.

When planning the unit, the teacher will first think in terms of weekly rather than daily lesson plans. The units will usually vary in length, depending on the subject matter to be covered, emphasis on different areas, films to be shown, and so on.

A SAMPLE UNIT. The following is a sample teaching–learning unit. Its format and ordering may differ slightly from the one suggested in this chapter. For example, objectives are stated as unit "aims," introductory activities are offered, and some important concepts that the students should acquire by the end of the unit are listed. Otherwise, the unit covers all the major areas in the teaching–learning unit described on page 66. The sample unit covers a five-week period on infectious diseases. The age level is approximately that of the ninth grade.

UNIT PLAN

Topic: Infectious Diseases   *Grade:* Ninth
Time: Five weeks   *Unit Sequence:* Given before noncommunicable diseases.

UNIT AIMS

Understandings (Cognitive Domain)

1. List three diseases and/or disabilities that are caused by environmental factors.
2. Differentiate between bacteria and fungi.
3. Describe the various routes through which bacteria may enter the body.
4. Identify the favorable conditions under which bacteria may grow and live.

[12] "Framework for a Teaching–Learning Unit" from *Teaching in the Secondary School,* 3rd edition, by Blount and Klausmeier. Copyright © 1953 by Harper & Row, Incorporated. Copyright © 1958, by Herbert J. Klausmeier. Copyright © 1968 by Nathan S. Blount and Herbert J. Klausmeier. Reprinted by permission of Harper & Row, Publishers.

5. Describe three major deterrents to infection in man.
6. Name at least five conditions under which man encounters most disease microorganisms.

Attitudes (Affective Domain)

1. To develop favorable attitudes toward maintaining and observing the health rules and regulations in the community for the preservation of health and the prevention of the spread of disease.
2. To develop favorable attitudes toward observing good habits of personal cleanliness in order to prevent the spread of disease.
3. To develop an interest in the need to control communicable diseases.
4. To emphasize the importance of immunization.
5. To develop an appreciation of the role one plays in disease control.

Habits and Skills (Action Domain)

1. To develop the skills of locating information concerning
   a. how to avoid disease.
   b. immunization time.
   c. how to recognize infection.
   d. methods of combating infection.
2. To develop the habit of seeing a doctor regularly.
3. To develop the habit of daily cleanliness.

POSSIBLE INTRODUCTORY ACTIVITIES

1. Present the film "Anatomy of a Disease."
2. Discuss some of the problems students have in controlling and preventing disease.
3. Give a brief history of disease from early times to the present.
4. Present current news articles and clippings on communicable diseases; have students envision what might occur if no methods of combating them were known.

UNIT INTRODUCTION

Every second of every day we are being constantly bombarded by an endless variety of one-celled organisms which fill the air we breathe, cling to our skins, and invade the water we drink, the rivers in which we swim, and the clothes we wear. No sooner do we finish washing than the organisms return, some to aid us, some to do us harm. But there are steps we can take to prevent infection. These include getting a regular physical checkup; maintaining a healthy balance between rest, play, and work; and preserving good nutrition and hygiene.

Yet even with these precautions we are sometimes still unable to protect ourselves from infection. In this case the human body has a marvelously effective method of taking care of itself. Let us look at this protection.

MAJOR SUBJECT MATTER CONTENT	LEARNING ACTIVITIES	STUDENT RESOURCES

How do the agents which cause communicable disease enter the body?
A. Person to Person.
B. Food.
C. Water.
D. Air.
E. Animal and human carriers.
F. Through the skin.
	A. Discuss some possible ways to eliminate these causative factors.
	B. Discuss questions
	  1. What is bacteria?
	  2. How do they live?
	  3. Why is the common housefly more than just a nuisance?
	(experiment for answers)
	C. Dramatize what a "carrier" is in an 8-mm film or in a play.
		Programmed text:
		Prevention of Communicable Disease
		Health Heroes Series
		  Louis Pasteur
		  Edward Jenner
		  Robert Koch
		  Edward Trudeau

Why is the sanitation of the milk supply one of the most important items of food control?
A. Milk spoils easily, protection comes through
  1. Healthy cows.
  2. Clean dairy.
  3. Pasteurization.
  4. Careful transportation.
  5. Sanitary bottling.
B. Protection of meat.
C. Protection of water.
	A. Discover laws for the pasteurization of milk (on state level).
	B. Discover diseases whose germs thrive in milk and meat.
	C. Debate the question of whether it is safe to drink from a well.
	D. Discuss what the government does to protect the public.
		Pamphlets on control of communicable diseases from local Department of Health:
		How Your Local Health Department Serves You
		How Your State Health Department Serves You
		Milk Sanitation
		Clean Water Is Everybody's Business

MAJOR SUBJECT MATTER CONTENT	LEARNING ACTIVITIES	STUDENT RESOURCES

The Body's Barriers
A. First-line barriers.
  1. Skin.
  2. Cila of nose.
  3. Reflex acts.
    a. Sneezing.
    b. Coughing.
    c. Vomiting.
    d. Diarrhea.
  4. Tears.
  5. Saliva.
  6. Tonsils.
B. Second-line barriers. If microbes or any other foreign particles succeed in breaking through the first-line barriers they are met by a complex internal system of defenses:
  1. Histamine.
  2. Leukocytes.
  3. Phagocytes.
  4. Fever.
C. Third-line barriers. (Immunity is the body's specific resistance to infection and is due to the presence of specific antibodies. Immunity can be obtained in one of two ways. Active immunity or passive immunity.)
	A. Film: *Defense Against Invasion* (10 min.)
	B. Follow-up discussion.
	C. Class investigation: What are some other possible first lines of defense?
	D. Start vocabulary chart.
	E. Discuss the three steps in the onset of disease—invasion, incubation, and infection—and how the body fights each stage.
	
	A. Film: *Body Defenses Against Disease* (10 min.).
	B. Discussion of other internal systems of body defenses.
	
	A. Invite local doctor to discuss with the class how immunity works and why it is important.
	B. Film: *Immunization* (11 min.).
	C. Students do individual immunity chart. List diseases they had and all past and recent immunizations.
		Control of Communicable Disease in Man
		How Your Body Fights Infection

Some Common Communicable Diseases

A. Common cold
  1. Causative agents.
  2. Symptoms.
  3. Treatment.
  4. Transfer methods.
  5. Prevention.

A. Film: *The Common Cold.*
B. Solve problem: what can be done to protect students in school and at home?

Cold Facts About the Common Cold
Common Cold
Let Your Cold Alone
Winter Enemies

B. Streptoccal Infection
  1. Causative agents.
  2. Symptoms.
  3. Treatment.
  4. Transfer methods.
  5. Prevention.

A. Construct cartoon strips, "The Biography of a Streptococcus."

C. Influenza.
  1. Causative agents.
  2. Symptoms.
  3. Treatment.
  4. Transfer methods.
  5. Prevention.

A. Construct a "Fight Influenza" campaign. Have students decide what local agencies could cooperate in the effort, what publicity would be necessary (posters, radio and TV commercials, etc.), and how each segment of the population could be reached.

Influenza

D. Tuberculosis
  1. Causative agent.
  2. Symptoms.
  3. Treatment.
  4. Transfer methods.
  5. Prevention.

A. Film: *Tuberculosis* (11 min.) and/or *Are You Positive, Rancher Glen's Secret.*

Climate and TB
Crusade of the Christmas Seal
How Your Body Fights Tuberculosis
Tuberculosis Through the Teens
TB—Basic Facts in Basic English
What You Need to Know About TB
What You Can Do About Tuberculosis
Long Adventure

MAJOR SUBJECT MATTER CONTENT	LEARNING ACTIVITIES	STUDENT RESOURCES
Veneral Disease A. Syphilis 1. Causative agents. 2. Symptoms. 3. Treatment. 4. How it is transferred. 5. Prevention.	A. Discuss venereal diseases, how they spread, how they are treated. B. Study effect of venereal diseases on history of mankind. C. Learn work of Public Health Service in fighting venereal disease.	*Teenagers and Venereal Disease*
B. Gonorrhea 1. Causative agents. 2. Symptoms. 3. Treatment. 4. How it is transferred. 5. Prevention.	A. Film: *A Quarter Million Teenagers* (16 min.).	*Strictly for Teenagers* *Syphilis and Gonorrhea* *Some Questions and Answers About VD*
Prevention of the Spread of Communicable Disease (Steps that can be taken to prevent serious complications of some of the more common communicable diseases of young people. Maintaining good health. B. Having periodic health examinations. C. Recognizing early sign of communicable diseases. D. Receiving vaccinations at appropriate times.)	A. Consult newspapers and current magazines for accounts of recent advances against disease. B. List personal habits which affect prevention of these diseases. C. Discover measures followed in the school which protect the pupils from the spread of communicable disease. D. Films: *Preventing the Spread of Diseases* (14 min.); *Your Health; Disease and Its Control* (11 min.):	*Protect Your Family Through Immunization* *Common Sense* *The Science Book of Wonder Drugs*

IMPORTANT CONCEPTS

1. Everyone has the potential for disease at all times.
2. A disease may become established long before it may be recognized.
3. Communicable diseases are still a major health problem of the individual.
4. There are certain steps the individual can take to prevent and control communicable diseases.
5. A great majority of disease is controlled by the body's natural defenses.
6. Disease-retarding factors within the body may be bolstered by immunization.
7. A disease may be prevented or its effects can be lessened through sound health practices.

SOME POSSIBLE MEANS OF EVALUATION

1. Discuss with the class the aims of the unit; see which ones were best met, which least.
2. Observe the growth in attitudes, skills, and knowledge of the students.
3. Present a knowledge test before and after the unit.
4. Ask for student comments about the knowledge gained.
5. Prepare with the class a list of unanswered questions.
6. Have the class prepare a health campaign for their school. Structure it much as the learning activity for influenza but have it much broader in scope and limit the "audience" to the school's physical area.

TEACHER RESOURCES

BOOKS

Adams John M. *The Virus Diseases*. New York: Macmillan Publishing Co., Inc., 1960.

Anderson, Gaylord W., and Margaret G. Arnstein. *Communicable Disease Control*. New York: Macmillan Publishing Co., Inc., 1962.

Curtis, Helena. *The Viruses*. New York: American Museum Science Books, 1966.

Fiennes, Richard. *Man, Nature and Disease*. New York: Signet Science Library Books, 1965.

Health Concepts: Guides for Health Instruction. Washington, D.C.: American Association for Health, Physical Education, and Recreation, 1967.

Krugman, Saul, and Robert Ward. *Infectious Diseases of Children*. St. Louis: The C. V. Mosby Company, 1964.

Morton, R. S. *Venereal Diseases*. New York: Pelican Books, 1966.

School Health Education Study. *Health Education: A Conceptual Approach to Curriculum Design*. Minneapolis: 3M Education Press, 1968.

PAMPHLETS

Cause, Spread and Cure of Syphilis. U.S. Government Printing Office, Washington, D.C. 20402.

Common Cold. Equitable Life Assurance Society, Bureau of Public Health, New York, N.Y. 10009.

Gonorrhea, Its Cause, Spread and Cure. U.S. Government Printing Office, Washington, D.C. 20402.

Guarding Your Family's Health. John Hancock Mutual Life Insurance Co., Health Education Services, Boston, Mass. 02116.

Home Care of Communicable Diseases. John Hancock Mutual Life Insurance Co., Health Education Services, Boston, Mass. 02116.

The News About Tuberculosis. John Hancock Mutual Life Insurance Co., Health Education Services, Boston, Mass. 02116.

Protection Against Communicable Diseases, Equitable Life Assurance Society, Bureau of Public Health, New York, N.Y. 10009.

Seminar Reference Material on Disease Prevention Through Immunization. U.S. Dept. of Health, Education, and Welfare, Public Health Service, Communicable Disease Center, Washington, D.C. 20203.

Syphilis, the Invader. Public Affairs Committee, Inc., New York, N. Y. 10016.

TB—The Killer Cornered. National Tuberculosis Association, New York, N.Y. 10019.

Tuberculosis. World Health Organization, Washington, D.C. 20001.

Why Let It Burn? American Social Hygiene Association, New York, N.Y. 10019.

Winter Enemies. John Hancock Mutual Life Insurance Co., Health Education Services, Boston, Mass. 02116.

FILMS

Anatomy of a Disease. National Tuberculosis Association; 1740 Broadway, New York, N.Y. 10019.

Are You Positive? National Tuberculosis Association; 1740 Broadway, New York, N.Y. 10019.

Body Defenses Against Disease. Encyclopaedia Britannica Films, Inc., 425 N. Michigan Avenue, Wilmette, Ill. 60091.

Common Cold. Encyclopaedia Britannica Films, Inc., 425 N. Michigan Avenue, Wilmette, Ill. 60091.

Defense Against Invasion. Department of State, Albany, N.Y. 12225.

Immunization. Encyclopaedia Britannica Films, Inc., 425 N. Michigan Avenue, Wilmette, Ill. 60091.

A Quarter Million Teenagers. Churchill Films, 662 North Robertson Blvd., Los Angeles, Calif. 90069.

The Innocent Party. Calvin Productions, 1105 Truman Road, Kansas City, Mo. 64106.

The Invader. Distributed by Center for Mass Communication, Columbia University Press, 1125 Amsterdam Ave., New York, N.Y. 10027.

Rancher Glen's Secret. National Tuberculosis Association; 1740 Broadway, New York, N.Y. 10019.

Tuberculosis. Encyclopaedia Britannica Films, Inc., 425 N. Michigan Avenue, Wilmette, Ill. 60091.

Your Health: Disease and Its Control. Coronet Instructional Films, 65 E. Southwater St., Chicago, Ill. 60601.

STUDENT RESOURCES

BOOKS

American Medical Association. *Today's Health Guide.* Chicago: American Medical Association, 1965.

Bauer, William W., et al. *The New Health and Safety.* Glenview, Ill.: Scott, Foresman & Company, 1966.

Igel, Haller B. *American Health and Safety Series: Prevention of Communicable Disease.* Palo Alto, Calif.: Programmed Learning Text, Behavioral Research Laboratories, 1965.

Townsend, R., K. Townsend, and L. Doss. *Building a Healthy Body and Healthful Living.* Austin, Tex.: Steck Health Series, Steck Company, 1960.

Williams, Dorothea M. *Building Health.* Philadelphia: J. B. Lippincott Co., 1959.

Wright, Betty L., and Reuben D. Behlmer. *Living in Safety and Health,* Philadelphia: J. B. Lippincott Co., 1966.

PAMPHLETS

Climate and TB. The National Tuberculosis Association, 1740 Broadway, New York, N.Y. 10019.

Cold Facts About the Common Cold. Aetna Life Insurance Co., Farmington Ave., Hartford, Conn. 06105.

Common Cold. Equitable Life Assurance Society, Bureau of Public Health, 393 Seventh Ave., New York, N.Y. 10009.

Control of Communicable Disease in Man. American Social Hygiene Association, 1740 Broadway, New York, N.Y. 10019.

Crusade of the Christmas Seal. National Tuberculosis Association, 1740 Broadway, New York, N.Y. 10019.

Health Heroes Series. Metropolitan Life Insurance Co., 1 Madison Ave., New York, N.Y. 10010.

How Your Body Fights Infection. American Medical Association, 535 N. Dearborn St., Chicago, Ill. 60610.

Influenza. U.S. Department of Health, Education, and Welfare, 330 Independence Ave., S.W., Washington, D.C. 20203.

Let Your Cold Alone. American Medical Association, 535 N. Dearborn St., Chicago, Ill. 60610.

Long Adventure. National Tuberculosis Association, 1740 Broadway, New York, N.Y. 10019.

Man Against Disease. Metropolitan Life Insurance Co., 1 Madison Ave., New York, N.Y. 10010.

Protect Your Family Through Immunization. U.S. Public Health Service, 330 Independence Ave., N.W., Washington, D.C.

Strictly for Teenagers. (Ask your State Board of Health.)

Syphilis and Gonorrhea. (Ask your State Board of Health.)

TB–Basic Facts in Basic English. National Tuberculosis Association, 1740
Broadway, New York, N.Y. 10019.

Teenagers and Venereal Disease. American Social Hygiene Association, 1740
Broadway, New York, N.Y. 10019.

Tuberculosis Through the Teens. National Tuberculosis Association, 1740
Broadway, New York, N.Y. 10019.

What We Need to Know About TB. National Tuberculosis Association, 1740
Broadway, New York, N.Y. 10019.

What You Can Do About Tuberculosis. John Hancock Mutual Life Insurance
Co., Health Education Services, 200 Berkeley St., Boston, Mass. 02116.

Winter Enemies. John Hancock Mutual Life Insurance Co., Health Education
Services, 200 Berkeley St., Boston, Mass. 02116.

THE DAILY LESSON PLAN

A daily lesson plan is nothing more than an expanded portion of a unit
plan. It is planned on a day-to-day basis and telescopes some aspect or
aspects of the unit to give further magnification.[13] Although the lesson plan
is an expansion of certain portions of the unit, it in no way alters or changes
the order in which the unit is to be taught.

Lesson plans are especially helpful to new teachers because they offer
them a detailed daily schedule to follow. These plans also involve a greater
amount of planning in terms of specific teacher goals and methods. Unlike
the unit plan, which gives a guide to what will be taught over a particular
period of time, the lesson plan is much more detailed and gives actual topics
to be covered on a particular day and specific activities to be used in
motivation and learning.

There are also considered disadvantages to the daily lesson plan. One
is that it is time consuming; it removes the teacher from giving his time to
other important aspects of the teacher–learning situation. Another is that
a detailed lesson plan tends to hold the teacher to a rigid course of instruction, whereas the unit plan allows for more flexibility. These problems
can be overcome if the teacher recognizes that there is a need for a healthy
balance between unit planning and daily lesson planning. Where certain
situations warrant more detailed preparation, the teacher should not hesitate
to do so.

Preparation of the daily lesson plan. Basically, there is no one
way of planning the daily lesson. There are a number of reasons for this.
One is that in creative teaching, the teacher must be allowed the flexibility
to plan in a way which best meets the needs of his or her teaching situation.
A second factor is that the subject matter will often dictate the type of
lesson plan needed. A third factor concerns the students involved. Consideration must be given to grade level, student backgrounds, learning
abilities, achievement groupings, and previous learning activities. Callahan

[13] A brief history and general nature of the daily lesson plan can be found in
William H. Burton, *The Guidance of Learning Activities*, 3rd ed. (New York: Appleton-
Century-Crofts, 1962), pp. 322–324.

agrees that no two lessons must have identical organization, but he does feel that the teacher should give attention to seven important factors while preparing a daily lesson plan. These he gives as follows:

1. Specific objectives.
2. Specific procedures.
3. Use of time.
4. Materials and resources.
5. Assignments.
6. Evaluation.
7. Relationship of a particular daily lesson plan to its parent unit.[14]

Callahan suggests further that the beginning teacher should experiment with different types of lesson plans to determine just how these seven points can best be covered.

To illustrate one way in which a daily lesson plan may be developed, an outline of a junior high school lesson plan on venereal disease will be used. Let us suppose that the motivating factor in devising this plan got its impetus from a newspaper article which stated that the incidence of teenage venereal disease was rising throughout the country. As the unit involved was communicable disease, the students began asking questions about the article. The teacher, therefore, felt it important to expand the unit in order to give more emphasis to venereal disease.

Before the teacher began working on a lesson plan, she asked the students to list questions they had concerning venereal disease. She then developed the following outline.

LESSON PLAN

Topic: Venereal Disease   *Grade:* Ninth
Time: Approximately three days, fifty minutes a period, three periods
       a week.

UNIT AIMS

Understandings (Cognitive Domain)
1. Differentiate between syphilis and gonorrhea.
2. Identify and describe the four stages of syphilis.
3. Identify the major source(s) of:
   a. syphilis.
   b. gonorrhea.
4. List the potential results of untreated:
   a. syphilis.
   b. gonorrhea.
5. Identify potential complications of (a) syphilis and (b) gonorrhea
   in pregnant women.
6. Identify signs and symptoms of gonorrhea and syphilis in men and
   women.

[14] Sterling G. Callahan, *Successful Teaching in Secondary Schools* (Chicago: Scott, Foresman, 1966), p. 172.

7. List forms of treatment of:
   a. syphilis.
   b. gonorrhea.

Attitudes (Affective Domain)
1. That students realize venereal disease is a threat to good health.
2. That students understand that venereal disease must be cured in its early stages in order to prevent further complications.
3. That young people be made to feel they cannot allow "shame" to prevent them from seeking competent help.
4. That there is an obligation on the part of a contaminated person to see that those with whom he has sexual contacts get competent medical help.
5. That students develop an appreciation of the role they can play in the reduction of venereal disease.

Habits and Skills (Action Domain)
1. To develop the skills of locating information with particular emphasis upon:
   a. Causes of syphilis and gonorrhea.
   b. The effects of the diseases on man.
   c. Signs and symptoms of gonorrhea and syphilis.
   d. How venereal disease can be cured.
2. To develop judgmental skills with particular emphasis on:
   a. The ability to evaluate signs and symptoms of venereal disease.
   b. The ability to recognize that certain steps must be taken to prevent the spread of venereal disease.
3. To exercise the habit of taking every possible precaution in avoiding venereal disease.

First Day of Lesson Plan

WHAT TO TEACH	TIME	PROCEDURES	RESOURCES
	10 min.	Briefly review some of the basic facts of communicable disease which were covered in class earlier in the unit.	
	5 min.	Discuss some of the causes for the rise in teen-age venereal disease.	Pamphlets: *Why the Rise in Teen-age Gonorrhea? Why the Rise in Teen-age Syphilis?*

I. Syphilis
  A. Caused by spirochete.
  B. Transmitted by
    1. Intimate contact.
	20 min.	Main discussion on syphilis	*VD Claptrap*

2. Congenital
syphilis.
C. Not transmitted
through door
knobs, toilet
seats, or objects
exposed to air
and sunlight.
D. Signs and symp-
toms
1. Primary
stage.
2. Secondary
stage.
3. Latent stage.
4. Tertiary
stage.
E. Results of failure
to treat syphilis.
F. Diagnosis.
G. Treatment.

10 min. Discuss student questions.
cover written questions students handed in earlier that
hadn't been answered in
the lecture.

1. Why are blood tests
for syphilis required in certain states before marriage?

2. Where did syphilis
originally come from?

3. How can a baby be
protected when a pregnant
mother has syphilis?

4. Can keeping clean
keep you from getting
syphilis?

5. How can a person get
syphilis without having sexual intercourse?

5 min. Hand out booklet for stu-   *Student Manual on*
dents to do assigned work   *Venereal Disease*
in.

Give assignments for next
period.

Answer last-minute ques-
tions.

Assignments:
1. Have students do Part I in their *Student Manual on Venereal Disease* for the next
class.
2. Hand out pamphlet *Today's VD Control Problem* for students to read and prepare
questions from the first part of next class.

Second Day of Lesson Plan

WHAT TO TEACH	TIME	PROCEDURES	RESOURCES
	10 min.	Go over answers to Part I in manual, using teacher's handbook.	*Teacher's Handbook on Venereal Disease Education*
		Discuss pamphlet.	
II. Gonorrhea	15 min.	Main discussion on gonorrhea.	
A. Caused by gonococcus.			
B. Transmission			
1. Intimate contact.			
2. Baby's eyes infected during birth.			
C. Symptoms			
1. Male.			
2. Female.			
D. Results of failure to seek treatment.			
1. Sterility.			
2. Blindness.			
3. Crippling.			
E. Diagnosis.			
F. Treatment.			

	5 min.	Discuss student questions handed in earlier.
		  1. How is gonorrhea diagnosed?
		  2. Why is gonorrhea harder to detect in females?
		  3. Can gonorrhea simply "go away?"	

	14 min.	Show film—discuss.	
	6 min.	Give assignments for next class.	*VD Questions,* *VD Answers*

Assignments:
1. Have students do Unit II in their *Student Manual* for the next class.
2. Remind them they may hand in questions they may have concerning the film seen that day.
3. Hand out pamphlet *Venereal Disease—A Renewed Challenge* for students to read for the next period.

THIRD DAY OF LESSON PLAN

WHAT TO TEACH	TIME	PROCEDURES	RESOURCES
	10 min.	Go over answers to Unit II in *Student Manual*.	
		Cover questions about film, pamphlet.	

III. Individual and Community Responsibility
A. Education
  1. Role of the home.
  2. Role of the school.
  3. Role of the health department.
  4. Role of family doctor.
	10 min.	Discuss on Individual and Community Responsibility.	

	13 min.	Film	*When Love Needs Care*
	17 min.	Discuss film in relation to the last three days.	
		Answer questions from students.	
		Hand out leaflets.	*Syphilis and Gonorrhea* *Strictly for Teen-agers* *Some Questions and Answers About VD*

TEACHER RESOURCES

Baumgartner, Leona, M.D. "What Parents Must Know About Teenagers and VD.," *McCalls* (January 1963), pp. 44, 118.

Dennie, Charles C. A *History of Syphilis.* Springfield, Ill.: Charles C Thomas, 1962.

Deschin, Celia S. *Teenagers and Venereal Disease—A Sociological Study.* Atlanta: U.S. Department of Health, Education, and Welfare, Public Health Service, Communicable Disease Center, 1961.

Galton, Lawrence. "Why VD Is on the Increase," *Cosmopolitan* (January 1963), pp. 10–11.

Teacher's Handbook on Venereal Disease Education. Washington, D.C.: National Education Association, 1965.

Terry, Luther L. "VD's Alarming Comeback," *Look,* December 4, 1962, pp. 82–85.

The Eradication of Syphilis. A Task Force Report to the Surgeon General, Public Health Service, on Syphilis Control in the United States. Washington, D.C.: U.S. Department of Health, Education, and Welfare, PHS Publication No. 918, U.S. Government Printing Office, 1962.

VD Blues. New York: Avon Books, 1973.

Venereal Disease Education. A Report of the Special Subcommittee of the Public Advisory Committee on Venereal Disease Control. Washington, D.C.: U.S. Department of Health, Education, and Welfare, PHS Publication No. 1190, U.S. Government Printing Office, 1964.

Warshofsky, Fred. "The Vicious Chain," *Today's Health* (August 1963), pp. 24–29.

FILMS

VD Questions, VD Answers. 16 mm, color, sound. Produced by BFA Educational Media, 2211 Michigan Ave., Santa Monica, Calif. 90404.

When Love Needs Care. 16 mm, color, sound. Produced by Leonard C. Schwarz, P.O. Box 3241, Stanford, Calif. 94305.

STUDENT RESOURCES

Student's Manual on Venereal Disease—Facts About Syphilis and Gonorrhea. Available from NEA Publications, Sales, 1201 16th St., N.W., Washington, D.C. 20036.

Syphilis and Gonorrhea, Strictly for Teenagers, and *Some Questions and Answers About VD*. Available from State Board of Health.

Today's VD Control Problem. Published by the American Social Health Association, 1740 Broadway, New York, N.Y. 10019.

Venereal Disease—A Renewed Challenge. Public Affairs Pamphlet #292A; 381 Park Ave. So., New York, N.Y. 10016.

VD Claptrap. Syracuse, N.Y.: Ed. U. Press, 1972.

Why the Rise in Teenage Syphilis? and *Why the Rise in Teenage Gonorrhea?* Available in reprints from the American Medical Association, 535 N. Dearborn St., Chicago, Ill., 60610.

SUMMARY

Because there is so much knowledge to be assimilated by students, effective methods of presenting information must be used by today's teachers. The most effective way to present this information is through the unit plan. This type of preplanning involves a correlation of objectives, materials, and activities around one area of information. All units generally include six elements necessary for complete preplanning. These elements are included because each (or several) can influence some phase of how a student actually learns.

The resource unit is primarily for teachers and includes many sugestions for activities and resources that are constructed for one broad topic. Similar to the resource unit in form is the teaching–learning unit, but more than one of this type of unit can be constructed from a topic as broad as the one around which a resource unit is built. Teaching–learning units include objectives, materials, and activities that will broaden or influence the students' understandings, attitudes, habits, and skills.

The daily lesson plan is an offshoot of the teaching–learning unit. It relates, in a more specific manner, what will occur in a single learning situation. It can be made as individual as the teacher and the class dictate, and it serves as an important guideline for new teachers who need to keep unit goals in view.

It is a matter of speculation whether the unit plan will always be the preferred way of organizing varied areas of knowledge. With teaching innovations made daily, there is every possibility that a new method, less demanding of a teacher's time, might be put to good use.

REFERENCES

A *Climate for Individuality*. Washington, D.C.: American Association of School Administrators, 1965.

Birney, Robert C., et al. *Fear of Failure*. New York: Van Nostrand-Reinhold Company, 1969.

DeCecco, John P. *The Psychology of Learning and Instruction*. Englewood Cliffs, N.J.: Prentice-Hall, Inc., 1968.

Esbensen, Thorwald. *Working with Individualized Instruction*. Belmont, Calif.: Fearon Publishers, 1968.

Fairfield, Roy P. (ed.). *Humanistic Frontiers in American Education*. Englewood Cliffs, N.J.: Prentice-Hall, Inc., 1971.

Herrscher, Barton R. *Implementing Individualized Instruction*. Houston, Tex.: ArChem Company Pub., 1971.

Kirkendall, Lester A., and Ruth F. Osborne. *Teachers Questions and Answers Book on Sex Education*. New London, Conn.: Croft Ed. Services, Inc., 1969.

Kohl, Herbert R. *The Open Classroom*. New York: Vintage Books, 1969.

Learning About Learning. Washington, D.C.: U.S. Printing Office, Superintendent of Documents, 1966.

Mager, Robert F. *Developing Attitude Toward Learning*. Palo Alto, Calif.: Fearon Publishers, 1968.

Popham, W. James, and Eva Baker. *Establishing Instrutional Goals*. Englewood Cliffs, N.J.: Prentice-Hall, Inc., 1970.

———. *Systematic Instruction*. Englewood Cliffs, N.J.: Prentice-Hall, Inc., 1970.

Schulz, Esther D., and Sally R. Williams. *Family Life & Sex Education: Curriculum and Instruction*. New York: Harcourt, Brace & World, 1969.

5
■ THE CREATIVE
USE OF
INSTRUCTIONAL MEDIA

The Random House Dictionary of the English Language (1967) gives the following as one definition of *medium* "an intervening substance, as air, through which a force acts or an effect is produced." It is easy to imagine literally hundreds of examples of media in this sense. For a geologist it is his rocks, for an artist his paints, for a jockey his horse, for a surgeon his scalpel. Obviously, for a teacher it could be a myriad of objects, techniques, ideas, etc.

Instructional, or *educational,* media include all the aids that appeal to the learner through his senses: sight, sound, touch, taste, and smell. They are those devices through or by which one can accomplish learning. Those available today generally appeal to only two of these senses and can be classified into *audio* and *visual* categories, with an overlapping area containing both. A general diagram would look something like that shown in Table 5–1.

To discover every advantage that could be gained through the proper use of the various educational media, one must first be prepared to dispense with it. In other words, everything audio and visual outside of the teacher and his pupils must be disposed of. Included in this impressive experiment (and excluded from the classroom) must be posters; pictures; phonographs; books of every kind; magazines; overhead, opaque, and movie projectors; a television set; all games, "educational" and otherwise; abacus, number-line, and alphabet cards; a tape recorder; building and Montessori-type blocks and materials; and so on. Looking at a completely bare classroom, devoid of any "sensual" stimulation, one can easily prove one advantage of educational media—they are necessary to give a continual stimulation to the senses.

TABLE 5-1 INSTRUCTIONAL, OR EDUCATIONAL, MEDIA

AUDIO	AUDIOVISUAL	VISUAL
Tapes	Sound motion pictures	Mirror
Records	Television	Classroom television camera
Radio	Dramatic plays	Slides
Listening labs	Sound filmstrips	Charts
Telelectures	Sound-on-slides	Posters
Instruments	Slide-tape series	Cartoons
	Talking books	Filmstrips
		Teaching machines
		Telewriting
		Books
		Newspapers
		Magazines
		Transparencies
		Maps
		Globes
		Simulation games

It is a creative teacher who can remain in a classroom with twenty-eight or more restless minds and bodies and give them sufficient stimulation to keep them curious and productive for hours. Even using such techniques as group discussions, problem-solving sessions, and calisthenics will not suffice; a teacher must use aids of some kind. Children and young adults, as well as all other people, need exposure to a variety of objects, information, pictures, noises, and so on, to keep their minds in gear and receptive to new learning situations. A student will consider only one point of stimulation, the teacher, dull.

A second factor is that various media expose a student to experiences they could not possibly have or know in their usual routines. One graphic example can be noticed in children of all ages and socioeconomic levels. This is the influence of television. Children have become consumers, critics, cowboys, private eyes, villains, and superheroes. Of course, books, films, and other media serve a similar purpose. The teacher should use these media to enrich every subject by exposing his class or group to more than one view of a given topic. A unit on drug use, for example, can be made more effective by showing a film on the effects drugs have upon the body; collecting and reviewing newspaper and magazine articles on users, pushers, and legal cases; listening to tape-recorded sessions of a pot party; and so on. Such devices help a student to make up his own mind whether or not to use drugs. Through their use he can be quite certain what a drug will do to him, even though he has never tried one personally.

The media do an important job of bringing back the past. Various resources in both categories of media can trace the history of disease, bringing in the pathological, sociological, and historical influences diseases have had upon man. One cannot avoid being interested in what might have happened if President Harrison had not died of pneumonia two weeks after his inauguration, if the first successful heart transplant had been performed thirty years ago, or if syphilis in the United States had been eradicated.

What could be better to arouse curiosity than showing a class the middle episode in a film on premarital pregnancy? Or a teacher might present slides of "miracle remedy" equipment and let the class decide what it is seeing and for what purposes this equipment is used. (An overhead projector, pictures, posters, and so on, could be equally effective for this.)

Another important advantage is that these media help to encourage thinking. Thinking is complex even at the lowest level but can be organized into several classifications. These include memorization, translation, interpretation, application, analysis, synthesis, and evaluation.[1] Being able to select a medium or method that will evoke a specific kind of thinking and help the student train his mind in the process should become a natural talent to a conscientious instructor. Knowing the statistics on how many traffic accidents occurred at a given local corner can be the first step in a student-sponsored safety campaign. Discovering the sources of the original information and deciding how to use that information are the students' mental tasks. The critical thinking that could be applied in such a situation is the epitome of the thought processes, as it encompasses all of them beyond the memory category.

Finally, the media enable students to be independently creative. Just as a careful, thoughtful teacher accomplishes his educational goals through various audiovisual aids, so, too, a student can develop new insights while engaged in a learning situation: ". . . the individual is a dynamic and open system. The teacher enters as a clinician improving the environment so that the system can gather together its energies and release its powers of self direction."[2]

A student need not be involved in a project that requires some physical action in order to release his creativity. Analyzing the information he has gained from books, pamphlets, films, and graphs, he can mentally seek fresh alternatives. He can predict future health hazards arising from today's negligence and construct alternatives. The student can evaluate his judgments periodically as new information is presented to him through the media; he can extend his mental horizons and discover new, fruitful areas for his thoughts and projects.

---

[1] Benjamin S. Bloom (ed.), *Taxonomy of Educational Objectives* (New York: Longmans, Green, 1956).

[2] Calvin W. Taylor and Frank E. William (eds.), *Instructional Media and Creativity* (New York: Wiley, 1966).

Misuse of Media

It cannot be said that there are disadvantages to any given medium. It is a fact, however, that many teachers overuse some types of media and that hardly any teacher gets maximum efficiency from the devices available to him. There are common cases like that of Mrs. Q. She was delighted when she found her new classroom's walls were the type into which she could press pins. She began the year with her walls covered with pictures, artwork graphs, health posters, and three-dimensional figures. As weeks went by, however, she could not keep up with her other work, and the bulletin-board areas remained the same. Still more weeks passed and the walls were unchanged. When she finally took time to put up one new bulletin-board display, one child commented to an enthusiastic friend, "Why are you looking at that now? You'll have half a year to see it." If Mrs. Q. had saved some of her original wall projects and put up just one at a time at frequent intervals, she could have been assured of a curious and receptive audience. If she had periodically selected a few children to construct a bulletin-board display on a relevant topic, she could have saved herself time and involved the class too.

Ms. R.'s problem had to do with her inattentive class. Because she was unable to control her class and teach a health lesson at the end of every day when it was scheduled, she relied upon films to keep her rambunctious class quiet those last few minutes. After three weeks of films on everything from brushing teeth to tuberculosis, she received an especially good movie on glue sniffing. It fit perfectly into a short unit she had wanted to begin on drugs, but unfortunately the class was no longer receptive to the film medium.

Ms. R. could have used her projector every day for three weeks, each day in a different way, if she had not attached a "functional fixation" to it. She and her class had settled upon the projector as a machine-which-showed-motives-from-the-audiovisual-department. Unaware that she could use it in a wide variety of ways, the teacher soon exhausted the health film library and her students' interest in films. It can suffice to say that all instructional devices can be similarly misused.

A final example can show the hazard of using media with little regard for the outcome. Mr. M. did his method planning quite thoroughly. He designated uses for every conceivable type of gadget at his disposal. His high school health class was busy with students engaged in taping sessions, poster making, film production, and other projects that kept the students fully interested and occupied. At the same time, Mr. M. was utilizing equipment by breaking all boundaries of their "functional fixations." However, his projects became progressively more numerous and extensive, until they lacked both quality and depth. Nutrition was given as much involved attention as drug abuse. The projects were accomplished and displayed without serious consideration of what the students had gained through doing them. Conclusions and generalizations gleaned from the outcomes of the activities were often ignored in the enthusiasm of beginning another project. Mr. M. could have used more thought and fewer projects involving audiovisual media. Stressing a few important units by in-depth coverage can often bring about more learning than can spectacular teaching techniques.

INSTRUCTIONAL MEDIA IN PERSPECTIVE

There is little doubt that the various instructive media are gaining more and more favor with educational systems throughout our country. There are several reasons why this "hardware revolution" is here to stay. One reason is that the American culture equates mechanization with progress. If a school has projectors, phonographs, learning machines, listening centers, and so on, it is an indication of modernization. New schools are built to include numerous bookshelves, bulletin and chalk boards areas, and individualized learning centers of various types and degrees of elaborateness.

It is also true that several big businesses have considerable investments in educational-machine production, and their influence upon administrators and other educational personnel is considerable. The adoption of more and more mechanical and electronic devices for school use is plainly increasing.

What will be the influence of these media upon the students now enrolled in school and upon those who will be exposed to such media in the future? Two factors will determine this influence. Obviously, the first factor is the use the teacher will make of the media. In order to make media-directed learning experiences meaningful to a class, he will need to know the kind of audience that will be receiving stimuli from the devices. Planning an elaborate bulletin board on venereal disease for a fourth-grade class in a middle-class suburb is a wasted effort. Topics and their method of presentation must be related to the background and interest of the class if they are to be effective.

Second, in addition to knowing the backgrounds of the students, the teacher should know some of the psychological basis of creativity. Each student learns in a highly individual manner, but types of reactions to learning situations have been recognized. The outcome of a given learning situation depends a great deal upon attitude toward error. If a teacher believes that any question, if properly phrased, must require a yes or no answer or that any given statement can be evaluated as true or false, he is considered right–wrong oriented. He is the type that believes $3 + 2 = 5$, not $3 + 2 = 4 + 1$ or $3 + 2 = 10/2$. The numeral 5 is right. The number 5 represented by $4 + 1$ is not as acceptable. He will be actually training his students to reject areas where error occurs and leading them to seek accepted interpretations of the area under study. In other words, students will be cautious about making mistakes. This error rejection training is commonly done by such devices as teaching machines, programmed text-books, battery-operated match-the-item bulletin boards, and so on.

This type of error-rejection approach [3] is fine for programs in reading, mathematics, and other so-called exact sciences, but does it answer the needs of all students? Most important, what can it contribute to creativity?

There exists a second attitude toward error besides that of "right–wrong." That is error tolerance. A teacher possessing insights into his individual students' intellectual personalities might notice that those who seem the most innovative and creative are those who are more casual toward the possibilities of error. Because these students are not as afraid of making mistakes, they are more free to experiment with fresh alternatives to old problems or to discover new problems. These error-tolerant students can benefit from films and film making, production of dramatic plays, book selection, art projects, and bulletin-board displays.

One might wonder whether there are only two kinds of students, those who can tolerate error and those who cannot. Wallach feels that some students can shift from one attitude toward error to the other and can function at a high level in both creative and analytical situations.[4] Other students have such a strong attitude of error rejection that they cannot function creatively at all; and some students are so tolerant of error that they do not work well in situations requiring exact answers (analytical situations). Finally, there are those students who work at low levels in both creative and analytical areas. Naturally, there are degrees within these categories and no one student can be rigidly classified in one of them.

If the preceding categories are further substantiated by current research,[5] there might be a tendency for the instructional media to train further those who are already strong in error-rejection attitudes and thereby prevent them from becoming creative. At the same time, the media will neglect or even penalize those who are strong in error tolerance.

Viewed in this perspective, it turns out, ironically enough, that automated instructional devices, for all their modern hardware, may well constitute an anachronism. By underplaying the side of human thinking that involves conjecture and invention—a side that, as we have seen, has come increasingly into focus as performing a central role in man's mathematical, scientific, and aesthetic activities—automated instructional devices may lead educational practice back to a one-sided, overly rationalistic view of how thinking proceeds.[6]

---

[3] For a detailed discussion of the error-rejection–error-tolerance factors read Michael A. Wallach, "Creativity and the Expression of Possibilities," in Jerome Kagan (ed.), *Creativity and Learning* (Boston: Houghton Mifflin, 1967).

[4] Ibid., pp. 45–56.

[5] Michael A. Wallach and Nathan Kogan, *Modes of Thinking in Young Children* (New York: Holt, 1965).

[6] Wallach and Kogan, op. cit., p. 55.

EXPANDED USES OF SPECIFIC MEDIA

It would be presumptuous to call the following "examples of *creative* uses of media." Many of these described have been merely adapted to an area in health education, but with an emphasis on presenting a newer, expanded use of a medium. Creativity is a product of an individual's response to a specific situation, and in teaching, so many variables exist that methods cannot be exactly duplicated. However, there can be adaption; and what better circumstances avail themselves for creativity?

Medium: The film   *Age Group:* Tenth through twelfth grade.
Project: The making of an 8-mm film on "The Acid Experiment" (or preferably, a suitable title decided upon by the students).

As the start of any project must consider the outcome, the first task of the class must be to decide the purposes of making the film. These will determine the structure of the plot and the development of the script. Perhaps the students will attempt to show that drugs are bad, no matter what the circumstances. Maybe the class will want to ensure that the conclusion matches a real-life situation and that ultimate decisions are necessarily left to the individual. Whatever is decided would not take an unreasonable length of time, as the production itself should be as efficiently planned as possible.

To shorten the plot development, a plot triangle can be constructed by the whole class. This usually consists of three statements that provide the setting and characters, tell the incident that provides the turning point, and show the conclusion. See example of this shown in Figure 5–1. After the skeleton plot has been constructed, a script can be written to fill in the rest of the triangle.

In the meanwhile, the class can preview available films on drugs, decide what materials will be needed, and begin to film trial segments to become accustomed to the 8-mm camera. Committees must be designated to make sure that what goes on in the film is factual and authentic.

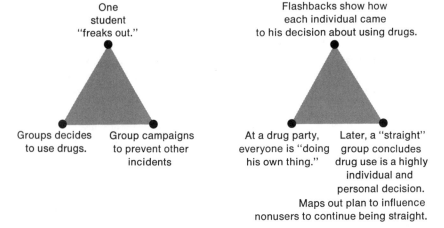

Figure 5–1. *Plot triangle.*

This might sound like an arduous process, but after a teacher has endured the pitfalls of a first trial, subsequent "productions" can run smoothly, with time left to innovate. It must be kept in mind that the objectives planned for the film activity must not be overlooked during the process.

Medium: Television.   *Age group:* All levels.   *Project:* Use of the television camera.

It has been noticed that the effectiveness of television instruction decreases as the grade level increases. That is, this medium is more successful in grades 3 through 9 than it is in high school or college.[7] If one has a hookup to an educational station, many benefits can be had through the carefully prepared lessons of the television instructors. Unfortunately, because health per se is seldom carried on these networks, the classroom teacher must discover for himself what programs in science (or history) could be relevant to an area in health. Of course this could lead to disjointed lessons unless the programs could be videotaped and replayed during a coordinated learning experience.

It is possible that some schools, particularly high schools and colleges, might have in-classroom television cameras, which can be helpful in showing details during an instructor's lecture. The camera is mounted above a table on which an object is displayed. As the instructor talks he can draw attention to the object, whose image is transferred in a magnified state upon the screen of the room's television set.

The day is not far away when high school health teachers will be instructing students in classes of human sexuality and sex education. A high school teacher could discuss the psychological and social reasons for contraception (and against contraception) and display the various contraceptive devices. Precious instruction time can be saved by letting the class see the devices without letting them be passed around. Various pills for a drug unit, isolated parts of whole pictures, microscope slides, and medicinal labels are all among the many other "props" whose magnified forms can be effectively used in a learning situation.

Medium: Tape recorder.   *Age Group:* Intermediate—High school. *Project:* Role-playing vignettes from taped interviews.

Students of all ages, not excluding adults, love to act out roles. Many of us know people for whom role playing is a way of life. Junior high and high school constitutes a time in most adolescents' lives when role playing is very close to reality. To aid the students in distinguishing and defining their personal feelings about health issues, role playing is a useful technique. The instructor can assign a role to an individual, and that individual can interject his personal interpretations and thoughts into the part.

The type of lesson we will describe will require the students to prepare, for they will need to know some facts about smoking and alcohol

[7] Wilbur Schramm, "What We Know About Learning from Instructional Television," *Educational Television: The Next Ten Years* (Stanford, Calif.: Institute for Communication Research, 1962).

usage. If the teacher plans the tape sessions as a culminating activity, the sessions need not be "anticipated" with the students. Often the pupil responses are more revealing if they are spontaneous.

The teacher, along with a small committee of students, can select the topic and subjects for the tapes. The subjects can be students in or outside the class or adults in the community. They will be playing roles also, but not being present in person can add an authentic touch to the staging.

Tape 1: An older person speaks to his two sons. "Now, boys, I've seen you both sneaking cigarettes here and there, but you've reached the age where you can make a public decision about smoking. I've smoked for twenty-five years, and you can see it has had no ill effects on me."

Roles: One son who wants to continue to smoke and his brother who has tried it and wants to convince his brother to quit.

Tape 2: A "judge" reads the case against an eighteen-year-old veteran of Viet Nam who was arrested for buying beer in a liquor store.

Roles: One defense lawyer; one prosecuting lawyer (or a jury who must decide the consequence).

Tape 3: The background sounds of a party are heard. There are loud laughs and the buzz of conversation.

Roles: Several teenagers in another part of the house. The opening dialogue will begin something like this:

ONE: How disgusting to hear our parents carrying on that way!

ANOTHER: Not disgusting at all! They're just having some fun. That's all.

A THIRD: What's wrong with having fun with V-8 juice or ginger-ale?

A FOURTH: Hold it now. What are you, your parents' keeper? Just because they let down a few times, you are practically condemning them as alcoholics!

The group continues, debating the issue of social drinking. Smoking could also be included.

The general procedure would be to play the tape and then let the students begin their roles. As other members of the class feel involved, they can pull their chairs closer and join in, taking the side they feel is most akin to their own feelings. Ideally, all three tapes could be going at once in various parts of a large area, so that only a small group would be involved in each situation. The groups could rotate; roles could be changed; and discussion could be started again after a given period of time.

Medium: Bulletin board. *Age group:* Elementary *Project:* Stimulate interest in proper nutrition.

Children often need to discover not only what foods are essential to good health, but also what some of the available foods are and how they taste. For an elementary unit on nutrition, one bulletin board can be used the entire time. This bulletin board can be constructed by having each student make a door and attach it on the board. On each door could be his personal knob, with his name on the outside of it. The board could be titled, for example, "Open the Door to Proper Nutrition" or "Find the Key to Good Health." Behind each door there might be a picture of the type of food being studied, like fruits, vegetables, or dairy products. Below the door could be placed two columns of small pictures of foods. The columns could be labeled, for example, "Do Like" and "Don't Like."

The children can aid in securing pictures and samples of the various foods. For instance, vegetables are an important source of essential vitamins and minerals. The students can decide what vegetables they have had that they like or do not like and can put the pictures or words for the pictures in the appropriate column. Then, with the help of the teacher, they can discuss vegetables like cauliflower, kale, and eggplant, which perhaps many students have not tasted. The simple preparation of these foods in the classroom with a pan and hot plate can provide an interesting opportunity to learn food preparation, serving, and table manners.

Fruits such as the avocado, fresh pineapple, and coconut can be handled in much the same way. Enterprising teachers of older pupils can have them bring in easy recipes which include a vegetable or fruit that might help the students move it from the "don't" to the "do" column.

The board can be a challenge for the students to discover various sources for the pictures or to make pictures of the vegetables in various stages of growth or preparation. It can also show substitute sources of the ingredients of vegetables that the children cannot move from the "don't" to the "do" column.

These same lessons are only four of the hundreds of uses of media. Using a combination of media would produce hundreds more. Of course each lesson involving media is individual, simply because of the physical limitations of facilities or of the amount of control a teacher has.

WHERE TO GET INFORMATION CONCERNING EDUCATIONAL MEDIA

Teachers and curriculum planners should review sources of information, selected references, periodicals, and journals concerned with educational media. The following list of sources of information on educational media is designed to aid the teacher and other school personnel in the selection and classroom use of the best modern instructional techniques and materials.

Where to Look for Audiovisual Materials

The following is a listing of some of the more useful references the health educator may use in locating audiovisual materials.

FILMS

Educational Film Guide. Edited by Josephine S. Antonini. H. W. Wilson Co., 950 University Avenue, New York, N.Y. 10452. Annual supplements. Indexes and describes alphabetically by title and by subject 22,949, 16-mm motion pictures in all instructional subjects.

Educators Guide to Free Films. Educators Progress Service, Randolph, Wis. 53956. Revised annually. Provides title, content description, length, running time, whether silent or sound, date of release, information on distributors, and limitations on distribution for 4,339 currently available free films.

The Educational Media Index. McGraw-Hill Book Company, 330 West 42nd Street, New York, N.Y. 10036. Describes all nonbook instructional materials.

Educational Television Motion Pictures: Descriptive Catalog Containing Series Data, Subject, and Use Level Index for 16-MM. Educational Television Programs. NET Film Service, Audio-Visual Center, Indiana University, Bloomington, Ind. 47401. Lists and describes 1,403 educational television programs available to schools, organizations, and individuals for non-television and nontheatrical use. Gives title, content description, length, film characteristics, grade classifications, and rental and purchase information.

Library of Congress Catalog: Motion Pictures and Filmstrips. Washington, D.C. 20540. Quarterly with annual and quinquennial cumulations. Includes listings by title and a subject index of all the educational motion pictures and filmstrips released in the United States and Canada. Short annotations of each title are provided.

U.S. Government Films for Public Educational Use. Office of Education, U.S. Department of Health, Education, and Welfare, Washington, D.C. 20402. Available from the Superintendent of Documents, U.S. Government Printing Office, Washington, D.C. Price $2.75. Describes and indexes alphabetically by title and by subject motion pictures and filmstrips of U.S. government agencies and departments available for public use.

FILMSTRIPS

Educators Guide to Free Filmstrips. Compiled and edited by Mary Foley Horkheimer and John W. Diffor. Educators Progress Service, Randolph, Wis. 53956. Revised annually. Lists and describes 270 silent filmstrips, 305 sound filmstrips, and 51 sets of slides available for use free of charge.

Filmstrip Guide. Edited by Josephine S. Antonini. H. W. Wilson Co., 950 University Avenue, New York, N.Y. 10452. Four-year cumulated supplement, 1955–58. Annual supplements, 1960–62. Provides an alphabetical listing by title and a subject index for 13,141 sound and silent filmstrips in all instructional subjects.

RECORDS, TAPES, AND TRANSCRIPTIONS

Audio Cardolog. Edited by Max U. Bildersee, Box 1771, Albany, N.Y. 12201. 1958 to date. Monthly except July and August. Provides more than 400 cross-indexed cards each year and gives complete data on selected records and tapes.

Children's Record Reviews. Box 192, Woodmere, N.Y. 11598. October 1957, to date. Issued five times per year. Includes listings of children's records featuring stories, fairy tales, and so on.

Educators Guide to Free Tapes, Scripts and Transcriptions. Compiled and edited by Walter A. Wittich and Gertie Hanson Halsted. Educators Progress Service, Randolph, Wis. 53956. Revised annually. Lists and classifies 138 free tapes, 287 free scripts, and 83 free transcriptions available to educators.

SOURCES OF INFORMATION ABOUT EQUIPMENT

The Audio-Visual Equipment Directory, 8th ed. edited by James W. Hulfish, Jr., 1962, 331 pp. National Audio-Visual Association, Fairfax, Va. 22030. Fee.

Audio-Visual Equipment Manual, by James D. Finn, 1958, 363 pp. Holt, Rinehart and Winston, Inc., 383 Madison Ave., New York, N.Y. 10017. Fee.

HEALTH CURRICULUM GUIDES (PARTIAL LIST)

Arizona, Mesa. Mesa Public Schools. *Health Education Student Terminal Goals, Program Goals, and Behavioral Objectives.* n.d. 41 pp. n.p.

Massachusetts, Springfield. Springfield Public Schools. *School Health Policies— Health and Safety Guides.* Revised 1970. unp. n.p.

———— Worcester. Worcester Public Schools. *Health and Safety K–3. Curriculum Guide.* 1971. 78 pp. n.p.

———— Worcester. Worcester Public Schools. *Health and Safety 4–6. Curriculum Guide.* 1971. 126 pp. n.p.

Minnesota, Rochester. Curriculum Dept. Independent School Dist. 535, Rochester Public Schools. *Health Course of Study: A Course of Study in Health for Kindergarten.* 1965. 22, 14 pp. n.p.

———— Rochester. Curriculum Dept. Independent School Dist. 535, Rochester Public Schools. *Health Course of Study: A Course of Study in Health for Grade One.* 1965. 26, 14 pp. n.p.

———— Rochester. Curriculum Dept. Independent School Dist. 535, Rochester Public Schools. *Health Course of Study. A Course of Study in Health for Grade Two.* 1965. 36, 14 pp. n.p.

———— Rochester. Curriculum Dept. Independent School Dist. 535, Rochester Public Schools. *Health Course of Study. A Course of Study in Health for Grade Three.* 1965. 38, 14 pp. n.p.

———— Rochester. Curriculum Dept. Independent School Dist. 535, Rochester Public Schools. *Health Course of Study. A Course of Study in Health for Grade Four.* 1965. 34, 14 pp. n.p.

———— Rochester. Curriculum Dept. Independent School Dist. 535, Rochester Public Schools. *Health Course of Study. A Course of Study in Health for Grade Five.* 1965. 72, 14 pp. n.p.

———— Rochester. Curriculum Dept. Independent School Dist. 535, Rochester Public Schools. *Health Course of Study. A Course of Study in Health for Grade Six.* 1965. 43, 14 pp. n.p.

—— St. Paul. Mounds View Schools. *"Issues in Life"*: *An Interdisciplinary Approach to Health Education at the Tenth Grade Level.* n.d. 12, 24, 32, 65 pp. n.p.

Missouri, St. Joseph. The School District of St. Joseph. *Health Guide for Grades 1–6.* 1970. 34 pp. n.p.

New Mexico, Los Alamos. Los Alamos Schools. *Health Education Curriculum Guide. Grades K–6.* n.d. unp. n.p.

—— Los Alamos. Los Alamos Schools. *Living Now, Transitional Health— Education, Curriculum Guide. Grades 7–12.* n.d. unp. n.p.

New York, Brooklyn. New York (City) Board of Education Bureau of Curriculum Development. *Health Education in Elementary Schools.* 1969– 1970. #3, 249 pp. Fee.

—— Rochester. City School District. *Science, Health, Safety Curriculum Guide——Unit Revision for Family Living Curriculum Guide K–6.* 1971. 39 pp. n.p.

Pennsylvania, Philadelphia. The School District of Philadelphia. *Environmental Rat Control, Primary Unit, Grades 1–3.* 1970. 34 pp.

—— Philadelphia. The School District of Philadelphia. *Environmental Rat Control, Intermediate Unit, Grades 4–6.* n.d. 47 pp. Fee.

—— Philadelphia. The School District of Philadelphia. *Health Education, Grades 10–11–12. (Senior High School.)* 1968. 218 pp. Fee.

—— Pittsburgh. Penn Hills School District. *First Grade Health Curriculum Guide.* 1971. 56 pp. n.p.

—— Pittsburgh. Penn Hills Schools District. *Health Curriculum Guide— Second Grade.* 1971. 52 pp. n.p.

—— Pittsburgh. Penn Hills School District. *Health Curriculum Guide— Third Grade.* 1971. 73 pp. n.p.

Tennessee, Chattanooga. Hamilton County Department of Education. *Nutrition Education Grades K–1.* n.d. 22 pp. n.p.

—— Chattanooga. Hamilton County Department of Education. *Nutrition Education Grade 2.* n.d. 20 pp. n.p.

—— Chattanooga. Hamilton County Department of Education. *Nutrition Education Grade 3.* n.d. 17 pp. n.p.

—— Chattanooga. Hamilton County Department of Education. *Nutrition Education Grade 4.* n.d. 21 pp. n.p.

—— Chattanooga. Hamilton County Department of Education. *Nutrition Education Grade 5.* n.d. 17 pp. n.p.

—— Chattanooga. Hamilton County Department of Education. *Nutrition Education Grade 6.* n.d. 16 pp. n.p.

—— Chattanooga. Hamilton County Department of Education. *Nutrition Education Guide Grades 7–12.* n.d. 22 pp. n.p.

Virginia, Norfolk. Norfolk City Schools. *Building Healthier Youth.* n.d. unp. Free.

West Virginia, Charleston. Kanawha County Schools. *Health Education Units for Grade 7.* 1971. 52 pp. n.p.

Printed Media: Books

Printed media are said to function well in directing attention, in presenting a model of the student's performance, in guiding thinking, and in giving feedback.[8]

Because books can and do change behavior they should be selected wisely. The problem is that about half the states have some regulations regarding the selection of basal textbooks, with a few states having a single textbook–adoption policy. The new teacher should investigate both the system's regulation concerning adoption policy and the availability of textbooks. Equally important, the new teacher should look into the resources which are available for securing additional supplementary references. For, although his particular situation may prevent him from selecting the basal text to be used, *no* system prohibits enriching the program through the use of additional texts of his own.

There are a large number of health texts (and health series) available for grades K–12. One should review current periodicals for reviews of texts, obtain complementary copies when possible, and inquire about various texts through fellow colleagues.

Most important, one should first review potential texts before their final use in the classroom. Wesley M. Staton provides us with a practical guide to book reviewing.[9]

I. *Content*

1. Does the book/article deal with a problem or area of sufficient professional significance to justify publication?
2. Has the material been adequately covered in previous publications, or does this presentation bring out fresh facts, new concepts, or improved techniques?
3. Has the writer made new and significant recommendations, or has he simply pulled together existing material without careful analysis and evaluation?
4. Is the content scientifically accurate and adequately supported by documentation or prima facie evidence?
5. Does the author use references that are essential and germane to his subject, or does he use them excessively, uncritically, and without regard for variances in their relative significance?
6. Is the philosophy sound, rational, and logical—based upon the latest and best evidence—or is it inconsistent with biosocial data, theory and logic?
7. Are false statements or misleading recommendations presented?

[8] Robert M. Gagné, *The Conditions of Learning* (New York: Holt, 1965), p. 284.

[9] Wesley M. Staton, "Literature: Lifeblood of the Profession," *School Health Review*, July/August 1973.

8. Is the content drawn from a diversity of fields and areas, or do the author's sources appear to be narrow and limited?
9. Are the proposals made consistent with basic human motivations, or do they fail to recognize contemporary value systems and the implications for what people want and what they will do to fulfill these wants?

II. *Organization, Coverage, and Emphasis*

1. Is the order of presentation of topics sound from both the logical and psychological standpoints?
2. Does the author introduce his material with a beginning chapter/section that motivates the reader and emphasizes the importance of the area or field he is dealing with?
3. Does the author adhere to the central purpose and area of concern of his book/article, or does he tend to depart from what should be the major thrust of the presentation?
4. Is the relative emphasis of various topics appropriate to, and consistent with, their importance to the basic purpose of the book/article?
5. Is the subject adequately covered in the book/article, or are important topics omitted or dealt with inadequately?
6. Is the book/article too long? If so, where could it have been cut without affecting its professional value and usefulness?
7. Is the material organized into chapters or sections on the basis of logical interrelationships and sequence of content?
8. If a book, are concise summaries, pertinent references, provocative questions, and realistic problems or projects provided at the end of chapters?
9. If a book where scientific and technical terms are extensively used, is there a glossary with a guide to pronunciation?

III. *Presentation and Style*

1. Does the author express his ideas clearly and concisely, or is his writing fuzzy, vague, and wordy?
2. Does the author tailor his sentences so they say precisely what he means, or does he settle for tiresome platitudes, worn cliches, and overused block phrases?
3. Is the ratio of ideas to words relatively high, or does the author "talk a lot without saying anything"?
4. Does the author write objectively and explicitly, or does he resort to emotionalized bias or vague exhortation?
5. Does the author write directly to the reader in a stimulating, personal manner, or is the style and vocabulary stiff, pompous, and pretentious?
6. In controversial areas—drugs, sex, alcohol, smoking, and health care plans—is the author's approach fair and objective, or does his presentation betray personal, religious, racial, or political prejudice?
7. If the author criticizes a professional policy, practice, group, or indi-

vidual, is he objective and impersonal, or does he go beyond the bounds of good taste and professional dignity?

8. Is the level of presentation consistent; that is, does the author avoid writing alternately to students and sophisticated professional colleagues?

9. Are quotations used effectively and pertinently, or are they used indiscriminately to impress the naive reader?

10. If there is a preface—as there should be in all books—is it brief, crisp, and succinct, telling clearly what the book is about, for whom it was written, and how it's organized; or does it ramble, claim too much, and credit an overlong list of people who "helped"?

IV. *Format*

1. If a book, is it attractively designed in terms of cover, size, illustrations, and use of color?

2. Are the illustrations essential, appropriate, and up-to-date, or are they used chiefly for artistic effect without adding to the communicative value of the work?

3. If graphs, charts, diagrams, pictographs, or symbols are used, are they really necessary, accompanied by concise captions, and explicitly referred to in the text?

4. If anatomical transparencies are used, do they actually help the reader develop concepts that could not be learned as well with other kinds of illustrations (i.e., are they simply a sales gimmick)?

5. Is the type of a size and style that is both attractive and readable?

6. Are the headings and subheadings set in a style and size that clearly delineates the important segments of the text?

7. Is the page layout and letter spacing and size conducive to easy reading (i.e., a two-column large page is generally more readable than a single column small page) or do paragraphs, sentences, and words seem to run together?

V. *Publisher and Author*

1. Is the publishing house recognized as one of quality and experience in the professional literature, or is it a publisher with an eye for quick profits—inclined toward mediocre manuscripts and vanity publishing?

2. If the publisher is a professional association or society, is it well established and highly regarded in the field, or is it one of the fringe organizations attempting to take advantage of the public and professional interest in drugs, sex, and certain other provocative areas of health science?

3. Is the author well qualified in the field or area discussed, or has he simply pulled together material from the works of authorities and restated their views without giving new and meaningful interpretation?

4. Does the author's professional affiliation appear to qualify him as an authority in the specified area of the book/article?

5. Does the author have previous books or articles, or is this his first? If

this is a first effort, did it come in the early stages or at the end of a professional career?

6. If an article, is it an "official" point of view by an office holder of a professional association? Would it have been published elsewhere without the authoritative mantle of political office?

7. Is the author presently involved with the area and problems he discusses, or is he commenting as an outsider or professional dilettante (e.g., health science text authors who have not taught the basic college health course for many years)?

8. Does the author or publisher appear to have a commercial or other vested interest in the philosophy and proposals advanced?

Selected References Concerned with New Educational Media

Arbuthnot, May Hill. *Children and Books.* Chicago: Scott, Foresman and Co., 1964.

Audio-Visual Research Institute. *The A-V Index: A Guide to Instructional Materials Information in Selected Publications.* Detroit: The Institute, 1961.

Brown, James, et al. *A-V Instruction: Technology, Media & Methods.* New York: McGraw-Hill Book Company, 1973.

Dale, Edgar. *Audio-Visual Methods in Teaching.* New York: Holt, Rinehart and Winston, Inc., 1969.

Freedman, Florence B., and Esther L. Berg. *Classroom Teacher's Guide to Audio-Visual Materials.* Philadelphia: Chilton Co., 1961.

Huck, Charlotte S., and Doris A. Young. *Children's Literature in the Elementary School.* New York: Holt, Rinehart and Winston, Inc., 1968.

Larrick, Nancy. *A Teacher's Guide to Children's Books.* Columbus, Ohio: Charles E. Merrill Books, Inc., 1963.

Learning Directory. New York: Westinghouse Learning Corp., 1972–73.

Wittich, Walter Arno, and Charles F. Schuller. *Audio-Visual Materials: Their Nature and Use.* New York: Harper & Row, Publishers, Inc., 1967.

A Selected List of Journals Concerned with Educational Media

American Library Association Bulletin. American Library Association; 50 East Huron Street; Chicago, Ill. 60611. Monthly, except bimonthly during July–August.

Audiovisual Communication Review. Department of Audiovisual Instruction, National Education Association, 1201 16th Street N.W., Washington, D.C. 20036. Bimonthly.

Audiovisual Instruction. Department of Audiovisual Instruction, National Education Association; 1201 16th Street N.W., Washington, D.C. 20036. Monthly.

Booklist and Subscription Books Bulletin. American Library Association; 50 East Huron Street, Chicago, Ill. 60611. Semimonthly.

Educational Screen and Audio-Visual Guide. 230 East Ohio Street, Chicago, Ill. 60611. Monthly.

Film World and A-V World News Magazine. Sidale Publishing Co., 672 South Lafayette Park Place, Los Angeles, Calif. 90057. Monthly.

Journal of the University Film Producers Association. University Film Producers Association, The Ohio State University, 1885 Neil Avenue, Columbus, Ohio. 43210. Quarterly.

N.A.E.B. Journal. The National Association of Educational Broadcasters, 119 Gregory Hall, Urbana, Ill. 61801. Bimonthly.

School Libraries. Published by American Association of School Librarians, 50 East Huron Street, Chicago, Ill. 60611. Four times a year—January, March, May, and October.

The Journal of Communication. The National Society for the Study of Communication, Central Michigan University, Mt. Pleasant, Mich. 48858. Quarterly.

Sources of Reference on Where to Find Free and Inexpensive Materials

Audio-Visual Committee. *Some Sources of Free and Inexpensive Teaching Materials for Health, Physical Education and Recreation.* Washington, D.C.: The Committee, American Association for Health, Physical Education and Recreation, 1967.

Aubrey, Ruth H. (ed.) *Selected Free Materials for Classroom Teachers.* Palo Alto, Calif.: Fearon Publishers. Revised biannually.

Beyrer, Mary K., et al. *A Directory of Selected References and Resources for Health Instruction.* Minneapolis, Minn.: Burgess Publishing Co., 1966.

Educator's Guide to Free Science Materials. Randolph, Wis.: Educators' Progress Service. Annual.

Educator's Index to Free Materials. Randolph, Wis.: Educators' Progress Service. Revised annually.

Elementary Teachers' Guide to Free Curriculum Materials. Randolph, Wis.: Educators' Progress Service. Revised annually.

Free and Inexpensive Learning Materials. Nashville, Tenn.: George Peabody College, Division of Surveys and Field Services.

LeFevre, John R., and Donald N. Boydston. *Free and Inexpensive Health Instruction Materials.* Carbondale: Southern Illinois University Press, 1959.

Miller, Bruce. *Sources of Free and Inexpensive Teaching Aids.* Riverside, Calif.: Bruce Miller, 1962.

Salisbury, Gordon. *Catalog of Free Teaching Materials.* Riverside, Calif.: Gordon Salisbury, 1965.

Schain, Robert L., and Murray Polner. *Where to Get and How to Use Free and Inexpensive Teaching Aids.* Englewood Cliffs, N.J.: Prentice-Hall, Inc., 1963.

Wescott, Howard E. *A Guide to Teaching Materials in Elementary Health Education.* San Francisco: Chandler Publishing Company, 1959.

SUMMARY

Imagination and resourcefulness add valuable dimensions to teaching, and various instructional media are tools through which these two can find numerous opportunities to develop. Media can help provide constant sources of stimulation, give experiences not usually encountered in every-day living, and show opposing points of view. In addition, they can help reconstruct the past, develop academic curiosity, encourage various ways of thinking, and enable students to become independently creative.

Media methods can be overused or substituted for necessary teacher exposure and defeat their own purposes. They can be used to "train" children in much the same way as machines are programmed, paradoxically achieving results that are the opposite of a creative ideal.

One can see that merely stockpiling audio and visual media equipment does not ensure creative processes. Using any medium means careful consideration of not only objectives but also possible outcomes. Above all, these uses must stress the flexibility inherent in the medium, as educating for creativity necessarily involves helping both student and teacher to become aware of alternatives.

REFERENCES

Bending, C. *Communication And The Schools*. New York: Pergamon Press, 1970.

Cook, Myra B. *The Come-Alive Classroom*. West Nyack, N.Y.: Parker Publishing Co., 1967.

Coppen, Helen. *Aids to Teaching and Learning*. New York: Pergamon Press, 1969.

Davis, Harold S. (ed.). *Instructional Media Center*. Bloomington: Indiana University Press, 1971.

DeKieffer, Robert E. *Media Milestones in Teacher Training*. Washington, D.C.: Educational Media Council, 1970.

Garrison, Cecil. *1001 Ideas for the Classroom Teacher*. Berkeley, Calif.: McCutchan Publishing Co., 1968.

Gunselman, Marshall (ed.). *What Are We Learning About Learning Centers?* Oklahoma City, Okla.: Eagle Media, 1971.

Haviland, David S. *Multi-Media Classrooms Revisited*. Troy, N.Y.: Center for Architectural Research, Rensselaer Polytechnic Institute, 1971.

Miller, Richard. *Selecting New Aids to Teaching*. Washington, D.C.: Association for Supervision and Curriculum Development, 1971.

Nelson, Leslie W. *Instructional Aids: How to Make Use of Them*. Dubuque, Iowa: W. C. Brown Co., 1970.

Saxe, Richard W. *Schools Don't Change*. New York: Philosophical Library, 1967.

Tanzman, Jack. *Using Instructional Media Effectively*. West Nyack, N.Y.: Parker Publishing Co., 1971.

Taylor, Calvin W., and Frank E. Williams (ed.). *Instructional Media and Creativity*. New York: John Wiley & Sons, Inc., 1966.

Tickton, Sidney. *To Improve Learning*. New York: R. R. Bowker Co., 1970.

PART III

Creativity in the Classroom

"For in spite of his lonely past, Jonathan Seagull was born to be an instructor, and his own way of demonstrating love was to give something of the truth that he had seen to a gull who asked only a chance to see truth for himself."

—RICHARD BACH,
Jonathan Livingston Seagull

6 ■ THE NATURE OF CREATIVE TEACHING

Emerson once said, "Imagination is not a talent of some men but is the health of every man." This imagination, or creativity, is a natural quality inherent in all human beings, but few can express this essential virtue fully. Emerson's assertion can be easily applied to education, but educators must be aware of their own creative abilities before they can hope to maintain the health of the imaginative minds entrusted to them.

This is not nearly as simple as it would at first appear. Although there is considerable agreement that the educational environment should place a high value upon creative behavior both for the teacher and for the students, little is known about the principles whereby such an environment can be created in the classroom. Moreover, research has yet to show whether the environment can influence the individuals in this type of classroom to seek new, original understandings or discovery methods.

Our interest in this text, therefore, will be to search for, formulate, and develop principles for (1) creating an environment which places a high value on creativity, (2) presenting teaching techniques in specific areas of health education, and (3) guiding the evaluative behavior of the teacher. It will be up to each reader to ascertain how effective these principles will be for him.

THE HEALTH TEACHER NEEDS TO BE CREATIVE

One may well ask whether the subject of health affords a great outlet for creative activity. The fact is evident that there is quite possibly no field of human knowledge that affords a greater outlet for creative teaching than health. The primary responsibilities of health education are to encourage the student to explore his own habits, attitudes, and behavior; to discover for himself the need for good health; and to pursue a course of action, based on current knowledge, for experiencing the "good life." These goals deal with values and behavior on such a personal level that they must be presented in a vital, imaginative way in an atmosphere that will encourage uninhibited discussion and introspection. Only then can health make an impact on the student's quality of life.

Few students today are willing to accept being told the cold facts of health. The depersonalized statistics of death, cancer, and heart disease or the "hard sell" of washing before meals and brushing one's teeth after eating destroy the very personal nature of the subject. Unlike some other areas of education that tend to be more abstract and remote from living, health is an essential and individual subject which readily lends itself to student involvement if presented without the limitations of *cold facts*. The teacher must bridge the gap that may exist between the student and the subject. One way to do this is to emphasize "pupil discovery" rather than "telling." If the student is allowed to discover for himself the solutions to the barriers to a healthy life, then he will feel the pride and satisfaction that come with the discoveries. This fact has been emphasized by John Gardner.

All too often we are giving our young people cut flowers when we should be teaching them to grow their own plants. We are stuffing their heads with the products of earlier innovation rather than teaching them to innovate. We think of the mind as a storehouse to be filled when we should be thinking of it as an instrument to be used.[1]

THE CHARACTERISTICS OF CREATIVITY

The Romans coined the phrase *Ignotum per ignotius*, which means "explanation of a difficult matter with a still more difficult explanation." It fits very well in trying to define and explain creativity, for merely giving many examples of creativity can well lead to confusion. It is known that creativity can seldom be consciously controlled, but it is found in almost all human activities. The discoveries made by creative people vary in kind, according to the limitations of the activity in which the person is involved and according to the individual's innate talent. A poet has a far broader range of alternatives for innovation than does an electrician who must keep his wiring techniques within standard safety limits.

Smith articulated a common definition quite simply. "Creativity is sinking down taps into our past experience and putting these selected experiences together into new patterns, new ideas, or new products."[2]

[1] John Gardner, *Self-renewal* (New York: Harper & Row, 1965), p. 21.
[2] James A. Smith, *Setting Conditions for Creative Teaching in the Elementary School* (Boston: Allyn and Bacon, 1966), p. 4.

This is an excellent definition, for it simply explains what small children most commonly do when left to entertain themselves. On a higher educational level it is called synthesis.

But what does creativity involve? Kneller stated, "creativity seems to involve certain mental abilities. These include the ability to change one's approach to a problem, to produce ideas that are both relevant and unusual, to see beyond the immediate situation, and to redefine the problem or some aspect of it." [3] The health teacher who teaches creatively is one who has an exciting, inventive approach to health, who is less likely to be bound by the usual. The health student who receives impetus from the creative teacher can synthesize new solutions to old problems and discover for himself areas of understanding that are new to him. Creativity involves helping oneself to see what has not been seen before by the individual.

To be even more precise, some specific examples of what creativity is and what it is not follow.

CREATIVITY IS A PERSONAL EXPERIENCE. The creative teacher must encourage the student to find good health and self-fulfillment within himself and to solve his problems by tapping his personal experiences. This is the theme in Laotzu's poem.

> There is no need to run outside
> For better seeing,
> Nor to peer from a window. Rather abide
> At the center of your being;
> For the more you leave it, the less you learn.
> Search your heart and see
> If he is wise who takes each turn:
> The way to do is to be.[4]

THE CREATIVE MOMENT IS UNIQUE. To say that creativity is unique means that whatever has been produced must never have occurred in that exact way before and can never exist again. If it were reproduced, then it would cease to be creative. One might wonder, then, how critics of some Shakespearean plays can praise "creative" performances, because the same lines have been performed since the seventeenth century. Here the uniqueness lies in an actor's interpretation of the drama. Mouthing the same words and gesturing can be mechanical and devoid of any meaning supplied by the actor. Giving the words new stress, with accompanying inflections and relevant gestures, can result in a truly creative performance. This is only one example of an endeavor that is limited somewhat by its natural

[3] George F. Kneller, *The Art and Science of Creativity* (New York: Holt, 1965), p. 13.

[4] Copyright © 1944 by Witter Bynner. Reprinted from *The Way of Life According to Laotzu*, translated by Witter Bynner, by permission of The John Day Company, Inc., publisher.

form but that is nevertheless capable of new interpretation. The difference between reproduction and interpretation is one of creativity.

CREATIVITY IS NOT CONFORMITY. Creativity involves original ideas, different and new points of view, and openness to fresh alternatives. Conformity simply means doing something repeatedly in the same manner as it has been done before.

Another important feature of creative situations is the use of sometimes unusual means to achieve practical ends. Conformity in thinking cannot envision a brick used in 100 different ways; a creative mind can, and enables an individual to use the object for anything from a door stop to a lithographic stone.

CREATIVITY DOES NOT ALLOW A SET SYSTEM. A system implies fixed standards or ways of doing things. This would stifle creative teaching. Because every situation in education is different, flexibility is required in order to extract maximum value from each learning opportunity. An example of this can be seen in the "new math." Children have no greater difficulty learning to change points of reference in arithmetic than they do in learning fixed facts, but the first method allows an infinite amount of variation because it is flexible. For example, until recently, a white stick of a designated size was always equal to 1, a red stick twice as large was equal to 2, and so on. Now students merely learn that red is twice as large as white (and white half the size of red), so that a teacher can give white (or any other color) any value he chooses. If white = 3, then red = 6; or if red = 16, then white must be half that value (8). Is this a new system? No. It is simply a different way of working with values. This is why so many parents have trouble when they attempt to work with the new math; they have lost the flexibility necessary to examine a problem.

CREATIVITY IS THE HERITAGE OF EVERY HUMAN BEING. Once more we can return to Emerson's quote. Creativity is within the nature of every individual. It simply needs to be stimulated in those who lack the confidence to discover this fact for themselves. Once this imagination is stimulated, immediate and gratifying results, both for the teacher and the student follow. A growth in independence is readily seen. Students will soon refuse to accept some of the given reasons for or solutions to current problems. Is the air pollution plaguing our cities a necessary evil that must merely be kept in check? Can the public's acceptance of gasoline-powered cars be changed in time to prevent "national suffocation"? Can the solution be found in the industries' methods of waste disposal? Are the answers to these questions really plausible?

CREATIVE TEACHING IN HEALTH

When the health teacher begins to apply these principles to the classroom, he may start by presenting a body of relevant facts or ideas. From these facts and ideas the students are led to make correct inferences about unstated facts and concepts. This challenges the student to find out for himself the generalization or inferences that the subject matter contains. They are the product of his own thinking and his manipulation of basic knowledge. Thus, the student becomes personally involved in his own learning, with enough detachment, however, to allow for critical evaluation of the results. One of the important results of this discovery is that the student is not simply a storehouse for a set of conclusions stated by the teacher.

SETTING CONDITIONS FOR CREATIVE TEACHING

Teachers have often decried establishing a creative atmosphere in their classrooms because they equate creativity with a license for permissiveness. They believe they must involve the students to the extent that the students can decide what is relevant and necessary for their own education. No one can refute the fact that students lack knowledge and experience. It would be unreasonable to let a sixth-grade math class decide its own curriculum. However, math can be learned more thoroughly by students under the guidance of a creative teacher than it can be in a classroom which discourages innovation and offers few direct-involvement activities. It should be noted that creativeness occurs when a motivated student discovers something completely new to him.

To enable this freedom of thought, many factors must be removed that currently are believed to stifle spontaneity. Unfortunately, the climate in some classrooms serves to place obstacles in the path of creative teaching and learning.

Clark, in his book *Brainstorming*, set up an effective list of "killer statements" or ways to stop the flow of creative thinking, which follows.

KILLER STATEMENTS

OR

How to Stop the Flow of Creative Thinking [5]

We've never done it that way before . . .
It won't work . . .
We haven't the time . . .
We haven't the manpower . . .
It's not in the budget . . .
We've tried that before . . .
We're not ready for it yet . . .
All right in theory but can you put it into practice . . . ?
Too academic . . .

Production won't accept it . . .
They'll think we're long-haired . . .
Engineering can't do it . . .
Won't work in my territory . . .
Customers won't stand for it . . .
You'll never sell that to management . . .
Don't move too fast . . .
Why something new now? Our sales are still going up . . .
Let's wait and see . . .

[5] *Brainstorming* by Charles Hutchison Clark (Garden City, N.Y.: Doubleday & Company, Inc., 1958).

What will the customers think . . . ?

Somebody would have suggested it before if it were any good . . .

Too modern . . .

Let's discuss it as some other time. . .

You don't discuss it at something like this . . .

You don't understand our problem . . .

We're too small for that . . .

We're too big for that . . .

We have too many projects now . . .

Let's make a market research test first . . .

It has been the same for twenty years so it must be good . . .

What bubblehead thought that up . . . ?

I just know it won't work . . .

Let's form a committee . . .

Let's think it over for awhile and watch developments . . .

It's not our responsibility . . .

Yes, but . . .

It will increase overhead . . .

It's too early . . .

It's too late . . .

That's not our problem . . .

The union will scream . . .

Here we go again . . .

Let's put it in writing . . .

I don't see the connection . . .

Won't work in our industry . . .

We can't do it under the regulations . . .

Nuts . . .

Political dynamite . . .

Sounds good but don't think it will work . . .

It's not in the plan . . .

No regulations covering it . . .

We've never used that approach before . . .

It's not in the manual . . .

It'll mean more work . . .

It will offend . . .

It won't pan out . . .

Our people won't accept it . . .

You don't understand the problem . . .

No adolescent is going to tell me how to run my business . . .

We have never done it that way before . . .

Let's wait until next week . . .

Gardner Murphy provides an excellent illustration of an uncreative environment in a school where

children are found who sit in rows with an adult in front, who are required to learn things which they do not wish to know, and who are forced for the most part to look forward in the room, not at one another or out the windows. They are required to recite—that is, to give back what they have read or been told. When the overwhelming excitement of something that has happened outside of school comes up, and the impulse is to talk about it, they are told that they can take care of that when school is over. . . . Their interest in things which are not laid out in the curriculum at the particular time and place is pushed aside as inappropriate and irrelevant. It is the task of the adult to know what the children are to learn. What they are learning all the time outside of school is regarded as an annoyance, a distraction, or even a sign of rebellion against the standard good behavior required of the school.[6]

This description may sound a little extreme, but this type of educational philosophy persists today. Accompanying it is a cloth to snuff out any flicker of creativity which may surface from time to time in the class-

[6] Gardner Murphy, *Human Potentialities*, 2nd ed. (New York: Basic Books, 1961), pp. 101–102.

room. Let us, then, consider those influences which will provide a more effective background for creativeness.

A CLIMATE FOR CREATIVE TEACHING–LEARNING

If the health teacher is to be concerned with creative teaching, he will discover that it takes more than a conglomeration of facts, ideas, and activities to produce it. Even the most creative ideas can die in an environment which lacks stimulation. Think, for example, of the teacher who wanted her students to break up into small groups for a critical debate but did not carry through with the assignment because she feared that it would "disrupt her classroom." Some teachers become unsettled by any situation which may disturb the status quo. They are threatened by excessive noise, lack of agreement, argumentative questions, and other situations which may have overtones of "disorder."

Smith has listed five conditions that tend to develop creativity: (1) intellectual conditions, (2) physical conditions, (3) social–emotional conditions, (4) psychological conditions, and (5) educational conditions.[7] By conditions of creativity the author means the techniques or environmental stimuli that cause original behavior, uncommon responses, and a continual flow of ideas.

Intellectual Conditions

A vital need in health education and in all teaching is to influence the student to draw warrantable conclusions, relate concepts, discover central ideas, and utilize as wide a range of resources as possible for developing insights. Some of the conditions which can lead the student to this desired end include his constant use of new evidence; his stress upon ideas, not facts; the development of creative thinking; his utilization of personal experiences; and his linking of key ideas. Because these conditions are closely linked to a free academic atmosphere, let us examine them more closely.

THE CONSTANT USE OF NEW EVIDENCE. By the time a new textbook rolls off the press today it is, at best, probably two years old. This fact is critical in a field such as health education, where medicine and research move at such a rapid rate that it is almost impossible to keep up, much less allow for a possible time lag of two years. Consequently, health teachers should take advantage of current periodical literature, new supplementary booklets, popular magazines, newspapers, and other media such as television to keep abreast of current information. Used to full advantage, this new information can provide an endless stream of meaningful classroom activity. For one, the teacher can frequently present the pupil with new evidence that apparently conflicts with previous information. The pupil then can integrate this information with previous knowledge and propose theories to

[7] Smith, op. cit., p. 120.

account for the discrepancies in the two sources. For example, the differences in the numbers of people who are killed in auto accidents from one year to the next or die of cancer or heart disease may warrant an investigation into why these trends exist. Has the inclusion of safety devices on automobiles had an effect on highway accidents? If not, why have they not? Has the antismoking campaign had any effect on the deaths from smoking-related diseases?

THE STRESSING OF IDEAS, NOT FACTS. There is a tendency in health education to bombard students with facts instead of encouraging them to see the significance of the completed puzzle. Food calories, names of muscles and bones, and leading causes of death can become much more relevant if students are motivated to look for their implications. For every principle that a student learns he should see at least one implication. By doing this he is able to use each principle as a spring-board to further inquiry. Facts (such as enamel being the hardest, most durable material in the body) are meaningless by themselves. The teacher who concerns himself with learning facts is simply concerning himself with a lower-level mental process. The teacher who uses data and stimulates the student to translate, interpret, or apply it is dealing in higher-level processes. In the lower mental process there is an emphasis upon the student receiving material, memorizing it, and reproducing it without a flaw. In the higher mental process there is an assimilation of facts, a synthesis of the material into something not there before, and a presentation of it in such a way as to make it a new idea.

THE DEVELOPMENT OF CREATIVE THINKING. Possibly everyone has seen the situation where the teacher says, "What do you think the answer to this question might be?" Generally such a teacher is not really interested in what his class thinks the answer might be, but whether they can guess what *he* thinks the answer is. The winner of the game to guess what answer the teacher wants usually receives the highly praised, "That's right, Johnny." This is about all the child does receive, because he lost any opportunity for creative thinking.

The reverse of this situation would be one in which a teacher leads his students to the point that not one but many answers are plausible. This, of course, often unsettles some teachers, for the result is not always predictable. But the multianswer technique does have its bright side, which affects the other, for it offers the students a chance to develop the skill of seeking alternative solutions. Trying to second-guess a teacher can be frustrating for a student who needs to find the worth of his own ideas.

THE UTILIZATION OF PERSONAL EXPERIENCES. The more the student can incorporate what he has learned into his own personal experiences, the more meaningful the learning process becomes. To give each learning situation a chance to become part of the student's world, teachers must have a thorough knowledge of each and every individual in his class so that he can include some "local color" in the teaching–learning situation. (See

Chapter 2 for a discussion of this point.) Because of this, students are often able to grasp the relationship between sound health practices and personal modes of life. With the threat of nuclear war and interracial strife, students will not be content with long monologues on what the instructor alone thinks is important. Not only must teachers see to it that students are exposed to the varied concepts of good health, but they must also be certain that these concepts are presented in such a way as to be both *relevant* and *honest*.

THE LINKING OF KEY IDEAS. Students should not be made to think of health in terms of isolated parts, but as many interlinking factors having a direct or indirect bearing on one's state of well-being. If, for example, a student is learning about good dental care, he should view good dental health not only as brushing one's teeth, but also as an aspect of personal appearance (psychological health), nutrition (Vitamin A), consumer awareness (obtaining a dentist, purchasing toothpaste), and infection and disease (possibility of mouth infection spreading to other parts of the body).

Creativity is more than a topic that is incorporated in a few lessons daily. It must be developed much like any other attitude, and it cannot grow in an atmosphere not prepared to nurture it. The intellectual conditions described here cannot alone provide the climate for creativity, but they are—along with the physical, social–emotional, psychological, and educational conditions—necessary to the process.

INTELLECTUAL CONDITIONS

AIDS TO CREATIVE TEACHING	OBSTACLES TO CREATIVE TEACHING
1. The teacher constantly stays tuned in to new ideas.	1. The teacher limits his discussion to the textbook.
2. The teacher leads the students to discover ideas and concepts instead of teaching them just facts.	2. Students are expected to memorize facts for future tests.
3. The teacher contrives situations where creative thinking is necessary for the student.	3. The teacher does the interpreting for the student.
4. The teacher utilizes the personal experiences of the students as much as possible.	4. Students' observations and personal exeriences are unexamined.
5. The teacher attempts to show the interrelatedness of subject matter areas.	5. The teacher deals in isolated facts.

Physical Conditions

In many traditional secondary schools today classrooms, lunchrooms, and hallways are almost barren of any type of decoration except for an occasional peeling of plaster or a no-smoking sign. Why is there such physical drabness? Probably the best answer is that "it has always been that way." One almost has the impression that the best type of education is that which takes place in surroundings which lack any aesthetic appeal.

But things are changing, however slowly. More and more schools are stressing the importance of beautiful surroundings, both for exteriors and for interiors of buildings. Classrooms are now equipped with both blackboards and bulletin boards, colorful and movable desks, centers inside and outside the classroom for different types of learning (see Figure 6–1), floors that are completely covered with carpeting so that children can sit down on it if desired, large windows, and fluorescent lighting. In some schools one can even hear the playing of soft music in the hallways. All of this, of course, could be considered the ideal, and any teacher would be happy to be blessed with one of these pleasant additions to his classroom.

But even the teacher who finds himself in an almost bleak situation where none of the above is available can provide students with a creative and stimulating atmosphere. The area of health is especially rich in possibilities for enriching the environment with such materials as the following:

Booklets	Mobiles
Books	Motion pictures
Brochures	Music
Bulletin boards	Newsletters
Cartoons	Newspaper clippings
Chalkboards	Opaque projector
Charts	Overhead projector
Closed-circuit television	Permanent mounted screen
Comic strip drawings	Phonographs
Drawings	Posters
Encyclopedias	Programmed instruction
Exhibits	Puppets
Filmstrips	Radio—AM-FM
Flannel boards	Scrapbooks
Flash cards	Simulating games
Flat pictures	Slides
Folders	Specimens
Graphs	Tables
Leaflets	Tape recorders
Magazine clippings	Teaching machines
Magnetic boards	Transparencies
	Videotape

Certain materials, such as pencils, paper, chart paper, maps, bulletin boards, and posters, should be available or on display at all times. Other

ADVANCED DESIGN FOR AN ELEMENTARY SCHOOL
Utilizing Media Systems and Team Teaching
to Achieve Individualized Instruction

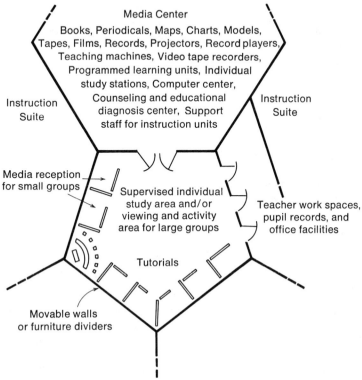

Media Center
Books, Periodicals, Maps, Charts, Models,
Tapes, Films, Records, Projectors, Record players,
Teaching machines, Video tape recorders,
Programmed learning units, Individual
study stations, Computer center,
Counseling and educational
diagnosis center, Support
staff for instruction units

Instruction Suite

Instruction Suite

Media reception for small groups

Supervised individual
study area and/or
viewing and activity
area for large groups

Teacher work spaces,
pupil records, and
office facilities

Tutorials

Movable walls
or furniture dividers

Figure 6–1. *Advanced design for an elementary school.*
Source: *Committee for Economic Development.* Innovation in Education,
1968, p. 57.

materials should be available as the situation demands. Chapter 5 discusses the creative use of many of these materials and lists sources for gathering information relevant to these materials.

Obviously, the preceding conditions plus the physical organization of students in the class will contribute greatly to the creative environment. Students who are afforded little or no freedom in the class feel excluded from any physical involvement in what is going on. The opposite of this is an environment in which students participate actively in setting up bulletin boards, exhibits, classroom activities, and some lesson plans. Seating arrangements should be determined less by tradition and convenience and more by the particular lesson that is being presented that day. Remember also that changes in surroundings are a welcomed improvement and can often stimulate students, especially when they are able to participate in the change.

PHYSICAL CONDITIONS

AIDS TO CREATIVE TEACHING	OBSTACLES TO CREATIVE TEACHING
1. Students are encouraged to move desks when situations demand. 2. Students have access to a variety of materials in the classroom. 3. Students are allowed to move about at predetermined times. 4. Students have opportunities to collect and display health materials.	1. Students are prevented from moving desks, because of teacher and/or physical surroundings. 2. There are few materials available in the classroom. 3. Students have little or no freedom of movement. 4. The teacher presents all materials to the class.

Social–Emotional Conditions

Andrews, in *Creative Education: The Liberation of Man,* states that if a teacher desires to establish an emotional–social climate conducive to creativity he must

allocate time for experimentation, for exploration, for the incubation of thoughts and feelings, and for discovery. He must encourage the individual to find the true, the good, and the beautiful within himself; to solve his problems with more than the literal-rational mind; to relate his own feelings and his own beliefs but not to disregard conventions, rather to hold them in reservation; to tolerate strangeness but also to question bias and prejudiced opinions.[8]

Reading through a number of books one will find that a nonconforming environment, free use of imagination, humor and lightheartedness, acceptance, and sensitivity to needs are factors which help to produce healthy social–emotional conditions for creativity in the classroom.[9] On the other hand, such conditions as emphasis on grading, pressure to conform, teacher-centered authority, and sanctions against questioning inhibit creativity.

An interesting aspect of the social–emotional situation is that a child showing a high development of creativity is often pressured to reduce his productivity. The sensitive teacher can help such a situation by praising originality while designating tasks which stress free use of imagination. By giving creatively inhibited students a chance to produce with no threat

[8] Michael F. Andrews, *Creative Education: The Liberation of Man* (Syracuse, N.Y.: Syracuse University Press, 1965), p. 33.

[9] See A. Cropley, *Creativity* (London: Longmans, Green, 1967). Calvin Taylor (ed.), *Creativity: Progress and Potential* (New York: McGraw-Hill, 1964), p. 98. E. Torrance, "Developing Creative Thinking Through School Experiences," in S. J. Parnes and H. F. Harding (eds.), *A Sourcebook for Creative Thinking* (New York: Scribner, 1962).

of disappointment, an instructor can help the spontaneous individual become more acceptable to the group.

SOCIAL–EMOTIONAL CONDITIONS

AIDS TO CREATIVE TEACHING	OBSTACLES TO CREATIVE TEACHING
1. The classroom atmosphere is one of mutual respect and acceptance.	1. The classroom is autocratic.
2. Students have opportunities to discuss and ask questions of the teacher.	2. Free discussion and/or "irrelevant" questions are not allowed.
3. The teacher accepts the students' attempts to think creatively.	3. The teacher rejects the students' efforts to think creatively.

Psychological Conditions

Smith lists four factors that appear essential for the development of a psychological creative environment:

1. A physically and emotionally healthy classroom.
2. An atmosphere which allows student freedom.
3. The proper motivation and tensions to agitate creative thinking and creative production.
4. A faculty and administration which understands and supports creativity.[10]

A PHYSICALLY AND EMOTIONALLY HEALTHY CLASSROOM. Much of what was stated under social–emotional conditions applies here also. In addition, a creative environment should alleviate the students' fear of participating orally in class, set realistic expectations, provide productive work and a variety of stimuli, induce a sense of trust in the teacher, and establish a cooperative rather than a competitive climate.

CREATING AN OPEN CLASSROOM. To open the door to creative teaching–learning, the teacher must allow the students to question, explore, work independently, test, evaluate, apply, and express their ideas. This does not mean that there are no controls to behavior in the classroom. It does mean that limits are both clearly visible and flexible enough to adapt to the activity. As activities vary, so limits must vary with them.

Sometimes in creative teaching a teacher may find that certain situations may not lend themselves to a completely open environment. In this case he may find it just as rewarding to arrange special "creative teaching–learning periods," such as on Monday, Wednesday, and Friday from 1:00 to 2:30 P.M.

10 Smith, op. cit., p. 131.

In his article "The 'Open' Classroom Concept Has Some Authoritarian Implications," Radebaugh brings out beautifully the contrast between the "open" and "traditional" classroom (Table 6–1).

TABLE 6–1. "OPEN" VERSUS "TRADITIONAL" CLASSROOM

AN "OPEN" CLASSROOM	A "TRADITIONAL" CLASSROOM
1. A casual and friendly exchange occurs between teacher and pupil; there is an absence of hostility.	1. There is hostility between teacher and pupil.
2. There is intense involvement of students in things they seem to care about.	2. There is much student apathy.
3. The classroom is nonauthoritarian.	3. The classroom is authoritarian and oppressive.
4. Teachers give up power.	4. Teachers are obsessed with power.
5. Teachers deal with each situation as a communal problem; an "open" classroom is *not* a permissive environment.	5. Teachers legislate annoying behavior out of existence and retain authority over student behavior.
6. Students are considered reliable, predictable, moral, friendly [implied].	6. Students are considered a reckless, unpredictable, immoral, and dangerous enemy.
7. Students enjoy school.	7. Students hate school.
8. Teachers do *not* dominate their classes.	8. Teachers dominate their classes.
9. The classroom spills out of the building into the streets, neighborhood, city.	9. Almost all activities are confined to the classroom [implied].
10. Teachers become involved in creating things in the classroom.	10. Teachers engage in little creative activity in the classroom [implied].
11. An open, democratic mode of existence is found in the classroom.	11. A closed, authoritarian mode of existence is found in the classroom.
12. Students are provided with workable alternatives.	12. Students are *not* provided with workable alternatives [implied].
13. The role of the teacher is to enable pupils to make choices and pursue what interests them.	13. The role of the teacher is primarily that of controlling pupils; choice making is denied to students.
14. "Professional" knowledge about the class is deliberately avoided.	14. "Professional" knowledge about the class is sought out and used.

SOURCE: Byron F. Radebaugh, "The 'Open' Classroom Concept Has Some Authoritarian Implications." *The Journal of Teacher Education* (Spring 1973), p. 45.

15. The teacher cultivates a state of "suspended expectations" about the class.
16. Teachers take chances; spontaneity is considered important.
17. Teachers "go with the class"; argument, disagreement, conflict, give-and-take are present.
18. Disagreement is accepted and integrated into the whole; teachers are mediators and arbitrators.
19. The classroom has a variety of resources but no prearranged structure is evident.
20. Teachers believe there is no one way to learn, nor are there specific stories or experiments all young people *must* go through.
21. Lesson plans are guides to options and a means of understanding and assessing where students are and where they seem to be going.
22. Time is *not* rigidly structured; digressions are considered valuable.
23. Fighting among students should be an affair in the lives of men— not a breach of discipline.
24. No grades; no punishment; teachers abandon absolute pronouncements.

15. The teacher has developed definite expectations about the class [implied].
16. Teachers minimize chance occurrences; routine prevails [implied].
17. Teachers follow a set plan; students obey teacher imposed rules.
18. Teachers legislate disagreement out of existence; teachers are judges and executioners.
19. The classroom is prearranged and orderly. A definite structure is evident.
20. Teachers believe there is one *best* way to learn and students must meet certain minimum standards [implied].
21. Lesson plans are "traps" for teachers.
22. Time is rigidly structured; digressions make the teacher feel guilty.
23. Fighting among students must be punished.
24. Grades given; punishment given; absolute pronouncements frequent.

MOTIVATING FOR CREATIVITY. One of the most vital components of creativity is motivation.[11] In motivating for creativity, the teacher sees his role as being less that of a provider of fixed and inflexible facts and more that of a resource person that students can tap from time to time.

In an extremely negative environment where only "correct" solutions are acceptable, facts are important and uniformity of behavior is expected. In such a situation motivation for creative endeavor is absent.

Positive motivation for creativity results when the teacher encourages students to look outside of an environment where discipline regulates behavior and outcomes are rigidly predicted.

A FACULTY AND ADMINISTRATION THAT UNDERSTANDS AND SUPPORTS CREATIVITY. Extracurricular or cocurricular activities, team teaching,

[11] See Taylor, op. cit., p. 24.

varied class size, provisions for individual study, and resource centers all nurture creativity. But without the support and encouragement of other teachers and the administration, a teacher finds it difficult, if not impossible, to carry out some of his ideas by himself.

Through faculty and administration support each teacher will become exposed to the creative work of others, provide for an environment which nurtures creativity, and encourage experimentation and innovation.

It is astonishing how the teaching becomes alive when both faculty and administration are linked in the common purpose of creativity. This common condition can infect students and reticent teachers alike.

PSYCHOLOGICAL CONDITIONS

AIDS TO CREATIVE TEACHING	OBSTACLES TO CREATIVE TEACHING
1. The classroom atmosphere is one which promotes student discussion and a sense of trust, respect, and acceptance.	1. The teacher demands attention and quiet and rejects student ideas.
2. The teacher allows students to voice opinions and participate in activities.	2. The teacher rejects student efforts to participate in planning or student-directed activities.
3. The teacher encourages students to be creative.	3. Little attention is paid to the creative activity of students.
4. Teachers and administration are sensitive to the creative needs of students.	4. No effort is made in the school to understand creativity.

Educational Conditions

The educational conditions are really the *modus operandi* of creative teaching. These methods of creative teaching will be discussed at length in subsequent chapters.

One of the key terms relating to educational conditions is *student readiness*. This refers to the ability of the student to grasp concepts, use materials, interpret, and so on. The teacher who has a knowledge of students' needs, interests, and development is equipped to recognize individual student readiness and to organize the teaching–learning situation in a more creative manner. For instance, there is no reason why children in elementary school should not be allowed the opportunity to discuss the beneficial and/or harmful effects of some drugs. However, their unreadiness to consider the physical, psychological, and social implications of narcotic drugs seems obvious. With children of this age it would be better if the teacher could begin with a discussion of some of the harmful drugs that can be found in the home, such as ammonia, paint spray, certain glues, gasoline, aspirin, and others. In this way the pupils would gain meaningful concepts and at the same time be able to form a personal association with the drugs discussed. The building of some background in drugs has begun. By the time the students are older and ready to discover the physical–social–psychological bases for heroin use, they will have a good concept of what a drug is and what powerful drugs can do.

TEACHING CONTROVERSIAL ISSUES

If health education is to be truly based on the needs of the student and society, then it is clear that the curriculum must embrace some of the so-called controversial issues which face us today. Fraser offers an excellent definition of what a controversial issue is:

A controversial issue involves a problem about which different individuals and groups urge conflicting courses of action. It is an issue for which society has not found a solution that can be universally or almost universally accepted. It is an issue of sufficient significance that each of the proposed ways of dealing with it is objectionable to some sector of the citizenry and arouses protest. The protest may result from a feeling that a cherished belief, an economic interest, or a basic principle is threatened. It may come because the welfare of organizations or groups seems at stake. When a course of action is formulated that virtually all sectors of society accept, the issue is no longer controversial.[12]

Under this definition three subject areas in health education stand out as controversial: sex education, venereal disease education, and drug education. Many parents (and teachers) feel that any type of education in these areas will lead young people down the path to immorality by teaching them "how to do it."

There are, of course, a number of reasons why one or more of the subjects are not being taught. Two factors are a lack of qualified teachers and pressure applied to administrators by parents.

Once the schools are able to get over the first hurdle of whether or not to include sex education, venereal disease education, and/or drug education in the curriculum, three other far more important questions arise: Who should do the teaching? When should these areas be taught? How should they be taught?

Who Should Do the Teaching?

Any instructor who plans to teach sex, venereal disease, and drug education for the first time needs two important background elements. The first is thorough *knowledge of subject matter* and the second is *sensitivity*. The first is much easier to gain than the second. To gain knowledge one must

---

[12] Dorothy M. Fraser, *Deciding What to Teach* (Washington, D.C.: Project on the Instructional Program of the Public Schools, National Education Association, 1963), p. 153.

read, think, and discuss the facts concerning these three areas as much as possible. It is sad but true that many misconceptions are started by the teacher. To become well versed in these areas requires a complete knowledge of the physical, social, emotional, medical, and legal implications of the topics. To think of sex education as merely reproductive biology is to misrepresent totally the concept of what constitutes human sexuality. Other concerns in sex education include such areas as social relationships, physical and mental health, language, mass media, contraception, and so on.

Gaining sensitivity is difficult. First, let us explain what we mean by sensitivity. Sensitivity involves an ability to feel intuitively what is happening at any given time, to sense when an individual is unhappy, confused, or elated; to realize the importance and meaning of introspection. In the areas of sex and venereal disease education, sensitivity means being at ease with one's own sexuality as well as that of others, especially young people. If, for example, a teacher who has not come to grips with his own sexuality attempts to teach in the area of sex education, he may find his efforts completely wasted, regardless of his intentions. Students are quick to identify and ignore those who are negative in their approach, guarded in their answers, or limited in their range and depth of discussion.

One can gain sensitivity or desensitization in a number of ways. In sex and venereal disease education talking with students, parents, other teachers, doctors, psychiatrists, and others will help to expose the teacher to varying views. Course work in psychology, sociology, and family living and summer workshops in the areas of sensitivity and group interaction are also valuable sources of exposure. Most important of all are, of course, informal meetings with young people.

In drug education the teacher will want to talk with students, parents, doctors, psychiatrists, police, and others who have possibly had a personal connection with drug users. Workshops, teacher–parent meetings, and meetings with local drug authorities are also valuable. A worthwhile experience for any teacher who may be involved in drug education is being able to talk with past as well as present users of drugs in order to get views from the "other side."

When Should These Areas Be Taught?
Such topics as sex education and drug education should logically start in the home. A child's first interest in sex may come as early as two or three. Parents should be equipped to handle questions arising from this interest.[13] Ideally, the school should be prepared to continue what the parents have covered. They should begin a program of sex education in kindergarten and continue it all the way through high school (and college).

---

[13] See Marion O. Lerrigo and Helen Southard, *Parents' Responsibility* (Chicago: American Medical Association, 1967), and *Parents Guide to Facts of Life for Children* (New York: Child Study Association of America, 1965).

Drug education is no different. Young children are quite aware of the smoking, drinking, and pill-taking habits of their parents. Questions are sure to arise. Drug education should, therefore, begin in the home and also continue through high school (and college). At the elementary grade levels discussion can begin with some of the common drugs and chemicals that can be found around the home, such as aspirin, cough medicine, glue, paint thinner, and so on. The list is endless.

It is vitally important that programs of education in these areas be made available for students K–12 and through college. The programs must be continuous, uninterrupted. They must be made a normal part of the health curriculum and not be "special subjects." Finally, they must be taught by competent teachers.

How Should They Be Taught?

This question can be applied to two areas: (1) what one should consider in planning a program in the so-called controversial areas, and (2) what to consider when teaching.

What to Consider in Planning a Program

1. Secure strong support from such groups as the PTA, outstanding community leaders, local medical organization (or local doctors), mental health association, churches, and so on.

2. Try to secure the support of the parents in advance of the program. Here you may wish to do a "needs" and "interests" survey in the community you are serving. If possible, before starting the actual school program have a planned program of education for the parents on what will be taught. If neither of these is feasible (or wise), you may wish to provide a program based on "parent consent." That is, parents must consent to allow their child to participate in the program. One way of doing this is through the use of a parent consent form such as the example shown in Figure 6–2.

3. Personally involve the students as much as possible in the planning and preparation of the program. When feasible, ask older students what they would like to have learned about the subject matter when they were in the grade for which the program is being planned.

4. Allow time for those who are going to instruct the program to gain a certain degree of "desensitization" prior to teaching in the area being considered. Briefly, what is being said here is that teachers who are going to teach in the area of human sexuality, for example, should first come to grips with their own personal feelings regarding their sexuality, to feel comfortable about their sexuality and the sexuality of others.

5. Be sure that enough lessons are planned in the program to cover the subject adequately and that time is provided for students to ask or discuss questions and to allow for evaluation and feedback.

_____ Elementary School

Date

Dear Parents:

The teachers, parents and several interested members of the community have cooperated in the development of a modern health and safety curriculum. One aspect of the family living unit includes basic concepts and understandings of sex education. We hope to establish a pilot program in our fourth grade next year. This will be the only grade in our building that will have a formalized sex education aspect in its course of study. (_____) has been

name of teacher

selected to coordinate this fourth grade pilot program. We believe that there will be innumerable benefits to those children who will be members of this program.

If you wish your child to be able to take advantage of this opportunity, please fill out the permission slip below and return it to your child's teacher.

Please feel free to call me if you have any questions regarding this course of study.

Sincerely yours,
(Principal)

_____

I request that my child _____ be taught the aspects of sex education as outlined in the district curriculum.

I understand that this program is voluntary and no penalty will be given to any child for not participating in the program.

_____

Signature of Parent or Guardian.

Figure 6–2. *Example of a parent consent form.*

Source: *Donald Shookhoff, "Establishing a Sex Education Program Parents Will Want," in James J. Lewis, Jr., et al.,* Critical Issues in Education. *Englewood Cliffs, N.J.: Prentice-Hall, Inc., 1972, p. 147.*

6. Plan to present a variety of sources—including guest speakers, films, pamphlets, and so on.

7. Plan into the program the opportunity for student–teacher–parent meetings. One or two of these at the end of the program may help parents, teachers, and students to see views and opinions from another vantage point.

8. Make sure that guest speakers are open to discussion and opposing points of view. Young people are quick to identify and ignore those who are totally negative in their approaches.

What to Consider When Teaching

1. Make your approach more positive than negative. Do not try to prove that all drugs, for example, are "no good" or that premarital intercourse is "immoral." Rather, aim at helping young people to make respon-

sible value decisions based on adequate knowledge of the positive and negative effects of drugs.

2. Do not just present facts. Aim toward forming positive attitudes, behaviors, and value decisions as well.[14]

3. Establish a positive climate for discussing values. At all times cultivate a genuine respect for the ideas, questions, and values of students so that the fullest degree of communication may take place.

4. Be open to any and all relevant questions. In this way students will get answers they are seeking, and the teacher will gain insights into what concerns students.

5. Provide time at the end of your program for follow-up. In this way you will be able to evaluate the success and/or failures of your program.

6. Be constantly open to new ideas.

SUMMARY

Teaching students to take a personal and immediate interest in their health requires more than a thorough knowledge of subject matter and course objectives. It must encompass the ability to motivate pupils into individual involvements with the subject. This ability is not presently seen in a majority of classrooms, but the potential for this ability is inherent in almost every person.

The health instructor should meet the challenges presented in creative teaching by thinking beyond the realm of pure science to that of questioning the social–moral–emotional implications of his field. To do this the teacher must have a solid foundation of knowledge in the physical, social, and psychological aspects of health as well as an ability to be free of convention while expecting something new and exciting. The creative teacher must have confidence in his own abilities as well as believe in the natural talents of his students. Finally, the creative teacher must recognize the need for creativity in all men. "The creative mind in its day-to-day functioning must be a critical mind. The ideal would be not merely to be aware, but to be aware of our awareness."[15]

REFERENCES

Arnold, J. E. "Useful Creative Techniques," in Sidney J. Parnes and Harold F. Harding (eds.). *A Source Book for Creative Thinking.* New York: Charles Scribner's Sons, 1962.

Borton, Terry. "What Turns Kids On?" *Saturday Review* (April 15, 1967), pp. 72–74.

---

[14] See Donald A. Read, "Developing Sexual Awareness: A Humanistic Approach," *The Journal of School Health* (June 1972), pp. 330–333.

[15] Aaron Copland, *Music and Imagination* (New York: Mentor Books, 1952), p. 55.

Bruner, J. S. "Learning and Thinking." *Harvard Education Review*, Vol. 29 (1959), pp. 184–192.

Derell, G. R. "Creativity in Education." *Clearing House*, Vol. 38 (October 1963), pp. 67–69.

Dixon, F. B., and C. H. Spain. "The Search for Creativity." *Clearing House*, Vol. 39 (November 1964), pp. 165–168.

Guilford, J. P. "Frontiers in Thinking That Teachers Should Know About." *Reading Teacher*, Vol. 13 (1960), pp. 176–182.

Henry, J. "Working Paper on Creativity." *Harvard Education Review*, Vol. 27 (1957), pp. 148–155.

Miel, A. (ed.). *Creativity in Teaching: Invitations and Instances*. San Francisco: Wadsworth Publishing Company, 1961.

Moustakas, Clark. *Creativity and Conformity*. Princeton, N.J.: D. Van Nostrand Company, 1967.

Meyers, R. E., and E. P. Torrance. "Can Teachers Encourage Creative Thinking?" *Education Leadership* (December 1961), pp. 156–159.

Rogers, C. R. "Toward a Theory of Creativity." *ETC*, Vol. 11 (1954), pp. 249–260.

Sample, Robert E. "Kari's Handicap—The Impediment of Creativity." *Saturday Review* (July 15, 1967), pp. 56–57, 74.

Zirbes, L. *Spurs to Creative Teaching*. New York: G. P. Putnam's Sons, 1959.

7

CREATIVE
■ TECHNIQUES IN
AFFECTIVE TEACHING

An increasing number of educators are focusing less on the cognitive, or content, but instead are introducing programs dealing primarily with psychological development. Such programs are generally called affective, humanistic, confluent, or psychological education. They aim chiefly at enhancing self-concept, increasing achievement motivation, promoting creative thinking and behavior, clarifying values, and promoting better human relations. To borrow a quote from Combs in *Educational Accountability: Beyond Behavioral Objectives*:

> Modern education must produce far more than persons with cognitive skills. It must produce *humane* individuals, persons who can be relied upon to pull their own weight in our society, who can be counted upon to behave responsibly and cooperatively. We need good citizens, free of prejudice, concerned about their fellow citizens, loving, caring fathers and mothers, persons of goodwill whose values and purposes are positive, feeling persons with wants and desires likely to motivate them toward positive interactions. These are the things that make us human. Without them we are automatons, fair game for whatever crowd-swaying, stimulus-manipulating demagogue comes down the pike. The humane qualities are absolutely essential to our way of life—far more important, even, than the learning of reading, for example. We can live with a bad reader; a bigot is a danger to everyone.[1]

By whatever term one wishes to use, however, this approach to teaching holds tremendous potential for improving education by creating an environment in which both student and teacher become agents in learning

[1] Arthur W. Combs, *Educational Accountability: Beyond Behavioral Objectives* (Washington, D.C.: Association for Supervision and Curriculum Development, 1972), p. 23.

137

—with boundaries amebically changing, rebuilding, disappearing, reawakening. It implies teacher as student, student as teacher, group as leaders, searching and sharing together. In short, it implies that education is much more than the frenzied acquisition of knowledge for knowledge sake.

THE AFFECTIVE IN EDUCATION

Affective or humanistic education has been defined as the integration of cognitive learning with affective learning. George Isaac Brown, in his book *Human Teaching for Human Learning*, uses the term "confluent education," which he describes as "the integration or flowing together of the affective and cognitive elements in individual and group learning." [2]

What the above-named phenomenon is, is no easier to describe than to name. Yet there are some identifiable elements in the educational use of humanistic education:

1. *Feelings.* Sensitivity (education) training deals with the "right now" feelings of learners: what their feelings are, the true expression of them, and learning how to cope with them. The inner world of the learner as well as his relationships become subject matter.
2. *Values and Attitudes.* Opportunities for value examination are created or seized, options are compared and contrasted, and deliberate value choices are made and acted upon.
3. *Concerns.* The concerns of learners are treated with the same respect as the concerns of teachers and others. All concerns are legitimate in these programs, not just those related to "school work."
4. *Process.* This kind of education focuses on the processes with which an individual may deal with his feelings, values, attitudes, and concerns.
5. *Self-Actualization.* The common broad goal of these programs is full humanness; not "the educated man," not "normality," but the best that man can become, the fully alive, authentic, "becoming" person.[3]

Actually humanistic education has been around, and in use, for generations, being practiced by those rare human teachers who can be found in the one-room schoolhouse and on the sprawling inner-city campus. One of the major differences between the humanistic teacher and the purely cognitive, dictatorial teacher is that the humanistic teacher provides for a climate that allows for *lots* of solutions and answers to a given question; a climate that allows for and encourages the open mind to be creative, to come alive. In addition the humanistic teacher often must have a willingness, and ability to

[2] George Isaac Brown, *Human Teaching for Human Learning: An Introduction to Confluent Education* (New York: Viking, 1971), p. 4.

[3] Harold C. Wells, "To Get Beyond the Words . . ." *Educational Leadership* (December 1970), p. 241.

- accept tension and conflict from time to time, rather than to avoid them.
- be open to new experiences every day.
- stand alone and to be courageous.
- have faith in oneself and in others, especially students.
- allow for individuality and individual experiencing.

In the words of Viola Spolin in *Improvisation for the Theater*:

If the environment permits it, anyone can learn what he chooses to learn; and if the individual permits it, the environment will teach him everything it has to teach. . . . It is highly possible that what is called talented behavior is simply a greater individual capacity for experiencing.[4]

BRINGING FEELING INTO THE CLASSROOM
A teacher in ninth grade wants to talk about genetics. A sixth grade teacher decides to turn the attention of his class and the individual student's attention to the matter of nutrition and health. A student wants to discuss the process of reproduction in man.

For those teachers who lack faith in their students and their innate powerful learning and creative processes, the above-mentioned subjects are often thought of as something to be ingested and then regurgitated in a predictable and thoroughly comprehensible manner. These teachers often worry about losing "respect" by allowing the class to choose the subject to be learned and the path by which they would like to learn the subject.

In humanistic education one is able to bring together (to integrate) both the intellectual and the feelings in a classroom situation.

One important beginning is to start to accept students as *real, feeling, worthy, responsible,* and *valuable* human beings. That is to say, the teacher begins to relinquish his role as authority figure and begins to assume the role of facilitator. This "advocates that we begin to look upon people (students) as whole human beings who have feelings—feelings which directly influence their intellectual growth." [5]

Conceding that personal (feelingful) concrete experiences often provide a more realistic and functional perspective, how can we, in health education, release the creative energy—the creative potential—in our students and at the same time teach more humanistically? Here are but a few suggestions:

1. *Learn to accept students as they truly are.* Don't set about "changing" student behavior. If a group of your students smoke don't try to get

---

[4] Viola Spolin, *Improvisation for the Theater* (Evanston, Ill.: Northwestern University Press, 1963), p. 3.

[5] Harold C. Lyon, Jr., *Learning to Feel—Feeling to Learn* (Columbus, Ohio: Merrill, 1971), p. 5.

them to stop. In this way they become nothing more than targets for your personal antismoking campaign. Instead, attempt to provide them with "alternative models," and let them make the choice.[6]

2. *Work toward the building up of self-concept in students.* Provide students with experiences that will help them find their strengths and build on them. Instead of dealing with the negative aspects of health, allow students to search out the positive aspects and to relate them to themselves. Each student has something he does well and which benefits his health and well-being. Let him relate it to the class.[7]

3. *Suspend judgment and encourage individual differences.* There are so many ways to do one thing—just lots of ways. It is important to allow students to clarify their values from time to time. In this way they begin to see, and feel, the importance of thinking and doing for themselves and standing up for what *they* believe. It gives them something to believe in—themselves.

4. *Allow for a variety of values and life-styles.* It is one thing for the teacher to allow personal values to be voiced in the classroom, still another to be nonjudgmental. Allowing all values to be aired and shared, and not criticized, lends itself to greater openness in the classroom.

5. *Allow for a variety of work styles.* Alone, in small groups, in lively groups, with and without the teacher. Releasing creative potential means allowing for individuality and difference, both in and outside the classroom.

6. *Be open to new and creative answers to questions.* Do not manipulate students to elicit the answer you wanted in the first place. Do not insist that your answer is the only answer. In the one-answer-type classroom, students often feel their ideas are of little or no value.

7. *Developing trust in the classroom.* An important ingredient in the humanistic approach to teaching is the development of *trust* in the classroom. This trust development has a number of facets: (a) that each student trust himself—what he feels, what he values, how he acts and responds in various situations; in short, that he not feel constrained or threatened by self or others; (b) that each person develop this same degree of trust in others that he has in himself; and (c) that the teacher share in this trusting—that he trusts and is trusted.

APPLYING HUMANISTIC TECHNIQUES TO HEALTH EDUCATION

It should be made clear that the techniques given below represent but a brief survey of some of the humanistic education techniques that are being developed and used by teachers in various levels and subjects today. Al-

[6] See, for example, Allan Y. Cohen, "Alternatives to Drug Use," *The PTA Magazine* (September 1972), p. 20.

[7] See William W. Purkey, *Self Concept and School Achievement* (Englewood Cliffs, N.J.: Prentice-Hall, 1970).

though many of these techniques have been used by the authors, most of them were not developed by them. References are listed at the end of this chapter.

Some Familiar Starting Points [8]

Teachers who have been successful in their efforts to establish a climate of openness and trust in their classrooms will often find it possible to deal with affective material simply through use of the old-fashioned general discussion format. This is particularly true in small classes of twenty-five or less in which circular or horseshoe-shaped seating arrangements can be used to increase the feeling of intimacy and involvement on the part of the class. Under these conditions the posing of an appropriate discussion question and the provision for sensitive, nondirective leadership will provide the learners with the opportunity to reveal, to share, and to examine their feelings regarding value-laden topics. The major limitation to this relatively simple scheme is that such classroom features as openness, trust, intimacy, and involvement are not simple to establish. A good affective discussion can develop a good classroom climate—and a good classroom climate can facilitate a good affective discussion. The teacher can resolve this "chicken-or-the-egg" situation by taking the first step; by applying good affective discussion techniques and maintaining them until the students realize that their feelings are important and their comments will be appropriately received.

Discussion Techniques

The specific techniques that are used in affective discussions vary to fit individual teaching styles. However, they basically represent the application of the general suggestions as provided above to the specific task of class discussion. Some of the main procedures are:

- Provide a clearly stated discussion question that is meaningful to the students, one that lends itself to a wide variety of viewpoints. For example, "Should a trial marriage system be established in which the couple involved can easily terminate or fully confirm their relationship after a given period of time?"
- Give the class time to respond; learn to tolerate periods of silence. When it finally becomes necessary to prod the class, a simple restating of the question will usually suffice.
- Be accepting of virtually all student responses in your words, tone, and actions; you asked the students how they feel and they are telling you—feelings have their own validity.

[8] Many of the basic ideas expressed in this section closely follow those found in Charlotte Epstein, *Affective Subjects in the Classroom* (Scranton, Pa.: Intext Educational Publishers, 1972).

- Distribute participation as much as possible; always remain alert for the opportunity to bring a heretofore silent member of the class into the discussion, but also give students who are verbally attacked a chance to reply.

Even though the comments students contribute to such discussions may sometimes seem frivolous and poorly conceived, the value of providing them with an appropriate forum for the expression of their feelings should not be underestimated. Beyond this intrinsic value lie the added benefits that can be realized when the resulting involvement and motivation is used to guide students into a search for more information and a deeper understanding of the topic discussed. Under these circumstances students have both the opportunity to gain a keener awareness of the emotions and feelings attached to a particular topic, and to develop a better cognitive understanding of the concepts and issues involved. This combining of the affective and the cognitive is the real essence of confluent education.

Small Groups

The degree of involvement and participation in any discussion technique can usually be increased by organizing the class into smaller groups. The basic procedures for accomplishing this are similar to those for the buzz-session technique as described on pp. 162–163; however, the purpose and nature of the ensuing group interaction differs considerably. The traditional purpose of the buzz-session has been to mobilize the knowledge available within a group and apply it to a problem, thereby sharing cognitive information and understandings in the process. The emphasis in the affective small group discussion is placed on the sharing of values, feelings, and opinions. As in the large group discussion the essential requirements for success are a climate of trust and a well-formulated discussion question.

The teacher, of course, will not be guiding each discussion; therefore, the students should be asked to give everyone a fair chance to speak and to adopt a generally accepting attitude toward the views of their classmates. Once the discussions are underway the teacher can help by circulating among the groups, listening in a nonjudgmental fashion, and interrupting only to lead students out of "dead-end" situations wherein there is a prolonged reiteration of antagonistic views.

The degree of success that may be expected from the initial use of this technique with a particular classroom group will be heavily affected by the amount of prior experience the students have had in the general types of affective experiences described in this chapter. The class members may at first be quite reluctant to reveal their real feelings and generally unaccepting of points of view that differ from their own. However, if the teacher will use every appropriate opportunity to reinforce the ideas that the existence of differing value systems among people is a normal phenomenon, that each person needs opportunities to express his views, and that such expressions deserve a respectful hearing, then he will very likely see significant growth in the qualities of openness and tolerance among his students.

Dramatizations

The playing or acting out of a role particularly in the spontaneous setting of the sociodrama can provide excellent opportunities for students both to become better acquainted with their own feelings and to communicate these feelings to others. Also, when assigned the task of acting in the role of some other person such as a parent, teacher, or friend, the student can almost literally "step into other persons' shoes" and gain new insights into their moods and responses. In the more tightly structured playlet with its predetermined script these advantages are comprised somewhat to yield a different type of experience, namely, the chance for both actors and audience to communicate with the moods and feelings of the author of the playlet. Both the sociodrama and the playlet make highly useful additions to teaching repertories of those concerned with humanistic education.

THE SOCIODRAMA. When the sociodrama is used, student participants are each provided with basic descriptions of a role they are to play in a particular situation and are asked to respond according to their interpretation of how the action might transpire. At the appropriate time the teacher stops the sociodrama and the class discusses the issues depicted. This technique is highly effective provided the class is sufficiently motivated to overlook the limitation of the participants' acting ability and concentrate on the relevant implications. A detailed illustration of this technique is provided on pp. 198–202. The basic procedures are as follows:

1. Select situations for portrayal that are relatively simple, that are clear-cut, and, as mentioned, that involve personality traits or value judgments. Examples of typical situations are a high school junior who is offered marijuana at a party and a seventh-grade girl who ask her parents to allow her to go out on dates without adult supervision. It is usually best to involve no more than four actors in a given sociodrama unless the class has had considerable experience with the technique.

2. Select for the principal roles stable, intelligent students who are neither unduly extroverted nor introverted. This is particularly important when the technique is new to the teacher or the students. If the class has the opportunity to become familiar with the sociodrama, then much less care need be taken in the selection of participants.

3. Outline the basic situation and the characteristics of each actor to the class briefly but clearly. This information can usually be presented verbally to the total class, although it is occasionally useful to present all or certain aspects of a participant's role to him secretly by use of written or whispered instructions.

4. Provide the participants or actors with a small amount of planning time (two minutes is sufficient) to decide upon the basic approach they plan to use in their presentation. This is ordinarily accomplished by allowing them to move to the hallway or to the back of the room for their brief discussion while the teacher prepares the class by pointing out the more important things to look for in the presentation.

5. Use simple props, usually tables and chairs or the teacher's desk. This can add much to the effectiveness of the sociodrama if the setting is explained to the class. (Explain, for example, "Mother and Dad are seated on the sofa," or "The personnel manager is seated at his desk.") Elaborate preparations are not necessary if the verbal description is clearly expressed.

6. During the actual presentation the teacher may have to assist the actors occasionally with their responses by reminding them of their roles and how such a person might react. The most important function of the teacher, however, is to decide when to terminate the action. This action is usually signaled by the portrayal of a particularly relevant point that demands immediate discussion or, more commonly, when it appears that the presentation is slowing down.

7. During the follow-up discussion it is important to keep the comments focused on the content of the sociodrama in terms of the words and actions of the participants rather than upon the quality of the acting. Besides being more relevant to class objectives this takes the pressure off the performers and makes it easier to recruit volunteers for this activity in the future.

THE PLAYLET. When it becomes necessary to present a dramatic portrayal of a health concept or situation in a predictable way, the playlet may be used. It differs from the sociodrama in that the dialogue is planned before the performance; however, in many instances little or no rehearsal is necessary. In some situations, such as assembly programs, it may be desirable to stage a full-fledged performance; however, for purposes of health education, the playlet may be presented in the classroom by simply providing scripts to reasonably alert students and asking them to "walk through" the action. This technique, of course, lacks the spontaneity of the sociodrama but provides the teacher with the opportunity to prepare more thoroughly for the follow-up discussion.

Probably the best source of playlets is the teacher's own creative ingenuity. He is in the best position to know the maturity level, the interest patterns, and the educational needs of his particular students. What his efforts lack in professional polish they will usually make up for in their particular appropriateness to his situation. Properly motivated students can often turn out effective playlets, particularly when they are also charged with the responsibility of staging the performance. The teacher can help them most appropriately by providing technical assistance on any scientific aspects that may be involved; the students can usually handle the plot and the dialogue with little if any outside aid. Some commercially prepared scripts are available but it is usually difficult to find those that match the teacher's needs regarding grade level, socioeconomic conditions, and health content.

Value Clarification Techniques

Among the more exciting teaching innovations of recent years have been the various value clarification techniques. One of their distinct advantages is the element of precision or structure they introduce to the relatively nebulous process of affective communication; each technique was developed to meet a well-defined purpose. Also, many of these exercises may be evaluated through use of an "I learned . . ." statement. This simply means that students are asked to think about or share "I learned . . ." statements (in reference to a particular exercise they have experienced) by expressing them verbally to the class, writing them on paper for themselves, etc. Additional type learning statements can be supplemented:

> "I discovered that I . . ."
> "I noticed that I . . ."
> "I relearned that . . ."
> "I was pleased that . . ."
> "I found out that . . ."

It is hoped that the few selected activities briefly described below will "prime the pump" of the reader's creative potential.

SELECTED ACTIVITIES
Activity
THE PERSONAL NAME TAG

Purpose
To develop a more "first name" close atmosphere. To get students to know each other more quickly.

Procedure
Supply students with 5" x 8" plain cards. Have them write their name with a felt pen across one side of the card (first name only). Next have them section the card off into threes with a pencil or pen. Now, in the left section have them list five things that they like about themselves. In the middle section have them list five things starting with the statement "I am happy most when . . ." In the last, or right, section have them list eight things that they enjoy doing and which they feel contribute to their health and well-being. An example is shown below. After they have finished, have them pin the card on their shirts so that everyone may be able to see their name. "First name" calling becomes more simple here.

Analysis
Allow students an opportunity to "look" at the cards of others. Some may wish to share their listings.

Class Age
All ages.

Precautions
Don't make students share if they don't want to.

Activity
A HEALTH RANK ORDER OR PRIORITY ORDER

Purpose
To increase student awareness of what is most to least important to them. It also shows students what their priorities are in terms of health.

Procedure
Give each student eight 3″ x 5″ cards. On each card have the students list one thing that they feel is important to their health. For example: exercising, eating good food, being happy, etc. Each card will have one "good health" thing on it. When they have finished, have them put these cards in rank order from the most important thing to the least important.

Analysis
Have students share (voluntarily) their listings. Comment on various responses to the question.

Class Age
All classes.

Precautions
None.

Activity
SAFETY FIRST (SEAT BELTS)

Purpose
To have students observe more closely their feelings concerning the use of seat belts. To have students examine their feelings about individual safety.

Procedure
Stick a strip of masking tape down the middle of the classroom floor. Indicate verbally that one end of the tape represents "Belt-in Harry," who is so safety conscious that he wears his seat belt while his car is in the drive-in movie. The other end of the continuum represents "Cut-'em-out Walt," who does not use a seat belt at all. In fact, if he gets into a car that has seat belts he cuts them out. In the middle is Mr/Ms Undecided. It's really not committing oneself to anything. So—see if you can get students to commit themselves to an either-or. Have individual students (those who are willing to share) stand up and position themselves on the tape. Have them share "where they stand" statements. At the end have the whole class position on the "tape."

Analysis
Discuss the class response to "who stood where" and what it means in terms of highway safety. Also mention the difference (if one is noticeable) in class response to this activity.

Class Age
All ages.

Precautions
None.

Activity
THINGS I LOVE TO DO

Purpose
To get students in touch with things they love to do (and hopefully are health-related things) that they will realize they "don't do" so often.

Procedure
Have students draw a line down the middle of a piece of paper. On the left side of the paper have them list twenty things they really love to do and which they also feel may benefit their health and well-being. To those who say, "Gee, I can't think of twenty," say "Try—really try." (They most often come up with twenty.) After they have finished, have them code the twenty things with (put next to each):

        $ — those things that cost you more than $1.00.
        * — those things that contribute to your good health and well-being.

+ — those things that you feel you could do with someone else.

65 — those things that you think you will be doing when you are 65 years old.

= — to those things that you have done in the last two weeks.

Analysis

Ask and discuss "I learned . . ." statements. Do you and your students feel close enough to share such statements as "I learned . . ."? This can be a real high for the class.

Class Age

Junior high and high school.

Precautions

Don't require students to share.

Activity

FORCED CHOICE (AND STICK TO IT)

Purpose

To enable students to make choices between competing alternatives.

Procedure

Students are asked to check one of the following: Which do you think would be the worst?

_____ To be poor.

_____ To be very sick.

_____ To have no friends.

Choose the one that best fits what you would do.

_____ give money to a friend who needs it to obtain an abortion.

_____ make yourself available to counsel a friend with a sexual problem.

_____ verbally and visibly support a friend whose sexual practices have been maligned.

Which do you think is the worst? (rank order: 1 = worst.)

_____ to become (or get someone) pregnant and be unwed.

_____ to be dependent on hard drugs.

_____ to date someone from another race.

Analysis

Have students share "I learned . . ." statements.

Class Age

Senior high/college.

Precautions
None.

Activity
ABORTION CONTINUUM

Purpose
To determine whether a difference does exist between male and female students concerning their views on abortion.

Procedure
Hand out 3" x 5" cards and have students put M (Male) or F (Female) on their individual card. Have them draw a continuum line: Example:

1	2	3	4	5	6	7	8
Right to live							Abortion on demand

Have the students indicate on the line the point where they feel they fall in terms of the abortion issue.

Analysis
Draw a continuum on the blackboard and make a tally of M/F responses (female responses above the line—male below). Have students share reactions.

Class Age
Junior high/senior high/college.

Precautions
None.

Activity
I WOULD LIKE TO BE A MAN/WOMAN BECAUSE . . .

Purpose
Consciousness-raising in the classroom.

Procedure
Have the girls complete either or both "I would (would not) like to be a man because . . ." For the boys, substitute "woman."

Analysis
This should indicate what the students see as the privileges and burdens of each sex, and how they perceive the division of roles. Have students share "I learned . . ." statements in class.

Class Age
Junior/senior high.

Precautions
Bring positive feelings into the classroom at the end of this exercise.

Activity
IF I WERE A BOY/GIRL I WOULD LIKE TO . . .

Procedure
An alternate phrasing of the above—"If I were a boy (girl), I would (like to) . . ." Do the students feel that they can't do or become these things, given their actual sex? For instance, if a girl says, "If I were a boy, I would climb trees and play baseball," she should be asked if she does climb trees and play baseball. Why not, if she doesn't. Would she like to? What makes her think she can't?

Analysis
Share "I learned . . ." statements.

Class Age
Elementary/secondary.

Precautions
None.

Activity
BRAGGING

Purpose
To enhance positive self-concept.

Procedure
Ask students to form groups of 5 or 6. Instruct them that they have a total of 25–30 minutes in which to brag and boast about anything in their life they can think of.

Analysis
Ask the students to make "I learned . . ." statements. Did they enjoy it? Were they uncomfortable? How did they feel when others were bragging? Did they feel competitive? Did they want to make "killer statements" to different people in the group? To whom? What brought on these feelings?

Class Age
Junior/senior high.

Precautions
None.

Activity
CONTINUUM TO LOOK AT GROUP (AND INDIVIDUAL) BEHAVIOR

Purpose

This exercise is useful after any task-group or small-group experience. To expand capacity to look at own behavior. To expand capacity to give and receive feedback. To check out self-perception with the way in which one is perceived by others.

Procedure

Explain what a continuum is. Using tape, run a continuum line down middle of classroom floor. Example:

Withdrawn	Indecision	Dominating
Sue		Francie

Direct the students to place themselves on the continuum, in terms of the way in which they behaved in the group today. Give class members time to check out perceptions of their own behavior. Next have class members state where they felt other class members would be on the continuum. Did they feel that certain class members placed themselves where they would have placed them?

Analysis

Questions: Did others place you at some point on the continuum as you placed yourself? Did you see yourself as other members of the group saw you? Did you see others as they saw themselves? Is the way you behaved today your usual way of behaving in the group? Use "I learned . . ." statements.

Class Age

Upper elementary through high school.

Precautions

None.

Activity

CURRENT EVENTS

Purpose

To help students to become more critical readers. To clarify student values on current events.

Procedure

Choose certain issues relating to the topic under discussion. Condense so that students can read them quickly. Example:

Golden Gate Bridge authorities have beefed up security to delay as long as possible the inevitable 500th fatal leap from the western hemisphere's most infamous suicide spot.

Authorities don't doubt someone will jump from the 6,451-foot span that stands at the gateway to San Francisco Bay. Number 499 took the 240 foot plunge Monday—and Dr. Richard H. Seiden, who is conducting an intensive three-year study of bridge suicides, said he half expected someone obsessed with a bizarre kind of fame of being number 500 to take the leap right afterward.

Bridge directors are currently considering an eight-foot-high fence of pencil-thick steel rods to replace the present low barrier. Its estimated cost is $800,000.

Dale W. Luehring, the bridge general manager, said, "my mail is running three to one against a suicide barrier."

Reason for opposing the barrier, he said, range from those who say bridge officials don't have any authority to tell people whether they should live or die to those saying the $800,000 should be put into new mass transit facilities for people who want to live.

—*Source:* AP, Sept. '73

Analysis

Questions: Do you feel that persons with authority have the right to tell people whether they can or cannot commit suicide? How do you think the $800,000 should be spent?

Class Age

With appropriate material, all ages.

Precautions

None.

Activity

FALLOUT SHELTER

Purpose

To help students gain insights into other people. Developing and exploring individuals' emotional responses to others. Learning to debate and live with others who have different values.

Procedure

Hand out ditto sheets to each student containing various roles each will play. Example:

1. Female "pot head"—college dropout with no apparent interests.
2. Salesman—40-year-old alcoholic; gets along well with other people; natural organizer, enterprising, with extensive business skills.
3. Female—25-year-old chain smoker; wants only to have large family but has nervous, irritable disposition.
4. & 5. Married coupled—mid 30's; both "need" an evening cocktail; wife is unable to have children; hypochondriac, on uppers and downers most of the time. He is a practical person, contractor. They will not be separated.
6. Male—semiheavy drug freak (LSD, methadone); at 27 he is a clinical psychologist, natural-born mediator and warm and understanding; not very productive since college.
7. Male—black minister, 40 years old; just out of jail for militancy; just recently rehabilitated heroin user.

Direct students to choose roles. State that in twenty minutes there will be a devastating nuclear attack. There is only one bomb shelter that holds ONLY four people. They must decide in twenty minutes who will stay and who will be able to get into the bomb shelter. This works best in group of seven so that each person has a chance to play a role.

Analysis
Share "I learned . . ." statements in large group.

Class Age
Any age depending on situation used.

Precautions
None.

Activity
SUPREME COURT

Purpose
To help students clarify their values concerning drugs. To help students to seek out important information concerning certain health issues.

Procedure
Set up a mock Supreme Court with nine class members sitting on the bench. Divide remaining students into two groups: those who are in favor of the legalization of marijuana—those who are not. Have both groups gather evidence to support their argument and present it to the Court. Conclude by having the Court render their decision.

Analysis
Have students discuss the decision. Was it just? What facts was it based on? What effect does the ruling have on the people?

Class Age
Depending on the topic under consideration, all ages can participate.

Precautions
None.

SUMMARY
The goal of humanistic education is for long-term life changes, not short-term gains in mastery. Through the humanistic approach to teaching in health, students are able to increase long-term operant behavior *as well as* respondent behavior. Additionally, a greater emphasis can be placed on examining alternatives for the achievement of a more satisfying self-concept, respect for one's body and one's well-being. In the words of Jerry

Rubin, "To love your body, to accept yourself, to know your own personal rhythm, to go inward, gives you getter control of your own life." [9] Humanistic education shares this feeling.

REFERENCES

Borton, Terry. *Reach, Touch and Teach*. New York: McGraw-Hill Book Company, 1970.

Brown, George Isaac. *Human Teaching for Human Learning: An Introduction to Confluent Education*. New York: The Viking Press, Inc., 1971.

Combs, Arthur W. (ed.). *Perceiving, Behaving and Becoming*. Washington, D.C.: Association for Supervision and Curriculum Development, 1962.

Dennison, George. *The Lives of Children: The Story of the First Street School*. New York: Random House, Inc., 1969.

Fantini, Mario, and Gerald Weinstein. *Making Urban Schools Work*. New York: Holt, Rinehart and Winston, Inc., 1968.

Gregory, Thomas. *Encounters with Teaching*. Englewood Cliffs, N.J.: Prentice-Hall, Inc., 1972.

Heath, Douglas H. *Humanizing Schools*. New York: Hayden Book Company, Inc., 1971.

James, Muriel, and Dorothy Jongeward. *Born to Win*. Reading, Mass.: Addison-Wesley Publishing Co., Inc., 1971.

Jones, Richard M. *Fantasy and Feeling in Education*. New York: New York University Press, 1968.

Lederman, Janet. *Anger and the Rocking Chair: Gestalt Awareness with Children*. New York: McGraw-Hill Book Company, 1969.

Leonard, George. *Education and Ecstasy*. New York: Delta Books, 1968.

Luft, Joseph. *Group Processes: An Introduction to Group Dynamics*. Palo Alto, Calif.: National Press Books, 1970.

Lyon, Harold C., Jr. *Learning to Feel—Feeling to Learn*. Columbus, Ohio: Charles E. Merrill Publishing Co., 1971.

MacMillan, Donald L. *Behavior Modification in Education*. New York: Macmillan Publishing Co., Inc., 1973.

Metcalf, Lawrence (ed.). *Values Education: Rational Strategies and Procedures*. Washington, D.C.: NEA, 1971.

Moustakas, Clark. *Teaching as Learning*. New York: Ballantine Books, Inc., 1972.

Nyberg, David. *Tough and Tender Learning*. Palo Alto, Calif.: National Press Books, 1971.

Otto, Herbert. *Group Methods Designed to Actualize Human Potential*. Chicago: Stone-Brandel, 1967.

———, and John Mann. *Ways of Growth*. New York: Grossman Publishers, Inc., 1968.

Perls, Frederick S. *Ego, Hunger, and Aggression*. New York: Random House, Inc., 1969.

---

[9] Jerry Rubin, "From the Streets to the Body," *Psychology Today* (September 1973), p. 71.

————. *Gestalt Therapy and Human Potentialities.* Esalen paper No. I. Big Sur, Calif.: Esalen Institute. (no date)

————. *Gestalt Therapy Verbatim.* Lafayette, Calif.: Real People Press, 1969.

————. "Group vs. Individual Therapy," *Review of General Semantics,* Vol. 24 (1967), pp. 306–312.

Polanyi, Michael. *The Tacit Dimension.* Garden City, N.Y.: Doubleday & Company, Inc., 1966.

Postman, Neil, and Charles Weingartner. *The School Book.* New York: Delacorte Press, 1973.

Raths, Louis E., Merrill Harmin, and Sidney B. Simon. *Values and Teaching: Working with Values in the Classroom.* Columbus, Ohio: Charles E. Merrill Publishing Co., 1966.

Rogers, Carl. *Freedom to Learn.* Columbus, Ohio: Charles E. Merrill Publishing Co., 1969.

Schrank, Jeffrey. *Teaching Human Beings: 101 Subversive Activities for the Classroom.* Boston: Beacon Press, 1972.

Schutz, William. *Joy.* New York: Grove Press, Inc., 1967.

Simon, Sidney B., Leland W. Howe, and Howard Kirschenbaum. *Values Clarification: A Handbook of Practical Strategies for Teachers and Students.* New York: Hart Publishing Co., Inc., 1972.

Stevens, John O. *Awareness: Exploring, Experimenting, Experiencing.* Lafayette, Calif.: Real People Press, 1971.

Thelen, Herbert A. *Education and the Human Quest.* Chicago: The University of Chicago Press, 1972.

8

CREATIVE
■ TECHNIQUES IN
COGNITIVE TEACHING

As was described in the preceding chapter it is both impossible and undesirable to make a clear-cut distinction between cognitive and affective
behavior. George Isaac Brown, in his book *Human Teaching for Human
Learning*,[1] pulls them both together into what he calls "confluent education." (See Chapter 7 of the present book.) However, individual learning
tasks, although they always include elements of both domains, are often
distinctly weighted either toward such cognitive outcomes as understanding and analyzing, or affective behaviors such as accepting or appreciating.
Consider, for example, the following two objectives which might be found
in a unit on human sexuality:

1. The student can discuss common sexual problems in a normal
classroom situation without displaying obvious signs of embarrassment.
2. The student can list and describe three factors that predispose the
human fetus to an adverse Rh reaction (erythroblastosis).

The first objective obviously deals with the student's affective feeling
toward discussion of sexual topics and would not be very effectively taught
by reading assignments, lectures, programmed learning devices, or other
techniques. These devices, however, might work very well for the second
objective, which is focused on the relatively complex Rh factor. The fact
that the teacher is not charged with the responsibility of helping the
student "show concern for" or "recognizing the seriousness" of the Rh

[1] George Isaac Brown, *Human Teaching for Human Learning: An Introduction
to Confluent Education* (New York: Viking, 1971).

156

situation but only for the rather unemotional actions of listing and describing, clearly places the emphasis on the cognitive aspects of this topic.

THE ROLE OF COGNITIVE LEARNING

Within such teaching fields as science, English, and history cognitive learnings have traditionally been regarded as ends in themselves, whereas in health education they are commonly viewed as handmaidens to the higher goals of attitudinal and behavioral change. This view is justified to a certain degree, but its validity is lost when overly simplistic strategies are used in its implementation. Students have been taught about the marvelous efficiency of the cilia lining the respiratory tract and the threatening activities of the lactobacilli that reside in the oral cavity, not because these topics have any intrinsic significance (which they do have), but simply to encourage young people to stop smoking and start brushing their teeth. When it became apparent that this approach wasn't yielding the desired results, cognitive learning activities were often reduced to a minimum in favor of predominantly emotional appeals for behavioral change.

The Importance of Cognitive Outcomes

Although there is a tendency for individual teachers or district-wide programs to become aligned at the opposite poles of either "good hard subject matter" or "getting the message across at all costs," the most desirable policy appears to lie between these extremes. The affective elements are valuable in some instances as ends in themselves and in others as means to heighten the involvement of students with the subject matter. Although the usefulness of cognitive material is often not readily apparent, it frequently meets a wide variety of education needs in unique and unpredictable ways. The study of the development of the human embryo might be included in the program mainly because of the appropriateness of human beings learning the facts concerning their own biological origin. To one student this information might have little meaning, but to another it might serve to build a positive attitude toward prenatal care, and to still another it might provide the motivation to investigate medicine as a possible career choice.

Another reason for placing due emphasis on cognitive learnings is found in the basic complexity of many health issues. Instruction that encourages students to place high values on good nutrition and weight control without also providing a workable understanding of how to reach these goals simply makes them easy prey for the food quacks and diet faddists. To impress sexually active adolescents with the dire consequences of venereal disease without teaching them specific means of precaution and procedures for obtaining treatment will only increase their reliance on the dictates of youthful folklore. The tasks of making intelligent contributions to public opinion and responding appropriately to proposals concerning such issues as nuclear power plants, methadone maintenance programs, and tax-supported medical care often involve the analysis of complex issues. In these, as in other examples, good attitudes and a sound value system are essential, but also needed is the ability to weigh the various pros and cons in a dispassionate manner.

The Selection of Cognitive Techniques

When a particular objective calls for cognitive behavior, the teacher should generally place emphasis on "cooler" modes of presentation which provide "light" rather than "heat." Films, filmstrips, audiotapes, programmed material, and simple reading assignments can provide systematic instruction in complex topics. When not abused, short lectures have their place; however, the time allotted to verbal interaction between teacher and class is usually better reserved for questions and discussion of material that students have previously covered by the aforementioned techniques. Several student-centered techniques also lend themselves to systematic coverage of complex topics. Committee-type investigations that may involve library work, small-group field trips, or independent experiments often provide optimum combinations of adult guidance and student involvement. These are but a few of the many techniques appropriate for the cognitive domain.

OVERVIEW OF BASIC TEACHING TECHNIQUES

The proper selection of specific teaching techniques involves much more than a consideration of the cognitive or affective nature of the content involved. The maturity level of the student, the time allotment, the materials and equipment available, and the personality and background of the teacher are of equal importance. In the chapters that follow, these factors will be discussed as they apply to specific content areas, and in several instances detailed examples will be provided. However, the consideration of these specific situations will be more worthwhile if preceded by an overview of some of the teaching techniques that are particularly useful to cognitive learning tasks.

Discussion Techniques

GENERAL DISCUSSION. Most teachers oriented toward creativity attach considerable value to the factor of "student involvement," which is often obtained through use of such techniques as field trips, problem-solving activities, and laboratory-type experiences. Unfortunately, these techniques often require a good deal of advanced planning, special materials, and class time for their proper use. A good open-ended class discussion with broad class participation can generate a good deal of "instant involvement" without the use of elaborate procedures. When properly conducted it can provide students with the opportunity to review facts and form meaningful generalizations that have practical applications to health problems.

Two preliminary conditions greatly affect the degree to which the benefits of class discussion may be realized. These are (1) the existence of a favorable classroom environment that permits the students appropriate freedom of expression and (2) the possession of sufficient information by the student to discuss the topic involved in a meaningful way. The first condition results more from the teacher's general approach or attitude than from specific procedures. It is illustrated by teachers who give proper credit to students for good answers, who often reinterpret contributions that are slightly incorrect or irrelevant, and who handle grossly incorrect responses in a manner that minimizes the student's embarrassment. In short, a good discussion environment is produced by the teacher who avoids the use of ridicule and generally regards any sincerely offered student response as a useful contribution to the discussion. The second condition, concerning adequate knowledge, is important if one is to avoid the rambling and unproductive "pooling of ignorance" type of discussion. Although there are certain situations that call for a brief airing of student opinions and misconceptions, major discussions for the purpose of building concepts can only take place if the students possess the necessary raw materials in the form of pertinent facts. For this reason discussions are usually more successful after the students have done some reading, viewed some films, heard some resource speakers, or participated in other such activities.

Once the discussion gets under way, then specific leadership techniques become important. There are probably an infinite number of tips or guidelines for discussion leaders. The following are a few of the more useful ones:

1. Turn questions back to the group if there is a reasonable chance of eliciting a good reply; students learn far more when they actively participate than when they listen to answers provided by the teacher.
2. Distribute group participation, thus involving as many of the class as possible. When more than one hand is raised, the student who has not yet spoken generally should receive preference.
3. Do not follow a student's reply with a harder question that he may not be able to answer. If you wish to ask a follow-up question, direct it to the rest of the class. For example, "That's correct, now can someone else tell us. . . ."
4. Give students whose contributions have been challenged or ridiculed a chance to reply if they wish. A teacher may often overlook this simple courtesy as he seeks to distribute participation.
5. Be alert to "dead-end" situations in discussions, where sufficient facts are not available to resolve differing opinions. Recognize the

disagreement and move on to more promising aspects of the topic.

6. Provide occasional facts where they are needed to keep things moving. The discussion leader should generally avoid drawing conclusions or making generalizations for the class, but often a simple fact or two will help students in discussing the larger aspects of a particular topic or issue.

Any teacher who establishes a good classroom learning climate and challenges students with a meaningful discussion question will soon discover many more good discussion tips as he begins to develop his own style of leadership.

SYMPOSIUM. The symposium is a technique wherein a small number of students first present brief oral reports on a given topic, then serve as "resource persons" in a general class discussion which follows the individual reports. The members of the symposium panel—by means of library work, field trips, interviews, or other similar activities—bring information to the class that is otherwise not available. When properly conducted this technique can be extremely rewarding as a learning activity that makes only moderate demands on the teacher in terms of advanced preparation and organization of participants. The opportunity that the symposium provides for the questioning of student "experts" often produces lively discussions, for there is less tendency for class members to accept passively something they do not believe from one of their peers as compared with a presumably knowledgeable adult. The specific procedures for this technique vary according to such factors as topic, grade level, availability of resources, and individual styles of teaching. However, those presented in the following paragraphs generally apply.

1. Because the key to a good symposium lies in the quality of the initial reports, it is generally best to select as speakers only those students who have the ability and willingness to do a good job. This procedure is of particular importance at the secondary level, where the development of health knowledge and values, rather than speech skills, is the health teacher's primary responsibility. There are many alternate activities that are much more appropriate for those students with poor speaking ability. At the elementary level, however, where there is much more emphasis on the integration of subject matter, it may sometimes be necessary to compromise the quality of the health lesson to provide all types of pupils the opportunity to gain speaking experience.

2. Unless unusually good student leadership is available, the symposium committee will usually need teacher help in dividing its report topic into logical subtopics. This procedure will tend to minimize overlapping or neglected coverage and will produce a report with a more logical format. When it is practical to do so, this task can be best accomplished with a short meeting with the committee during a study hall, during a home room period, after school, or at some other time when the committee and

the teacher are free. If no mutually free time is available, then basic organizational help can be provided in class at the time the assignment is made.

3. In addition to basic guidance from the teacher, the student participants also need some time to meet on their own to organize their presentation further. In some situations students will have the opportunity and the willingness to meet during their out-of-school hours; however, it is often necessary for the teacher to provide some help with this task. Some school libraries provide conference rooms for student groups; some modern school plants provide small conference rooms adjoining regular classrooms. Even without these conveniences it is often possible to help students set up meetings during the health period in a nearby vacant room or other appropriate area in the school building.

4. Another way the teacher can raise the quality of the reports is by guiding the participants toward good sources of information. This might be a recent issue of *Today's Health*, a pertinent article in a news magazine or newspaper, television special, or a special book in the library. With only moderate effort, the teacher can provide each student reporter with one or two good suggestions that can form the nucleus of the report. The specific amount and nature of this help should vary considerably with the background and ability of the students. Some slow students will need very specific help, whereas strong students are often best left to their own devices. The average student can usually be counted on to bring in a good report if he has received one or two good tips and encouragement to search on his own.

5. Thus far the descriptions of this technique have centered on the importance of the student's search for information; the teacher's next task is the encouragement of the effective delivery of this information. The mechanics of the actual presentation of the symposium should vary with the specific situation; however, the following points generally apply:

a. The individual presentations should be short; three to five minutes is generally appropriate.

b. Each report should focus on one or two interesting and relevant points rather than attempt a systematic coverage of detailed material.

c. Strongly encourage students to report in their own words in conversational tones; notes are needed for reference but reports should not be read.

d. Encourage the use of illustrations, charts, models, and other props that aid interest or clarity to the presentation.

e. Allow a student leader to chair the general discussion if a reasonably capable one is available, otherwise assume leadership of the discussion but refer questions to the panelists. Be a leader, not a lecturer.

Buzz session. Large-group discussions often provide opportunities for only a few students to participate with any degree of effectiveness. The buzz session calls for placing students in small groups of three to six where all will have an opportunity to express their views. These discussions usually extend for three to fifteen minutes, after which the class is reassembled to hear reports given by buzz-group representatives and to discuss further the same material as a total group. This technique may be used either as a regular device to cover course content or as a means of facilitating student planning of class activities. Its main value lies in the opportunity it provides for broad student participation in somewhat uninhibited discussions. The basic procedures are described in the following paragraphs.

1. The discussion question for the buzz session should be chosen with particular care, as it will be discussed without benefit of teacher leadership. It must be appealing, clearly defined, open-ended, and relevant to educational objectives. A special effort should be made to develop high interest in the general topic of study just prior to placing the students in their groups. This may involve the use of a film, newspaper clippings, or simply a lively class discussion.

2. The membership of the small groups can be determined on an arbitrary basis, alphabetically, by rows, and so on. This system will often work if other factors in the total situation are good, such as class morale and the general academic orientation of the students. However, the effectiveness of the buzz session can be improved if group memberships are preplanned to ensure a reasonable distribution of ability and leadership. Some attention should also be given to social factors. Most teachers seek to avoid either putting whole cliques together as groups or isolating individual students from any of their friends. Once the groups are established they can be used repeatedly for future buzz sessions on other topics and for other techniques involving small groups. If activities requiring small groups are frequently used, it is often useful to reshuffle them occasionally to expose students to fresh points of view.

3. Prior to placing the students in their groups, the teacher should (a) present the discussion question clearly, (b) designate a recorder for each group, (c) charge the group with the responsibility to submit a verbal and/or written report, and (d) establish definite time limits.

4. Once the small-group discussions are under way, the teacher can usually help most by moving about the room to provide facts, clarify the task, or motivate lethargic groups. It is often necessary to extend or shorten the time allotted as groups become more involved in a topic, or perhaps achieve an early consensus. Obviously, it is better to err on the short side if one hopes to have some of the usual lively enthusiasm typical of small-group discussions carry over into the large-group discussions that follow.

5. Once the class is reassembled for the follow-up discussion, the general procedure is for the recorders for each group to report. Usually the

general discussion is then directed toward the resolution of any conflicting views between the individual reports and the development of a class consensus. Many teachers also require that the recorders submit the notes they took during the discussion as a further means of evaluating the small-group discussions. For suggestions regarding other types of culminating activities and a detailed illustration of the buzz session see pp. 209–213.

Narratives

THE PROBLEM STORY. If the truth were known, we would probably find that most of our students acquire their real health concepts and attitudes outside the classroom as they come to grips with real-life situations. Through use of the problem story, an attempt is made to examine and discuss typical situations in the classroom, where mature and knowledgeable guidance is available. This technique is also known as the case-problem or case-study technique, and in a more refined form it is known as the critical-incident technique.[2] Basically it consists of presenting the students with a narrative account of a meaningful life situation, then challenging them with provocative questions concerning possible courses of action. The following is an example of the topic of safety for kindergarten or first-grade pupils:

A RIDE WITH A STRANGER

Two second-grade boys, Jim and Bill, were walking home from school on a very warm afternoon. Although they had only three blocks more to go, they were hot and tired because of the warm weather and their busy day at school. At this moment, a car pulled up beside them and the nice-looking stranger at the wheel of the car said, "Hop in boys, I'll give you a ride home." Jim started to get in, but Bill said, "Don't, Jim. We'd better walk."

The children could be asked such questions as, "Would you act like Jim or Bill?" and "What should you do after you get home?" (report incident to parents). An illustration of the use of a narrative for the elementary level is also presented on pages 203–207. Regardless of the grade level involved, the procedures are basically simple.

1. There are several ways to obtain appropriate narratives and each method offers certain advantages. Teacher-written narratives can be tailored to local situations, interest patterns, and specific instructional objectives. What they lack in professional polish is usually more than offset by these advantages. Another way is to let the students write them. This adds a new dimension to this general technique. In this case we ask young people to assimilate pertinent health facts and concepts, analyze their value in terms of real-life situations, and then express them in a creative fashion. This can be quite profitable in terms of both the individual's experience in writing

[2] Cyrus Mayshark and Roy A. Foster, *Methods in Health Education* (St. Louis: Mosby, 1972), pp. 1–12.

the narrative and the class's experience in discussing the better ones. The use of newspaper stories is a less creative but often a more practical way to obtain good stories for discussion. It pays to remain alert and keep the scissors handy throughout the year in order to build up a good file. Magazines and books, both fiction and nonfiction, are also good sources; however, written permission is generally required for duplication of this type of material.

2. Short narratives can simply be read to the class. However, if the narrative is at all long or involved, it should be duplicated so that students may refer to a written account. In some cases it is also useful to number the lines of the story along the margin for convenience during discussion. Some teachers also prefer to include the main discussion questions in the duplicated account or to list a series of possible solutions or actions for evaluation during the discussion.

3. The simplest way to organize the discussion is (a) introduce the topic briefly, (b) distribute the written narratives, and (c) begin the discussion after the class has had sufficient time to read the narrative. In some cases it may be best to have the students take them home for study prior to the next class meeting, but usually they can be read in class. A very useful variation is to combine the buzz-session technique with the problem story. When this version is used it is usually best to read the story to the entire class first, then place the students in small groups and distribute one copy of the story to each group for reference. The small groups will be more task-oriented if they are provided with definite questions to discuss.

THE OPEN-ENDED STORY. A technique that is quite similar to the problem story is that of the open-ended story. It consists simply of presenting students with the first part of a story, then asking individual students to supply their own version of a suitable ending. These efforts are then discussed and evaluated by the total group. Other than the obvious benefits of active participation, there are several advantages to the use of such a technique. It offers a favorable balance of teacher guidance versus creative pupil endeavor. The child's efforts are channeled into productive directions by the structure of the story, which the teacher controls. The students have greater incentive to listen closely and remember the important facts when they know that they may be called upon to finish the story. In creating their own endings the students often express, directly or indirectly, many of their basic attitudes and concepts concerning the theme of the narrative. This often provides the teacher with insights into the needs of individual students that might not otherwise be apparent.

Like the problem story, the narratives for the open-ended story can be either obtained from some outside source or written by the teacher. It is often easier for the teacher to make up an appropriate story than to search for a ready-made version. This is particularly true for the elementary grades, where elaborate plots are not necessary or desirable. However, even at the secondary level, teachers can write effective open-ended stories without undue effort, and once a good story is developed it generally has value for a number of years. (See pages 252–255 for an illustrated example of this technique.)

Community Resources

The essential function of the school is to prepare the learner for life in the world beyond the classroom walls. Consequently it is easy to think only of the school's role in serving the community while overlooking the many highly useful ways in which various individuals and organizations within the community can directly serve the school in its educational functions. The concept of the community as a learning environment, while somewhat neglected over the past 10 to 15 years, has recently reemerged in a highly useful and viable form. In speaking specifically of the urban environment the Group for Environmental Education, an organization that champions the "Schools Without Walls" concept, states:

> Education has been thought of as taking place mainly within the confines of the classroom, and school buildings have been regarded as the citadels of knowledge. However, the most extensive facility imaginable for learning is our urban environment. It is a classroom without walls, an open university for people of all ages offering a boundless curriculum with unlimited expertise. If we can make our urban environment comprehensible and observable, we will have created classrooms with endless windows on the world.[3]

Although the resources of many smaller towns and communities fall considerably short of the ideal "boundless curriculum with unlimited expertise," virtually every community has much of value for the well-motivated and properly oriented student. In their *Yellow Pages of Learning Resources* the aforementioned group expands the concept of community resources considerably beyond the common visits to the firehouse or police station and points out the educational potential of many heretofore neglected persons and facilities. For instance, they include sections entitled "What Can You Learn at a Restaurant?" "What Can You Learn from a Taxicab Driver?" and "What Can You Learn at a Cemetery?" The key to the use of these opportunities is the ability to ask the right questions. Under the section for Cemetery, for example, the student is advised:

> Look at tombstones and notice especially the dates on them. Has the material they are made from changed? What has been the effect of time and weather? Have epitaphs changed? Look at tombstones from the same year. Are there differences in stone or style among them? Did people seem to die at a younger

---

[3] Group for Environmental Education, Inc., *Yellow Pages of Learning Resources* (Cambridge, Mass.: MIT Press, 1972).

age a hundred years ago? Is there one year that has many deaths? If so, check in City Hall for records of a plague or epidemic. Look at the architecture of large tombs. Can you distinguish differences in religion, social and economic class, and time from the words and materials? Who composes the message on the tombstone? [4]

Few teachers have the opportunity or the inclination to focus their entire program on community study; however, suitable applications can add considerable interest and realism to almost any health topic. A number of specific techniques may be used either to bring the community into the classroom, as with resource speakers and exhibits, or to send the student to the community through use of surveys or field trips.

THE SMALL-GROUP FIELD TRIP. A class field trip is one of the best ways to add realism to a unit of study, but it is frequently difficult to arrange and may be completely impractical. The small-group field trip can often provide a satisfactory alternative (see pages 375–377 for a detailed example). Using this technique, student volunteers visit health-related facilities in the community and report their experiences to the class. Each visit is made by two to four students who prepare themselves for the visit by prior work in the library. In the class meeting following the visit, the committee presents a brief oral report to the class, and then a discussion period follows during which all students have an opportunity to question the committee members. In this manner the class hears about and discusses firsthand experiences of other students. Young people often learn more this way than when they are all herded through, with the four or five keenly interested students at the front doing all the learning. The small-group field trip consists basically of sending these students and leaving the rest at school. The basic procedures are as follows.

1. At the beginning of the school year, review both the health education units to be covered and the local health facilities that might possibly be visited. These might include local health departments, mental health clinics, food-processing plants, water treatment plants, ambulance services, and so on. Once the appropriate facilities are selected, conduct a telephone survey to determine whether the personnel of specific facilities encourage visitors and what they have to offer. If encouraging information is received on these basic points, then make further inquiries concerning:

    a. Limitations on the number and frequency of visits.
    b. Most desirable days of the week and hours of the day for visits.
    c. The best length of time to allot for each visit.
    d. The availability of public transportation to the site if appropriate.
    e. The possibility of having pamphlets or brochures about the facilities sent to the school.

[4] Ibid, p. 19.

As this information is gathered, it should be recorded for future reference. Once it is initially obtained, it can be updated from year to year with little effort.

2. Details of the actual assignment can be tailored to meet specific situations, and well-motivated student groups will often devise their own embellishments; however, here is one pattern that generally works well:

    a. Ask the committee to review a number of pertinent magazine articles or other selected readings containing general information on the type of facility or type of health problem their visit involves. Require them to meet and pool the information their individual library efforts provided so they will develop a reasonably good background for their visit.

    b. The student committee should usually take responsibility for its own transportation arrangements, particularly at the senior high school level. At the junior high and upper elementary grades, parents will often provide transportation because only two to four students are involved. Although the trip is often expedited by releasing students from one of their health classes and/or study halls, most such trips are scheduled for after-school hours or for weekends.

    c. During the first class meeting following the visit, the committee should submit a ten- to fifteen-minute prepared report in the form of a symposium (see page 160). Very often the balance of the period may be spent in profitable discussion of the findings.

Although this technique can yield meaningful results, it requires well-motivated students to carry it out. Teachers can stimulate this motivation in different ways according to their individual philosophies and the realities of their teaching situations. Some teachers rely on appeals to intrinsic interest and generally solicit volunteers after a good film or lively discussion. Those with a more conservative approach require every student to carry out at least one "project" per term, a requirement that can be met in several ways, including field trip participation. Others choose to use an extra-credit system to help involve students in more demanding assignments.

THE LARGE-GROUP FIELD TRIP. The large-group field trip is "strong medicine" in a methodological sense. When used for an appropriate educational purpose and conducted effectively, it can add substance and meaning to a unit of study far beyond that offered by more indirect devices. However, an ill-conceived trip can easily become an expensive, time-consuming, and even dangerous outing that serves little worthwhile purpose. Thus, in most schools the large-group field trip should be used infrequently and only when its educational potentials are thoroughly utilized. A successful trip results only from careful planning.

The necessary planning for the large-group field trip can be roughly classified into two categories: (1) educational considerations and (2) logistical considerations. The educational considerations usually produce the following type of procedures:

1. Generally, the large-group field trip should be planned as the focal point of an entire unit of study. A visit to a state mental hospital, for instance, might properly involve a class or several classes of students in extensive study and preparation for three or four weeks prior to the visit. This study might include both general background information on mental illness, its prevention and treatment, and information on the treatment facility to be visited.

2. In addition to acquiring background information, the students should participate in planning the specific information they should gain for the trip. They might learn from their library work that most progressive mental hospitals are moving toward a "therapeutic community" concept characterized by efforts to make the hospital environment as normal as possible. They might also read of severe shortages of psychiatrists and other professional personnel and of an emphasis on group rather than individual therapy. These might be identified as specific points to investigate. The assignment of specific responsibilities might also be planned by the students. Who is going to investigate what? Often it is impossible for everyone to visit all components of a large and complex facility; in these instances, student subgroups, properly balanced with respect to talent and leadership, can be planned prior to the trip.

3. During this preplanning stage the teacher can often communicate with the personnel of the facility to make special arrangements for the coming visit. Often small changes in the way time is spent during the tour can produce big dividends. If, for example, a few of the students are permitted to sit in on a group therapy session with patients as actual participants, this experience may provide insights into the therapeutic process that can be profitably shared later in the class sessions that follow the visit. These kinds of special experiences are more likely to be made available when those serving as hosts realize that a visiting group has made a serious effort to prepare themselves as knowledgeable visitors.

4. After the visit there should be a systematic debriefing to evaluate, interpret, and consolidate the information gained on the trip. If the class was organized into subgroups for the visit, then a series of symposiums (see page 160) might be appropriate. If students from different classes or sections were involved, it is often worthwhile to arrange for a sharing of information and experiences among these normally isolated groups. This can be accomplished by exchanging symposium groups between sessions meeting at the same hour or by combining sections into assembly meetings.

The educational benefits also depend on the proper handling of the logistical aspects of the trip. As with most other aspects of teaching, these procedures vary considerably from situation to situation. However, in virtually all instances, the teacher's first step is to discuss the possibilities of a field trip with the building principal or some other appropriate administrative representative. Such a person should be of good help concerning the practical aspects of the field trip, which normally include provisions for

a. Securing parental permission for student participation.
b. Excusing students from other classes on the day of the trip.
c. Providing for additional adult supervision, if indicated.
d. Transportation arrangements, school buses, parental car pools, and so on.
e. Contingency plans for possible problems such as missing students, illness, accidents, or student misbehavior.

THE RESOURCE SPEAKER. It is often simpler and more effective to bring part of the community into the classroom in the form of a resource speaker than it is to take classes of students into the community. As with the field trip, maximum benefits will be derived from the resource speaker only if the students have prepared themselves to be knowledgeable listeners. For this reason the appearance of the guest speakers is best scheduled later in the study unit so that the students will have an opportunity to become acquainted with both the general area of study and the specific topic the resource speaker will present. Procedures are as follows:

1. Invite as resource speakers only those persons who can offer substantially better coverage of a particular topic than the regular teacher. The time and effort involved usually do not justify the use of this technique merely for a change of pace. Try to assess the potential speaker's general effectiveness beforehand; if this is impossible, then set up a small-scale appearance for his first visit, such as one period with a single class rather than all day with large groups. Give particular attention to the possible interaction of the speaker and the group. A public health officer with good technical knowledge and poor speaking ability might do little for a flighty group of eighth-graders, but he might provide an excellent experience for a group of college-bound seniors sophisticated enough to draw him out.

2. Once a speaking commitment from a person of proved effectiveness is secured, every effort should be made to provide for his maximum exposure. When the speaker makes himself available for the entire school day, sections that meet concurrently can be combined. If the speaker will be at the school for only a short period of time, it is sometimes worthwhile to arrange for an assembly hour for the entire grade level or perhaps the entire student body. If such measures are impractical, then one or two representatives from other sections may be excused from other obligations to attend the single presentation and report to their regular health sections later. At the very least, a tape recording or, where available, a videotape should be made so that all or part of the presentation can be played back to other health classes.

3. When the resource person is contacted, he should be informed as to the size of his potential audience and its age, sex, academic ability, and general interests. Also, of course, he needs to learn of the students' background in his speaking topic. Often outside experts assume that any audience they speak to knows nothing about their topic. This assumption should not apply to the class of any conscientious teacher. Arrangements for any possible audiovisual needs should also be discussed at this time.

4. When the resource person visits, the teacher should introduce the speaker and his topic adequately but briefly. Time is usually short and student response is generally based primarily on the visitor's actual presentation rather than on any fascination with his prestigious credentials. Once the speaker begins his presentation, the teacher should note pertinent points for later discussion either during a question-and-answer period following the speaker's talk, or in a succeeding class session. Occasionally, the teacher may need to step in and provide leadership during a discussion period that the speaker is attempting to conduct, but this action should not be taken too hastily, as the speaker may wish to use his own format. An especially inept speaker may start to flounder badly with a particular group, in which case the teacher should move in and convert the presentation to a discussion session. Fortunately such occasions are rare.

5. The teacher and students should express their appreciation to the speaker following his presentation. Shortly after the visit the teacher should send him a note of appreciation. In addition to being courteous, this procedure may make it easier to secure his services again in the future.

Audiovisual Techniques

THE OVERHEAD PROJECTOR. In recent years the overhead projector has developed into an extremely popular and versatile teaching tool. It consists basically of a lighted stage upon which transparencies are placed and a specially designed lens which projects the transparency material on a screen.

The transparency generally consists of a sheet of clear acetate, approximately 8½ by 11 inches, mounted on a cardboard frame. Through the use of either commercially prepared or homemade varieties, printed material, diagrams, and illustrations can be effectively displayed. One of the more attractive features of this projective technique is that the teacher is able to remain at the front of the room and retain eye contact with his class while using the projector. Many teachers also like the projector because it can be used in a fully lighted room and because the teacher can control the material by revealing only part of the transparency at any given moment.

These features make the overhead projector a "teacher-oriented" system. This basic characteristic immediately accounts for the overhead projector's principal strength, weakness, and popularity. It provides highly effective support to the traditional lecture–discussion approach. Teachers who are used to doing most of the talking take quite readily to this technique and find that their sometimes tedious presentations are much improved. Although the overhead projector is compatible with a teacher-centered approach to methodology, it does not have to lead in this direction. Through the use of properly prepared transparencies, concepts can be presented and questions posed which can initiate lively, student-centered class discussions. As long as this technique is used to encourage more, rather than less, student participation in the teaching–learning process, it can be a highly effective addition to a creative teacher's bag of tricks. Basic procedures are as follows:

1. Commercially prepared transparencies often come in sets of ten to twenty, covering a single health topic; a teacher's guide is usually included. The material must be reviewed thoroughly and a decision made on whether to use the whole set or select only those transparencies particularly pertinent to one's course of study. This decision should be based on the similarity of the package to the content to be covered and the extent to which other methods will be used.

2. The creative potential of this technique can be best realized by use of teacher-prepared transparencies. Few other media are so adaptable to the amount of time, skill, and interest possessed by the individual teacher. Somewhat crude but remarkably effective transparencies can be made from a few sheets of acetate and a grease pencil. Satisfactory results have been achieved by using a few sheets of old X-ray film and a typewriter correction pencil. At the other extreme, sophisticated reproduction processes, color-lift techniques, adhesive color film, and other specialized materials make it possible for the teacher to produce transparencies of professional quality. Although the technique of transparency production is relatively simple, the variations are endless. Information provided by such sources as the Minnesota Mining and Manufacturing Company plus the teacher's ingenuity and experimentation are all that are needed for effective handling of the material involved, so no attempt will be made to cover that aspect here. However, some general points merit special emphasis:

a. The basic rule to keep in mind is *one idea to a transparency*. The primary information should be clearly and simply stated and set apart by color underlining from supportive or secondary information.
b. Secondary information should be kept to a minimum and used only to clarify or dramatize the main idea. Written material should be kept to the minimum. Complex explanations, interesting sidelights, and so on, should be presented by the teacher or drawn out in class discussion rather than embodied in the transparency.
c. Letter size should be large enough to permit easy reading from the back of the room; the smallest letter on the screen should have a height of at least 1 inch for every 30 feet of viewing distance.
d. Whenever possible, use simple illustrations and diagrams rather than text. Be willing to experiment with your own "amateurish" drawing, for the projective technique adds a certain professional quality to any

material you place on the transparency. The important consideration is the effectiveness with which the drawing communicates the idea.[5]

3. In most classrooms, the screen should be placed on an angle in a front corner of the room, preferably on the window side. This arrangement enables the teacher to remain at the front of the room without obstructing the view of any student. The screen should be placed as high as possible and, if its construction permits, the top should be tilted forward to minimize distortion of the image (keystoning). Although these procedures are desirable, transparencies simply projected on a wall can still convey an idea effectively.

4. In addition to displaying information simply and effectively, the overhead projector enables the teacher to reveal only a portion of the information at any given moment. This is accomplished by use of (a) the revelation technique, (b) overlays, and (c) the on-off switch. It is important for the teacher to learn to use these devices properly. The revelation technique involves covering certain portions of the transparency with cardboard or heavy paper until the proper time for its presentation. In its simplest form, it consists of merely sliding a piece of opaque material off a transparency in successive stages from the top down as the discussion proceeds. Overlays are simply additional transparencies that are placed over the first to add new elements to the image on the screen; the teaching considerations that govern the use of the revelation technique also apply to the use of overlays. Release new material only when you are ready to discuss it to avoid distracting the student with a transparency that does not apply to the immediate point. The periodic exposure of new information helps sustain the interest of the class. When the material is not needed, the projector should be turned off. This enables the class to redirect its attention to the teacher or to students participating in a class discussion.

EDUCATIONAL FILMS. The conventional 16-mm sound film is one of the most commonly used teaching aids in health education. In addition to the inherent attractiveness of this medium, much of its popularity among health teachers is due to the great variety of health-related films that are generally available. Dozens of organizations of all types, including commercial firms, governmental and voluntary health agencies, and charitable foundations, produce health films which they make available to schools at little or no cost. Unfortunately this profusion of film tends to encourage film abuse, as well as film use. Some teachers subject their classes to a quick succession of films containing complex and sometimes irrelevant material, while providing them with little time to discuss or properly digest the bewildering array of facts and ideas. Students may be shown the same film three or four times as they progress through the grades in a single

[5] Adapted from Morton J. Schultz, *The Teacher and Overhead Projection* (Englewood Cliffs, N.J.: Prentice-Hall, 1965), pp. 28–29.

school system, or they may arrive in class for the second day of a unit on drug abuse only to be greeted with a nutrition film that arrived two weeks after they completed their study of that topic.

As with other teaching techniques and materials, films should be employed for appropriate and well-defined purposes. These purposes can be reduced to two broad categories. The first concerns the ability of film to illustrate all manner of complex phenomena more conveniently and effectively than by other means. Microscopic and time-lapse techniques can be used to show the entire process of cell division or the entrance of a sperm cell into an ovum. The student may also see exactly what happens to manikins with and without seat belts during an auto collision. A series of schematic illustrations supported by a well-conceived narrative may provide the student with a clear concept of the immunity process. Many such technical subjects can be effectively presented in a film. However, all complex phenomena are not physical or biological. Films are often more effective than words in conveying real understanding of such concepts as hostility, maturity, or affection.

A second major purpose films can serve is that of providing health material with emotional impact. Whether it be the panic and tragedy of an auto accident or the pleasure and delight of a young mother holding her newborn child, the valid presentation of emotional situations is necessary if health concepts are to be conveyed effectively and realistically. Films can probably do this better than any other technique. A word of caution is needed; emotional content in films serves little useful purpose unless (1) it contributes to an accurate and well-balanced presentation of a topical area, and (2) it is interpreted properly and backed up with practical information concerning related health behavior.

Two of the most important considerations in the selection of films to meet these purposes are their relevance to the topic and appropriateness to the maturity level of the students. With regard to relevance, the teacher should bear in mind the breadth of most content areas in health education. A 40-minute film showing the manufacturing of flu vaccine is obviously related to the topic of communicable disease, but this does not make it relevant to a unit of study calling for heavy emphasis on venereal disease. Films designed to teach medical students about various skin disorders might have some perverse entertainment value for eighth-graders but would probably do little for their practical needs. The quality of the acting, authenticity of the setting, and up-to-dateness (hemlines, auto styles, etc.) are important considerations when an impact on attitudes or values is desired. These considerations are of lesser importance when the main emphasis is on cognitive objectives.

Some idea of the degree to which a particular film meets the criteria for selection can be obtained from the film description and from other secondary sources; however, a final decision is seldom justified until the film is previewed. In addition to determining the film's basic fitness for use, the teacher can also identify the relevant points covered by the film and note those aspects that the student will want to question or discuss. Once a good film is selected and previewed, the proper handling of the film in the teaching situation is greatly simplified. The following are some commonly used procedures:

- The film should be presented at the appropriate time within the teaching unit. Films that are short on content but long on interest values should come early in the unit. Those that present complex subject matter might well be delayed until the students have developed some grasp of the preliminary concepts; those with a culminating or summarizing quality are normally placed at the end of the unit.
- The basic purpose of the film should be explained to the class briefly but clearly immediately before it is viewed; alert them to the basic points of the film by either a verbal itemization or a printed film guide.
- Extensive note taking should generally not be required during the film; the action is often fast and the room dark.
- The early part of the follow-up discussion usually should be reserved for student-initiated questions and comments. After this is completed or begins to lag, the teacher can undertake a brief but systematic review of the film's highlights.

The basic mechanics of handling the equipment may require very much or very little of the teacher's attention, depending on the type of audiovisual service available. Fortunate teachers will receive highly effective help from an audiovisual coordinator or his assistants; others will be virtually on their own. Regardless of the situation these basic considerations apply:

- Competent operation of the equipment is essential for a good educational experience. If good operators are not available, the teacher must train himself in the use of the equipment.
- If at all possible, have the film set up and all components tested well before class begins: Is the film threaded properly? Does the lamp work? How's the focus? Is the room dark enough? Is the sound adjusted properly?
- If practical, delay the rewinding operation until after class dismissal so as not to detract from the follow-up discussion.
- The astronauts are fond of referring to "Murphy's Law," which cautions that "if something can go wrong, it will." Remember that the film may not arrive. The equipment may arrive without an extension cord. The lamp may burn out. Take all precautions and have an alternate lesson planned.

Although films are available from many sources (see page 104), the most convenient source is the school or district film library. Encourage the purchase of films that will not quickly become dated, such as those presenting basic scientific concepts. Films of current interest should be obtained on a loan or rental basis.

TELEVISION. The many obvious advantages of television as a medium of communication would make it appear to have exciting potential for all fields of education. However, after several years of relatively ambitious experimentation, this potential is still largely unrealized. Many of the early disappointments seemed to result from (1) an underestimation of the demanding nature of quality television teaching, and (2) inappropriate attempts to use television as a substitute for good classroom teaching. Now that these hard lessons have been learned, educational television in both its open-circuit (ETV) and closed-circuit (ITV) versions is becoming increasingly valuable as an instructional aid. A fairly common pattern seems to be developing in districts where it is routinely used in the classroom as a supplement to health education. Often a public school or university teacher whose teaching style and personal qualities lend themselves to television will be featured in a series of twenty-minute programs which parallel the course of study. These programs are viewed by the students during their regularly scheduled forty- or fifty-minute health class. Because the class is viewing what is essentially a "health film," the teaching procedures are similar to those for conventional sound films.

- Review the content of the program carefully before it is presented and preview it if this is possible.
- Select for use in your classroom only those programs that will present material you cannot present more effectively by other means. In most situations, the classroom teacher controls the on-off switch.
- Prepare students for the programs and plan appropriate follow-up activities.
- Note taking is possible with this medium, so encourage students to take notes if the material lends itself to this activity.

The many programs on health topics prepared for conventional home viewing provide an effective but often neglected source of supplemental information for the health education class. These are commonly offered as documentaries or as part of a series focusing on contemporary problems. The teacher can learn of such programs through conventional television guides and, although previewing is impossible, some reasonable assessment can usually be made from preliminary descriptions. Some possible ways to make use of these programs are the following:

- Announce the date, time, and channel of promising programs in all health classes and encourage students to view them.

- When the program topic happens to apply to the present unit of study, secure volunteers or assign one or two students from each section to view the program and report to the class; encourage as many as possible of the other class members to view it on their own.
- Knowledge of particularly well-recommended forthcoming programs or series of programs will occasionally warrant reshuffling of the course calendar to coordinate a unit of study with the television offerings.

Programmed Instruction

Although taking many forms, programmed instruction commonly embodies certain well-defined characteristics. Information leading to a precisely defined objective is released to the student bit by bit while he is constantly required to make some type of overt response. As Schramm describes:

> His response may be to fill in a word left blank, to answer a question, to select one of a series of multiple choice answers, to indicate agreement or disagreement, or to solve a problem and record the answer. As soon as he has responded to the item, he is permitted to see the correct response so that he can tell immediately whether his response has been the right one.[6]

Generally, programs are designed so that the student is correct more than 90 per cent of the time even though he is gradually being led deeper into subject matter with which he is unfamiliar. This constant and usually positive feedback appears to keep most students well motivated and highly involved while working largely on their own.

The most common type of programs are linear or Skinnerian, programs, which generally utilize "fading" as their principal technique. New terms are first described in a clear-cut and familiar context. Then the student is asked to apply these terms to a series of situations in which the clues to their use gradually become less obvious. Soon the student finds himself using the new term or fact properly with no artificial cues from the program. A second major type of program is the Crowder, or branching type of, program. This type of program generally features a multiple-choice format combined with a more sophisticated way of dealing with wrong responses. The Skinnerian program usually corrects a wrong response by immediately supplying the proper answer; in a similar situation the Crowder program generally provides a brief explanation of why the response is incorrect and sends the student back for another selection. This often increases the time needed for the student to complete the program but, by providing responses tailored to his particular misconceptions, presumably

[6] Wilbur Schramm, *Programed Instruction Today and Tomorrow* (New York: Fund for the Advancement of Education, 1962).

accommodates his individual needs. Occasional student errors are thus regarded as useful responses in the Crowder system, whereas Skinnerian programmers seek to hold them to an absolute minimum.[7]

Programs come in a great variety of packages—some in the form of books or booklets, some as material for simple teaching machines, and still others for use in highly sophisticated computer-assisted instruction. Although these modes of presentation vary somewhat in efficiency and cost, the principles governing their construction and use remain essentially the same.

During the past few years there has been a great rush by various commercial firms to develop and market programs for public school use. As one might suspect, a great many of these "rush jobs" are of doubtful quality and few of any type are available for the field of health education. Many teachers are fully capable of devising their own programs after a brief exposure to the fundamentals of construction (the authors have seen decent programs resulting from a three-semester-hour course). However, program construction is a time-consuming task. At the present time, the most practical strategy for most teachers is to remain alert to the appearance of good health education programs on the market or, if the resources are available, to cooperate with other teachers on a district-wide basis to construct programs for local needs.

The basic guidelines for the incorporation of programmed instruction into classroom activities are not well defined; however, the following are a few basic hints that seem valid at this time:

- In their present stage of development, programs generally are more effective in presenting cognitive material that lends itself to precise definitions as compared with content heavily weighted with attitudes or value judgments.
- Programs appear useful as a means of providing remedial instruction to students who failed to gain important knowledge because of extended absences, poor class performance, and so on.
- Programs also can serve as a means of enriching a program for students who can profit from content more challenging than that provided by regular class activities.
- Programs may be used to relieve the teacher of the burden of routine instruction by "handling" one portion of a class while he works with the remaining students.

Ideally, programs develop into disciplined and efficient automated tutors that may free the teacher for the more challenging and creative aspects of teaching.

[7] James W. Armsey and Norman C. Dahl, *An Inquiry into the Uses of Instructional Technology* (New York: The Ford Foundation, 1973), p. 56.

REFERENCES

Ahrens, Maurice R. "Methods Can Make a Difference," *Educational Leadership*, Vol. 30, No. 8 (May 1973), pp. 700–705.

Armsey, James W., and Norman C. Dahl. *An Inquiry into the Uses of Instructional Technology*. New York: The Ford Foundation, 1973.

Dale, Edgar. *Audio-Visual Methods in Teaching*. New York: Dryden Press, 1954.

Erickson, Carlton W., and David H. Curl. *Fundamentals of Teaching with Audiovisual Technology*. New York: Macmillan Publishing Co., Inc., 1972.

Esbensen, Thorwald. *Working with Individualized Instruction*. Belmont, Calif.: Fearon Publishers, 1968.

Evaul, Thomas W. "The Automated Tutor," *Journal of Health, Physical Education and Recreation*, Vol. 35, No. 3 (March 1964).

Franenkel, Jack R. *Helping Students Think and Value: Strategies for Teaching the Social Studies*. Englewood Cliffs, N.J.: Prentice-Hall, Inc., 1973.

Hurt, Tom. "Conventional Versus Systems and Linear Versus Intrinsic Models for Developing Self-Instructional Materials for Health Education," *Journal of School Health*, Volume XLII, No. 9 (November 1972), pp. 542–547.

Mayshark, Cyrus, and Roy A. Foster. *Health Education in Secondary Schools*. St. Louis, Mo.: The C. V. Mosby Co., 1972.

Means, Richard K. *Methodology in Education*. Columbus, Ohio: Charles E. Merrill Publishing Co., 1968.

Murphy, Judith, and Ronald Gross. *Learning by Television*. New York: Fund for the Advancement of Education, 1966.

Prentice, Marjorie. "Systematic Instruction," *Educational Leadership*, Vol. 30, No. 8 (May 1973), pp. 706–709.

Schramm, Wilbur. *Programmed Instruction Today and Tomorrow*. New York: Fund for the Advancement of Education, 1962.

Schrank, Jeffrey. *Teaching Human Beings: 101 Subversive Activities for the Classroom*. Boston: Beacon Press, 1972.

Schultz, Morton J. *The Teacher and Overhead Projection*. Englewood Cliffs, N.J.: Prentice-Hall, Inc., 1965.

Smith, James A. *Creative Teaching of the Social Studies in the Elementary School*. Boston: Allyn & Bacon, Inc., 1967.

Springfield, Charlotte Ann. "Learning Centers—Stations—Places," *Educational Leadership*, Vol. 30, No. 8 (May 1973), pp. 736–737.

PART IV
Creative Teaching Applied

"It must be remembered," said Vaihinger, "that the object of the world of ideas as a whole is not the portrayal of reality—this would be an utterly impossible task—rather to provide us with an instrument for finding our way about in this world more easily."

9 MENTAL
■ HEALTH I:
FOUNDATIONS

For a number of years the National Association for Mental Health has presented statistics that cannot help but make an impact on anyone who gives them a moment's consideration. Each year in our nation more than one million persons are admitted to hospitals for psychiatric care; at least 50 per cent of all medical and surgical cases of any type involve emotional problems as an important factor.[1] Impressive as these facts are, they still do not reflect the many instances of divorce, suicide, and delinquencies and repetitive crimes of various types involving persons with mental illnesses that are never diagnosed or treated.

We are also told by the National Association for Mental Health that one out of every ten Americans is in need of psychiatric treatment. In view of the difficulty of determining exactly who is disturbed enough to warrant professional care and who is simply exhibiting a harmless personality quirk, many persons view the one-in-ten estimate as another exaggeration presented by a fund-raising organization. But let us look at one of the better-known investigations of the mental health status of our population. Researchers for the Mid-Town Manhattan Study sought to determine the mental health of 175,000 persons living in a 200-square-block area of Manhattan through the use of psychiatric interviews.[2] According to their criteria, they placed the majority of this population (58 per cent) in the "mildly to moderately disturbed" category. They found less than one in five (18.5 per cent) persons "essentially well in terms of mental health." Those remaining (23.5 per cent) were classified as "marked or severely"

[1] The National Association for Mental Health, *Facts About Mental Illness* (New York: The Association, 1972), p. 1.

[2] Leo Srole et al., *Mental Health in the Metropolis: The Mid-Town Manhattan Study* (New York: McGraw-Hill, 1962), p. 138.

disturbed and presumably strong candidates for professional help. A more recent study of a similar design sampled the population of a Long Island community and identified from 26 to 35 per cent of the subjects as likely to be psychotic cases, depending on the specific screening procedures used.[3] A review of 26 such studies of this type completed during or since 1950 yields a median prevalence rate for psychiatric disorders of 15.6 per cent.[4]

These studies make the one-in-ten estimate of the National Association for Mental Health appear quite conservative, rather than exaggerated. Although the process of psychiatric diagnosis admittedly falls far short of being an exact science, these and other indications strongly suggest at the very least that the mental health status of the average person falls far short of the ideal. Also, it seems clear that large numbers of the mentally ill are undiagnosed and untreated.

The Crucial Years

But what about the school-age child? Most of us accept the fact that adolescence is fraught with potential for emotional trauma that may produce lifelong scars on adult personalities, but we tend to dismiss the problems of the elementary school child as unimportant. There is a tendency for the normal, immature, boisterous, and often irrational behavior of children to mask the symptoms of emotional disturbances exhibited by a small but significant minority. The following case dramatically illustrates some important aspects of the mental health needs of children in this age range:

In the fading days of the summer of 1965, in our Nation's capital, an 11-year-old boy was found spending his nights huddled in an apartment hallway with the only friend he knew—a stray dog. As millions of his young fellow citizens were beginning their zestful return to school, he devoted his full attention to the quest for survival—managed, somehow, through the haphazard handouts of food and drink from curious tenants, and the affection of the dog he had claimed as his only companion.

Taken finally by police to a detention home, the now retarded boy's story unfolded: Through his meager decade of life, begun in a broken home, he had ricocheted from court to welfare department, from mother to foster home, from institution to psychiatrist. He had been tested but never treated, examined but never loved. So it was that he had long begun to spend his own love on dogs, not people.[5]

During the ten years or so since this particular case was reported there has been, first, a concerted effort to develop more community mental health

---

[3] Bruce P. Dohrenwend, "II Psychiatric Disorder in General Populations: Problem of the Untreated 'Case'," *American Journal of Public Health*, Vol. 60, No. 6 (June 1970), p. 1055.

[4] Ibid., p. 1052.

[5] U.S. Department of Health, Education, and Welfare, *Mental Health of Children*, PHS Publication No. 1396, Washington, D.C., 1965, p. 1.

clinics and, more recently, some retrenchment of this endeavor; unfortunately, the phrase "tested but never treated, examined but never loved" still applies to many children who develop mental illness. Facilities are often jammed and waiting periods are long. When the treatment is finally forthcoming, it is too often superficial and ineffective.

Some communities have made vigorous efforts to attack their problems of mental illness, and the sharp criticism expressed above admittedly does them an injustice. However, where this general problem is addressed realistically, it soon becomes obvious that no one program or no one approach can do more than scratch the surface in terms of real community needs. Virtually every aspect of community life has an impact on the mental health of its citizens either directly or indirectly; therefore, a broad-front approach is needed if mental health is to be promoted or mental illness is to be prevented or treated. According to the needs of a particular situation, the attraction of new industry to provide employment, the development of new parks and recreational programs, or the addition of psychiatric services to community health care clinics might all make equally important contributions to the cause of mental health. Within any given community the general physical, economic, and social environment, the quality and quantity of mental health services, and the information propagated on the topic of mental health represent the major categories of, what is in effect, a total mental health program.

Prevention and Promotion

The practical application of this philosophy to the school program involves attention to (1) mental health services, (2) the emotional environment of the school, and (3) the teaching of mental health content. It is the third category, of course, that this text is most concerned with, but some knowledge of the first two is necessary if instructional needs are to be viewed in proper perspective.

MENTAL HEALTH SERVICES. The need for psychiatric treatment for advanced cases of mental illness has been discussed earlier. However, effective personal guidance of an informal nature on the part of well-trained and sympathetic teachers often leads children away from self-defeating behavioral patterns long before their problems reach the clinical stage. The more difficult problems in this subclinical category may often be handled by guidance workers or by school nurses who are trained in this area. In addition to these direct services, school personnel can serve an important preventive function by identifying and referring children who appear to need psychiatric help. When this is done effectively, many potentially serious cases are brought to treatment at a time when help is most beneficial.

THE EMOTIONAL ENVIRONMENT. As an important living environment, the school is rivaled only by the home in terms of contact time or of presenting crucial challenges to the child's adaptive capabilities. Recognition of this importance during recent years has resulted in increased efforts to structure the total school environment in a manner designed to have a positive effect on mental health. This has included everything from changes in the basic architectural design of elementary schools to make them less massive and threatening to children, to changes in general classroom procedures, assignments, and discipline methods to produce a healthier emotional climate. Considerable attention has also been given to the scheduling of the school day to balance classroom work and activity periods and to provide an adequate lunch period. The teachers themselves constitute another crucial aspect of the school environment. By staffing the school with teachers with adequate professional training in their particular specialties, in the characteristics of children, and the mechanics of teaching, many potential cases of school maladjustment can be avoided.

THE ROLE OF HEALTH EDUCATION. A third major part of the school's total effort in behalf of mental health is in teaching young people about personality development, habits of mental hygiene, and ways to handle emotional stress. This is the phase of the program that involves the teacher most directly and, unfortunately, this is the phase that generally receives the least support. The specific aspects of mental health teaching are covered in the remainder of this chapter, beginning with a closer examination at the objects of our attention—the children themselves.

THE MENTAL HEALTH CHARACTERISTICS OF CHILDREN AND ADOLESCENTS

Although the teacher needs to be thoroughly knowledgeable about the specific age levels with which he comes into contact, some familiarity with the whole pattern of personality development is needed to view any particular age group in proper perspective. It is beyond the scope of this text to present an intensive discussion of this major topic, but a brief review may increase the meaningfulness of the teaching recommendations that follow.

The Preschool Period

If the primary child is fortunate, he will have a solid base to work from as he tackles the social challenges of school. During his preschool period, he will have sought to become a "little person" in his own right within the home and within his neighborhood play groups. If he succeeded, he will enter kindergarten or first grade with an appropriate sense of his self-identity. The extent to which this has been accomplished will in large part determine how well he progresses in his next stage of development.

The Fundamental Task

From a social and emotional standpoint, the fundamental task that elementary school children must accomplish can be stated quite simply if one is permitted to overgeneralize to some extent. They must learn to draw a significant amount of their emotional support from their peer groups, particularly from their companions of the same sex. This basic need immediately leads to a whole series of complicated events. There will be a corresponding decrease in the support needed from the parents. The primary child will shift considerable dependence to the classroom teacher and this new-found source of strength will gradually be dropped in favor of the gang during the intermediate grades and the gang demands that children qualify for membership by demonstrating a reasonable degree of independence and personal identity. "Momma's boys" and "Teacher's pets" are generally excluded.

The elementary child's task is complicated by the need to preserve his status with both his age-mates and the significant adults in his life. Consciously or unconsciously, elementary children are aware of their need for the emotional and physical support of parents and teachers while at the same time sensing that their future lies with their age-mates. The conflicting demands that these two groups place on the child are well known, as is the fact that most children somehow manage to accommodate these conflicting forces. This is generally not accomplished without squabbling, disappointments, occasional threats to leave home, and other symptoms of distress but, after all this, we find that the normal child has developed a reasonably secure spot for himself within the gang structure. This then serves as a point of departure for his journey into the unknown world of heterosexual activities during adolescence.

Values and Standards

Stone and Church, in their book *Childhood and Adolescence*, highlight an important characteristic of elementary school children that often does not receive proper emphasis—their "moralistic" quality, their tendency to react strongly to anything that appears inconsistent or unfair.[6] Issues are "right or wrong," "black or white," and children tend to pass severe judgment on those who violate the rules. Later on, in the true "gang state," they tend to develop strict codes which may or may not be formalized in writing, as in the constitution of a "secret society."

The inflexible quality of their standards while they are still busily internalizing adults standards and values probably makes it difficult for children to avoid frequent violations of these requirements. This provides some explanation for their tendencies toward rationalization, denial, and self-justification, for their secretiveness and argumentativeness. When these measures fail to prevent or release the anxiety that results from being unable to meet the rigorous standards set by both adults, peers, or oneself, it may be expressed through other less appropriate outlets. It may take the

---

[6] L. Joseph Stone and Joseph Church, *Childhood and Adolescence*, 2nd. ed. (New York: Random House, 1968), p. 414.

form of fear of some nonexistent thing or situation, or perhaps exaggerated fear of some real but minor factor. Excessive fantasizing, shyness, or, at the other extreme, excessive boisterousness or bullying may result.

Degrees of Success

A few children handle the challenges of this period in outstanding fashion; these fortunate ones sail on into adolescence unencumbered by unresolved conflicts or emotional scars that might limit their development. A few, at the other pole, fail miserably and wind up on the waiting list of community mental clinics. But the vast majority meet with indifferent or mediocre success, and they go on to mediocre careers as adolescents. They then become the adults displaying the characteristics that enable researchers to classify large portions of the population as mildly to moderately mentally ill.

It is impossible to determine the exact status of the mental health of the population in general, or of elementary school children in particular. By definition, most children are normal, but it is apparent that "normal" is far from "ideal." Almost all children show the need for improvement in their mental and emotional traits. Health educators generally feel that direct educational efforts can contribute significantly to this improvement.

The Fundamental Task of Adolescence

"Who am I?" "Where am I going?" "How do I get there?" "Will I ever get there?" As the individual moves out of the typical gang stage of the upper elementary school years and through the stormy years of adolescence, these questions become increasingly important. Much of the adolescent's behavior is accounted for by his struggle to find answers for these questions or relief from the tensions they produce. The adolescent is searching for his own personal identity and independence; he may not be conscious of this search in a manner that enables him to express this need in any articulate way, but it will appear in many other forms. One of these is found in the changing role of the peer group.

PERSONAL IDENTITY. The typical gang of the elementary school child serves mainly to provide emotional support and companionship for its members. The fifth-grader, for instance, is generally content merely to belong, to be accepted. Belonging and being accepted are also vitally important to the adolescent in meeting his immediate needs; however, he also looks to the future. The temporary nature of the gang now becomes increasingly apparent to him. As he becomes more aware of the nature of adult society, he wishes to develop a more individualized role; he must make his mark, find his place. These feelings tend to produce a self-awareness or self-consciousness greater than that of either the small child or the adult.[7] The fifth-grader can decide that he is going to be an astronaut and

---

[7] Paul H. Mussen, John J. Conger, and Jerome Kagan, *Child Development and Personality* (New York: Harper & Row, Publishers, Inc., 1969), p. 623.

beat down all criticisms of his decision; the ninth-grader, however, soon realizes that if he does not figure out some way to handle first-year algebra many professions may be closed to him. The fifth-grader may decide that he never wants to get married or that he may someday marry a movie star; the ninth-grader fears that if he does not find something to cure his acne, he may never get a date.

In his efforts to move toward his version of competent adult status, the adolescent is seeking independence, on the one hand, and accurate guidance, on the other. He now uses his age-mates as a reflective device; he studies their reactions closely for clues to the true nature of his own emerging personality. He uses adults in the same way, only the process is more complicated. He must gain information from this segment of society without becoming subservient to it. This ambivalent attitude toward adults is most apparent in the adolescent's typical view of his parents, which is aptly described by Stone and Church as one in which parents who intervene in the child's life are "snoopy and domineering," whereas those who do not are "neglectful and uncaring." [8] It is not surprising that parents and teachers alike find the secondary school youth a challenging individual with whom to deal. The young person's problems with the basically sexual aspects of his behavior will be discussed in later chapters. The sex drive provides many general implications for mental health.

A MATURE SEX ROLE. The development of the sex drive in its mature or genital form serves as a constant reminder of the adolescent's growth toward adult status and responsibilities. Its arrival tends to close the doors of childhood and add a sense of urgency to the task of developing a relatively mature masculine or feminine role. A closely related problem of the teen-ager is found in the simple need to master the sex drive and channel it into constructive pursuits. Regardless of the views of the adolescent or his parents toward sexual behavior, few adolescents release more than a small portion of their sexual tension through sexual intercourse, and many, of course, release none at all in this way. Although medical and psychiatric authorities have pointed out the fallacies inherent in folklore concerning masturbation, this practice still produces guilt feelings among those who use this form of physical release.

Havighurst [9] and others who accept the concept of neutralization or sublimation of sexual energy feel that our society requires the adolescent to learn to channel the sex drive into such things as academic, vocational, or athletic pursuits. Another important outlet lies in participation in heterosexual activities such as informal discussions, recreational games, and social dancing. When properly managed, these things can reduce rather than increase sexual tensions.

[8] Stone and Church, op. cit., p. 447.
[9] Robert J. Havighurst, *Developmental Task and Education*, 2nd ed. (New York: Longmans, Green, 1952).

Although mastery of the physiological component of the sex drive constitutes perhaps the most dramatic need of the adolescent, the development of other aspects of the mature sex role is also formidable. The teenager seeks to develop those qualities of manliness or womanliness that he or she considers ideal in the adult. The fact that some of the attempts to assume adult mannerisms are painful, clumsy, and inept serves to remind the teen-ager of how long and difficult the path to adulthood is. Many adolescents seek to develop such attributes as courage, forthrightness, decisiveness, integrity, and a social consciousness in a short span of time. And, of course, they want to incorporate all the mannerisms and little marks of sophistication that they associate with adulthood. It is little wonder that they often tire of the struggle and find relief in periodic binges of childish behavior.

INDIVIDUAL VARIATIONS. Although it is not difficult to identify the basic pattern of emotional development in the adolescent, it is virtually impossible to discuss the many variations displayed by individual children as they grapple with the complex problems involved. Many junior high school students appear to prefer the role of the competent child to that of the struggle of the incompetent adult-to-be; this temporarily simplifies things for both the child and the adult dealing with him but merely delays rather than solves any problems. Some adolescents exhibit ambivalence or problem-centered behavior throughout their secondary school careers; others who seemingly show little distress may be adjusting smoothly or may be covering up serious conflicts by directing them inward in a pattern likely to produce psychosomatic ailments or long-term personality scars. Regardless of the apparent presence or absence of maladaptive behavior, or the student's individual style of handling the problems of this stage, health educators generally feel that these tasks can be made easier for the student if he is provided with an opportunity to develop a basic understanding of the forces that influence his behavior during this period.

INSTRUCTIONAL APPROACH

The specific task of teaching young people about mental health begins with a decision on the necessity of and the specific manner in which it will be incorporated into the total health education curriculum. Because of the extremely broad and ill-defined nature of the content in this area, many educators have questioned the practicality of teaching mental health as a specific content area. A few still choose to ignore it completely and concentrate on the purely physiological aspects of health. Others omit it as a specific area for exactly the opposite reason: they see mental health as too large and relevant a topic to be confined to a single unit or content area. The personnel of the School Health Education Study took this latter approach and designated the mental aspect as one of the three basic dimensions of health, along with the physical and social.[10] Following this scheme, mental content is integrated throughout the curriculum with personality development taught as part of the general concept of growth and development, mental illness taught as part of the disease concept, and so forth throughout the total curriculum.

Separate versus Integrated Mental Health

A brief look at the rationale for these differing points of view can provide a clearer understanding of the importance of mental health. As educators probe into the real essence of self-damaging health behavior in such areas as human sexuality, drug abuse, and obesity, they tend to find that emotional disturbances in the form of frustrations, feelings of inadequacy, and damaged self-concepts consistently appear as possible root causes. For example, an eighth-grade boy with a strong fear of girls and the prospects of dating might express these fears in the form of drug use, heavy eating, excessive fantasying, or extra attention to his schoolwork. Extreme cases of this type, of course, need professional counseling rather than education, but all persons can benefit from some understanding of the underlying dynamics of these and similar situations. And rather than deal with such content in a fragmented or repetitious way within successive units on drug abuse, human sexuality, and nutrition, it seems logical to consolidate such learning experiences under the general heading of mental health.

According to the opposing point of view, the study of mental health per se tends to become a relatively uninviting consideration of abstractions such as needs, responses, conflicts, ego structures, and so forth. It has no reality until it is viewed within the context of something concrete such as a sexual or drug-oriented problem, so why bother with it as a separate area of study. However, before one becomes too embroiled in the controversy it is well to recognize that either mode of organization can function effectively, provided that other more fundamental factors are sound. In the final analysis, the total content of the health curriculum is more important than the particular way it happens to be organized. A good learning experience is a good learning experience regardless of the title of the unit of study in which it occurs.

General Goals

Although it seems logical that people should learn something about anything as important as mental health, it is difficult to identify a clear relationship between classroom experience and any favorable impact on the quality of mental health itself. The question arises of just what an educa-

[10] School Health Education Study, *Health Education: A Conceptual Approach to Curriculum Design* (St. Paul, Minn.: 3M Education Press, 1967).

tional program in mental health is designed to accomplish. Any given health educator or health curriculum committee would usually answer such a question differently, with the differences often being extreme. There are several logical ways to categorize the desired outcomes. Those discussed below are offered merely to illustrate some possible areas to consider.

PERSONAL BEHAVIOR. Much of the material presented to students on the topic of mental health, as it is with other health topics, is designed to help the learner solve or prevent personal health problems. The adolescent, for instance, can learn that his parents are seeking to provide his life with a needed degree of structure and discipline while he is seeking an equally essential measure of independence and autonomy. He can also learn that moods and feelings are occasionally subject to unexplainable swings that border on depression or euphoria and, while knowing about these phenomena will not prevent problems and conflicts from occurring, they can often prevent or minimize the hopelessness and confusion that frequently lead to overreaction. The ignorant person often finds himself with a seemingly unique problem that seems destined to last forever, whereas the educated person often knows that many others are "in the same boat" and that most conflicts and depressions eventually die a natural death if they are not unduly aggravated. The minimizing of problems through the simple application of knowledge and understanding does not yield the sudden dramatic results of encounter therapy, for instance, but its long-range benefits should not be overlooked.

Another example of the application of knowledge of mental health occurs when students refer themselves to teachers, counselors, and similar professionals for help. This requires a basic knowledge of the availability of help and some assurance that their overtures will be sympathetically received. It is true that many of the students that need help the most cannot be effectively reached in the classroom, but some can be encouraged to avail themselves of mental health services, and it does not take many such cases to make the whole effort worthwhile. Many students who do not need counseling or therapy for themselves can sometimes become effective in guiding others to help once they learn what sort of problems should be referred and where services can be obtained. These efforts may range from the simple encouraging of a distressed classmate to talk to a school guidance counselor to the use of subtle influence to get an unstable parent to visit a community mental health clinic.

COMMUNITY BEHAVIOR. In their intense concern for the personal needs of the learner, health educators frequently overlook his potential as a voter and contributor to that somewhat vague but important entity termed "public opinion." It is seldom appropriate for the school to advocate specific ways of voting on referendums or candidates, but it is very appropriate for the school to equip young people with the tools needed to take informed positions on important social issues. Each year Congress and many state legislatures, town councils, and school boards make decisions on such issues as the support of research in mental health, the treatment of the criminally insane, and the education of mentally retarded children. In his attempt to describe the addictive qualities of our most popular drugs, Menninger says "the trouble with alcohol is that it works." In a certain sense the same could be said for "democracy." When a public consensus develops and persists long enough, elected officials usually seek to accommodate the public will. In the long run, social progress depends on a sensitive and informed citizenry; scores of community decisions have significant impact on the mental health of all members of the community.

FEELINGS AND EMOTIONS. The development of the skills and insights needed to deal effectively with one's own feelings and emotions as well as those of other persons is closely interrelated with personal and community behavior in mental health. Despite this close relationship the idea of dealing directly with feelings and emotions has become somewhat of a controversial issue among teachers, parents, and administrators. And this controversy takes its most intense form when such terms as "sensitivity training," "sensitivity education," or "encounter therapy" are used to describe the learning experiences involved.

Although much of the concern and criticism has been unwarranted, in some cases they have been well founded, particularly when a too thoroughly therapeutic approach has been used under the guise of classroom instruction. Psychotherapy, even under the best of conditions, involves significant risk as the patient's personality structure is systematically dismantled in order to uncover the sources of the trouble; just as the patient in surgery accepts a reasonable degree of risk as part of the treatment aimed at the relief of his symptoms, so must the psychiatric patient expose himself to at least the possibility of excessive trauma or deepening depression that occasionally occurs when the therapy goes awry. Although the risk of damage is small, most parents understandably object when they get the impression that therapeutic procedures are being administered to their essentially normal children by persons who are supposedly trained to educate rather than treat them.

Part of the problem, of course, lies in the difficulty in drawing a distinction between educational and psychotherapeutic procedures, and this problem applies to the environmental and service aspects of the school health program as well as the instructional phase. Most good mental hospitals today incorporate the "therapeutic community" concept wherein every part of the patient's daily routine is viewed as part of his therapy; likewise, within well-administrated schools the emotional environment is structured to nurture the wholesome personality growth of the child. Within the realm of health services, school counselors often find it difficult to determine where academic guidance and "band-aid" counseling end and inappropriate therapy begins. Within the health classroom this dilemma arises in those cases where teachers seek to deal with values, beliefs, emotions, feelings, and similar factors that comprise the affective life of the learner.

As was described in the preceding chapter, every teaching procedure involves some degree of emotional involvement and some amount of cognitive information. The balance between the affective and the cognitive may appropriately vary to meet the objectives of any given class session. The topic of "basic trust in people," for example, may be studied in an intellectual manner with technical descriptions of how it normally develops during early childhood, how it serves to humanize the child, and what types of pathology are associated with its absence. Here students might obtain considerable useful information about trust without gaining any new awareness as to what trust feels like. The "feeling" aspect of trust might be experienced in an activity initiated by a teacher well versed in affective techniques wherein students are placed in situations in which they must place their faith in a classmate to save him from embarrassment, discomfort, or loss of some classroom prize. Here they might experience a trusting relationship directly and gain some appreciation of its value in a specific situation. However, they would have little chance to gain any understanding of the broader role that trust plays in the total personality of the individual.

The logical resolution of this apparent conflict between cognitive and affective goals requires the inclusion of both within the program. According to the needs of any particular objective, the learning activity might be primarily directed toward an intellectual understanding, an emotional experience, or more often, some combination of both.

Suggested Concepts

Once the general scope and purposes of a curriculum area such as mental health have been established, the next step is the selection of the content to be covered. Concepts are one of the most widely accepted means by which to express the content of any given health curriculum. Although the specific facts and information presented to help the learner develop a given concept may vary from year to year, the concept itself represents a broad and meaningful idea that tends to endure on into the foreseeable future. The concepts suggested below are based on a review of several sources.[11] Although we feel that these are representative of those commonly found in school health curricula, they should be examined carefully in terms of local needs before they are used in any specific program.

[11] Most helpful were *Health Concepts: Guides for Health Instruction* (Washington, D.C.: National Education Association, 1967); "Mental Health in the Classroom," special issue of *The Journal of School Health*, Vol. XXXVII, No. 5a (May 1968); and School Health Education Study, *Health Education: A Conceptual Approach to Curriculum Design* (St. Paul, Minn.: 3M Education Press, 1967).

The Nature of Personality and Behavior

1. *People possess many similar personality traits, yet each person is unique.* Each person is distinctive in some way from anyone else in the world. It is useful to classify and study various characteristics; it is often beneficial to emulate desirable qualities we see in others. Even when this is done, a certain degree of individuality always remains.

2. *An individual's personality includes many internalized concepts, values, and modes of expression which produce a certain degree of consistency in his behavior.* A wide variety of structured and unstructured learning experiences account for a large portion of one's personality structure. Although personality is constantly developing or undergoing modifications, changes tend to take place slowly.

3. *Much of human behavior consists of habits that can be cultivated or eliminated with proper practice.* Like tooth brushing and table manners, larger aspects of personality such as concern for others and self-reliance can be developed to the point that they occur without conscious effort.

4. *Emotions are expressed in many different ways.* Persons who lack confidence sometimes behave as if they feel superior; extreme happiness sometimes brings tears; parental love sometimes takes the form of severe discipline.

5. *Mood changes and swings represent a part of normal behavior.* Almost all persons find themselves very depressed sometimes and very elated at other times; it is often difficult to understand why these changes happen.

6. *As people mature, their behavior generally becomes more effective, constructive, and self-directed.* This occurs as a result of physical growth and development, learning experience involving both adults and playmates, and a good deal of individual effort; this change benefits both the individual and those around him.

The Determinants of Behavior and Personality

7. *"Human behavior is determined by mental, physical, and social factors; it is complex and characterized by adaptability."* [12] Thoughts, feelings, and actions result from a complex interaction of natural forces. Although behavior is always directed toward some form of need satisfaction, it may be either adaptive or maladaptive in its effects.

8. *"Self-acceptance is fundamental to sound mental health."* [13] Self-acceptance and self-respect are based on a realistic appraisal of one's values, abilities, and other important attributes. Although others can help in this process, these qualities must ultimately come from within.

[12] *Health Concepts: Guides for Health Instruction* (Washington, D.C.: National Education Association, 1967), p. 42.
[13] Ibid., p. 43.

9. *A basic understanding of the dynamics of human behavior facilitates constructive reactions to interpersonal conflicts and other similar problems.* Those who direct their attention to the underlying causes rather than the external manifestations of undesirable behavior are generally more effective in producing desirable modifications.

10. *Affection and companionship are essential to good personality development and the maintenance of mental health.* Because of one's dependence on others during infancy and possibly because of innate factors, friendships and affection become deep human needs that are commonly satisfied by a wide variety of interpersonal relationships.

11. *The nature of one's personal acceptance and adjustment to the inevitability of death has important effects on the strength and effectiveness of one's personality.* Man is perhaps the only living creature that must live with the knowledge of his own mortality; although this knowledge can be threatening and unpleasant, the act of accommodating to it can add meaningfulness and zest to one's existence.

Society and Personality

12. *Both individual and group values are important to a sound personality structure.* Some values are common to the large majority of one's society. Others are unique to certain segments, such as ethnic groups or individual families, and still others may be unique to the individual. Personal values should be appropriate to one's situation and generally should not bring one into serious conflict with society.

13. *Society's expectations of behavior vary according to the age of the individual.* Behavior that might be appreciated and rewarded when exhibited by a young child may be viewed as part of the normal responsibility of the older child. As each person matures, people keep expecting more from him; if he should fail to show this progress, disappointment and conflict often result.

14. *Regardless of the influence of external forces, society generally holds the individual responsible for the behavior he displays.* As one matures, he is expected to show increasing degrees of control, or self-discipline; the development of this quality generally serves the interests of both the individual and society.

Mental Illness

15. *Mental illness appears to represent maladaptive reactions to emotional or organic stress.* Although cases of mental illness may be grouped into various categories, each case is unique in terms of its apparent determinants, specific symptoms, and indicated therapy.

16. *Appropriate therapy generally reduces or eliminates the symptoms and disabilities associated with mental illness.* Effective treatment measures exist for most cases of mental illness; the effectiveness of these measures is greatly enhanced by prompt and thorough application.

REFERENCES

Allensmith, Wesley, and George W. Goethals. *The Role of the Schools in Mental Health*. New York: Basic Books, Inc., Publishers, 1961.

Cahn, Lorynne, and Robert Petersen. "Education and Mental Health: A Need for Interdisciplinary Involvement," *Journal of School Health*, Vol. XLIII, No. 4 (April 1973), pp. 218–220.

Cameron, Norman A. *Personality Development and Psychopathology*. Boston: Houghton Mifflin Company, 1963.

Ellis, Albert. "Teaching Emotional Education in the Classroom," *School Health Review* (November 1969).

Erickson, Erik H. *Childhood and Society*. New York: W. W. Norton & Company, Inc., 1963.

Glasser, William. *Schools Without Failure*. New York: Harper & Row, Publishers, Inc., 1969.

Havighurst, Robert J. *Developmental Tasks and Education*, 3rd ed. New York: David McKay Co., Inc., 1972.

Joint Commission on Mental Illness and Health. *Action for Mental Health*. New York: Basic Books, Inc., Publishers, 1961.

Jourard, Sidney M. *Healthy Personality*. New York: Macmillan Publishing Co., Inc., 1974.

Kaplan, Louis. *Education and Mental Health*. New York: Harper & Row, Publishers, Inc., 1971.

Lowenfield, Viktor. *Creative and Mental Growth*, 6th ed. New York: Macmillan Publishing Co., Inc., 1975.

Mantz, Genelle K. "Can Mental Health Be Taught," *Journal of School Health*, Vol. XLII, No. 7 (September 1972), pp. 398–399.

Maslow, Abraham H. *Motivation and Personality*. New York: Harper & Row, Publishers, Inc., 1970.

"Mental Health in the Classroom," *The Journal of School Health*, Vol. XXVIII, No. 5a (May 1968, special issue).

Mussen, Paul H., John J. Conger, and Jerome Kagan. *Child Development and Personality*. New York: Harper & Row, Publishers, Inc., 1969.

Romey, William D. *Risk-Trust-Love: Learning in a Humane Environment*. Columbus, Ohio: Charles E. Merrill Publishing Co., 1972.

Smith, James A. *Creative Teaching of the Social Studies in the Elementary School*. Boston: Allyn & Bacon, Inc., 1967.

Stone, Joseph L., and Joseph Church. *Childhood and Adolescence*. New York: Random House, Inc., 1972.

Teper, Lynn. "Emotional Education," *School Health Review*, Vol. 3, No. 2 (March–April 1972), p. 24.

———. "Role Playing as a Tool in Mental Health Education," *School Health Review* (February 1971), p. 31.

Thorpe, Louis. *The Psychology of Mental Health*. New York: The Ronald Press Company, 1960.

10. MENTAL ■ HEALTH II: APPLICATIONS

The most crucial phase of the total school health education program takes place in the classroom when teacher and pupil interact within the context of learning experiences. Even the most logical and thorough curriculum development effort will go for naught if the teacher doesn't "deliver" at this moment of truth. Specific techniques must be selected which are appropriate both to the instructional objectives and the particular classroom group involved in a particular class session. Many adjustments and decisions are commonly needed as the learning activity unfolds in the classroom which make heavy demands on the teacher's ingenuity and leadership. This process is indeed challenging; however, it does guarantee that each class session will be unique. The skills involved are never totally mastered, for improvement is always possible. Teaching competence can only be acquired by actual experience; however, the examples described in this chapter may make the process of developing techniques and polishing teaching skills somewhat easier.

SELECTION OF TECHNIQUES

The subject matter involved within the study of mental health is inherently abstract. No one has actually seen self-confidence, happiness, responsibility, and love, yet these are fundamental concepts we deal with in this content area. Because of this abstract quality, the teacher should be sure that the examples used are real to the learner. The old axiom of selecting content from the learner's realm of immediate experience should be applied whenever possible. The teacher should link basic concepts of mental health with common school situations. Once identified, these events can either be used for incidental teaching at the time they occur or worked into a formal presentation on the topic of mental health.

196

Elementary Level

Role playing and other short dramatizations serve to illustrate concepts in concrete form while at the same time capitalizing on the elementary school child's natural inclination to imagine and pretend. This also provides for a certain degree of freedom and movement, at least for the actors, which the children will enjoy. By keeping the individual playlets short and rotating the various roles, it is possible to involve most of the class actively while conforming to the restricted attention span typical of young children.

Practical considerations will require that the children adopt a more passive role during many of the instructional sessions. In such cases, pictures can help to add realism and at least a vicarious type of involvement. These can range from simple stick figures on the blackboard, to magazine clippings, to elaborate presentations involving projectors of various types. When these are combined with active classroom discussion, a favorable learning situation will likely result.

As children move along into the upper elementary grades, the textbook becomes increasingly useful as a teaching device. However, textbook material, although useful as background information, probably does not make any real impact on the child's attitudes, values, or behavior until it is discussed and examined. This appears to be particularly true in the case of concepts related to mental health and personality development.

Secondary Level

Interest in mental health topics tends to increase as students progress to higher grade levels.[1] However, it will be found that their interest will usually be restricted to practical situations involving interpersonal relationships or individual problems as opposed to psychologic theory. This is particularly true at the junior high level. There is little that can be done with the facts and principles of personality development or mental illness until they are translated into meaningful examples or illustrations. Once this is accomplished, a wide variety of teaching approaches can be used. Techniques that involve a high degree of student involvement, such as role playing and problem solving, still provide the most impact and should be emphasized, particularly at the junior high level. However, these can be interspersed with such traditional devices as library assignments and class discussions. These provide the advantage of covering more content per unit of time, thus broadening the scope of the unit.

TEACHING EXAMPLES

This section includes eight specific examples of how teaching leading to the development of specific mental health concepts might be handled. Al-

---

[1] Ruth Byler, Gertrude Lewis, Ruth Totman, *Teach Us What We Want To Know* (New York: Mental Health Materials, Inc., 1969).

though each individual description involved a specific grade level, the technique involved often has application to many other levels above and below the one depicted, provided that appropriate modifications are made. Therefore readers whose interests are restricted to either the elementary or secondary level are advised to review all the examples for possible applications to their own teaching.

I. UPS AND DOWNS

The ability to exert a moderate degree of control over one's emotions constitutes an important characteristic of the healthy, mature personality. One common way in which this trait is manifested is in the avoidance of overreactions to temporary moods of anger or depression; if this can be accomplished, the process of getting rid of these unconstructive patterns will not be complicated by ill-chosen words or actions that often deepen the undesirable mood. The mature person learns that anger soon passes if it is allowed to and that time often rids one of depression. Knowledge of the transient nature of most mood states often makes the unpleasant ones more endurable and tends to strengthen one's efforts to defer irrevocable actions until a better state prevails. Everyone probably learns this to some extent, sooner or later, as a result of normal living experiences, but this process can be improved with the proper type of formal study.

Concept
Mood changes and swings represent a part of normal behavior.

Pupils
Developed for third-grade boys and girls of average socioeconomic status; also recommended for grade four.

Technique
Sociodrama.

The general procedures for use of the sociodrama were described in Chapter 7 (pp. 143–144); only certain specific points require attention here. The third-grade child usually responds well to this technique because he often combines the primary child's love of make-believe with sufficient maturity to act out various role situations effectively. The teacher should keep the character descriptions brief and restrict the content of the drama to familiar situations. The action should be brisk and extend no more than two or three minutes.

THE EXAMPLE
Just as the class was finishing up its reading lesson, Mrs. Downey asked them to turn back to a page describing a family squabble.

"All right now, boys and girls, please turn back to page 28 and look at the picture of Jimmy talking to his mother." After everyone had found the page, she asked, "What is he saying to his mother in this picture?"

One of the boys answered, "He's calling her the meanest mother in the world."

After the small ripple of laughter that this produced died down, Mrs. Downey led the class in a brief discussion concerning the reasons for such a statement. The class generally agreed that Jimmy probably did not really mean what he said and that his mother also seemed to be in a cranky mood that caused her to be too hard on Jimmy that day. With the class thus drawn into the topic, Mrs. Downey began the main part of the lesson.

"Now let's see if we can find out why mothers act the way they do; I would like to have some of us act out some little plays or shows about mothers and their children."

Mrs. Downey had used this device successfully on previous occasions, so this announcement produced an air of pleasant anticipation among the pupils; a few hands were already up as the children attempted to volunteer for parts or roles in the "play."

A Swift Kick. Mrs. Downey selected Mary to play the part of the mother and asked Bill and Jessica to pretend that they were children playing at home on a Saturday afternoon. The "mother" was directed to use a make-believe dustcloth on the "furniture" (Mrs. Downey's desk) and the "two children" were seated at the "kitchen table" (a small table at the front of the room) playing with a set of interlocking construction blocks. Immediately after making these assignments in the presence of the whole class, she whispered some specific directions to each of the players, then asked them to begin.

"Mother" immediately became very busy dusting the make-believe furniture and the "children" started assembling some actual blocks in a hit-and-miss pattern. After a couple of moments the "children" got up and walked over to their "mother." Bill spoke first.

"Mother, we're hungry and thirsty; could we have some juice and cookies?"

Jessica could see that "Mother" was looking rather cranky, so she quickly added, "Please, Mother. We've been good all afternoon."

"Mother" puffed herself up and exclaimed, "You most certainly cannot have any juice and cookies! You've done nothing but make noise and get on my nerves all day! You can both march right to your room and pick up all that junk up there; I'm tired of doing all the work around here!"

With this, the two "children" turned around and walked off while making a rather corny effort to cry.

What's the Matter? Mrs. Downey intervened at this point. "I think this would be a good place to stop and try to figure some things out; that was a good job of acting that you three did! Can someone guess why 'Mother' was so gruff with the 'children'?"

Tom, who tended to be a chronic troublemaker, said that this was just the way that mothers are; he implied that no special reason was necessary to account for this reaction. There were a few nods of agreement among the other boys and girls, but Mrs. Downey also observed considerable restiveness on the part of the pupils who disagreed with this theory, so she asked, "Does anyone have a different idea?"

Angela thought that "Mother" probably had a cold or was feeling a little bit sick, and many of the pupils appeared to support this explanation.

"Would this be a reason for 'Mother's' crankiness?" asked Mrs. Downey.

After seeing that most of the class agreed, she said, "Let's find out."

She looked at Mary, who was still standing on the "stage" and asked, "Mother, were you feeling sick or ill today while you were cleaning the house?"

Before the sociodrama started, Mrs. Downey had whispered to Mary that "Mother" didn't like to clean house and that the house was very dirty that day, and also that the job had made her very tired and the "children" had been very noisy. With this information in mind, Mary answered a bit indecisively.

"No, I wasn't exactly sick or ill."

Mrs. Downey decided to reinforce this valid reason even though it happened to be incorrect in this case.

"I think most of us agreed that a cold or some other small illness could make a mother act harshly toward her children; that was a good guess Angela, but this time there was another reason. Does anyone have another idea?"

Bonnie, who had been very quiet throughout the whole discussion, raised her hand and said, "Maybe she was just tired from doing all that housework."

Once again Mrs. Downey queried "Mother" and this time Mary answered, "Yes, that's what the trouble was—you told me that I was supposed to pretend like I was very tired from cleaning house, and besides, I don't like house cleaning anyway."

"And how had the children been acting?" continued Mrs. Downey.

"They had been noisy all day," answered "Mother."

Mrs. Downey then asked the actors to return to their seats and she led the children in a discussion on how their own mothers might act in a similar situation. As would be expected, the majority of the children reported that their mothers tended to act the same way. Tom still maintained that mothers in general, including his own, were cranky all the time, but the total picture was kept in balance by a couple of the girls who maintained that their mothers seldom became cranky about anything.

Ice Cream and Cake. At this point, Mrs. Downey set up the next sociodrama, with Mary continuing in her part as "Mother" but with different pupils to play the part of the "children." The same "Mother" was used so that a change in the "Mother's" reactions might be related to situational factors rather than the personality of a different mother. Different actors were selected for the "children" simply to provide more pupils with the chance to become actively involved. The "children" received the same whispered instructions that the previous "children" had received: they were hungry and thirsty and they were to ask "Mother" to fix something for them. "Mother's" instructions were quite different this time. She was told that it was a pleasant sunny day; that "Father" was going to barbecue dinner on the outside grill this evening, thus relieving her of any cooking chores; and that the "children" had done a good job of cleaning their room without even being asked.

After a few moments with the blocks, the new "children" interrupted "Mother's" dusting with their request for some refreshments, and this time their reception was quite different.

"Of course you may have something, children; I don't have any cookies for you but there is some cake left and we might even put some ice cream on top."

"Oh, goodie!" exclaimed one of the "children." "I'd like a big piece please," and they both clapped their hands just like the real thing was forthcoming.

"Well now," began Mrs. Downey. "Things went quite differently this time, didn't they? I wonder why."

Stephanie, who was not too bright, excitedly replied, "I know! The 'mother' wasn't tired this time."

"I suspect that's part of the story, Stephanie, but there's probably some other reason, too," said Mrs. Downey.

"I bet the children have been quieter this time," volunteered Angela.

"Yes, they were quieter this time," affirmed Mrs. Downey. "But don't you think that there would have to be something even better than that to account for 'Mother's' especially good mood?"

Jessica had felt a little uneasy playing with the blocks during her previous acting stint with even an imaginary "Mother" house cleaning, because, at her home, she always helped her mother in some small way. This prompted her to say, "Maybe the children had been helping the 'mother' clean house."

"Is that right, 'Mother'?" asked Mrs. Downey. "Have the 'children' been helping you clean house today?"

"Yes they have," replied Mary. "They straightened up their rooms and I didn't even have to ask them, or nag them."

"I think we've finally found the most important reason, don't you, children?" asked Mrs. Downey. "How many of you think your mothers would feel good if you volunteered to help with the house cleaning?"

Most of the class answered "yes" by raising their hands and nodding agreement. At this point, Mrs. Downey realized that time was running short and that they would have to move faster if they were to complete the two additional dramatic sketches that she had in mind. She asked "Mother" to tell the class about her pleasant anticipation of an evening's relief from the main cooking chores. The class discussed this briefly and appeared to gain a bit more insight into the things that affect "Mothers'" moods.

During the second half of the session, Bill and Angela effectively depicted the classical situation wherein "Father" comes home after a hard day at the office only to be greeted by a wife with nagging requests and troubles to be unloaded. This produced a believable little spat and tearful retreat to the bedroom on the part of "Wife." The final skit presented the converse situation with Linda showing how a wife might safely make the same demands on her tired husband after first providing him with a cup of coffee and an opportunity to unburden a few of his troubles.

The lesson was completed with a four- or five-minute summarizing discussion in which the class concluded that moods are easily changed by many things. Some of these things are really very important, whereas others having equally strong effects often seem small and not important at all.

Mrs. Downey set up a fairly sure-fire situation for the class in this example. In this school district, the children were generally familiar with house-cleaning chores and their effect on mother's disposition. The same content could have been covered more quickly in a simple discussion with the children, but the use of the sociodrama probably produced a much higher degree of involvement. The action demanded their attention. The limitation of the player's acting ability in many instances proved advantageous as the children had to use their imagination in an active way to piece the stories together.

II. JUST LIKE ME—ALMOST

School-age children regardless of their particular stage of development need reassurance that they are "normal," that they are in some way unique and important, and that they have some distinctive qualities. The inherent conflict in these needs begins to disappear as children learn to understand them better. The lesson described here is designed to provide the pupil with a little better understanding of a desirable balance between common and unique qualities:

Concept

People possess many similar personality traits, yet each person is unique.

Pupils

Developed for second-grade boys and girls of average socioeconomic status in an urban setting; generally recommended for the primary grades.

Techniques

Still pictures or overhead transparencies.

The use of still pictures combined with class discussion is but one of several possible ways to handle content bearing on this concept, and within this technique several variations can be used. Study of the specific example presented here should provide ideas for broader applications of the content and techniques involved.

The pictures show children of approximately the same age as the class engaged in a wide variety of activities. Most of the activities are common ones with which the majority of the pupils are familiar. Specific pictures and typical discussion points include:

1. *"Helping set the table."* How many of you do this at home? Why do you? Why don't you? Do you like to? Why? Why not? Should boys do this chore? Why not?
2. *"Packing for a family vacation."* Where do you usually go? Do you like it? Why? Why not? Where would you rather go? Does your father have a good time? Does your mother have a good time?
3. *"Playing a game."* Do you play this game? Do you like it? Why? Do you play it well?
4. *"Caring for a pet."* Do you have this sort of pet? Are they fun to own? Do you take care of it? What other pets are nice?

The discussion of such activities as these provides the children with the opportunity to discover many things that they share in common with their classmates and to strengthen their sense of security in so doing; however, they also can discover the existence of many individual likes, dislikes, habits, and capabilities along with some logical reasons for these differences. This awareness can help children respect the individual differences they perceive in themselves and in others.

III. DOES HE REALLY FEEL THAT WAY?

The small child's habit of freely exhibiting his emotions probably constitutes one of his more charming aspects. When he is happy, he is happy, and he lets everyone know about it. His sad or angry moods can be unpleasant, but the adult that manipulates him out of his darkness is quickly rewarded with his smiles and laughter. However, a little maturity soon changes this situation; the older child, or the adult, soon learns not to wear his emotions on his sleeve. Instead, he learns to adopt a variety of façades which often make it difficult for those around him to gain any true indication of his feelings. Although this practice often serves useful ends, it also tends to cut him off from the sympathy and understanding of those who might offer their help. If we are to react in a sensitive and constructive way to those around us, we must learn to look behind these façades and see how people really feel.

Concept
Emotions are expressed in many different ways.

Pupils
Developed for fifth-grade boys and girls of lower socioeconomic class in an urban setting; generally recommended for grades four through six.

Technique
Problem story.

In the following example, the teacher utilized his special knowledge of the needs and interests of his pupils in the writing of a problem story (see pages 163–164) tailored to both the special characteristics of his class and the specific concept he wished to develop. Although his narrative was somewhat amateurish in quality, it was tailored for his situation. Because the story was short, the issues clear, and the reading ability of the pupils low, he simply read the story to the class. Under different conditions, he might have duplicated the story and provided a copy for each pupil.

THE EXAMPLE

"It ought to be simple to develop an interesting story to illustrate this concept," thought Mr. Valke. "If I can just think of a common emotional situation and then describe the reactions of two or three persons, I think the kids will get the idea."

At this point, the complaints of a couple of the local merchants in the area of the school about the conduct of some of the pupils in their stores after school suddenly came to mind. With the basic theme thus provided, the rest of the narrative quickly took shape. Within fifteen or twenty minutes Mr. Valke had the story "roughed out" in a form suitable for presentation.

The next day in class Mr. Valke began the health lesson with a short discussion of "moods" or "feelings."

"Yesterday we learned quite a bit about 'moods' and 'feelings'; can anyone tell me what we decided about their importance?"

"It's just nice to be 'happy' or 'satisfied' most of the time," volunteered Mitzy. "Nobody wants to be angry or sad very often."

"And we can sometimes learn to control our moods a little bit," added John. "So that we can keep from blowing our top or feeling down in the dumps too often."

"That's right, isn't it, children?" confirmed Mr. Valke. "Some moods are much more pleasant to have than others, aren't they? But wasn't there at least one other important thing we learned?"

"I know," said Dick. "They make you do things sometimes."

"Dick has thought of another important reason," said Mr. Valke. "Who can tell us a little more about how moods affect the way we do things?"

After a couple of more exchanges the role of moods as modifiers of behavior was clarified and the review of the previous day's material was completed. Mr. Valke then introduced the main activity of the current lesson.

The Story. "Let's see if we can find out something new about moods and feelings. I'm going to read a story to you that I think you'll enjoy and after I'm through I'm sure there'll be some questions about it. Let's see who can answer them. This story is about three fifth-grade boys who lived in a city something like ours."

Mr. Valke then read the following narrative:

Hank, Bill, and Kev liked to hang around Mr. Richards' drugstore in the afternoon after school. They would sometimes buy a root beer or even a milk shake when they had enough money but the real attraction was the well-stacked magazine rack up near the front of the building. The three boys would read comic books for hours if they could get away with it. Mr. Richards didn't like people reading his magazines without buying them, so he would often run them out of the store. But the boys found that if they were quiet, they could get in a lot of reading before they were discovered, especially if Mr. Richards had many prescriptions to fill. This was really starting to bother Mr. Richards; the comic books were generally out of place, sometimes torn up, and lately it seemed that some of them were missing.

Mr. Richards decided to investigate; the next day he slipped out the side door into the alley and walked around to the front of the store just as the boys were coming out. Each of them had a brand new comic book in his hand, one that he hadn't paid for. Mr. Richards had faced this situation before. Because it was near closing time anyway, Mr. Richards decided to lock up his store and take the boys home to their parents and talk things over with them. Hank was the only one that did any talking in the car.

"We were going to pay for them, Mr. Richards, we just got talking and forgot. How can you call that a crime? You shouldn't be taking us home like this. It's practically kidnapping!"

Hank went on and on but Mr. Richards hardly even answered him. Meanwhile Bill started to cry; he didn't make much noise, just a little sob now and then, but he couldn't hide the tears that were streaming down his cheeks. Kev just sat and stared straight ahead and he was very, very quiet.

The three fathers acted differently when they heard Mr. Richards' explanation. Hank's father used a big stick that he kept in the garage for such occasions and poor Hank was nursing some big welts as he went to bed that night. Bill's father seemed equally upset but he talked to Bill for an hour or more about honesty, character, and the importance of thinking about one's future. Bill felt bad to start with and he felt much worse after all that. Kev's father, after hearing that Kev had taken a total of ten comic books, simply told him that he was to stay away from the drugstore for the rest of the school year except for one trip per week to turn over his allowance to Mr. Richards. This was to continue until Mr. Richards was paid for his magazines, time, and trouble.

The Discussion.   After he had completed the story, Mr. Valke asked the class how they thought the boys felt when they found out that Mr. Richards, the druggist, was going to take them home to their parents. Dick answered this question with the general observation that they were probably scared.

"But one of them wasn't scared," countered John. "One boy was busy trying to talk the druggist out of taking them home."

"I think you mean Hank," said Mr. Valke. He then reviewed what Hank had said and confirmed the fact that "Hank was very talkative."

"But sometimes people talk a lot when they are scared," argued Marv. "I think they were all scared."

The other pupils expressed their agreement with Marv that all the boys in the story were scared, and it became apparent that this was the class consensus. Mr. Valke then asked the class if they thought that the boys showed any other important moods or feelings. After some discussion, the class decided that the boys were sorry about their actions, and at least part of this sorrow was due to shame or disappointment in themselves.

Mr. Valke then switched the discussion to the question of how the fathers felt.

John provided the predictable reply, "They were pretty angry, especially Hank's father who gave him a whipping."

Mr. Valke then moved into the same pattern as in the previous sub-discussion by asking if the other fathers were also angry. This time the pupils could not agree on whether or not Bill's and Kev's fathers were very angry. This prompted Mr. Valke to try still another approach.

"Suppose Bill's and Kev's fathers became real angry at their boys for some other reason; do you think they would give Bill and Kev whippings?"

This new approach was rewarded with some thoughtful replies that indicated that the pupils had become effectively involved with the problem.

"I don't think those fathers believe in whippings."

"Some grown-ups don't like to let on how they feel."

"My mother tries to act mad at me sometimes when she really isn't."

"My father gets real quiet when he's mad—then I have to watch out!"

Mr. Valke concluded the session with a brief summary in which he called attention to two main points that the class uncovered in the course of the discussion: (1) people don't always show their anger, shame, or other feelings in the same way, and (2) people sometimes try to hide their real feelings for many different reasons.

There are a few interesting points about Mr. Valke's techniques that can be profitably reviewed at this point. It should be noted that, although he had clearly decided on the concept he wished to present, he did not present this concept directly to the class. Instead he sought to lead the discussion in such a manner that the pupils, both individually and collectively, would discover this concept. The most important learning took place when the pupils were actively reacting to the comments of their classmates and formulating replies in their own minds. This process had considerable value regardless of whether or not they got a chance to express their reactions. The information that Mr. Valke expressed directly, such as his paraphrasing of the concept in the summary, was of secondary importance. It was useful in crystallizing many of the important points of the discussion, but its value was dependent on the learning that preceded it.

This class lesson also illustrated some astute handling of a moral question. Mr. Valke kept the class on the topic of the moods and feelings and seemingly ignored the fact that the characters in the story had committed an act that is generally condemned in our society, but the nature of his narrative and the manner in which he conducted the discussion linked thievery with "shame" and "disappointment." This resulted in a moral "fringe benefit" without distracting from the basic purpose of the lesson.

Much of the success of Mr. Valke's narrative was undoubtedly based on its appeal to some of the baser emotions of the class. It involved theft, fear, tears, and physical punishment. These elements are not pleasant, but neither are many emotional situations that one must learn to handle in the process of maturing socially. In a small way and at their own level, Mr.

Valke's pupils were attempting to look behind the overt actions of the characters under discussion and react to the real motives and emotions involved.

IV. GREAT EXPECTATIONS

"Why do children keep wanting to grow up? If they were smart, they would realize how lucky they are." This is a very common adult reaction to the seemingly incessant striving of children to gain the privileges, responsibilities, and status of adulthood. Although these efforts often seem misguided, they are very real; they are virtually universal among young people and represent normal, healthy phenomena. However, impatience and restiveness with this slow process do at times create problems and frustrations among children and youth at all stages of development from infancy through adolescence. Education can help alleviate these problems by providing the child with a broader perspective of the basic task of growing up.

Concept

Society's expectations of behavior vary according to the age of the individual.

Pupils

Developed for sixth-grade boys and girls of above-average academic ability and socioeconomic status; also recommended for average to above-average groups of grades seven through nine.

Technique

Group art project.

One of the major difficulties involved in helping children develop this concept is that it requires that they focus their attention on several different points in time simultaneously. Even when one is dealing with adults, some graphic means of portraying the occurrence of events in time is very helpful; among elementary school children it is practically essential. The technique described in this section involves the use of a mural composed of a series of individual pictures, each depicting important instances of independent or dependent behavior of children at different ages. This type of mural is more technically termed a frieze, because the pictures are designed to be viewed in sequential order rather than as one elaborate composition.

The use of an appropriate commercially prepared frieze or mural would be useful but only in a limited sense, because much of the value lies in the actual creation of this visual aid. This type of project provides the opportunity to combine artistic expression with the study of health and thus justifies the allocation of additional class time to the project. This project could be accomplished in four class sessions as follows:

1. Present some general information concerning the privileges and responsibilities associated with various stages of growth. Appropriate

selections from assigned readings, a short film or filmstrip, or a newspaper or magazine article are common sources for this sort of material. Invite the class to express opinions on what privileges and responsibilities are proper for their age groups and how their views differ from those of their parents. Any type of discussion in this area is generally very interesting to elementary pupils and should result in good pupil involvement. Lead the class toward a decision to pursue the topic further the following day.

2. Write seven headings across the top of the blackboard: (1) Infancy, (2) Toddlerhood, (3) The Primary Grades, (4) The Intermediate Grades, (5) Junior High School, (6) Senior High School, and (7) Adulthood. Assign each pupil to a committee; distribute the academic ability, artistic talent, and leadership ability as equally as possible. Designate a chairman and a recorder for each committee. Ask each committee to compile a list of important things that people in their category normally can and cannot do without outside help. Allot approximately twenty-five minutes to this task. If conditions permit, allow one member of each committee to go to the library to select resource material; provide them with a list of possible selections or arrange for assistance from the librarian to be available during this time period. At the end of the allotted time, collect the lists and alert the class to the beginning of the art phase of the project during the next day. Ask them to discuss their task with parents, brothers, sisters, and so on, before their next meeting.

3. During the time scheduled for health education, ask the committee to meet and (a) consider any new suggestions, (b) review the total list and select the best example of independent behavior and the best example of dependent behavior. After approximately fifteen minutes, have the class meet as a total group to review the selection of each committee. Place each item on the blackboard as it is reported and approved by the class. The resulting entries might look like this:

STAGE	INDEPENDENCE	DEPENDENCE
Infant	chooses from among various toys in his playpen	Mother must pick up his toys and put them away
Toddler	uses her own spoon to feed herself	Mother must put the food on her plate
Primary Child (second-grader)	cares for her dolls and other toys	needs a baby-sitter when the parents are away
Intermediate Child (fifth-grader)	buys a "coke" with his friends	needs Mother's help when buying clothes
Junior High Student	cares for children as a baby-sitter	must rely on others for auto transportation
Senior High Student	reads and understands about political candidates	cannot go to the polls and vote
Adult	cares for his children when they have a cold	calls for the doctor when the illness is serious

On the same day during the art period, ask each committee to plan and draw in pencil a picture depicting each of the two situations in its category. Generally two children will be available for each picture. If so, one can work on the background and the other on the figures on separate pieces of art paper; the two parts can be cut out and combined later. Help the groups achieve some uniformity in size and style. This is the time to use the services of an art coordinator, or consultant if such a person is available. Classes with a good background in artwork can attempt realistic scenes and those with lesser skills can do an effective job with a "stick-figure" schematic approach. After the pencil drawings are completed, colors should be selected and approved; then the students can go on to the painting. Generally the paintings must dry overnight before they are assembled or mounted.

4. On the fourth day of the project, have each committee assemble its two drawings. The finished pictures for each stage may then be attached, by paste or staples, to a long piece of butcher paper for display along a wall of the classroom. If a large bulletin board is available, the pictures may be attached to it. Labels or captions may be kept to a minimum because the entire class should be familiar with the content and meaning of the pictures. Once the artwork is completed, the way is clear for a profitable discussion of its meaning and interpretations in greater depth. The mural or frieze may serve to illustrate related ideas or concepts that are studied in succeeding lessons.

The project as described here requires good deal of advance planning to ensure its success. It also requires sixth-graders with some experience in committee work and a reasonably good background in art work. However, where these conditions prevail, a project such as this can result in a highly meaningful experience. Its usefulness as a means of developing the stated concept will vary directly with the intensity of the pupils' efforts to examine and evaluate typical behavior for each age category. The suggested schedule calling for the completion of the mural in four sessions is a rigorous one; individual teachers may wish to set a more leisurely pace if additional time is available.

V. EVERYBODY'S DOING IT

Parents and teachers alike have often lamented over the seemingly irresistible drive of adolescents to gain status with their peers through conformity to all manner of popular, yet often ill-advised, behavior patterns. These group norms, fads, or whatever you wish to call them take their most obvious forms in new fashions of dress, expressions of speech, and tastes in music. Behavior in these categories is generally harmless or merely irritating; however, when popular innovations in dating behavior, use of stimulants and depressants, use of automobiles, and vandalism or quasi-legal activities begin to take radical directions, then the consequences become more than merely irritating. The efforts of adults to intervene in these situations are complicated by the fact that a reasonable degree of conformity to peer group norms is essential to normal personality development in the young person. The answer does not lie in merely encouraging adolescents to resist peer pressure but in teaching them to evaluate the type of behavior that conformity will involve.

Concept
Both individual and group values are important to a sound personality structure.

Students
Developed for ninth-grade girls with average academic ability; also recommended for girls or co-ed groups of grades eight and ten.

Technique
Buzz session.

The buzz session, as described in Chapter 8 (pp. 162–163), involves the placing of students in small groups, generally of three to six, for brief but intensive discussions. Probably the most important single factor contributing to the success of the buzz session is the selection of an appropriate topic. If students are to deal with the topic in small discussion groups not directly supervised by the teacher, they must have something interesting to discuss.

In the following example a ninth grade teacher uses the buzz session to help her class of girls examine fads as a means of learning about an immediate concern while also developing a more abstract concept related to individual versus group values.

THE EXAMPLE
Mrs. Reynolds was not too impressed with the concept she found underlined in the left-hand column of her curriculum guide. "I can't picture my ninth-graders getting excited over a philosophical comparison of individual versus group values," she thought to herself. However, one of the suggested learning opportunities caught her eye. It stated, "Have students develop guidelines for the evaluation of fads; use buzz sessions or a more permanent type of committee organization for this task." "That's more like it!" she thought. "Those girls of mine would go for something like that, and, if there is anything they need, it's to learn how to use a little common sense in thinking about these goofy fads!"

Mrs. Reynolds had always been aware of the way the ninth-grade girls would follow the latest "in" thing popular with the high school crowd. Some of the more mature and popular ninth-grade girls were dating senior high school boys, and these girls, who were envied by many of the other students, served as a ready means of communication between junior high and senior high society. All the fads, of course, were not inspired by high school fashions. The junior high schoolers were fully capable of originating their own ideas, but some of the most troublesome practices resulted from the tendency of the younger groups to adopt a fad originated by the older students and exaggerate it or in other ways apply it with poor judgment.

Generating Interest.   The next day in class Mrs. Reynolds began by reviewing with her students a colorfully illustrated article on teen-age clothing fashions in different sections of the United States. This article was found in a popular magazine devoted to teen-age life, and Mrs. Reynolds noticed that in addition to fashions in clothing it also made frequent reference to such items as "kookie" pins, pierced earrings, bleached hair, and so forth. Mrs. Reynolds let individual members of the class express their opinion on a few of the more interesting aspects of the article in a general way for five or six minutes to let them get involved and build enthusiasm for the topic. It was not hard to get them discussing clothing fashions. They were ready to discuss that topic all period, but that was not what Mrs. Reynolds had in mind. One of the girls had just finished clarifying her previous comments on the type of outfits she felt went well with chain link belts when Mrs. Reynolds said "I doubt whether we could get the whole class to agree on the proper use of chain belts if we talked about it all period. Let's talk about fads in things other than clothing. Who can name some?"

Several hands went up and Mrs. Reynolds recognized each girl in turn. Before the class had exhausted its ideas, several good examples of fads had been presented. They mentioned two or three fad diets, the recent revival of "knock, knock" jokes, new types of dances, ear piercing, and a number of others.

"You've mentioned plenty of interesting examples, now can you tell us if these fads serve any useful purpose?" asked Mrs. Reynolds.

Jeannie offered the first comment. "I don't think they serve any purpose, but who cares, they're fun.

"But fun *is* a purpose," countered Marcia. "What would life be worth without fun?"

"That's quite profound Marcia; now that you have given us your philosophy, let's get specific. Why *are* fads fun?" asked Mrs. Reynolds in a somewhat teasing fashion. She knew that Marcia was bright and irrepressible and a person who responded well to a little pressure.

"Well—they're something new and different, they keep you from getting bored," said Marcia.

"That sounds reasonable, life does get monotonous at times," replied Mrs. Reynolds. "Now can someone else think of any other purposes?"

During the next two or three minutes a number of other purposes were mentioned, but only two of these had direct relevance to mental health, namely, that fads make one feel like "one of the gang" and that some fads involve knowledge or physical skills that may be useful.

Mrs. Reynolds summarized this brief subdiscussion and then issued instructions for the main activity of the period.

Launching the Groups.   "Those are two very worthwhile purposes. I think that you are beginning to discover some of the more important characteristics of these things we call fads. Now I want to give you a chance to discuss this topic more thoroughly in small groups."

"Here's how we'll do it, girls," directed Mrs. Reynolds. "I would like these instructions followed closely. First, are all the recorders here today? Raise your hands, please."

Noting that all were present Mrs. Reynolds proceeded. "I would like the recorders to copy this down. The others should be listening so that you'll be ready to come up with some good ideas as soon as your group is assembled. Develop five to ten good rules to help one decide whether to follow a certain fad or to avoid it."

Mrs. Reynolds repeated the statement describing the task one more time to ensure that the recorders had an opportunity to copy it accurately. She then emphasized that she wanted each group to turn in a good list of guidelines at the end of the discussion period. She designated six areas of the room for the group meetings, asked if anyone had forgotten the group to which they were assigned, and told the students to move to their areas and begin immediately. There was a brief commotion as the students moved to their places, but as the six tight little circles formed, the noise moderated to a tolerable level that permitted easy communication between group members.

Troubleshooting. Mrs. Reynolds directed her first supportive efforts toward those who seemed to be slow at getting organized and beginning the task. This involved prodding a couple of the girls to move their chairs into their circles and getting one group back on the topic that was discussing a pair of steadies that the vice-principal had chastised for displaying too much affection in the hallway. "Come on, girls," she chided. "You'll have all noon hour to talk about that but you've only nine minutes left to finish this assignment, so get going!" With these minor disturbances taken care of, Mrs. Reynolds proceeded to assist individual groups dealing with their discussion task. She circulated around the room answering brief questions to clarify the assignment. Most of these dealt with superficial points that could be handled quickly; however, she found the members of one group arguing vociferously over the basic nature of the guidelines. She pulled a chair into the circle, redefined the assignment, and served as discussion leader for a few exchanges as a means of getting the group moving in the right direction.

By this time some of the faster-moving groups had several guidelines on their lists. Mrs. Reynolds reviewed these briefly and made constructive criticisms that stimulated further efforts toward improvement. One group had included only negative characteristics without listing any positive reasons to try a fad; another had a twelve-item list with many duplications. These groups were busy with their revisions and one or two of the other groups were just beginning to make progress at the end of the scheduled ten minutes.

"This is the most interest this bunch has shown in anything all year," thought Mrs. Reynolds. "They could put another few minutes to good use." She called for their attention and asked, "How many groups need more time?" After receiving the expected answer from all of them, she said, "Okay, let's take three more minutes, but hurry and get finished."

During this stage of the activity, Mrs. Reynolds watched the groups closely for signs of waning interest and used this factor, rather than her watch, as the main key to her decision to terminate the small-group activity. When the students returned to their regular seats, they proceeded to a productive summarizing discussion for the final ten minutes of the period.

The teacher in this situation was able to lead a group of volatile ninth-grade girls into an activity that permitted considerable freedom of expression, yet channeled student behavior in useful directions. This was accomplished by (1) selecting a topic with natural appeal to the class, (2) introducing it properly, and (3) setting up a learning activity with a firm but flexible structure.

The activities following this small-group discussion could take different forms depending on particular needs. If there was a need to move on to other topics, the highlights of the buzz groups could be reported and discussed in the last ten or fifteen minutes of the period, as just described. This is the simplest culminating activity and probably the one most appropriate to the average situation. If there appeared to be a need to spend more time on the buzz topic, the following class period could be devoted to the development of a composite list of guidelines representing a pooling of the best ideas of the individual groups. The examination and selection of the best guidelines through group discussion and consensus could lead the participants to a significant degree of individual commitment.

A more elaborate follow-up would be to use the interest so generated as a lead-in to a full-scale problem-solving activity. This would involve setting up a relatively permanent committee structure to examine fads more deeply. This could logically involve the class in library research into the psychological and sociological bases of fads, a survey of student opinion and participation, and interviews with school personnel. This would result in recommendations based on carefully gathered information and the learning involved would obviously extend beyond the specific topic of investigation.

VI. FAMOUS PERSONALITIES

The term *personality* is an exceedingly difficult one to define. As a health topic, it incorporates breadth, abstractness, and importance in a challenging combination. One of the more practical approaches is to regard personality as the totality of one's behavior. Although this view certainly does little to narrow the topic, it does provide the opportunity to deal with something concrete. We observe what people do in various situations, and when behavior patterns emerge we start applying labels such as *dependence, aggressiveness,* or *submissiveness.* Within such behavior patterns we tentatively identify normal ranges of variations and undesirable extremes. We find that certain of these characteristics affect one's chances for success in a specific occupation or affect the prospects for a successful married life with a certain person. The young person's behavior and eventually his personality is strongly affected by his identification with persons he admires or respects. Adolescents need to become aware of their own personality development process, gain some understanding of how it takes place, and develop the ability to exert some degree of control over the direction it takes.

Concept
An individual's personality includes many internalized facts, impressions, values, and modes of expression that produce a certain degree of consistency in his behavior.

Students
Developed for eighth-grade boys and girls with average academic ability and socioeconomic status; generally recommended for grades 7 through 12.

Technique
Symposium.

When dealing with a topic such as personality, where value judgments as well as simple knowledge acquisition are involved, it is wise to use teaching techniques that allow direct student-to-student discussion. The symposium (see pages 160–161) accomplishes this while still providing a tight structure of the class's activity. This technique typically involves three to five students who each report briefly to the class on a particular phase of a topic. These individual topic reports are then followed by a general class discussion to enlarge on and clarify the main points presented in the discussion. Several topics in the area of mental health lend themselves well to this technique, and the possible variations are virtually unlimited. One specific example is described in the following steps:

1. Recruit a student committee to report on a number of famous persons with whom the class as a whole is familiar. Have some suggestions ready but allow the committee reasonable freedom in choosing persons to report upon. Guide the group away from overemphasis on one type of person and toward a reasonable variety. Generally it would not be well to have reports on five pop singers unless the choice there appeared to be due to considerable variation in their basic traits. A more promising group might include a political leader, a professional athlete, an industrial leader, and an entertainer of some sort. The specific categories and persons selected would naturally vary greatly according to the interests of specific groups of students.

2. Provide the committee with suggestions concerning possible sources of information for their reports. In the case at hand, feature stories in various popular magazines would be promising. Biographies or, better yet, books containing short biographical sketches are common sources. Help the committee divide the reporting responsibilities. The simplest scheme would call for each student to report on one famous person; however, some groups might prefer to use a different type of organization. One alternative would be to have one reporter describe the childhood period, another the adolescent years, another the adult life, and so on, of all the persons being studied.

3. Ask the student reporters to concentrate on events and aspects that provide clues to basic character or personality. This often calls for emphasis on behavior in situations not directly associated with public life. What sort of family life does the person maintain? How does he relate to

his close personal friends? What form of recreational activities does he choose?

4. Although the nature of the follow-up discussion will naturally depend on the type of information presented in the individual reports, the following points generally merit attention:

    a. *Personality traits.* What traits seem most dominant within each personality? What traits seem to be real as opposed to those that appear to be artificial? What effects do specific traits have on the person's profession? his private life? What traits are held in common by the personalities studied? What traits are obviously missing in the personalities studied?

    b. *Value systems.* What things in life do the individuals value most— fame, power, achievement, family, religion? Do they seem to have long-term goals? How well defined are their goals?

    c. *Talent and ability.* What specific talents or abilities are most responsible for the success of the persons reported upon? How did these seem to be acquired? Do any specific talents seem common to successful people in general?

    d. *Major events.* What events seem to be of major importance in regard to personality formation, personal happiness, professional success? Were these events planned or did they happen by chance?

    e. *Present and future prospects.* Which persons appear to be gaining the most satisfaction from life? Which ones appear to adjust well to disappointments? Which ones appear to be headed toward lifelong satisfaction?

Time will not normally permit all these questions to be discussed in one class session, and other questions will arise spontaneously; however, these are the kinds of directions that a meaningful discussion might take. Eighth-graders will generally not be interested in exploring subtle details and ramifications; but they will be able to see some valid generalizations. If this is accomplished, they will become more aware of the direction in which their own personalities seem to be developing, and the groundwork will be established for a more sophisticated study of personality in later grade levels.

VII. SWING HIGH, SWING LOW

How can we bridge the gap between the abstract material which is often provided in standard health texts and the concrete life problems experienced by our students? This is always a problem with health topics but it can be much more acute when dealing with mental health content. In this example, we see how a teacher translated a rather complex concept into terms that had meaning for students of an urban vocational high school. He accomplished this by finding practical application for the scientific facts and principles related to the topic at hand. Few of the students developed much enthusiasm over the relatively technical discussion of human emotions presented in their textbook; however, when the teacher showed them how to study emotions in a realistic way, they became aware of the major factors that affect this aspect of mental health.

Concept
A basic understanding of the dynamics of human behavior facilitates constructive reactions to interpersonal conflicts and other similar problems.

Students
Illustrated here with eleventh-grade boys, with average to below-average academic ability; generally recommended for grades 10 through 12.

Technique
Self-appraisal technique involving a recording of personal mood changes.

Mood and emotion charting was originally developed as a teaching device by Robert E. Kime.[2] It is a procedure whereby each student records his general mood or feeling tone three times a day for a specified period of perhaps five to seven days. This chore is facilitated by the use of specially prepared charts (see Figure 10–1). Mood and emotion charting can be used effectively with most secondary school students regardless of grade level or general academic ability. Because of the graphic record it provides, the nebulous characteristics of moods and feelings are made much easier to deal with in the classroom. There is seldom any problem involved in drawing students into meaningful discussions of the information contained in a completed set of charts. The teacher's challenge lies in the task of motivating the student sufficiently to ensure his reasonable diligence in maintaining the charts. In our example, this challenge was met through use of a combination of positive encouragement, grade pressure, and persistent reminders.

THE EXAMPLE
Mr. Cohen had given his new group of students their first written quiz of the year on a chapter in the mental health section of their text.

"Boy! What a bunch of characters," he thought as he reviewed their scores. "I thought that this year's eleventh-graders were sharper than usual, but it sure doesn't show in this quiz. None of my sections have done well. Those questions weren't that hard; I wonder if the 'powers-that-be' have finally thrown reading completely out of the elementary school curriculum."

The thing that puzzled Mr. Cohen was the inconsistency of the poor scores with the reasonably good performance of his students during class

[2] Robert E. Kime, "Mood and Emotion Charting," *The Journal of School Health*, Vol. XXXV, No. 3 (March 1965), p. 138.

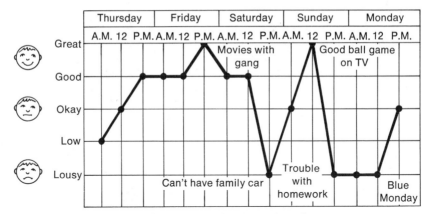

Figure 10–1. *Mood and emotion chart.*

Source: *Adapted with permission from material provided by Robert E. Kime, University of Oregon.*

discussion. On the first day of the unit on mental health, he had discussed with his students a few spectacular newspaper clippings concerning mental health themes. Although many of the comments reflected common misconceptions and biases, there were also a seemingly large number of thoughtful contributions. What Mr. Cohen did not realize was that, as a young and creative teacher, his techniques of discussion leadership were improving greatly from year to year. This factor, together with improved rapport and better classroom discipline, had enabled him to draw more out of his students. But although they responded better verbally, they were the same type of "low-achievers" that he had dealt with in previous years.

As a means of handling mental health concepts in a more concrete fashion, he decided to try "Mood and Emotion" charting. Mr. Cohen modified the standard five-point scale slightly to make the terminology more understandable to his type of students. He designated the five levels as "lousy," "low," "Okay," "good," and "great." He had prepared a ditto master of this modification with the chart extending sideways across the page. He had to cut an inch off the bottom of his ditto master so that it would fit in his portable typewriter at home; however, the remaining 8½ by 10 inches left sufficient space to prepare a chart with plenty of space to add comments. He could have simply drawn the chart with a ruler and printed in the letters but he elected to use the typewriter.

Poor Scores. As Mr. Cohen began the next weekly cycle of classes, he departed from his usual practice of returning and discussing the quizzes at the end of the class hour. This time he returned them at the beginning of class. He was firm and businesslike but not completely unsympathetic as he discussed the generally poor results with his first class. Some of the boys could not have cared less about a poor quiz score, but most were concerned. They had formed an attitude toward Mr. Cohen and his health class that was tentatively positive. He seemed to make things interesting and tried to give them a chance to do well in his course.

"Settle down, fellows," directed Mr. Cohen. "There's no sense crying about your scores. They're already in the book. Let's see what you can do on the next assignment."

With this he handed a supply of the charts he had prepared to the student who had the regular responsibility of distributing materials to the class. "Here, Bill, I want you and your assistant to distribute one of these to each member of the class." Mr. Cohen found that discussion of quizzes and tests generally left his classes a bit unsettled, so he wanted to get their attention focused on the next learning task. A slight murmur went around the room as each student received a blank chart.

Good Salesmanship. "Listen carefully, please. This chart is easy to work with once you get the direction straight. I really feel that most of you will do well once you find out what to do. You've been reading—that is, at least some of you have been reading—about things that affect people in general. This week we're going to forget about the textbook and study about *you* and the things that affect how *you* feel. And this chart can help you do it."

Following this introduction he went on to explain clearly and simply how to make entries in the chart. He asked them to print a two- or three-word explanation each time they marked the "great" or "lousy" level. By the time Mr. Cohen finished, the class was feeling fairly confident about the assignment. They thought they could tell when they felt "low" "okay," "great," or whatever, and it did not seem too difficult to print a brief comment occasionally. But Mr. Cohen knew it was not going to be that simple.

"We could really have an interesting discussion *if* you fellows can remember to keep your charts up to date. I'm looking forward to putting some good grades on your papers next week. Now how are you going to handle this job? Filling in the chart is easy but remembering to do it may be tough."

Mr. Cohen was aware of good tips about remembering things, but he wanted to hear them come from the group. Most of those students that ate breakfast decided to leave their charts on or near the table where the family ate its meals. Many of the "breakfast skippers" planned to keep their charts near the front door. A few highly enthusiastic students expressed their intention to carry their charts with them throughout the day, but most thought it would be better to make a "mental note" of their noontime mood and record it in the evening. Mr. Cohen was dubious about the accuracy of such entries but recognized the practicality of this scheme.

"If many of these guys try to carry these charts throughout the day, they'll either lose them or give them a ride through the wash in their shirt pockets," Mr. Cohen thought to himself. A final procedure the class agreed to was to remind each other about their mood charts when they met during the week.

Satisfying Results. During the seven-day period from one health class to another, Mr. Cohen had the same boys twice for physical education. During each "gym" class, he again reminded the boys of their mood chart assignment. He also pressured his students on the assignment as he met them informally before school, in home room, and at any other opportunity. As a result of this campaign, about three-fourths of the class produced completed charts as he opened class a week later. Mr. Cohen reminded them again to make sure their names were on their charts and asked Bill and Rich to collect the papers. As the students passed their charts sideways toward the center aisle, Mr. Cohen watched them closely. "All right! Don't get snoopy! If someone had a great time on his Friday night date, it's his own business," directed Mr. Cohen with mock sternness. He was serious when he nabbed Ralph in the back row trying hastily to fill in the last two days of his chart just before turning it in. "Forget it, Ralph. If you want credit for this assignment, pick up a new chart after class and try again next week."

Mr. Cohen returned to the front of the room and picked up the stack of completed charts that Bill had assembled and placed dutifully on his teacher's desk. The class settled down as they saw Mr. Cohen sit on his desk and leaf through the charts with apparent interest. He ignored a whispered comment from the back row concerning who was "snoopy." The class laughed as he remarked, "Boy! Some of you fellows really live a rich emotional life. It looks like many of you spend a pretty busy week!"

Now that he had the interest of the class focused, he said, "You know what I think? I think that this stack of charts might provide a good opportunity for two or three of you to make an interesting semester report. After I grade these, I'm going to remove the names and find a small group that would like to review these and report to the class next week. Just to make things a little more interesting I'll put my chart in the pile for their analysis. It's about time you guys found out how rough it is to be a middle-aged school teacher these days. Do I have any volunteers?"

As a result of their interest and their knowledge that Mr. Cohen routinely required one written or oral report from each student each term, six hands went up. Mr. Cohen selected George, Bill, and Greg, the three boys he thought would do the best job; he made George responsible for picking up the charts the next morning before classes began. He then asked all three of them to list the following items in their notebooks as things to include in their report:

1. The average number of "great" entries per chart and the three most commonly listed causes for this mood.
2. The average number of "lousy" entries per chart and the three most commonly listed causes for this mood.
3. The most common day and time for one to feel "great," and the most common day and time to feel "lousy."
4. The most common mood listed for the morning, for noon, for evening; the most commonly listed mood regardless of time.
5. Any other commonly occurring pattern of interest.

After directions were given and recorded, Mr. Cohen asked the newly formed committee to meet with him briefly after class so that he could help them schedule a meeting some time during the week for tabulating the charts and preparing the report. With the reports of this class thus set up for the following week, he proceeded to introduce the film he was showing for the day's regular lesson.

In this example we see a teacher who is apparently accomplishing a lot while teaching under circumstances that are far from ideal. His teaching duties are divided between health and physical education. He meets his health classes only one day per week, and his students are generally low in academic skills. Despite these handicaps he appears to have a series of interesting reports organized for his next series of weekly classes. He has three of his top students working with very concrete and meaningful material; they have specific instructions concerning the basic structure of their report, yet they have considerable leeway to add items of interest. It seems quite possible that the students hearing these reports may have the opportunity to acquire a good deal of practical and useful information concerning the dynamics of moods and emotions.

VIII. LIFE AND DEATH

Although the various disease agents and accident situations that threaten to cause death tend to be overemphasized in many health education programs, the actual reality of death itself is generally ignored or avoided both in the classroom and in society at large. Reasons for this omission range from the rather frivolous reluctance to bother young people with such an unpleasant subject to very strong beliefs that this sensitive topic should be left to the church and the home. However, health educators, particularly those heavily involved in mental health work, have come to realize that the individual's knowledge of the eventual death of himself and his loved ones has a real presence, not only when death is imminent or has occurred, but for most of his life extending from the first moment he is able to understand his mortal status.[3] There are many prominent examples of persons who have been forced to take a hard look at death, either because of their own close escape or the actual death of someone very close to them, who have found that the experience had a positive effect on their day-to-day capacity to live with zest and maturity. Although it is both impractical and inadvisable to duplicate the intensity of these real experiences in the classroom, many of the same positive benefits can result from learning experiences designed to help students "come to terms" with this important health topic.

Concept

The nature of one's personal acceptance and adjustment to the inevitability of death has important effects on the strength and effectiveness of one's personality.

[3] See Joan D. McMahon, "A Unit for Independent Study in Death Education," *School Health Review*, Vol. 4, No. 4 (July–August 1973), pp. 27–34, for a good overview of this topic together with detailed teaching suggestions and a comprehensive bibliography.

Students
Developed for twelfth grade, co-ed classes with average to above-average academic ability; also recommended for similar groups in grades 10 and 11.

Technique
Student interview project.

Although death is an important area of study, both the realities of modern medical progress and the aforementioned universal habit of avoidance have combined to make the topic quite remote and abstract to most high school students. Moreover, the beneficial changes in student behavior which would hopefully result from a study of this sensitive topic generally take the form of altered feeling tone, increased peace of mind, and so forth, rather than the overt change sought in the study of nutrition, disease control, and other more traditional health topics. Consequently the real teaching challenge here is to provide reality and impact to an essentially abstract concept. Somehow the various issues, understandings, and subconcepts related to the study of death must be translated into terms and situations with which students can readily identify.

One way this task may be accomplished is through the use of good films or videotapes that realistically present death-related content. These materials may be very effectively worked into any well-planned presentation if they are available; however, at this writing such materials are generally scarce. Another more practical approach in most teaching situations is to use a small group of students as the medium through which the needed material is conveyed to the class. This calls for the soliciting of three or four student volunteers from among those with better-than-average personal qualities (sensitivity, group acceptance, intelligence, etc.) who will then investigate the topic in a meaningful way and report it to the class. This general scheme can take many forms, depending on the particular conditions involved; however, the following description of specific steps may provide a useful basis for planning a teaching sequence in this area:

1. Arrange to meet with the student investigators for a minimum of five to ten minutes either at the back of the classroom during class time or at some mutually convenient time outside of class. During this meeting first acquaint them with the basic benefits that can result from the study of death such as the ability to

- provide effective support and comfort for aggrieved friends and family members who have recently lost loved ones through death.
- provide effective support and comfort to friends and family members who are facing imminent death by terminal illness.
- adjust effectively to the loss of one's own loved ones through death.
- adjust effectively to a situation involving one's own imminent death.
- experience greater happiness and zest for life by coming to terms with the reality of eventual death.

Ask each investigator to use these basic points or objectives as the basis for interviewing a minimum of three persons on their feelings and opinions concerning death, including at least one young person (their own age), one mature adult (parents' age or older), and one person whose work routinely involves contact with dying or aggrieved persons. This last category might include such persons as ministers, priests, or rabbis; nurses on cancer wards, attendants at nursing homes, or other appropriate medical personnel; and morticians and funeral directors. Also advise each investigator to read one or more good articles on the topic before their interview and suggest any specific references you know to be worthwhile. Ask them to meet once on their own before the interviews to coordinate their efforts and once again following the interviews to plan a 15- to 20-minute report to the class. Encourage them to incorporate instructive aids in the form of tape recordings, pamphlets, and so forth, into their presentation but allow them to use a simple symposium format if they wish.

2. During the class meeting immediately preceding the report of the student investigators, generally introduce the class to the topic and the possible benefits of studying it. This may be accomplished by first showing a short film or reading them a synopsis of a good article or news item that relates to some aspect of adjustment to death. After they have had an opportunity to discuss the film or article for three or four minutes, present the following questions by use of the chalkboard, overhead projector, or other means:

What does death mean to you?
a. The end; the final process of life.
b. The beginning of a life after death; a transition; a new beginning.
c. A joining of the spirit with a new cosmic consciousness.
d. A kind of endless sleep; rest and peace.
e. Termination of this life but with survival of the spirit.
f. Don't know.
g. Other.[4]

Ask each student to select one of the "a" to "f" selections if it seems reasonably close to what he or she believes and the "other" item if this is not the case. Following this, have each student write a paragraph in which his or her answer is more fully explained; allow them 5 to 10 minutes for this task. Next tally the choices by a show of hands for each of "a" through "g," but make it clear that any student may choose not to reveal his choice. Once the tally is complete allow willing students to read their paragraphs to the class beginning with those who chose the most common category and then moving to a consideration of the less popular choices. Allow general discussion of the points raised by each presentation. If the class seems ready in terms of understanding and interest, cut short the individual analysis of paragraphs 5 minutes before the end of the class period and lead them into a discussion of the following question: "What

---

[4] Taken from the questionnaire provided in Edwin S. Schneidman, "You and Death," *Psychology Today*, Vol. 5, No. 1 (1971), pp. 43–45, 74–80. Some teachers may wish to obtain and administer the full 28-item instrument.

effect can your beliefs about death have on your ability to live happily and effectively?"

3. Begin the following (second) class meeting with the reports of the student investigators. Unless the reporting team has devised a unique format, the general directions for the symposium (see pages 160–161) should apply to their presentation. Once the basic reports have been completed the class should be ready to explore interesting subtopics in some depth. Many of the questions that might be profitably discussed relate directly to the basic objectives presented in item 1 above such as:

- Through what stages must grief-stricken persons generally pass?
- How can one help the aggrieved person respond constructively to his grief? What words or actions should be avoided?
- What kinds of people combine zest for life with an acceptance of death? Do they have common occupations, religious beliefs, life experiences, and so forth, or are they diverse?

Other questions may be suggested by the categories of persons interviewed such as

- How do medical and hospital personnel generally seem to adjust to contact with dying persons?
- Are there apparent differences in how the younger versus older person feels about death?
- How do you think you would respond to news that you will die within six months?

These questions could be pursued in conventional class discussions or where conditions permit, in terms of time available and class readiness, these same questions could be explored by use of role-playing situations that they suggest.

REFERENCES

Clarke, Kenneth. "The Relevance Perspective in Drug Education," *School Health Review*, Vol. 3, No. 2 (March–April 1972), pp. 5–7.

Health Curriculum Guide in Mental and Social Health. Fall River, Mass.: Fall River School Department, 1971.

Jones, Herbert. "Exploring Emotions with Young Children," *School Health Review*, Vol. 4, No. 4 (July–August 1973), pp. 14–19.

Kime, Robert E. "Mood and Emotion Charting," *The Journal of School Health*, Vol. XXXV, No. 3 (March 1965), p. 138.

Leviton, Dan. "Death, Bereavment and Suicide Education," in Donald A. Read (ed.), *New Directions in Health Education*. New York: Macmillan Publishing Co., Inc., 1971, p. 179.

McMahon, Joan D. "A Unit for Independent Study in Death Education," *School Health Review*, Vol. 4, No. 4 (July–August 1973), pp. 27–34.

Ross, Elizabeth Kübler. *On Death and Dying*. New York: Macmillan Publishing Co., Inc., 1969.

11. HUMAN ■ SEXUALITY I: FOUNDATIONS

Throughout history sexual activity has served as a means of expressing some of mankind's best and worst emotions. The powerful motivations provided by the sexual instinct have resulted, in their most overt form, in highly compassionate and constructive behavior in certain situations and equally ruthless and destructive actions in other instances. For those who accept Freudian interpretations, the study of human sexuality becomes even more complex and paradoxical. According to this view, sexual activity represents the most elemental expression of one's basic life force, or libido, which serves as the underlying stimulus for most varieties of human behavior. But regardless of the differences found among individual interpretations of human sexuality, considerable agreement exists concerning the serious-ness and persistence of sex-related problems. The consequences of illegi-timate births, venereal disease, family instability, adultery, and divorce are viewed as serious by most responsible members of our society. The more positive and liberal members of this group are also disturbed about the generally negative and repressive attitude that some citizens exhibit toward a human force with such potential for constructive expression.

Historical Perspective
When such problems as illegitimate births, venereal disease, and family instability are viewed in historical perspective, it is easy to find support for a pessimistic view. A cursory review of human activities extending from the beginning of recorded history through Biblical times, the glory of Greece and Rome, the Dark Ages, and the Renaissance reveals instances of adul-tery, rape, and illegitimacy. Although it is possible to interpret modern trends in a manner that indicates that mankind is making progress in combating these and similar problems, the evidence is far from overwhelm-

ing and lends itself to various interpretations as determined by individual biases. Rising divorce rates are viewed by many as an indication that the family as a useful social institution is disintegrating in the face of modern stresses; others feel that the modern tendency to abandon an unsatisfactory arrangement is far better than the earlier practice of avoiding divorce at the cost of lifelong unhappiness and an affectionless environment for any children involved. Rising illegitimate birth rates are viewed by many as evidence of a deterioration of youthful morals; others feel that such statistics indicate an increased willingness to face the consequences of illegitimacy and deal with them in a more constructive manner than a forced marriage that often compounds the difficulties of the situation.

Throughout the twentieth century there have been efforts to deal openly and constructively with sex-related problems. The American Social Health Association, formed in 1914, supported an educational approach to combat the specific problem of venereal disease. The White House Conference on Child Health and Protection in 1932 called for educational programs that would direct the individual's sexual nature in a manner encouraging self-development and happiness while advancing the welfare of society.[1] In 1944 the National Congress of Parents and Teachers called for a well-planned program of "social hygiene instruction extending from the preschool years throughout K to 12 and on into adulthood."[2] In response to this growing concern many specific programs have been initiated. Public and private efforts to help the unwed mother have increased. Marriage counselors and family physicians are beginning to accept and deal with sexual conflicts as an important threat to family unity.

Although these efforts have been encouraging, this encouragement is based more on their potential rather than their actual accomplishments. In most instances the programs and services offered are meager in comparison with individual and community needs. Two factors appear to have played a large part in our failure to handle this situation. First, there was the almost total lack of scientific information concerning the sexual aspects of man that persisted throughout most of this century. The only comprehensive explanation of these phenomena that was based on anything resembling orderly investigation was that expounded by psychodynamic or Freudian psychiatrists and psychologists. Although this provided some useful insights, much of the data supporting it was based on clinical observations of neurotic adults. Useful implications for the important but less pathological problems of "normal" persons were often lacking. Coupled with this lack of comprehensive and reliable information has been the public's general unwillingness to accept the little information that was made available and

---

[1] White House Conference on Child Health and Protection, *Social Hygiene in Schools* (New York: Appleton-Century-Crofts, 1932), pp. 3–4.

[2] H. Frederick Kilander, *School Health Education* (New York: Macmillan, Inc., 1968), p. 192.

to respond objectively to the implications of this information. The Kinsey reports on the male, in 1948, and on the female, in 1953, represent cases in point. These pioneer efforts produced much useful information, yet the response of the public was often directed toward discrediting the results or reinterpreting them in a manner that would not disturb traditional views.

Recent Developments

The events of the past few years have given rise to new hopes that American society may finally come to grips with problems related to sexual expression in an effective manner. Sexual matters have gained increasing acceptance as a legitimate area of scientific inquiry. The work of Masters and Johnson [3, 4] and other less widely publicized investigators is beginning to provide the accurate and objective information that is vitally needed. Of perhaps equal importance is the growing willingness of the average citizen to discuss this subject openly and frankly. One result of this new openness has been a relaxation of both legal and informal restrictions on what can be discussed and shown in magazines, motion pictures, television, and other forms of mass media. The editors of *Time* magazine attribute a good deal of *Playboy* editor Hugh Hefner's success to his accurate assessment of this new post-World War II public attitude. In their words, "He was the first publisher to see that the sky would not fall and mothers would not march if he published bare bosoms; he realized that the old taboos were going." [5] These trends of course have proved disturbing to many people. Recently there have been increasing efforts on the part of conservative elements of our society to reaffirm the old legal restrictions and develop new and more readily enforceable legislation embodying stricter definitions of pornography. However, the practical difficulties in interpreting such laws, together with the relentless demand of the younger portion of our citizenry for freedom of expression in all spheres of activity, make it difficult to view these restrictive efforts as anything more than a delaying action. As the barriers continue to lower in the mass media, it is becoming increasingly easy to examine and discuss sexual matters in more formal situations, such as in the classroom.

In 1966 *The Journal of Social Issues* published a comprehensive review of American sexual attitudes and practices in a special issue entitled "The Sexual Renaissance in America." [6] In the summarizing article Ira Reiss pointed to the consistent agreement in the results of major studies which show that "although attitudes have changed considerably during the

---

[3] William H. Masters and Virginia E. Johnson, *Human Sexual Response* (Boston: Little Brown, 1966).

[4] William H. Masters and Virginia E. Johnson, *Human Sexual Inadequacy* (Boston: Little Brown, 1970).

[5] "Think Clean," *Time*, Vol. 89, No. 9 (March 3, 1967), p. 76.

[6] Ira L. Reiss (ed.), "The Sexual Renaissance in America," *Journal of Social Issues*, Vol. XXII, No. 2 (April 1966).

past 20 to 25 years, that many areas of sexual behavior, such as premarital coital rates, have not." [7] He cites the modification of attitudes to conform with actual practices as the single most significant change. Sexual practices have not changed; they are simply becoming accepted. Consequently, guilt is less frequent and intense than in past years. Reiss continues with a description of the effects of these trends on young people that carries obvious implications for health education.

Our young people are *not* less sure of their views than were their parents or grandparents—on the contrary they are probably more certain of their sexual attitudes. The difference is that they are more open, vocal and desirous of examining alternatives intellectually; thus awareness is increased.[8]

Reiss's assessment of young people's views toward their own sexuality is consistent with the more recent finding of Sorensen, who conducted a comprehensive study of both the sexual values and practices of teen-agers.[9] In regard to the "sureness" of personal views, 84 per cent of his subjects expressed the belief that they had "come to definite conclusions about what is right and wrong for them as far as sex is concerned." [10] In comparison with previous studies he found a moderate increase in sexual activity with 59 per cent of the males and 45 per cent of the females among his 13- to 19-year-old subjects reporting that they had experienced sexual intercourse. Although Sorensen avoided comparing his results with those found in studies of the past, presumably because of the many differences in the methodology used, he interpreted his findings as revealing a generally constructive view of contemporary teen-age attitudes toward sex. As one reads the report the tendency for young people to show genuine concern for the feelings and personal integrity of their sexual partners or potential sexual partners seems to be a consistently recurring theme. There appears to be a trend away from many of the selfish and predatory attitudes that were typical of the "double standard" philosophy that dominated the thinking of the past.

Many view these changing attitudes as evidence of a deepening problem. They would say that our sexual behavior has never been good and that now we have stopped feeling ashamed of our shortcomings. However, others welcome these developments as a refreshing change from the hypocrisy of the past. Regardless of the ultimate effects of this "new permissiveness," the new latitude given to public discussions of sexual patterns represents a positive gain for the health educator.

[7] Ibid., p. 126.
[8] Ibid.
[9] Robert C. Sorensen, *Adolescent Sexuality in Contemporary America* (New York: World Publishing, 1972).
[10] Ibid., p. 115.

The Role of the Schools

One concrete manifestation of this new opportunity is found in the generally improved attitudes of parents and school board members toward sex education. Within the past decade solid support and enthusiasm have developed for school programs of family life and sex education. Within many communities there has been a rapid shift in public opinion, from one of distrust and hostility toward such programs to one so positive as to produce an urgent demand for special courses in this sensitive area. Many of the better-organized and innovative school districts have been able to meet this demand with well-planned and effectively implemented programs that have been well received by all elements of the community. Many other districts, however, were caught unprepared. Here school authorities often found themselves pressured into crash programs in an area where persons possessing the competencies for quality teaching are still relatively scarce. Where these conditions prevailed, parents and other concerned persons were often highly critical of many of the methods and materials employed in teaching sex education. This understandable concern, combined with the less defensible reaction of those who simply view sex education as part of a general move toward permissiveness of all types, has produced some retrenchment in the rush to launch new programs. In a few cases even well-managed programs have come under severe attack. Despite these setbacks, the long-term trend appears to be toward increasing acceptance of sex education as an important part of the school curriculum.

It is not surprising that difficulties are sometimes encountered by those persons responsible for developing units or courses of sex education. Many of the subtopics are sensitive ones and community attitudes vary widely in regard to what content is acceptable or desirable. Another difficulty is that there are so few good programs in existence that might provide guidance for the development of new ones. Menstrual-hygiene education in the form of one or two lectures for girls only has been around for a long time and some districts have been providing basic sex education to boys and girls for many years. But the concept of comprehensive kindergarten-through-high school programs of sex education that provide the opportunity for the development of wholesome values and attitudes is comparatively new. In 1966 Mary Calderone, executive director of the Sex Information and Education Council of the United States (SIECUS) said, "Let me disclaim any authority in this field, where at this time there are probably no authorities." [11]

Since that time many new programs have been implemented and much has been learned; there are probably a few genuine authorities now and several communities whose programs appear comprehensive, popular,

[11] Mary Calderone, "The Development of Healthy Sexuality," *Journal of American Association for Health, Physical Education, and Recreation*, Vol. 37, No. 7 (September 1966), p. 23.

and effective. Only 17 per cent of Sorensen's subjects, for instance, were negative concerning the value of sex education courses in school.[12] But while effectiveness has improved, the fact remains that sex education will continue to be a sensitive and controversial area of study as long as sexual matters continue to evoke so many feelings of guilt and ambivalence in society at large. Educators commonly find themselves seeking to satisfy parents and other community members who are themselves very unsure of just how they stand. Although the trends are toward more openness and consensus, progress is slow, and the basic problem is large and complex.

In 1964 Kirkendall and Calderwood reviewed studies of the sources of sex information and concluded that adolescents were still getting the "majority of their insights about sex from each other." [13] They continued with a sweeping criticism of the programs in existence at that time. Some of their basic generalizations were:

1. When sex information is obtained from "appropriate sources," it is very limited in scope, meager in content, and always too late in coming.
2. The education received from the "appropriate sources" is much more aptly labeled "reproduction education" than "sex education."
3. What occurs between parent and/or teacher and youth in sex education is usually largely a matter of something being told.
4. Parents and teachers lack any clear concept of the outcomes they hope to achieve with sex education for youth beyond "keeping them out of trouble." [14]

It would be unfair to apply these criticisms in a general way today, because substantial progress has been made since this review. However, they still apply in many instances and they also serve to show the important problems that were virtually universal not too long ago. Another value of these criticisms is their use as a checklist of major errors to avoid in the development of modern programs of sex education.

A Positive Program

The four points previously listed effectively describe what sex education should not be. The task of describing what it should be is considerably more complicated. Our view of this curricular area will be expressed in the form of priority concepts and specific examples of teaching situations in this and the following chapter. As a means of developing a point of view for the consideration of these suggestions, some general points are worth noting.

[12] Sorensen, op. cit., p. 181.
[13] L. A. Kirkendall and D. Calderwood, "The Family, the School, and Peer Groups; Sources of Information About Sex," *Journal of School Health*, Vol. XXXV, No. 7 (September 1965), p. 290.
[14] Ibid., pp. 291–292.

1. Human sexuality refers to all those qualities that distinguish between maleness and femaleness. The physiological differences are both obvious and important, but in addition there are the equally important differences in attitude, behavior, and responsibilities that define the male and female role in American society.

2. A sound program of sex education provides young people with the opportunity to (a) obtain accurate and comprehensive information related to the physiological, psychological, and sociological aspects of human sexuality, and (b) develop effective *personal* values concerning the sexual aspects of their lives. The need to convey good information is obvious and widely accepted. What is sometimes overlooked is the fact that values are also important determiners of behavior, and behavior is what health education is all about. It is both unwise and impractical for a teacher or a program to attempt to impose preselected values on boys and girls; however, it is possible to help the individual to form a personal set of values within the range of his or her individual family, religious, and cultural backgrounds.

3. The task of developing one's proper sex role is infinitely complex and requires extensive time. There are appropriate concepts to acquire at each stage of one's development; therefore, sex education in its comprehensive sense is required at all school levels. Calderone expressed this view effectively: "if our aim is adults who will use their sexuality in mature and responsible ways, we cannot begin sex education later than earliest childhood." [15]

4. Sex education is taught most effectively as a part of, or in close relationship to, the broad area of family-living education. Within our society many of the most intimate and important aspects of the masculine or feminine role are expressed within the marriage context. In addition to sexual intercourse, such things as expressions of love and affection and the experiences and responsibilities of parenthood form an important part of family life. Many of these activities of a sexual nature that take place prior to marriage often affect the important attitudes that the individual brings to any future marriage relationship.

GROWTH AND DEVELOPMENT CHARACTERISTICS

A review of the growth and development characteristics of children and youth yields useful implications for school programs of sex education at this level. However, like most other aspects of this topic, one immediately encounters conflicting and controversial issues. One of the most obviously pertinent of these issues concerns the sexual or erotic nature of the preadolescent child. Many parents and educators do not accept, or will not accept, the fact that such characteristics exist. Our society generally pre-

[15] Calderone, op. cit., p. 24.

sumes that children are essentially free of any frankly sexual or erotic yearnings until the time of puberty. This assumption contributed to the ineffectiveness of many of the sex education programs of the past that were "almost always too late in coming." [16] Even today this misconception persists among the general public in spite of the views of most psychologists, sociologists, and anthropologists.

Childhood Sexuality

Much of the confusion can be blamed in part upon the propagation of the Freudian-based theory of psychosexual development. This elaborate system, with its well-defined and relatively inflexible stages, has been criticized severely and rejected in whole or in part by many behavioral scientists. Most of those parents and educators who did not initially dismiss the concept of psychosexual development on emotional grounds quickly accepted the technical criticisms of hostile professionals and laid the disturbing idea of childhood sexuality to rest with a sigh of relief.

What many persons overlooked, however, was the specific nature of the rebuttals to this Freudian-based theory. For the most part they did not deny the existence of preadolescent sexuality itself; what was rejected was the specific stages and the dynamics or pattern of causation advocated by the Freudian school. Broderick [17] illustrated this point very effectively in his references to the findings of both cultural anthropologists who studied sexually permissive societies, and surveyors of sexual behavior in American society, specifically Kinsey [18, 19] and Ramsey.[20] The evidence from both of these sources conflicted with the classical Freudian concept of latency because preadolescent children were shown to have *more*, rather than less capacity for erotic stimulation than Freud postulated. The children of all cultures exhibited considerable interest in sexual matters. Many engaged in such behavior as masturbation and homosexual or heterosexual sex play. The main difference between American children and those of more sexually permissive cultures was the American tendency to hide sexual interests from adults.

This type of evidence has led most thoughtful advocates of sex education to accept human sexuality, both in the broad sense of sex roles and in the narrow sense of capacity for erotic stimulation, as a quality that exists at every age level. In the words of Mary Calderone, "there must be full understanding and acceptance of the sexuality of all age levels, beginning

[16] Kirkendall and Calderwood, op. cit., p. 291.

[17] Carlfred B. Broderick, "Sexual Behavior Among Pre-Adolescents," *Journal of Social Issues*, Vol. XXII, No. 2 (April 1966), pp. 6–21.

[18] Alfred C. Kinsey et al., *Sexual Behavior in the Human Male* (Philadelphia: Saunders, 1948).

[19] Kinsey, *Sexual Behavior in the Human Female* (Philadelphia: Saunders, 1953).

[20] Glenn V. Ramsey, "The Sexual Development of Boys," *American Journal of Psychology*, Vol. 56 (1943), pp. 217–233.

with infancy and continuing throughout life." [21] The specific nature of the educational implications resulting from the acceptance of this concept of sexuality will vary according to individual interpretation of this concept. However, it seems clear that sex education at the elementary level is not so much preparation for some future situation as it is education for sexual beings in an active stage of development.

Adolescent Sexuality

Adolescence is traditionally, and rather accurately, characterized as a period of stress during which the young person often makes things difficult for both himself and those around him as he struggles with a unique set of problems. He may want more pocket money, greater freedom in his use of leisure time, less responsibility for household chores, and far less parental involvement in his personal affairs. Although individual patterns of adolescent concerns will often appear hectic and random, they will generally be found to be related to the basic task of achieving independent adult status. The problem of developing a mature sex role lies right at the heart of this task, and it is the sexual aspect of the adolescent's overall development that often presents the most difficulties. Television, movies, his peer group, and his observations of people in general provide information stressing the importance of properly managing one's sexual concerns, yet none of these sources provide very reliable or comprehensive guidance as to what he should do to handle problems in this area. Meanwhile the process of physiological maturity adds increasing urgency to the situation without providing useful insights into what behavior to adopt.

Even under the best circumstances, adolescent sexuality is fraught with difficult problems. In our society sexual maturity in a physiological sense normally occurs long before any socially acceptable outlet becomes available. Premarital sex on the part of school-age youth is regarded as immoral or dangerous by the majority of our citizens. Masturbation is deemed immature and undesirably introverted. Much of the sex drive is undoubtedly channeled into other activities, but it seems neither practical nor even desirable to handle the entire problem in this manner. These very real concerns are often seriously compounded by an artificial one. We seem determined to deny the adolescent any effective information or guidance concerning sexual behavior. Early in life his parents may provide him with a monetary allowance and guidelines for its use. He may find that he can discuss his personal financial affairs with his parents and receive useful advice. He may discuss academic and vocational problems with school guidance personnel with good prospects of receiving meaningful help. But if he should try the same sources for advice concerning his sexual problems, he will receive advice, but very often it will not deal forthrightly with his real concerns. He may find that both he and the parent or other adult

[21] Calderone, op. cit., p. 23.

advising him may evade the real issues. They may both find themselves participating in what has often been called a "conspiracy of silence."

CURRICULAR ASPECTS

Educational Needs

The present state of affairs regarding sex education remain somewhat discouraging, however, present trends are encouraging. Many factors are contributing to a new spirit of openness and full communication. The many newly emerging programs of education in family living and human sexuality at the secondary level are both a result of and a contributor to this new point of view. We now recognize that effective mass instruction in this area can both prevent many individual problems from developing and render others easier to manage. Beyond this lies the very real possibility of doing something in a positive way in the improvement of society's general attitude about sexual matters. Many health educators find this line of reasoning easy to accept in theory but difficult to put into practice. Although some of the difficulties are unusual, the process of developing a good program is similar to that of other topical areas in that the identification of specific needs is the first step.

HUMAN REPRODUCTION. As noted earlier in this chapter, the sex education programs of the past were often criticized for their preoccupation with the physiological aspects of conception and reproduction. Anything that touched upon the broader aspects of human sexuality that might provide implications for the formation of values or behavioral decisions was viewed as the responsibility of the home or the church. More recently, as a reaction to this imbalance, there has been a tendency to overreact in the opposite direction. In their efforts to embrace the broader and more sophisticated view, there has been a tendency for modern curriculum makers to neglect the basic facts of human reproduction.

Basic biological information concerning the reproductive system, sexual intercourse, ovulation, conception, prenatal development, and the birth process still represents an important element, if not the foundation, of school programs of sex education. Ignorance in this area often results in fears and anxieties that interfere with the normal development of wholesome attitudes and values related to the broader aspects of sexuality. The better programs include appropriate content related to human reproduction at each school level, from the primary through the high school grades.

Within this area, as is the case in most other health topics, it is important to stimulate the development of valid concepts before, rather than after, problems develop. For example, many of the serious concerns of adolescents pertain to the normalcy of certain physiological events, such as menstrual irregularities, untimely erections, markedly small or large genital organs, and so on. The intensity of these problems may be reduced in many instances when accurate information related to pubescent development is presented earlier at the upper elementary level. Unfortunately children in many elementary schools still receive only superficial menstrual education and this limited instruction is provided only to the girls. In these situations biological information should be provided at the secondary level as soon as possible.

THE SEX DRIVE. A blending of biological and psychosocial concepts is essential to an effective understanding of the sex drive. The groundwork for this complex topic may be effectively developed at the elementary level helping children to understand the importance and potency of sensual and erotic feeling in a general way. Here the emphasis can be placed on the significance of hugging, kissing, and caressing as ways of expressing affection within the family. At the secondary level it is appropriate to deal more directly with the sex drive in its genital form. Adolescents need some knowledge of the different forms it generally takes in the male and female. Within the male it is more specific and direct. It tends to be isolated from feelings of love and affection and directed more toward orgasm. Within the female the sex drive is more diffuse and is related to feelings of affection. Indirect stimuli such as sexual fantasies and provocative pictures have a much greater effect on the male than the female. For both sexes the intensity and mode of expression are affected by a wide variety of forces, including parental attitudes, religious teachings, general social values as depicted in the mass media, and the particular views and practices of one's close associates. A good program will give the young people an opportunity to explore these general points and to see how broadly they apply, what form they take in specific situations, and how to apply such information to personal decisions.

SEX ROLES. Much of what attracts the mature adult toward his or her fiancé or spouse consists of those personal qualities of masculinity or femininity that extend beyond mere attractiveness as a sex partner. Although these sex roles are still very important, the task of identifying their specific nature is fraught with difficulty and controversy. According to the traditional view, boys often seek sweet and compassionate qualities in the personalities of their feminine companions. Presumably they expect girls to have a feminine pattern of interests that typically lead them into involvement in the planning of school dances and social events, and away from participation in, for example, the school's auto club. Boys supposedly seek admiration from the girls rather than competition and attempt to gain this favored status by displaying high degrees of aggressiveness, independence, and early emancipation from the control of parents and other adults. These generalizations still apply in varying degrees to many of the more socially conservative localities of the country; however, the long-term trend appears to be toward reducing the heretofore sharp distinctions in societal expectations for masculine and feminine patterns of interest and behavior.

Despite the vigorous actions of many feminist groups, certain underlying physiological differences will undoubtedly place limits on this effort and preserve the meaningfulness of sex roles. But the archaic and unfair discriminatory nature of many sex-oriented attitudes and policies is becoming increasingly unacceptable. Many of society's expectations in this regard represent the aftermath of centuries of cultural experience wherein men typically made the family's living through hard, physical labor and women bore many children and spent long hours cleaning and cooking. Under these conditions many of the traditional role differences were useful and in some cases necessary for survival; however, many of them seem obviously counterproductive in today's world. Stone and Church express this view quite clearly when they state:

as parents, teachers, and social engineers, we see through the artificiality and even perniciousness of some of our sex-role expectations. We brutalize boys when we expect them to be cavemen living in a technological, educated, humane society, and we brutalize girls when we expect little from them in the way of intellect and creativity, and when, on the other hand, we expect them to be passive, docile, accepting, and cast in traditional roles.[22]

It seems clear that the task of correcting the very real problems and injustices in this situation will continue for many years. The future changes in the more superficial aspects of sex roles such as those regarding apparel, cosmetics, and social etiquette, however, are considerably harder to predict. It would not be surprising to see periodic returns to the "good-old-days" in these relatively harmless areas. But the changes that occur will be largely determined by social action—the formation of new customs and, in some cases, new laws rather than by the dictates of inherent physical differences. The provision of suitable classroom experiences, can prepare young people for more efficient participation in this important process.

FAMILY LIVING.   In spite of all the notoriety concerning the troubles of the American family, many couples avoid the well-published pitfalls and maintain good homes with effective and enduring affectionate relationships among the family members. Where do these fortunate people develop the knowledge, skills, and attitudes to accomplish this? The most widely supported view maintains that they acquired most of these qualities by participating in, or reacting to, their previous family life as children in the homes of their parents. This preparation does not, of course, take place in a single premarriage talk with one's parents. It occurs on a daily basis and encompasses thousands of learning experiences over perhaps twenty years of life as a junior family member. Consequently, if the school seeks to exert a favorable effect on this process, it must do more than offer a single unit on family living at the senior high level. Ideally, a school program of family-life education would parallel the child's career as a family member and assist him in learning from this experience.

[22] L. Joseph Stone and Joseph Church, *Childhood and Adolescence*, 2nd ed. (New York: Random House, 1968), p. 392.

Many children are exposed to family customs, practices, and attitudes that are far from ideal. A good school program can partially counteract these negative experiences by making the child aware of other alternatives; this can be done in a manner that does not involve undue criticism of his own family life. Every family possesses at least a few characteristics worthy of emulation. Learning experiences at school can increase the child's awareness of these desirable qualities and enhance the possibilities that they will be incorporated into his permanent value structure.

SOME ADMINISTRATIVE AND TEACHING CONSIDERATIONS

Are the facts and concepts we are teaching accurate? Are they relevant? Are they consistent with community attitudes and values? Are the teachers well trained? We hear such questions more often in conjunction with sex education than with any other health topic. Furthermore, many of the more thoughtful observers are expressing concerns over the need for children and youth to have the opportunity to discuss and examine their own feelings and values regarding sexuality. These represent legitimate and serious concerns but concerns which should apply to any other aspect of health education worth teaching. There is growing recognition that sex education should be handled in an effective but routine manner. The application of this generalization will be apparent in some of the specific aspects presented in this section.

PLACE IN THE CURRICULUM. The practice of offering family-living and sex education as separate courses is quite commonly advocated, even though this arrangement does not appear to offer a sound approach to the problem at the present time. Where this pattern is followed we generally find either a comprehensive semester course that reaches only a minority of the student body or a single short unit that is somehow inserted into the crowded secondary school curriculum. A joint committee representing the nation's school boards and administrators recently called attention to the impracticality of offering separate courses for every important health topic and also pointed to some specific reasons for avoiding this practice with respect to family-living and sex education.

Including sex and family life education with the other categorical health topics in one sound, interrelated, and sequential program not only saves time in an already-crowded curriculum but assures that all topics will be part of a long-range program and will receive more complete and detailed consideration at the appropriate level of the student's development.[23]

[23] Joint Committee of the National School Boards Association and the American Association of School Administrators, "Health Education and Sex/Family Life Education," *Journal of Health, Physical Education, and Recreation*, Vol. 39, No. 5 (May 1968), p. 16.

In addition to these advantages, the possibilities of correlating content with such related areas of mental health and growth and development is enhanced by retaining family-living and sex education within the regular health education program.

ADMINISTRATIVE ARRANGEMENTS. Who should do the teaching? Where should it take place? How should pupils be grouped for this instruction? Generally speaking, the answers to these questions are simple. Sex education should be taught by whoever teaches the other health topics; at the elementary level this is normally the classroom teacher. Instruction should take place wherever health instruction normally takes places, probably in the regular classroom. Pupils should be grouped the way they are normally grouped, which is usually in a mixed class of boys and girls. As is the case with any other topic, there are probably times when assembly programs or resource speakers are warranted, but these should not constitute the main focus of the program. It may be advisable for the girls to meet separately to consider the specific aspect of menstrual hygiene, but facts about ovulation, sperm production, and sexual intercourse have obvious importance to both sexes and should be presented to the class as a whole.

At the secondary level there is even less justification for segregating the sexes for sex education than there is at the elementary level. Unfortunately, students are commonly separated for health education at this level because of the traditional relationship between health and physical education. Therefore, teachers must be trained to teach in either type of situation. The teacher of sex education should possess a sound and wholesome personality, a good knowledge of content and method, and a teaching schedule that permits adequate preparation time for planning class activities. These are, once again, the minimum requirements for teaching any subject.

TIMING AND SEQUENCE. The problems of student response are greatly complicated by the too common practice of waiting until the onset of puberty before providing pupils with their first exposure to classroom sex education. However, when boys and girls experience sex education as a normal part of the curriculum beginning in the early grades, many of the sensitive topics lose their emotional charge and thus permit a degree of detachment conducive to serious consideration of sex-related matters.

In spite of the general endorsement of a K–12 program, elementary school teachers occasionally find themselves charged with the responsibility of providing fifth- or sixth-graders with their first experiences with sex education. In such situations the logical strategy is to devote considerable time in the early stages to discussion of topics with low stimulus value, such as reproduction in lower animals or simplified principles of heredity. Once the pupils become accustomed to this general area of study they are better prepared to deal with the more sensitive topics. This procedure, in effect, devotes the early part of the unit to the provision of the necessary background of experiences that the total program failed to provide in the lower grades.

At the secondary level the better curriculum guides and curriculum recommendations of authoritative bodies commonly advise a balanced approach with both biological and psychosocial content represented at both the junior and senior high school levels. Generally there is some content appropriate to each grade from each of the major subtopics such as growth and development, conception and birth, sex roles, sex drives, and family dynamics. However, it would probably not be wise to attempt to cover every subtopic every year. When the local curriculum pattern provides for some sex education every year, the recommended practice is to emphasize only one or two subtopics at each grade level to avoid duplication and fragmentation of subject matter. In a district where there is a strong program in the elementary grades, it might be appropriate to concentrate on "Life Within the Family" at the seventh-grade level, "Human Reproduction" (review in depth) at the eighth-grade level, and "Social Behavior," with emphasis on understanding and managing the sex drive, at the ninth-grade level. Here the goal would be to provide comprehensive coverage within the three junior high years through use of concentrated and meaningful units.

In well-organized programs we usually find recapitulation of the major subtopics at each school level. However, there are important changes in content emphasis and sophistication. The study of family structure and dynamics at the junior high level normally focuses on the student as an adolescent child in the family of his parents, whereas at the senior high level the emphasis is on the student's potential role as a spouse and parent. In the biological realm the junior high curriculum commonly seeks to provide a sound understanding of pubescent changes and the significance of one's newly acquired sexual capabilities. In senior high the concentration is often on the uterine life of the child and the birth process itself. In the social–emotional area we often find emphasis on the basic mechanics of dating behavior and some general consideration of desirable manly and womanly qualities in junior high, whereas senior high students are provided with an opportunity to examine the deeper meaning of affection and love.

THE TEACHER'S ATTITUDE. Perhaps the most important factor affecting pupil response to sex education is the emotional tone the teacher exhibits when presenting it. Once again the key is naturalness. Insofar as possible human sexuality should be treated as a routine health topic. It is an important topic, but so are the others. Some teachers adopt an artificially serious "great-mystery-of-the-universe" type of demeanor, which often serves to prevent breaches of decorum on the part of the pupils; however, it also effectively deters any serious discussion among preadolescents who cannot match this serious mood. It is also possible to err in the other direction, with the jovial "let's-have-some-fun-talking-about-sex" approach. This appears to be a defensive reaction on the part of teachers who feel uneasy with the topic. Although young children may not analyze it as such, they will probably react to its basic insincerity.

Teachers vary considerably in their general teaching style. What is appropriate and effective for one might be inappropriate and poorly received when imitated by another. Within this broad range of individual patterns, the most successful teachers are generally found to use the same matter-of-fact approach with this topic that serves them well with other health topics.

The complexity and broad scope of the subject matter in human sexuality are other sources of concern to many teachers of health. These qualities commonly produce undue worries concerning the adequacy of one's preparation. Although the teacher's subject-matter background should enable him to deal effectively with content appropriate to the grade level at which he is teaching, he should not feel compelled to combine the qualities of an obstetrician, psychiatrist, and sociologist. In this area, like many health areas, no one has all the answers, and every teacher must learn responsible ways of dealing with questions for which he is not prepared.

Suggested Concepts

The concepts presented in this section are based on a review of several sources.[24] An effort was made to develop a balanced list of those concepts that appear to merit particular emphasis in school health curricula. Persons charged with the selection of concepts for particular programs would be well advised to review several such lists as a means of identifying those most suitable for the needs of their specific situation.

Human Reproduction

1. *All living things reproduce their own kind.* Living things come only from similar organisms; reproduction is necessary for the preservation of life. Most animal forms of life are equipped with certain instincts designed to aid this process.

2. *The reproduction of many forms of life, including man, involves the uniting of male and female substances.* All mammals, together with most of the higher animals and many forms of plant life, reproduce by means of sexual reproduction wherein a male sperm is united with a female egg or ovum. In this manner both sexes contribute equally to the hereditary potential of the new organism.

3. *Human begins, like other mammals, carry out their early stages of development within the protective environment of their mother's body.*

[24] Most helpful were "The Sexual Renaissance in America," special issue, *Journal of Social Issues,* Vol. XXII, No. 2 (April 1966); "Growth Patterns and Sex Education," *Journal of School Health,* Vol. XXXVII, No. 5a (May 1967); *Health Concepts: Guides for Health Instruction,* American Association for Health, Physical Education and Recreation, 1967; and School Health Education Study, *Health Education: A Conceptual Approach to Curriculum Design* (St. Paul, Minn.: 3M Education Press, 1967).

The mother's uterus normally provides extremely favorable conditions for the child during its earliest and most delicate stage of development. The health practices of the mother are particularly significant during this period.

The Sex Drive

4. *Typical physiological changes take place as one approaches sexual maturity.* At a certain stage in one's physiological maturity, endocrine secretions are produced which stimulate the development of both reproductive capacity and secondary sex characteristics.

5. *The sex drive is an innate and powerful force that is related to human pleasure and reproduction.* Most animal forms of life possess certain instincts that encourage the reproduction process; in man, the sexual instinct lends itself to a high degree of voluntary control.

6. *Proper expression and control of the sex drive contribute to one's general well-being.* The satisfaction of the sex drive either by direct or indirect means involves behavior that may range from extremely detrimental to extremely beneficial in its overall effect on one's total living satisfaction.

7. *Sexual adjustment and responsiveness within marriage are influenced by a wide variety of premarital and postmarital factors.* The sexual relationship affects and is affected by other aspects of the total relationship of the couple involved. Past experiences of a sexual nature, whether direct or indirect, can exert a strongly positive or negative effect on the quality of sexual expression within marriage.

Sex Roles

8. *Boys and girls develop typical differences in their personalities, interests, and modes of behavior as they mature.* Physiological differences between men and women have traditionally led to different duties and responsibilities, which in turn have produced general personality differences. Although based on physiological factors, this process of role definition is largely a cultural process.

9. *Adolescent dating activities and other heterosexual social activities typically serve important functions in the process of personality development.* Properly controlled social activities during the adolescent period can drain off a certain degree of sexual energy in a useful way, thus rendering the sex drive easier to manage. Beyond this immediate need, social skills are developed which may serve the individual throughout life.

10. *Love and affection are complex human emotions which require substantial living experience for their full understanding.* Love and affection in their best form involve a high degree of genuine concern for the happiness and well-being of another person which transcends personal considerations. Considerable experience and maturity are required to produce the personal qualities this process requires.

Marriage

11. *The family serves as a means of satisfying many of the physical, psychological, and sociological needs of its members.* The infant receives vital physical care, the child receives training and guidance, adults find a socially sanctioned sexual outlet, and reciprocal affectional benefits are experienced by all family members; these and other important functions may occur within an effective family.

12. *The selection of a marriage partner is a crucial step which has important effects on the lives of the husband, wife, and future offspring.* When a marriage endures, the close personal interaction involved may provide the opportunity for deep human satisfaction or pose the threat of emotional impoverishment and distress. The dissolution of a marriage often produces adverse personality changes in the members involved.

13. *Effective family functions depend upon the appropriate behavior of each family member.* Each family member can contribute to the happiness and well-being of the others; misfortunes which render one member incapable of performing his role adversely affect all other family members.

14. *Each family develops a specific set of common attitudes, values, and modes of behavior which differ in some degree from those of any other family.* As a family is formed, each individual brings his own unique set of characteristics to the marriage; as the marriage develops, additional experiences interact with these characteristics in complex ways.

15. *Many factors affect the overall quality and effectiveness of the marriage relationship.* The development of mutual goals, the compatibility of personality traits, agreement on responsibilities and prerogatives, the effectiveness of personal communication are but a few of those having important effects.

16. *Persons who do not marry often develop valid life-styles that enable them to live productive and satisfying lives.* Although the family is the normative mode of satisfying many important human needs, these needs are often successfully met in other ways.

Parenthood

17. *Parenthood may provide an opportunity for emotional enrichment or the potential for the severe disruption of marriage life.* The responsibility of providing for the physical, social, and emotional needs of a child, if met successfully, becomes a maturing and satisfying experience. The reciprocal relationship between parent and child carries the potential for either mutual satisfaction or distress.

18. *The developing human being requires substantial medical supervision during its prenatal life, delivery, and neonatal period.* Although the process of uterine development, birth, and early infancy may proceed in a normal fashion with little or no medical help, there are special health needs and special threats to health associated with these events. These risks can be greatly reduced by proper care.

19. *Human beings require extensive parental care and attention throughout infancy and childhood if they are to achieve optimum development.* The human infant is one of the most helpless of all living things; it needs constant physical care for its survival. Children require a favorable psychological and sociological environment if they are to develop effective human qualities.

REFERENCES

Blaufarb, Marjorie. "Rap Sessions, Sexuality Resource People, & Teacher Team Training," *School Health Review*, Vol. 3, No. 2 (March–April 1972), pp. 20–23.

Bracher, Marjory. "The Martinson Report: Implications for Sex Education," *Journal of School Health*, Vol. XXXVII, No. 10 (December 1967) pp. 491–496.

Burt, John, and Linda B. Meeks. *Toward a Healthy Sexuality*. Philadelphia: W. B. Saunders Company, 1973.

Calderone, Mary S. "The Development of Health Sexuality," *Journal of Health, Physical Education and Recreation*, Vol. 37, No. 7 (September 1966), pp. 23–27.

Couch, Gertrude B. "Youth Looks at Sex," *Journal of School Health*, Vol. XXXVII, No. 7 (September, 1967), pp. 332–339.

Dalrymple, Willard. *Sex Is for Real*. New York: McGraw-Hill Book Company, 1969.

Fulton, Gere B. "Sex Education: Some Issues and Answers," *Journal of School Health*, Vol. 40 (May 1970), pp. 263–286.

"Growth Patterns and Sex Education," *Journal of School Health*, Vol. XXXVII, No. 5a (May 1965).

Johnson, Warren R. *Human Sexual Behavior and Sex Education*, 2nd ed. Philadelphia: Lea & Febiger, 1968.

Katchadourian, Herant, and Donald T. Lunde. *Fundamentals of Human Sexuality*. New York: Holt, Rinehart and Winston, Inc., 1972.

Kirkendall, L. A., and D. Calderwood. "The Family, the School, and Peer Groups: Sources of Information About Sex," *Journal of School Health*, Vol. 35, No. 7 (September 1965).

Lin, Barbara B., et al. "A Peek at Sex Education in a Midwestern Community," *Journal of School Health*, Vol. XLII, No. 8 (October 1972), pp. 462–465.

Ready, Jeny L. "The Current Status of Family Life and Sex Education in the Public Schools of Illinois," *Journal of School Health*, Vol. XLIII, No. I (January 1973), pp. 49–51.

Reiss, Ira L. "The Dilemma of Sex Education in the Public Schools," in Donald Read (ed.), *New Directions in Health Education*. New York: Macmillan Publishing Co., Inc., 1971.

——— (ed.) "The Sexual Renaissance in America," special issue, *The Journal of Social Issues*, Vol. XXII, No. 2 (April 1966).

Simon, Sidney B., et al. *Values Clarification*. New York: Hart Publishing Co., 1972.

Sorensen, Robert C. *Adolescent Sexuality in Contemporary America*. New York: The World Publishing Company, 1972.

Stone, L. Joseph, and Joseph Church. *Childhood and Adolescence*, 2nd ed. New York: Random House, Inc., 1972.

Williams, Sally R. "Family Life and Sex Education," *Bulletin of the National Association of Secondary School Principals*, Vol. 52, No. 326 (March 1968), pp. 49–55.

Willke, Dr. J. C., and Mrs. J. C. Willke, *Sex Education, The How-To for Teachers*. Cincinnati, Ohio: Hiltz Publishing Co., 1970.

12. HUMAN SEXUALITY II: APPLICATIONS

The broad scope of human sexuality as an area of study was illustrated by the concepts presented in the previous chapter. These ranged from the mainly biological, through the intensely personal or emotional, to such socially oriented concepts as the role of the family in contemporary society. The teaching techniques needed to present this content effectively naturally reflect this diversity and thus do not differ greatly from those used for most other health topics. The unique aspect of teaching in this area is the frequent need to avoid undue embarrassment or emotionality among the learners. This task is somewhat in contrast to that of other areas of study wherein the teacher often must work to achieve an appropriate degree of student involvement. The achievement of good pupil responses will depend most basically on the appropriateness of the content and the general quality of the teaching involved in its presentation; however, there are a number of considerations that provide some guidance to the selection and use of specific techniques.

SELECTION OF TECHNIQUES

Elementary Level

One general type of teaching technique that merits special attention is that of incidental or informal instruction. The practice of taking full advantage of spontaneous questions or unplanned occurrences that provide the opportunity for impromptu coverage of content provides a valuable means of supplementing any health topic on any school level. However, incidental teaching as applied to sex education at the elementary level assumes particular importance. Nothing seems quite as natural as a mature

244

adult rendering a sincere answer to a question of genuine interest to a child. Unfortunately, parents and other adults often respond to questions concerning sex with either false information or a complete evasion. Children have a right to expect better treatment from those persons with responsibility for imparting health information. The elementary school teacher who responds naturally and sincerely to the impromptu sex questions of children will be laying a sound foundation for a good total class response to any scheduled sex education that might occur in the future.

When selecting specific techniques for regularly planned teaching in sex education, one would do well to keep in mind Kirkendall and Calderwood's criticism of earlier programs, namely, that they have too often consisted "largely of a matter of something being told." [1] The use of techniques designed to stimulate pupil involvement in open discussions not only results in better learning, but also provides the teacher with constant feedback on how content is being received and what particular aspects of any topic are of most interest to the class. Such pupil-centered techniques designed to stimulate pupil involvement in open discussions not only results in better learning, but also provides the teacher with constant feedback on how content is being received and what particular aspects of any topic are of most interest to the class. Such pupil-centered techniques as buzz sessions, sociodramas, and problem stories are particularly useful when dealing with material pertaining to sex roles, sexual behavior, and the responsibilities of various family members. With these topics, the development of values and attitudes merits special stress; pupil involvement is needed if this task is to be accomplished.

Teacher-centered methods, such as the use of films and textbooks, are particularly appropriate in handling content that is basically scientific and noncontroversial, such as the structure of the reproductive organs, the prenatal development of the child, and the birth process. Films and other audiovisual aids can often be of particular use to the beginning teacher, because they can provide a professional touch to the handling of particularly sensitive areas. Simple classroom experiments, such as observing the birth of hamsters or guppies, also add much to the study of the biological aspects of this topic.

Although it is inadvisable to rely on resource speakers as the main way of presenting content in sex education, it is equally unwise not to take advantage of any good opportunities that might be available in this area. A well-trained school nurse may bring special expertise to certain topics in sex education as well as to other health topics. Occasionally, interested and willing obstetricians and pediatricians are available who have a knack for dealing with young people. They can often provide insights into aspects

[1] L. A. Kirkendall and D. Calderwood, "The Family, the School, and Peer Groups: Sources of Information About Sex," *Journal of School Health*, Vol. XXXV, No. 7 (September 1965), p. 281.

of prenatal care, birth, and infant care that have meaning and value to elementary children.

Secondary Level

In the secondary school curriculum, as in the elementary school curriculum, certain topics in the family-living and sex education area are essentially biological in nature. Prominent examples include basic reproductive anatomy, prenatal development, and birth. These topics lend themselves to teacher-centered techniques, with emphasis on overhead transparencies, films, and readings of various types. Where resources are available some laboratory experiences, such as examination of animal embryos and fetuses, can be very useful. Within this general portion of the curriculum the teaching task should focus on the transmission of accurate information; the development of attitudes and values plays a secondary role.

Other topics with a psychosocial emphasis such as those pertaining to the sex drive, sex roles, dating and courtship behavior, and basic dynamics of family living necessarily involve considerable examination and evaluation of different patterns of behavior. It is perhaps unfortunate that in this sensitive area of the curriculum, where young people need the most help, health teachers find that there is less solid information. When questions arise, such as "How much intimacy is permissible between dating high school couples?" or, "Should mothers work when their children are still in infancy?" there are seldom "correct" answers available that may be universally applied. For these and a host of other questions students must eventually work out answers that are right for them as individuals. Regardless of what the school does, they will somehow find answers and make choices. If no process is available for making a conscious choice, they may simply drift into a behavior pattern in a thoughtless fashion.

Student-centered techniques are considered to be highly useful when topics heavily weighted with value judgments and attitude formations are involved. Here young people need guidance more than instruction. For this reason buzz sessions, sociodramas, and symposiums are commonly chosen. These techniques provide students with the opportunity to express ideas, beliefs, and points of view that they may hold with varying degrees of commitment. Where mature guidance is available, this material can receive constructive criticism from the peer group, with the chance of producing favorable changes in the values and attitudes of all those participating.

PRACTICAL APPLICATIONS

The following examples are hypothetical and represent an effort to show the results that might be achieved with teaching techniques that are particularly appropriate to family-life and sex education.

I. SUZIE'S BABIES

The old-fashioned procedure of telling children about "the birds, the bees, and the flowers" has taken on undesirable connotations in this more sophisticated era. It implies that the child's real interest in the facts of human reproduction has been unsatisfied by diverting his attention to the lower animals. According to popular cartoonists and humorists, parents and teachers generally delay in providing even this meager substitute until long after the young person has been informed of the basic mechanics of human conception from other sources. Unfortunately, there has been a tendency to overreact to this situation by omitting any study of lower animals as a means of understanding human reproduction. As will be illustrated in the following example, animals can serve us well in illustrating certain principles of reproduction which apply to humans. The key to the validity of this general technique is the proper selection of main points or generalizations for emphasis and the manner in which questions are handled that have human implications. This approach also permits children to observe many aspects of the reproductive process directly; this has special value at the primary level, where concrete experiences are especially meaningful.

Concept
All living things reproduce their own kind.

Pupils
Developed for second-graders of average socioeconomic status; recommended for all primary grades.

Technique
Classroom observation.

One of the oldest and most useful ways to learn about natural phenomena is by careful and systematic observation. When carried on in a highly refined manner, we might term it *observational research* as opposed to *experimental research,* where some factor is varied to study a narrower aspect of the phenomena under consideration. The children in our example observe a white rat throughout her pregnancy and during the early days of her litter. During this time they also observe the development of frog eggs in an effort to obtain some concept of what was taking place within the womb of the expectant mother. Although the mature frog differs greatly from the rat and even more so from the human, there is considerable similarity in the embryonic development of all three organisms. Even at the high school and college levels frog or salamander eggs are useful for illustrating early cell cleavage, the formation of the blastula, the formation of the neural groove, and other important steps common to the development of the human embryo. As a means of illustrating much simpler content in the primary grades, the comparison of frog and man have even greater usefulness.

THE EXAMPLE

The arrival of Suzie the rat had produced a good deal of excitement among Miss Hannibal's second-graders. A sixth-grade boy and girl had delivered the interesting little animal to their room and showed them how to feed and care for it. Mr. Johnson's sixth-grade classroom was the school's unofficial science center, so he was able to provide the necessary cage, food pellets, and other items to get Suzie comfortably established in her new home. That afternoon and the next morning most of the children had a chance to get a close look at her, so they were much calmer the following afternoon when Miss Hannibal brought her in front of the class once more.

"In all of the excitement of her arrival yesterday, I didn't get a chance to tell you one other important thing about Suzie. In a little less than three weeks, she will probably have babies."

The children seemed excited at this prospect but not unduly so. A few of them were already somewhat familiar with this event because of the arrival of puppies or kittens in their homes; many others were too ignorant of the whole process to become very concerned. This resulted in quite a good emotional climate for class discussion. Miss Hannibal began the session with a carefully thought-out question.

"What do you think we would see if we could look inside Suzie and see the place where her babies are going to grow? Can anyone try to tell us?"

Marvin raised his hand and said that he thought that "we would find teeny-tiny rats inside of Suzie."

"Suzie will have little rats inside her just before they are born, but that won't be for several days," responded Miss Hannibal.

Betty was a bit more accurate when she said, "Babies start from little seeds like radish plants do, so Suzie's got seeds inside her now."

"That's quite a good answer, Betty," said Miss Hannibal. "Animals do grow from little things like seeds, only we call them eggs."

"Are they like chicken eggs?" asked Harvey.

"Well, they are quite a bit different from chicken eggs, Harvey. They are much smaller and have no shells."

Miss Hannibal felt that the time was ripe for her main proposal. She explained that although it was impossible to see inside Suzie, there were some animals, such as frogs, that laid eggs that the class could watch grow.

"Don't you think it would be a good idea for me to ask some of the sixth-graders to get some frog eggs for our classroom?"

Another Delivery. Needless to say, the children agreed to this suggestion and Miss Hannibal found Mr. Johnson ready to put a couple of his boys to work on her request. Two mornings later, as she was in her room preparing for the arrival of her pupils, the boys marched in with a gallon jar full of pond water and containing six masses of frog eggs. They also brought in five shallow glass dishes called finger bowls and five large magnifying glasses. These latter two items were on loan from Mr. Johnson's room.

After the children left that afternoon Miss Hannibal filled the five finger bowls with pond water from the large jar. She removed one of the twigs with its attached egg mass and snipped off a lobe containing fifty or so eggs and put it in one of the finger bowls. She repeated this procedure using a different egg mass for each bowl to minimize her reliance on any one mass that might be defective. She did notice that one group of eggs were oriented so that their light-colored side was uppermost, indicating that they were not fertilized. She selected these for one finger bowl.

Next morning the early-arriving children were once again rewarded with something new to inspect. It was interesting for them to get a closer look at the eggs than that provided by the gallon jar that they had seen the previous morning. By the time class resumed after lunch, most of the children had managed to observe the eggs under this new arrangement. This toned down their excitement somewhat, so they were able to listen to directions and carry out instructions in an orderly manner when Miss Hannibal gave out the magnifying glasses. In their normal classroom arrangement the children were seated at tables that accommodated four or five children each. Miss Hannibal asked one pupil from each table to get one finger bowl and carefully carry it to his table. Each child had an opportunity to view the eggs with the magnifying glass as the bowl was passed from pupil to pupil at Miss Hannibal's command. The children were directed to place the magnifying glass close to the finger bowl and to move it upward until they could see the eggs clearly. They were asked to look at the eggs closely so that they could tell about them later; they were also cautioned to keep their fingers out of the bowls and off the lens of the magnifying glasses. All this was accomplished with only a couple of minor spills.

Beginning the Experience Chart. After the finger bowls had been returned to their spot on the window ledge, Miss Hannibal asked the children to describe what they had observed. She asked each volunteer to describe any one thing they had noticed about the eggs. As each characteristic was reported she asked the other children if they had seen the same thing. After the reported fact was verified, it was recorded on an "experience chart" consisting of a large piece of paper that had been taped to the blackboard. Light lines had been drawn on the chart to guide the entries and plenty of room was allowed for future additions. After the first session the chart looked something like this:

Watching Frog Eggs Grow

First Day: The eggs are small brown and white balls.

At the close of the session Miss Hannibal told the children that starting tomorrow, the magnifying glasses would be left out and they would be able to look at the eggs during any of their free moments.

It was three days later, on Monday, before Miss Hannibal discussed the eggs with the children again. This time it was not necessary to have the children observe the eggs during the formal part of the lesson, because most of them had observed the eggs earlier in the day. However, she did have to use special care to screen out erroneous reports based on faulty memories or superficial observations. After some discussion the children agreed that the eggs had definitely changed shape and that each egg seemed to have a tail and a head. They also observed that part of the egg did not change; the white belly still looked like an egg. When it seemed as though the major points had been covered, Miss Hannibal made a second entry on the experience chart. It was numbered *Fourth Day,* because it was the fourth day since their first observation. The chart now looked like this:

Watching Frog Eggs Grow

First Day: The eggs are small brown and white balls.
Fourth Day: A head, tail, and white tummy can be seen.

The Male Frog. Miss Hannibal had been puzzled about one important aspect of the project ever since the first observation session, so she was relieved when one of the boys said, "One dish of eggs is not like that."

"What do you mean, Billy?" asked Miss Hannibal.

"That one over there on the end," answered Billy, pointing with his finger. "The eggs are still little specks and they're mostly all white."

"Did anyone else notice anything different about those eggs?" she queried.

Two other children confirmed Billy's report. At this point Miss Hannibal decided to impart some information of her own.

"I've been watching those eggs too, and I think I know what the trouble is." At this point she paused to see if the children were really interested, then continued. "I don't think there was any male frog around to help those eggs start growing."

This left many of the children puzzled. Billy, whose earlier question had started all this, asked again, "What does the male frog do?"

"He puts something special from his body in the water around the eggs to make them start growing into frogs."

"Won't those eggs ever change into frogs?" asked Jeannie.

"Let's watch them and the other eggs over the next few days and find out," suggested Miss Hannibal.

This arrangement seemed to satisfy most of the class. A few of the children seemed quite interested in the unfertilized eggs but the majority were more concerned with the eggs that were developing.

Tadpoles' Birthday. Two days later another discussion was held and the children reported the appearance of eyes and mouths in most of the developing tadpoles. This information was duly recorded on their experience chart. The children also noted that there was no change in the appearance of the unfertilized eggs. After another two days passed, Miss Hannibal once again called the class together to report on the tadpoles. However, everyone knew in advance what the main entry on the chart would be, for that morning one of the children found that a few of the tadpoles from one egg mass were swimming freely in the bowl. Some of the children were concerned because the tadpoles were so different from the frogs that they had apparently been expecting, but other class members who had raised tadpoles at home assured them that the "big feet" and the "big mouths" would someday arrive.

At this point Miss Hannibal obtained a small aquarium and a few water plants and transferred the tadpoles to this more suitable habitat. The water plants helped provide oxygen for the tadpoles and provided an interesting setting for their display. However, three days later, on Monday, the attention of the class shifted to new developments.

The Paper Collector. Monday morning a couple of the children who were responsible for Suzie's care were letting her run about on the counter top to get a little exercise when they noticed something unusual. She seemed very interested in a stack of art paper that was lying near her cage.

"Gosh, Miss Hannibal," said Jeff, "we'd better move those papers before she tears them up."

"You're right, Jeff," replied Miss Hannibal. "Let's get them out of reach, but I also think we'd better give Suzie some paper and see if we can tell why she's so interested in it."

Miss Hannibal tore a piece of paper toweling into narrow strips. Jeff placed Suzie back in the cage and dumped the handful of paper into her cage. Suzie immediately began dragging the strips over to one corner of her cage, much to the fascination of the children. They watched her for some moments before Jeff finally said, "I'll bet she's building a nest!"

"And you know what that means, don't you?" added Sarah, who had joined the group.

"Sure," replied Jeff, "her babies will come soon; maybe even today!"

According to Miss Hannibal's count Suzie still had three or four days to go, so she attempted to tone down the children's expectations. "It may be a few days yet, children, so don't get discouraged if the babies don't come right away."

In their next health lesson their discussion focused on the parallels between Suzie's pregnancy and a typical human pregnancy, which some of the children had observed in their homes. Miss Hannibal generally sought to lead the class toward an acceptance of the basic naturalness of the reproductive event. "Yes, we need to be gentle with Suzie, but we always should be gentle with her. . . . Expectant mothers should eat good, wholesome foods, but we should always eat good, wholesome foods. . . . Yes, it sometimes hurts when the babies are coming out, but everyone experiences some pain as part of living."

Watchful Waiting. During the next couple of days the children watched Suzie closely. Each child wanted to be the first to report the beginning of the birth process, but this vigilance produced only an occasional false report. Then, on the morning of Suzie's twenty-second day of pregnancy, Miss Hannibal arrived at the classroom before any of the children and discovered Suzie nursing her newborn litter. As the children arrived before class, they were naturally excited, but for the most part they were cautious about getting too close to her cage. They peered intently into the cage, hoping to obtain a glimpse of the babies, but there was little to see except Suzie's pink, beady eyes peering back at them out of a mass of white fur.

It was two mornings later before Miss Hannibal felt it was safe to remove one of the newborn babies so that the class could get a brief look. Suzie and her children remained with the class for the remaining five weeks of the school year. During the last two weeks of this period the young rats were weaned and placed in a separate cage. These lively young animals and the aquarium full of developing tadpoles contributed much to the general classroom environment long after Miss Hannibal had concluded her formal unit on reproduction.

A close analysis of this example would lead one to conclude that Miss Hannibal was not "teaching a unit" as much as she was "creating an environment" for incidental learning. Even in her formal sessions, she did not force-feed the children with information that might not interest them. Instead, she encouraged them to observe and report their findings. She guided them away from erroneous assumptions and toward accurate interpretations. She did not try to provide her class with a complete educational program in human reproduction. These were second-graders who still had a number of relatively calm prepubescent years before encountering the heterosexual challenges of adolescence, so she was content to work on the foundations rather than tackle the total structure.

The curriculum guide for her district did not call for direct teaching of the male role in reproduction at this grade level, thus permitting Miss Hannibal to take a flexible position toward this sensitive topic. The children asked what the male frog had to do to help the eggs, so she told them. This particular class did not inquire about the fertilization of the rat's ova, and she did not volunteer the information. If they had, Miss Hannibal would have told them that a male rat put something in Suzie to help her eggs grow and this probably would have been accepted without undue excitement by children of this age. Presumably, she would have been prepared to provide more details if any one had wished to pursue the matter further.

II. CHAIN REACTIONS

Those of us who are willing to give thoughtful consideration to what sociologists tell us about the dynamics of American family life sometimes despair of ever finding anything of practical use in their offerings. Yet although many aspects of family life seem to defy analysis, the concept of the interdependence of the health and well-being of the members within a family appears well supported. Negative factors affecting one member—whether physical illness, injury, or psychological stress or anxiety—have obvious and subtle effects on other family members. Positive factors are equally potent. The direction of the effect of a new occurrence of factor is not always the same for all family members. Mother's illness may give daughter a chance to acquire needed confidence in her ability to discharge responsibilities. Conversely, Father's promotion may burden the family with a new social status it is not prepared to handle. These things seem obvious, but people too often merely react to important occurrences and give little thought to the possibility of influencing the chain of events that they might produce. The teaching situation that will be described in this example illustrates how children might be made aware of family interdependence at an early.age.

Concept
Effective family functioning depends upon the appropriate behavior of each family member.

Pupils
Developed for first-grade children in an urban setting of average socioeconomic status; generally recommended for all primary grades.

Techniques
The open-ended story, overhead projector.

This example involves the use of the overhead projector (see pages 170–172) to provide interest and structure to the discussion preceding the main technique for the unit, which is the open-ended story (see page 164). Although overhead transparencies are ideally suited to this purpose, an attractive set of still pictures will also work quite well in the typical story-telling situation of the primary grades. Few facts or ideas actually need to be presented to help children develop a meaningful concept of "family interdependence." The pupils themselves can provide the facts; the teacher's task is to make the children sensitive to the knowledge that is already available to them. It is becoming so fashionable to emphasize the problem of poor home environments that one may overlook the fact that there are at least a few children who come from well-managed homes that maintain a wholesome climate. These children often carry the load in the discussion of family-living topics, but almost any pupil can make worthwhile contributions to this type of discussion if proper leadership is employed. The following procedures show how primary school children might be led toward an awareness of family interdependence.

1. Show the children a picture of a typical family by use of the overhead projector or still pictures; this picture should probably include a father, mother, and two or three children. One of the first topics to discuss would be the ways other families might differ from the one shown, such as (a) the absence of a father or mother because of death, divorce, or separation; (b) the presence of grandparents or other relatives living in the same dwelling; and (c) the difference in race or socioeconomic background. When possible, have transparencies ready to depict these common differences.

2. As part of the same discussion, or perhaps in a succeeding one, lead the children into a discussion of the role of each family member in terms of contributions to the happiness and welfare of the other family members. Examples: father (and perhaps mother) works to make money;

children help with chores where appropriate; help and sympathy are extended to troubled members; and most important of all, family members provide love for each other. The mechanical aspects of dividing work responsibilities within the family are simple and worth discussing. The more difficult aspect of emotional interdependence can be approached by asking the children to "tell about times that someone in your family helped them feel better when they were unhappy" or "tell if you have ever helped cheer up someone in your family when they were sad."

3. After the children have gained some understanding of variations in family structure and in family roles, they are ready to tackle the basic concepts of interdependence or family dynamics, provided that these concepts are presented in appropriate terms. The most logical approach is to set up a situation wherein the pupils can consider the effects of some change in the status of a family member. Examples: father loses his job; father gets promoted; mother is expecting a baby; a new baby arrives; grandfather comes to live with us. The following open-ended story portrays a simple and uncomplicated situation that many children are familiar with:

Typical lead-in: Today I'm going to tell you a story about a family. It's going to be a different kind of story because I'm not going to finish. I'm going to call on one of you to finish it for us, so try to remember each little thing in the story so that you can make up a good ending.

Story text: Billy, who was five years old, and Jo Ann, who was eight, lived with their father, mother, and little baby brother in a neighborhood something like curs right here. Billy and Jo Ann always enjoyed breakfast time at their house. Since father worked hard helping build big tall buildings, he needed a lot to eat in the morning, so mother always got them up early and cooked lots of good things, like bacon, ham, hotcakes, or waffles. Jo Ann helped mother by giving the baby his morning bottle. Billy helped mainly by dressing and getting ready for school mostly by himself. He thought that was pretty good for a kindergarten boy. It took Father a while to shave and get ready for work but he usually finished these chores in time to help Mother set the table. Most of the time Father had to rush away to work as soon as he finished eating, but Billy and Jo Ann had time to clear away the dishes before getting ready for their walk down to the school bus stop.

Billy came home at lunchtime, for he was all through with school by then. That was a special time for him, since he and Mother had lunch all by themselves. After lunch, he generally spent the rest of the time playing with his friend Kim, who lived just two houses away. Jo Ann was the next to get home; she generally started right in on her homework, because you have to work pretty hard when you are in the third grade. But the time both children enjoyed most was when Father came home from work. Billy always made sure that he was home from play by this time. As soon as the car stopped, he would run out toward the driveway, where Father would lift him up on his shoulder and carry him back to the house. Jo Ann usually wanted to tell or show him what she did in school that day. After kissing Mother hello, he would spend some time with them. One of their favorite things to do was to read the comics in the evening paper.

That evening while doing the dishes something happened to Mother. She had hardly touched her food during dinner because she didn't feel very well and afterward she started to shiver and shake all over. Father decided to call Dr. Powell to see what to do. Father hung up the phone and told Billy and Jo Ann, "I have to take Mother to the doctor's office. I'll see if Mrs. Marsh can stay with you while we're gone."

Mrs. Marsh, the next-door neighbor, was able to stay with them. Billy and Jo Ann were worried because their mother had never been this sick before. When Father and Mother returned, the children found out that she had a bad case of the flu and had to stay in bed for at least two days. Mother took some medicine that she and Father had picked up on the way home from the doctor's and went right to bed. Just then the baby started crying and Jo Ann said, "Golly, it's time for his night-time bottle already." Father asked if she could feed him and she said, "Yes, I can feed him if you can heat the bottle on the stove. Mother never lets me do that part." As Father put the pan of water on the stove, he said, "I think I'd better set the alarm a little earlier tomorrow. Things are going to be busy around here with Mother sick."

Next morning Billy and Jo Ann were still sleeping soundly when Father's alarm clock started ringing.

4. At this point the teacher could stop and call for volunteers to complete the story. First-graders will often overlook major points in their efforts to complete stories such as this. The following is a possible reply:

The little boy and girl got up and went downstairs and fixed breakfast. Then the father got up and shaved and came downstairs and they all ate a big breakfast. Then the little boy and girl went to the bus stop and father went to work.

One tactful way to handle this contribution, with its gross omissions, would be to say, "That's not a bad story for the first try, but someone else can probably make up a better ending now that they've heard yours." An ending with a little better quality might go like this:

Billy and Jo Ann got up and dressed very quickly because they knew they had a lot of work to do. Father got dressed very fast too and went right to the stove to warm the baby bottle. Jo Ann fed the baby and Father fixed breakfast and after breakfast Jo Ann helped get Billy off to school. Then Father stayed home with Jo Ann that day and they took care of the baby together.

This ending could stimulate worthwhile class discussion concerning such points as mother's care, which is still overlooked, and the practicality of father's staying home from work. Even first-graders know that this may result in loss of wages. Children at this level can also suggest possible good consequences that might result from mother's illness; for example, children learn how to do more things for themselves.

The teacher's role in a discussion of this type is to structure the discussion to lead the pupils toward and help them identify worthwhile generalizations. The children themselves can provide concrete and valid illustrations if they are provided with the leadership necessary to draw upon their collective experiences.

III. BOYS AND GIRLS—MEN AND WOMEN

Like most other areas of health education, the study of family living and human sexuality involves information and concepts drawn from both the biological and the behavioral sciences. Although there is some overlap in the type of teaching methods appropriate for both types of content, some categorization is possible. Ovulation, menstruation, sperm production, and conception are biological processes and lend themselves to a more traditional or technical approach than topics pertaining to sexual behavior and interpersonal relationships within the family, where student-centered methods are particularly effective. This example deals chiefly with biological information and involves the use of the 16-mm sound film, a very common and a very effective educational aid (see pages 172–175).

Concept

The reproduction of many forms of life, including man, involves the uniting of male and female substances.

Pupils

Developed for fifth-grade pupils of average socioeconomic status; generally recommended for grades 4 through 6.

Technique

Film and discussion.

Preparation of the Class. The better sex education films that are designed for the elementary level generally present basic information in a very simple and clear manner. Thus, it is seldom necessary to prepare the pupils with background information of an anatomical or physiological nature; the films handle this content quite effectively. However, the teacher can greatly improve the quality of the pupils' learning experience by helping develop a proper attitude or approach toward the material contained in the film. One way in which this is accomplished is by including the film as part of a unit of study which begins with topics that are important and relevant but that are of a lower stimulus value than sexual intercourse and conception. A unit might begin with a study of the special care needed for new babies; how fifth-grade boys and girls should typically react to these new arrivals; and what they can do to help. Another typical starting point is the study of the development of typical masculine and feminine interests and personality characteristics that become pronounced in the upper elementary school years. Either of these topics provides a natural approach to the biological aspects of reproduction.

In addition to these advanced preparations, much can be done in the minutes immediately preceding the viewing of the film to ensure a favorable reaction. At this time the teacher should first provide a very brief overview of the content of the film and then by means of a brief discussion or a few preliminary remarks link the content to be presented to the larger issues of the unit. The teacher's preparation for this preliminary segment of the lesson results mainly from a preview of the film. The film preview, which is always a sound practice regardless of the topic, becomes absolutely essential when dealing with the study of human sexuality. The teacher's remarks might sound something like the following:

Yesterday we discussed many of the common differences in the way boys and girls are ordinarily expected to think and act. We found it quite easy to see these differences in play and leisuretime activities and in the household chores that children of your age often do. Although many of these differences seem to result from custom or tradition, the physical differences in the bodies of men and women are also important reasons. This film will show us how and why these physical differences happen.

A somewhat more time-consuming, but more effective, lead-in would be to review the previous day's material with the children in a brief discussion. This would involve asking someone in the class to review the main points that had been covered and permitting others to add any items that had been overlooked. Just before starting the film it is well to remind the children to try to identify and remember things about which they would like to ask questions after the film.

The Follow-up Discussion. Perhaps the most challenging aspect in the use of sex education films for the teacher is the management of the discussion that follows the viewing of films which deal with human conception. Like so many others, this teaching situation is greatly affected by the events immediately preceding it and by the general setting in which it takes place. Was the film properly selected on the basis of content, grade level, and the technical quality of its production? Were the children properly prepared for the content of the film? Did the teacher establish a proper emotional climate for learning? Were the mechanical aspects of the film projection handled with a minimum of distraction? If these questions can be answered in the affirmative, then the teacher will have a good opportunity to guide a productive discussion. Good personal preparation resulting in a reasonable command of the subject matter involved is the main ingredient needed to take full advantage of this situation. However, the anticipation of the type of questions that are likely to arise is another highly useful procedure. The most effective and most obvious way to find out what sort of questions will be asked is to show the film and take one's chances on the first occasion. Many teachers have had to start this way; they experienced many awkward and embarrassing moments, but they generally survived and improved with succeeding groups of pupils in the years that followed. Fortunately the time has passed when the beginning teacher must acquire this information the hard way. Discussion guides accompany most of the good audiovisual aids assigned for sex education. These usually contain background information for the teacher as well as typical questions to expect from one's class. The *Journal of School Health,* in its special issue covering "Growth Patterns and Sex Education," [2] includes a list of commonly asked questions for each grade level. Examples of some of the more difficult questions for grade 5 are the following:

1. Does a sperm have to come from the man? How does this happen?
2. Can a sperm ever get into a woman if she isn't married?

[2] "Growth Patterns and Sex Education," special issue, *Journal of School Health,* Vol. XXVII, No. 5a (May 1967).

3. What if a woman has a baby before she is married?

4. Does the husband have to help to have the baby? [3]

Questions like the preceding require some planning with regard to choice of terms and phrases and what to emphasize. However, the majority of the questions generally require accurate knowledge rather than verbal adroitness in the teacher's response. Examples of these are the following:

1. How can one cell turn into so many?

2. Do boys grow the same way girls do?

3. Why doesn't my brother look like me?

4. What should you do or not do when you menstruate? [4]

The course work involved in one's professional preparation enables one to deal with many such questions; additional information may be provided by the many good sources available for additional study while on the job. Most teachers find that a reasonable investment of time in added personal preparation for their responsibilities in sex education pays handsome rewards in teaching satisfaction. However, in spite of these efforts, questions will arise for which the teacher is unprepared. It is somewhat paradoxical that the teacher who does the best job of creating a good learning environment is the one most likely to stimulate a wide variety of difficult questions from the class. However, such teachers soon develop various strategies for dealing with these questions. Often the questions will be obviously highly technical or not very meaningful to the class in general or even to the questioner. If a child asks, "What color is the medicine used when the mother has a 'spinal' at the hospital?" the teacher may often, but not always, perceive that it was rather lightly asked. It might be answered with a simple, "I'm sorry, I don't know." However, if the child inquires as to the effectiveness of drugs given to lessen the mother's pain, then either the teacher or some member or members of the class should seek an answer from a reliable source if the answer is not immediately available.

Some of the questions that involve value judgments or knowledge that many of the children probably possess are sometimes best turned back to the group. Such questions as, "Will my parents love me just as much when our new baby comes?" or, "How does the mother know when it's time to go to the hospital?" can usually be answered very effectively by pupil volunteers. In these cases the teacher's proper function is to guide the class toward acceptable conclusions. Other questions are likely to be too delicate for many classes to handle. The specific way to handle these questions varies greatly according to the social maturity of the particular class, their previous learning experiences, and the teacher's background and particular style of teaching. The following excerpts from the American Medical Association's *A Story About You* [5] booklet for the upper

[3] Ibid., pp. 31–32.

[4] Ibid.

[5] Martin O. Lerrigo and Helen Southard, *A Story About You* (Chicago: American Medical Association, 1971).

elementary grades illustrates one way to handle some of the more sensitive topics.

Sexual intercourse: At times love that a father and mother feel for each other makes them want to be alone, and to be very close in an act called mating, or sexual intercourse. When they lie close together in a loving embrace, the father's penis becomes erect and can fit into the mother's vagina. Then, if some sperm cells leave the father's penis, they can swim along the vagina in the semen, and can enter the uterus, and swim into the tubes.

Female anatomy: A narrow passage called the vagina connects the uterus with the outside of the body. The outside opening of the vagina is between the legs where it is protected by folds of skin and flesh. The body's opening for passing urine is in front of it, and the opening for bowel movements is some distance in back of it.

Girls and women have ovaries, a uterus, and a vagina. Boys and men do not have these parts of the body.

Male anatomy: When the sperm cells leave the testicles, they go into the part of the body called the penis. It is in front of the testicles, and is shaped something like a thumb. When a baby boy is born, he already has testicles and a penis. Girls and women do not have these parts of the body.

Erection and seminal emission: During these teen-age years, it may happen that a boy's penis becomes stiff and erect, and semen is discharged from it unexpectedly. Sometimes this happens at night while he is asleep. This is called a seminal emission. It is a natural thing to happen, and is just part of the changes that take place during the years when a boy is becoming a man. The ability of the penis to become stiff and erect is important, because a father's penis can fit into a mother's vagina and send out the sperm cells only when it is erect.

These examples are not intended to provide a comprehensive view of content in human sexuality, nor are they recommended as answers appropriate to all classes of fifth-graders. These excerpts do, however, provide an example of an acceptable style and tone for the presentation of content on human sexuality in the upper elementary grades.

IV. THE HEART OF THE MATTER

During the preschool and primary years the child develops a diffuse background of attitudes related to human sexuality. The child at this age probably gives little conscious thought to such specific matters as sexual intercourse. Many children remain ignorant of this act for all or a good part of these early years. However, many of the child's experiences still have important effects. The concern or lack of concern for modesty among members of his family, their attitude toward his instances of genital play, and their attitude toward sex-related words he may use are but a few of the many possible examples. During the upper elementary years children become increasingly concerned with many of the specific erotic aspects of human sexuality. For the majority of the girls and many of the boys, the physical evidence of their developing sexuality arouses natural curiosity about kissing, caressing, petting, and the sex act itself. Many of the boys become concerned about nocturnal emissions and masturbation. Even among the late-maturing pupils, considerable interest develops in these things as a result of their growing knowledge of the full implications of the adult sex role. Although there is considerable merit in covering these topics in a systematic manner through use of films, readings, and class discussion, this "shot-gun" coverage will always leave some individual questions unanswered. These questions must be asked before they can be answered; eliciting these questions is a challenging task.

Concept
The sex drive is an innate and powerful force which is related to human pleasure and reproduction.

Pupils
Developed for sixth-grade pupils of average socioeconomic status; generally recommended for grades 4 through 6.

Techniques
The question box and related techniques.

Ideally the pupil-teacher relationship should be such that the children will approach the teacher openly with their questions. Although one should always strive to achieve this high degree of rapport, it is helpful to provide alternative means of communication. The question box is perhaps the most widely used supplementary device for soliciting questions of a personal nature. The basic mechanics of this device are extremely simple. A slot is cut in a small wooden or cardboard box. This "ballot-type" box is placed in some accessible place in the classroom and children are encouraged to write questions of interest and place them unsigned in the box. This is indeed a simple procedure, and there are certain important ways to increase its effectiveness.

Emotional Environment. Like most other teaching procedures, the value of the question-box technique depends directly on the existence of good rapport between teacher and pupils. The use of the question box is no substitute for the difficult and thoughtful measures required to develop a climate of trust and freedom of expression within the classroom. If this does not exist, then little will be gained by use of this device. The truly meaningful questions will not be asked. If it does, then it will provide a useful complement to other important aspects of the family living unit.

Classroom Acceptance. One common characteristic of effective sex education programs is their natural acceptance as part of the regular school curriculum. Within the self-contained elementary school classroom, the teacher should normally avoid treating sex education and the procedures and techniques used in its presentation as something special. The question box is no exception. It is best not to install it in the classroom as a special adjunct to the family-living unit. Children also have personal questions to ask on other health topics; physical growth, cigarette smoking, and parental drinking problems are examples of other topics with potential for personal questions. Ideally, the question box should be established in the classroom at the beginning of the school year and be made available for questions on any topic.

Organizing the Questions. Advanced screening and planning are the key to the smooth handling of the questions submitted. Sometime prior to the health lesson the teacher should read the questions carefully and organize them. Some of the questions may fit logically into the content that is already scheduled for presentation. These questions might be best answered within the context of regularly planned activities. Others might be more appropriately answered during future presentations. If no more than two or three days are involved, then it would probably be best to wait until they can blend naturally into the program. Others that are related to content already covered or to content not normally included in the yearly program can be answered in a special presentation, usually at the beginning or the end of the regular health lesson. Occasionally pupils will submit questions designed to be needlessly "shocking" or obscene. The motivation for such questions often results from an "I-dare-you" attitude within peer groups or from simple curiosity concerning the teacher's reaction. Very often the teacher can revise the terminology and provide useful answers to these questions of doubtful sincerity. Extreme examples in this category sometimes must be ignored completely. Although this step may sometimes be necessary, it should not be taken lightly, for these questions often represent the outward manifestations of serious concerns that the pupil cannot express in any other way.

The Answers. Many of the questions of a particularly sensitive or technical nature probably should be answered directly by the teacher in conventional style. However, others related to content previously covered or information already in the possession of many of the children should be directed to the class. Many of these lead to fruitful discussions that sometimes range into other sensitive areas of importance.

ALTERNATE TECHNIQUES

The question box is just one of several possible techniques available for stimulating meaningful questions. The technique or techniques most appropriate for a particular class depend both on individual teaching styles and on the characteristics of the individual class and situation.

The Personal Essay. The assignment of an essay on topics related to family living or human sexuality can have many advantages. The pupils are provided with the opportunity to give some quiet and thoughtful consideration to important issues and to organize their ideas into some logical order. If the assignment is made near the end of the family-living unit, then many accurate facts and wholesome concepts may be reinforced in the process of writing them down. These papers also provide a rich source of information for the teacher in her efforts to familiarize herself with the values, concerns, and patterns of thought characteristic of her pupils. The careful reading of these papers will often reveal important personal problems that call for private consultation with the child involved. These papers may also reveal widespread misconceptions or concerns that merit the use of class time for specific attention to these topics.

Some examples of promising topics follow:

"The Kind of Teen-ager I Hope to Be"
"The Kind of Parent I Hope to Be"
"The Way Boys Should Act Toward Girls" (Boys)
"The Way Girls Should Act Toward Boys" (Girls)

The mechanical details of the assignment, attention to spelling and handwriting, and so on, should be treated as they might be in a typical assignment in language arts. The opportunities for correlating the essay with the regular activities of this area are obvious.

Personal Guidance. Children often wish to discuss questions that they feel are embarrassing with an adult whom they consider knowledgeable and sympathetic. Although the parents would seem to be the logical ones for them to approach, it has been observed that children quite often feel the need to discuss sensitive matters with someone outside their immediate family. The reasons for this are complex and not well understood; however, this preference is found among children who have a good relationship with their parents as well as among those who do not. The classroom teacher can provide a valuable service by taking the few simple steps necessary to function effectively in this role.

Beyond the basic need for good rapport is the need to be available. Generally, the normal school routine requires or encourages the teacher to be at his desk for thirty minutes or so before and after the regular hours of class. This provides an opportunity for individuals or small groups of pupils to present personal problems. To be really available, a teacher must be a good listener. This means, among other things, remaining alert for serious concerns that are camouflaged by a frivolous or indirect approach. It is well to regard every question as important until proved otherwise. When a serious discussion materializes, the teacher should obtain as much information as is practical, assess the emotional tone of the child, and make a judgment on the disposition of the matter. It may be obvious that a little information and support is all that is needed. Other cases may be serious enough to merit some continued attention. A good approach for these is to tell the pupil, "Be sure and let me know if this keeps worrying you." Occasionally, a problem will be encountered that requires referral to appropriate agencies or personnel. Some medical problems as well as such things as sexual molestations and unduly severe parental punishment fall in this latter category.

Resource Persons. The use of resource persons in any area of the health curriculum has obvious value in terms of the special expertise such persons may bring to the classroom. One additional advantage is that children may ask questions of a comparative outsider that they are reluctant to ask of their own teacher. Generally, the reverse is true; children will ask those with whom they are most familiar. But in some cases pupils show the same reticence toward discussing some personal matter with their teacher that they show with their parents. Other pupils may simply respond better to the particular approach that a school nurse, physician, or other resource person might adopt. Sometimes these questions are asked in the open classroom; in other cases these individuals are approached privately if they are available. It is well to recognize this particular role of the resource person and remain alert for any opportunity to make such persons available to one's pupils.

V. THE RULES OF THE GAME

A young adolescent's entry into the difficulties of dating and other activities with the opposite sex can be a difficult experience for both parent and child. In one sense, their objectives and expectations for this enterprise are similar; both the adolescent and his parents want him to develop social competencies that will contribute to his overall adjustment and maturity. However, when it becomes necessary to spell out just what these goals mean and what specific types of experiences are needed to achieve them, the agreement ends. The parent emphasizes the development of skills that will lead to successful courtship and marriage at some future time; the adolescent emphasizes the development of "cool" (or whatever the current term may be) and skills for future adventures. The adolescent lacks the long-range view of the parent, and the parent lacks understanding of the importance of current modes of behavior within adolescent society. The disagreements are most apparent between individual parents and their teen-age children when specific issues are involved. Very often groups of parents or groups of teen-agers can collectively develop and express much more reasonable views than can individuals. This example calls for the development of a code of behavior for dating among junior high students.

Concept

Adolescent dating activities and other heterosexual social activities typically serve important functions in the process of personality development.

Students

This example was developed for eighth-grade co-ed students with average academic ability and socioeconomic status; however, with modifications it may be applied to any secondary grade.

Technique

Committee work.

One of the immediate objectives of any unit on teen-age dating is to encourage the acceptance of reasonable standards of behavior for social activities of various kinds. These standards will be much more acceptable to adolescents if they are developed by their peers rather than imposed upon them by adults. Therefore, it becomes quite logical to select a group of mature students who have some status among their age-mates and to provide them with the opportunity to work seriously on this task. A project of this type could be conducted within a single classroom group or throughout all the health classes of a particular grade level; in an activity that goes beyond the concept of a classroom teaching technique, a school-wide committee can be used. The following suggestions illustrate one generally useful approach at the classroom level:

1. The committee should be appointed and started early in the unit that includes a study of dating procedures, but not before some introductory information on this topic has been presented. Students need to get some idea of the scope of the topic before they are asked to volunteer for a project related to it; an early start is needed if the committee is to finish its work and report to the class before the end of the unit.

2. Two of the most common ways to establish a committee of this type are (a) teacher selection from among those who volunteer, and (b) a classroom election. Both procedures have their advantages and disadvantages; the choice should be determined by local factors. In any case, work for the selection of committee members who are generally popular with their classmates, reasonable in their judgment, and relatively mature in their social development. Although it will seldom be possible to have every committee member meet these criteria, they represent practical goals for the collective nature of the committee.

3. Four to eight students usually represent the best committee size for effective work; membership should be divided equally among the sexes.

4. The committee should receive some help in arranging its meetings. In some modern schools these meetings might take place during class time in special conference rooms that adjoin the classroom or form part of the library complex. Homeroom or activity periods are often a good possibility; some groups may decide to meet in the classroom before or after school.

5. The first order of business should be the election of a chairman and, in most cases, a recording secretary. The next step consists of outlining the scope of their assignment, that is, spelling out specifically what they plan to accomplish. Typical subtopics for their report might include acceptable age ranges for dating, activities while on dates, days of the week and times of the day, transportation arrangements, dating patterns (going steady, double-dating, and so on), and the parent's role in supervision and chaperoning.

6. Once the task is accurately defined, a plan for gathering pertinent information needs to be established. The committee should secure some guidance from the teacher for this task. Appropriate sources include (a) magazine articles, (b) booklets designed for the teen-ager, (c) interviews with parents, (d) interviews of older students, (e) surveys of peer opinion, (f) a review of similar codes of other schools.

7. Once the committee has gathered its information it should prepare a report for presentation to the class. During this presentation the report should be thoroughly discussed; also modifications when needed should be made on the basis of majority opinion.

8. Further use of the resulting code should depend upon its quality and the nature of the school situation in which it was developed. Even if the project terminates with the class report, the students will have benefited a good deal through their participation in its development. Other possible uses would include its presentation to other classes for their

consideration or to a student government group as a possible stimulus for school-wide action on this issue.

VI. WHAT'S GOING ON AROUND HERE?

The ninth-grade is one of the more hectic school years for many students insofar as heterosexual adjustment is concerned. Many of the more mature girls will be dating very regularly and once in a while one will be engaged or think she is engaged. At the other end of the scale, many of the late-maturing boys will have had no dates and will be showing little concern about the situation. In between these extremes we find boys and girls at all stages of social development, many of whom are very greatly concerned about this phase of their life. As adults we know that most of these "worriers" are worrying unduly about behavior that is perfectly normal for their age but that a small minority do indeed have genuine problems that may have a detrimental effect on their total pattern of life. Classroom learning activities can do little for the really serious cases of arrested social development that have taken on pathological overtones; however, a good program can do much to prevent borderline cases from worsening and can do much to improve the adjustment of the "low-normals." Activities that provide the adolescent with some degree of perspective as to the various patterns of social behavior exhibited by his age-mates can often do much to reduce his anxiety. In this example, ninth-graders accomplish this with a well-conducted survey of their classmates' social and recreational activities within their family and with their peers.

Concept

Proper expression and control of the sex drive contribute to one's general well-being.

Students

Developed for ninth-grade co-ed classes of average academic and socioeconomic status, recommended for grades 9 through 12.

Technique

Student survey.

Polls and surveys are viewed with considerable suspicion by the general public and this suspicion is often well founded. A careful examination of the procedures used in many surveys and the conclusions drawn show that this poor reputation is often deserved. But this negative feature actually presents a strong argument for providing young people with some actual experience in the use of this much abused device. Through their attempts to conduct a survey they will have the opportunity to become aware of the limitations in the type of information that this technique can provide. Also, they may develop an understanding of the careful procedures that are needed to conduct a survey properly and thus learn to distinguish between surveys conducted by trained researchers as opposed to those conducted or sponsored by advertising agencies.

The first step in the conduct of any survey is the selection of the type of information to be gathered. In the present example we are dealing with social maturity and adjustment, with emphasis on heterosexual activities and their substitutes. Typical subcategories to survey might include such behavior as (1) extent and nature of one's solitary activities, (2) extent and nature of social activities within one's family, (3) extent and nature of activities with one's friends of the same sex, (4) incidental or informal activities with the opposite sex, (5) extent and nature of one's dating activities. The task of the student surveyors is to devise tightly worded questions to solicit information from within these general categories. The teacher's role in guiding this project consists of helping the students use the best possible procedures within the practical limitations of their situation and leading the students toward a cautious interpretation of their findings in accordance with these limitations. Both of these tasks are highly important to the validity of this type of learning experience. The following are some specific recommendations as to how they might be accomplished:

1. Because the quality of the learning experience for the total classroom group depends in large part upon the effectiveness of those particular students engaged in the project, this activity is quite properly restricted to the more capable students. Four to six students would seem to be about the right number to provide enough manpower for the committee without making it unwieldy.

2. The committee's first task should consist of searching the library for any possible information about (a) the results of similar studies conducted by trained researchers, and (b) examples or descriptions of surveying procedures. The sources in the latter category can provide help in the form of both good survey questions and ideas for the selection of methods and techniques for the conduct of the survey.

3. Following a review of this information, the committee's next step is the construction of an interview form. Such a form generally consists of a one- or two-page list of questions with appropriate spaces for recording the answers. These questions would normally be based on the basic behavior categories described—that is, solitary activities, family activities, and so on. After the interview form has been devised, each member of the committee should try it out on two or three subjects and then meet again to compare their results and make any revisions necessary to improve the clarity of the questions.

4. Next, plan how many subjects will be interviewed and who they shall be. Ten to fifteen subjects is a reasonable number for each member to interview. Thus an average-sized group can cover from forty to sixty subjects. Use some random system for selecting subjects. One method would involve assigning every ninth-grader a number and then selecting the subjects by a lottery-type procedure. Another simple procedure that is acceptable for this type of project is to select every tenth or every twentieth student from a list of the total class. Advise the investigators to conduct the actual interviews in private or semiprivate to minimize the number of "show-off" answers.

5. After the interviews have been completed, the committee should tabulate the results and prepare a report to the class. In the report the

highlights of the findings should be presented in a conversational style of delivery; also, any interesting comparisons with other studies found during their library work should be reported. A long recital of percentages should be avoided. Use statistics only when needed to support generalizations or conclusions.

6. During the class discussion following the report, the teacher usually should guide the class toward a cautious interpretation of the results. Encourage the point of view that "this information can give a general idea of the social activities of our students, but remember that it is even difficult for professional investigators to establish specific facts and trends." It is also generally a good idea to call attention to diversity or variability in the results if these are present. Realization of the wide range of "normal" behavior can serve to provide reassurance to many adolescents who are concerned with the appropriateness of their social pattern.

VII. LOVE AND/OR SEX?

Individuals have experiences. Out of these may come certain general guides to behavior—values—which tend to give direction to life.[6]

Most communities these days recognize the school's responsibility to provide young people with basic information concerning human reproduction. However, there is far less agreement concerning the school's role with respect to sexual attitudes and behavior patterns. Most professional educators and the large majority of our general citizenry feel that it is inappropriate for teachers to "moralize," that is, to attempt the direct indoctrination of specific ethical positions. In any but the most ideologically homogeneous communities, this practice can readily lead to undesirable conflicts between the teachers' version of morality and those of individual families. Even if complete agreement could somehow be achieved, the practice of "moralizing" can produce indifference or possibly a "behavioral backlash" on the part of students who often hear too much preaching from too many sources. Although most teachers know that they should not moralize, many of them do and maintain that they are teaching values rather than morals. They feel that somehow the use of different terminology makes their actions more acceptable. This practice is perhaps even more damaging to the real spirit of education than that of the outright offenders.

In matters of sexuality as with other areas of human conduct, the teacher's primary task is to help young people identify and evaluate their personal values. This should naturally lead to some modifying of old values and formulating of new ones; however, the teacher should place emphasis on the *process* of value development, not the *content* of the resulting values. Values, by definition, involve an emotional element and this factor is particularly strong when dealing with such topics as sexual activity and love. The approach presented in this example shows one way that ado-

---

[6] Louis E. Raths, Merril Harmin, and Sidney B. Simon, "Helping Children to Clarify Values," *NEA Journal*, Vol. 56, No. 7 (October 1967), p. 12.

lescents might be provided with an opportunity to clarify their feelings and understandings in this sensitive area. Although it is based on an essentially cognitive activity, the discussion that it will stimulate can provide the opportunity for the students to deal with the topic of sexuality with the degree of openness and frankness that they feel ready to handle.

Concept
Love and affection are complex human emotions that require substantial living experience for their full understanding.

Students
Developed for eleventh-grade co-ed classes with average to above-average academic ability; recommended for average and above-average twelfth-graders also.

Technique
Critical reading.

The concept of love and its relationship to sexual intercourse and lesser degrees of sexual activity are topics that textbooks (even special supplements and booklets) generally do not cover thoroughly or convincingly. For material bearing on these topics many health teachers have turned to good novelists or those authorities in the behavioral sciences with an appealing writing style. One good example of a selection that many senior high schoolers could profitably read is found in the following excerpt from Erich Fromm's well-known work *The Art of Loving.*

ERICH FROMM ON LOVE AND SEX

Line

Sexual desire aims at fusion—and is by no means only a physical
2 appetite, the relief of a painful tension. But sexual desire can be stimulated by the anxiety of aloneness, by the wish to conquer or be con-
4 quered, by vanity, by the wish to hurt and even to destroy, as much as it can be stimulated by love. It seems that sexual desire can easily blend
6 with and be stimulated by any strong emotion, of which love is only one. Because sexual desire is in the minds of most people coupled with the
8 idea of love, they are easily misled to conclude that they love each other when they want each other physically. Love can inspire the wish
10 for sexual union; in this case the physical relationship is lacking in greediness, in a wish to conquer or to be conquered, but is blended with
12 tenderness. If the desire for physical union is not stimulated by love, if erotic love is not also brotherly love, it never leads to union in
14 more than an orgiastic, transitory sense. Sexual attraction creates, for the moment, the illusion of union, yet without love this "union"
16 leaves strangers as far apart as they were before—sometimes it makes them ashamed of each other, or even makes them hate each other,
18 because when the illusion has gone they feel their estrangement even more markedly than before. Tenderness is by no means, as Freud
20 believed, a sublimation of the sexual instinct; it is the direct outcome

of brotherly love, and exists in physical as well as in non-physical
22   forms of love.[7]

There are several acceptable procedures for handling the details of
this type of assignment. The following are some general suggestions that
apply to most situations:

1. Usually the most practical way to bring this type of material to
students is by use of a duplicating process. This procedure is routinely
followed by teachers in many fields even though it is in technical violation
of copyright laws. Those who wish to avoid the risk this involves may write
the publisher for written permission covering the use of the desired material. Some school libraries make classroom sets of paperback novels
available or place several copies on reserve, thereby making them accessible to large numbers of students.

2. Appropriate preparation is essential if the class is to react constructively to the type of material presented in this example. Ideally, these
eleventh-graders would have developed a factual background in human
sexuality as a result of a comprehensive program beginning at the elementary level. In any event, this type of material is best presented toward the
end of teaching units on human sexuality in classes where good class
morale and rapport with the teacher prevail.

3. A class with a good background could profitably discuss this
material in a "spot situation," wherein the excerpt is simply distributed and
discussed after they have had a few moments to read it. However, the
quality of the learning experience would be greatly improved by providing
more extensive preparation for the class discussion. A more ambitious
procedure would involve (a) distributing the excerpts as homework during
the class meeting preceding the discussion, (b) beginning with buzz
groups on the day of the discussion (see pages 162–163), and (c) discussing the excerpt with the total class after the buzz session.

4. The task of discussion leadership in this instance varies little
from that of similar discussions involving textbook material. Some general
recommendations follow:

   a. The teacher should open the discussion by soliciting comments
      of a general nature on the most interesting or provocative points
      of the excerpt. Examples of workable lead-ins are, "Do you agree
      with Fromm's basic point of view?" or, "What points seem most
      accurate or truthful about this material?"
   b. The teacher should be ready to bring up specific points for dis-
      cussion after the students have had a chance to discuss the items
      of high interest. Also be prepared for questions about terms and
      concepts the students may not understand, for example, Fromm's
      brotherly love, Freud's *sublimation,* or the phrase *orgiastic, tran-
      sitory sense.*

[7] Erich Fromm, *The Art of Loving* (New York: Harper & Row, 1956), pp.
54–55.

c. Toward the end of the planned discussion it would be well to lead the class toward a consensus on the main points; during this process care must be taken to protect the rights of those with minority views.

VIII. MARRIAGE HOLLYWOOD STYLE

One of the factors that are often regarded as being responsible for hasty and ill-advised marriages is the so-called myth of romantic love. Although young people are often warned against placing undue emphasis on this factor during courtship, they seldom have an opportunity to examine the specific reasons that support this point of view. One way to meet this particular educational need is to analyze carefully some common examples of romantic love as found in the mass media. This can be done with popular novels, romance magazines, and television dramas. The example here deals with movies.

Concept

Many factors affect the overall quality and effectiveness of the marriage relationship.

Students

Developed for twelfth-grade co-ed students with average academic ability and socioeconomic status; also recommended for eleventh grade.

Technique

Committee work.

The example described here was first suggested in a special edition of the *Journal of School Health.* The recommendations were as follows:

Appoint a committee to analyze the last ten movies seen by any of the members in terms of the following:

a. number of instances in which the hero or heroine fell in love at first sight.
b. number of instances in which couples in love behaved in a manner which they would consider appropriate.
c. number of instances in which couples in love behaved in a manner which their parents would consider appropriate.
d. number of instances in which couples contemplating marriage would, in the committee's judgment, be likely to have a happy marriage.
Ask the committee to discuss the criteria they used in making the judgments involved in the analyses.[8]

Although this activity would hold the interest of most senior high school groups regardless of their background in family-living and sex education, it would be a particularly useful experience for groups that had a reasonably good background in family-living topics. Adolescents who

[8] "Growth Patterns and Sex Education," *Journal of School Health,* Vol. XXXVII, No. 5a (May 1967), pp. 117–118.

had had previous opportunities in the classroom to deal with the concept of love (as in example VIII, pp. 267–270) and to struggle with the distinction between infatuation and genuine love could, in discussing item (a), apply what they had learned to specific situations in the films. Items (b) and (c) refer to behavior during dating and courtship and would provide particularly good discussion material for classroom groups who grappled with such tasks as the problem of establishing dating standards as in example V (pp. 263–265). The key to good discussion leadership as applied to these items would be to get down to the real reasons for terming behavior appropriate or inappropriate. For example, "Why is a certain type of behavior inadvisable?" "What type of harmful consequences might occur?" "How does the risk compare with the favorable outcomes that might result?" This would be more useful than merely comparing the conduct observed with arbitrary standards.

Of the four subtopics listed, item (d) offers the best opportunities for bringing a greater proportion of "firm evidence" as opposed to value judgments into discussion. Considerably more scientific investigation has been directed toward identifying the factors related to successful marriages than toward determining appropriate dating behavior. Although this is certainly not the type of problem that lends itself to scientific proof, there is some solid ground to serve as a starting point. Blood and Wolfe,[9] for instance, have identified nine areas in which significant disagreements often occur between husbands and wives, specifically,

1. Money	6. Roles
2. Children	7. Religion
3. Recreation	8. Politics
4. Personality	9. Sex
5. In-laws	

In the discussions of the film couples, these nine factors could serve quite well as a means of structuring the discussion. Did the prospective spouses have any opportunity to become acquainted with each other's views concerning these areas? In which areas might there be disagreements? How serious might these disagreements be?

Although the example here deals with commercial movies, the same general format could be applied to other media. In many situations classroom films, television dramas, short stories, and novels or excerpts from novels would serve quite well. The opportunities for occasional correlation with English classes should also be kept in mind. Very often the same novel is assigned to total grade levels, or several sections in one grade level, thus providing many students with a common assignment that might be profitably discussed in a family-living or human-sexuality unit during the health class.

[9] Robert O. Blood, Jr., and Donald M. Wolfe, *Husbands and Wives: The Dynamics of Married Living* (New York: Free Press, 1960), p. 247.

REFERENCES

Burt, John S., and Linda Brower. *Education for Sexuality*. Philadelphia: W. B. Saunders Company, 1970.

Epstein, Charlotte. *Affective Subjects In the Classroom: Exploring Race, Sex, and Drugs*. Scranton, Pa.: Intext Educational Publishers, 1972.

Kilander, H. Frederick. *Sex Education in the Schools*. New York: Macmillan Publishing Co., Inc., 1970.

Rees, Floyd D. "Teaching the Valuing Process in Sex Education," *School Health Review*, Vol. 3, No. 2 (March–April 1972), pp. 2–4.

13 ■ DRUG EDUCATION I: FOUNDATIONS

The use of psychoactive substances in the form of alcohol, marijuana, the opiates, and stimulants such as the cocaine of the coca leaf, historically has constituted both a blessing and curse for mankind. The use of alcohol to encourage feelings of well-being and revelry extends back beyond the beginning of historical records; the ancient Greeks used opium in oral forms for the relief of pain, and these and other beneficial uses have traditionally been accompanied by equally detrimental abuses. The study of man's past involvement with mind-altering drugs brings to light a fascinating kaleidoscope of issues and events ranging from the triumph of anesthesia to the tragedies of alcoholism and heroin addiction. Most of these issues are, of course, still with us; little seems to have changed, yet the events of the recent past, perhaps the last ten years or so, represent what may come to be known as a unique turning point in American attitude and practices regarding this persistent aspect of life.

Since the middle 1960s the public has witnessed and endured a series of events and reactions to events that have combined to produce years of turmoil comparable to the prohibition era of the twenties and thirties. Some of the highlights of this recent period include:

- The blatant display of illegal drug use in campus demonstrations and rock festivals.
- The spread of marijuana and heroin use from city ghettos to middle- and upper-class suburban and rural areas.
- The extension of drug abuse problems into public school populations and downward into lower grade levels.
- The identification of the abuse of a legal substance, alcohol, as a problem ranking in seriousness with heroin abuse.

273

- The rise in popularity of somewhat exotic treatment modalities such as "self-help" Synanon-type communities, and methadone maintenance programs.
- The implementation of a rather massive drug educational effort in the public schools and the mass media.
- The use of periodic, extensive drug law enforcement campaigns at local, state, and national levels.
- The advent of emotionally charged public debates on such issues as decriminalizing or legalizing marijuana, executing "pushers," and allowing 18-year-olds to purchase alcohol.

A NEW AWARENESS

There have been many agonizing problems related to these events, and like most individual bouts of disease, this societal illness is partially the result of external agents—the drugs themselves—and partially self-inflicted by public overreaction and panic. A death from a heroin overdose or an alcohol-induced traffic accident is inherently tragic, but the blighting of a young person's life with a criminal record because of relatively innocuous drug experimentation is tragic only because society chooses to make it so. In some cases expensive law enforcement activities have served only to raise the going price for illegal drugs with a consequent fattening of the pusher's profits and an increase in drug-related burglaries and shoplifting to cover the user's added costs. The only identifiable result of many spectacular educational programs in public schools has been to heighten student interest in drugs and increase youthful experimentation. Often the treatment has produced as many problems as the disease.

A Calmer Period

Fortunately this turmoil has been followed by a period of moderating trends both in terms of actual drug abuse and in public reaction to the general problem. Because of the unreliable nature of the methods of estimating users, it is always dangerous to generalize on the extent of drug use, but this latest wave of abuse appears to have reached its peak and settled down to a relatively steady though still disturbing level. Also, because of increased sophistication, sheer exhaustion, or some combination of these and other factors, the general public seems less prone to overreact. News of the latest drug problem or craze fails to produce the panicky response common to the late sixties. We appear to have entered a calmer period characterized by both (1) grudging acceptance of the fact that drug abuse is here to stay—that it will be a significant problem for the foreseeable future, and (2) realization that society is still intact and functioning about as well as it ever has—that it seems to be enduring this latest threat to its fragmented integrity.

DISAPPOINTING RESULTS. Looking at the first of these points a bit more closely we find that after a decade of intensive educational efforts that were primarily abstinence-oriented, there is, if anything, more rather than less drug use among young people.[1] During this same period law enforcement efforts were characterized by expanded narcotics squads and sophisticated undercover techniques, yet the amount of illegal use continued to grow. Kaplan, in his *Marijuana: The New Prohibition*, asks us to shift our perspective backwards a bit historically and consider the rather dismal failure of our efforts to prohibit alcohol and cautions that we will do little better with marijuana.[2]

UNFAIR ASSESSMENTS. There are many persons who seek to use these observations to brand both drug education and law enforcement effort as failures, but this extreme view is as unrealistic as were the original expectations that accompanied the launching of these efforts. If we should give the police unlimited support in terms of the resources at their command and the latitude of their action, they might indeed reduce drug abuse to an insignificant level. Likewise if we should give the educators free reign in terms of staff, time allotments, and full use of the latest in behavior modification techniques, they too might "solve" the drug problem. But the simple facts are that neither of these groups is going to receive anything close to the massive support that might produce some sort of solution, much to the relief of most thoughtful persons. The current trend in both fields is toward retrenchment rather than expansion. There are other topics in the health curriculum that deserve equal attention; there are other crimes against which we need protection.

COEXISTENCE. If drug abuse is a thoroughly established part of American life, why are we not being overwhelmed by this unstoppable menace? Well, perhaps we are. The evidence that we can coexist with this problem is not insurmountable. However, there is considerable cause for hope. As the evidence regarding drug abuse continues to accumulate, beverage alcohol seems to be emerging as potentially the most harmful drug. Although this is disconcerting, it at least tends to reduce the problem to understandable dimensions. We know that alcohol can cause serious problems, but alcohol problems have been with us since the beginning of our society; even though the various statistical indices continue to rise each year, this familiar enemy is losing it's ability to panic us into self-defeating policies. Narcotic problems should not be taken lightly, but America has endured them at least since Civil War days. And they are not new to middle-class society. The Harrison Narcotic Act of 1914 was prompted in large

---

[1] Richard H. DeLone, "The Ups and Downs of Drug-Abuse Education," *Saturday Review of Education*, Sept. 11, 1952, p. 28.

[2] John Kaplan, *Marijuana: The New Prohibition* (New York: Pocket Books, 1971).

part by the presence of more than a quarter million addicts, many of whom were respectable citizens who purchased their drug, laudanum (an opium derivative), from their local apothecary or general store. Now after 60-odd years of federal law enforcement we seem to be about where we started; both society and drug addiction have survived.

But what about the infiltration of pot, pills, acid, and other exotic drugs into the mainstream of modern American life? Despite the doomsayers, we seem destined to survive these assaults as well, mainly because the large majority of these new drug users, like most alcohol users, manage to avoid self-destructive patterns of use. In 1968 Harvard psychologist Kenneth Keniston classified campus users into tasters, seekers, and heads, with only the latter incurring adverse behavioral effects from their drug use.[3] In this same year one of the more comprehensive studies on drug use in the public school population was conducted in Portland, Oregon.[4] It yielded figures for any use of marijuana of 24.9 per cent and 12.1 per cent for high school senior boys and girls respectively; comparable figures of 9.5 per cent and 5.0 per cent were reported for heroin use.[5] However the figures for 16 or more instances of use were much lower; the figures for heroin were 1.4 per cent and 0.3 per cent on this basis. More recently the National Commission on Marijuana and Drug Abuse determined that only one-third of an estimated 24 million persons who have tried marijuana continue to use it with any regularity, and of these only 500,000 (2 per cent of the total) use it heavily.

Although it is understandably disconcerting to find drug problems within the public schools, it appears that, as is the case with adults, there are more users than true abusers in the school population. In 1964 Maddox and McCall conducted a landmark study on teen-age drinking practices and found that the majority of drinkers in this group avoided serious problems; where alcohol-related problems did occur, a cause-and-effect relationship was not apparent.[6] In these cases alcohol abuse seemed to complicate behavior prompted by other factors. The comprehensive Portland study also surveyed the use of alcohol and found the incidence to be quite high with approximately 9 out of every 10 high school students reporting at least some contact with this substance; however, this high use was apparently not accompanied by a high rate of alcohol-related behavior problems. In a

[3] Kenneth Keniston, "Heads and Seekers: Drugs on Campus, Counter-Cultures and American Society," *The American Scholar*, XXXVIII, No. 1 (Winter 1968–69), United Chapters of Phi Beta Kappa, 1968.

[4] Kit G. Johnson, et al., "Survey of Adolescent Drug Use I—Sex and Grade Distribution," *American Journal of Public Health*, Vol. 61, No. 12 (December 1971), p. 2421.

[5] Ibid., p. 2425.

[6] George L. Maddox and B. C. McCall, *Drinking Among Teenagers: A Social Interpretation of Alcohol Use by High School Students* (New Brunswick, N.J.: Rutgers Center of Alcohol Studies, 1964).

study of high school use of drugs other than alcohol, Matchett found some-what parallel results. He studied a sample of 81 students and concluded that

there were two very different categóries of people who were using drugs in this school. One group was using them more heavily and seemed to fit the stereotype of an individual on the fringe of society. The other group was apparently only experimenting with drugs or using them socially, and were in fact more secure, inquisitive, and active than were their non-using peers.[7]

These results and observations illustrate a key point needed to put drug problems in proper perspective. Drug abuse more often contributes to or intensifies existing personal problems than it serves as a basic cause of such problems. If all drugs were somehow removed from the lives of Kenis-ton's campus heads, Maddox and McCall's alcohol abusers, or Matchett's high school drug abusers, they would still be people with serious problems. But in most cases, of course, the problems would become more manageable in the absence of drugs.

From all indications it appears that the problem of drug abuse will not be solved within the foreseeable future nor is it likely to show any great expansion. Although some recent surveys have shown sharply higher rates of alcohol abuse among children and teen-agers, these phenomena seem to represent more a shift in drug popularity within the same problem-ridden portion of the young population rather than any large increase in total abusers. Many of today's young adolescents who in previous years would have been attracted to pills and heroin are now finding beer and wine easier to obtain and less likely to produce serious encounters with law enforce-ment authorities. In another year or two we will undoubtedly be reading of some new threatening pattern of drug use, as young abusers find still differ-ent ways of expressing their deep-rooted problems. In short, what was once wildly epidemic now seems stubbornly endemic. The drug problem is still serious but it is now seen as one of several important adolescent problems rather than as the single overwhelming menace it once appeared to be.

Life in a World of Drugs

So it appears that drug abuse is a chronic social problem with historical roots and one that promises to extend into the indefinite future. It is not a fatal and overwhelming infection but a parasite that seems too clever to kill its host. More than ever before, drugs and drug-related issues promise to remain a significant aspect of the personal environment of every Ameri-can. The "pusher" with his wares, the drug advertiser with his promises, the physician with his prescription pad, the corner tavern with its fellow-

---

[7] William Foster Matchett, M.D., "Who Uses Drugs? A Study in a Suburban Public High School," *The Journal of School Health*, Vol. XLI, No. 2 (February 1971).

ship and cheer, and the backyard marijuana patch seem destined to survive our various efforts at eradication and control.

As human beings we live in a world of bacteria—some very helpful, some very pathogenic, and others of little significance. Our systems generally learn to adjust to this environmental factor and learn to live in harmony in a world of microorganisms. In a like manner most people have adjusted to life in a world of drugs and have to respond to drug-related situations in a way that achieves satisfaction within the context of his life-style and value system. Individuals who display apparently successful patterns of adjustment may vary from the devout Christian Scientist who eschews coffee, cigarettes, and the physician's medications to the stereotype member of the intelligentsia who, from time to time participates freely in cocktail and pot parties, and has no compunctions about receiving a little "psychoactive" help now and then from his doctor. Most of us feel more comfortable at some point on the continuum in between these two extremes; however, regardless of our position we all have educational needs regarding this significant aspect of American culture.

THE ROLE OF THE SCHOOL

Society's scenario of action, reaction, and new awareness was accompanied for the most part by parallel changes in the schools. The school personnel of all types of teachers, school nurses, and administrators were caught unawares in the middle 1960s by a rapidly escalating drug problem; they responded with massive programs, and while the problems appeared to have subsided, there was little evidence that these program efforts were of much value. Particularly discouraging was the consistent evidence that drug education not only failed to reduce the number of users but in some cases tended to increase them. Now, with the benefit of hindsight, we can see that this problem was partially a real one, as it reflected poorly planned and poorly presented programs, and partially an artificial one as it reflected the use of a false criterion for evaluating the success of these programs. Statistics regarding the number of users are not all that meaningful, since they treat both the one-time experimenter and the heavily dependent abuser on the same terms. Even data on the amount and frequency are not without serious limitations because the degree of exposure to a drug does not necessarily reflect the nature of its total impact on the individual's effectiveness. And on this latter point the evidence, pro or con, is extremely sparse.

New Principles

Although the better school programs of both drug education and health service related to drugs have changed in many ways in response to earlier failures and disappointments, three of these new trends or principles merit special attention.

DRAWING A DISTINCTION BETWEEN USE AND ABUSE. The earlier programs were for the most part abstinent-oriented in that they emphasized the distinction between simply use and nonuse rather than between sensible, constructive use and excessive or immoderate use. They saw the educator's main task as one of minimizing the use of alcohol and illegal drugs. All illegal drugs were uniformly bad; anything prescribed by a physician was O.K. regardless of the circumstances; the social drinker was regarded as an apprentice alcoholic; drug advertising was something to be studied purely as a matter of protecting the consumer's pocketbook.

Recently, however, the schools are coming to realize that virtually all their students are drug users in some degree, even if only at the aspirin tablet level, that drugs sanctioned by medical prescription are sometimes abused despite the physician's good intentions. Therefore the individual must learn to distinguish between proper use, abuse, and perhaps between various degrees of abuse. Seldom should he refuse his physician's pills, but he should know enough about psychoactive substances to cooperate with his physician in his attempt to protect him from a medically induced dependency. Whether he drinks or abstains he needs to know the difference between well-controlled alcohol use and dangerous drinking patterns. He needs to be able to make a sensible distinction between occasional marijuana use and heavy heroin use, whether he be the user involved, a friend of the user, or at some future time the parent of the user, or a voter responding to a drug-related referendum.

MEETING THE NEEDS OF THE NONABUSER. Surprisingly enough to many health educators the large majority of the students will not become drug dependent regardless of whether they are taught anything about drugs or not. As mentioned above, they need to know something about the normal socially acceptable use of drugs. Most students are or will be users of alcohol and prescription and over-the-counter drugs and thus they need to know of the pitfalls that occasionally threaten the normal user. An alcohol- or LSD-induced traffic accident is as likely or even more likely to occur on the first as it is on the fiftieth occasion of use. Furthermore, the simple possession of illegal drugs can produce serious legal consequences even if they never enter the bloodstream of the owner. And even stable, mature persons are occasionally exposed to drug overdose when medically prescribed drugs are combined with alcohol or someone else's prescription.

Another whole set of educational needs apply to all adolescents including those few who abstain from any drug use. As family members they sometimes must deal with alcoholism or drug abuse by siblings or by parents. As members of the school community they have responsibilities to fellow students who may become drug dependent or drug abusers. And, finally, as potential or, in some cases, current voting members of American society they have a vital role to play in forming public policy ranging from the enactment of logical drug control laws to the establishment of tax-supported programs of drug treatment. Government administrators seek to operate within a perceived "mandate of the people," legislation seeks to interpret "grass-roots sentiment," and judges often hand down decisions that reflect the "temper of the times." Cynicism aside, in our society, public opinions often lead to needed community action.

MEETING THE NEEDS OF THE POTENTIAL ABUSER. Possibly 10 per cent or less of the students of any class are potential heavy drug abusers. Although most drug and alcohol education efforts of the past have been explicitly or implicitly designed to serve this relatively small group, they have not served them very well. Much of this disservice seems based on the false assumption that young abusers typically blunder into drug dependency because of their lack of knowledge of the consequences. In actual fact the young drug abuser gravitates toward drugs in a futile effort to solve intense and prolonged problems related to his feelings about himself, his sense of worth, his confidence in his abilities, his relationship with his peers, his parents, and his teachers.

Although drug abusers commonly report specific reasons for their use of psychoactive substances such as peer pressures, disenchantment with contemporary society, or just for "kicks," these are at best visible manifestations of much deeper problems. The real causes of drug abuse are highly complex and present a unique pattern for each individual case; they are as complex as is personality development itself.[8]

The potential abuser can be helped in the classroom by teachers with some aptitude and skill in working in the affective domain with the emphasis not on drugs but on feelings about oneself and insight into oneself. But more than this he needs direct service through formal and/or informal counseling by a "caring" person. He also needs very badly a general school environment that will accommodate him. He needs educational tasks that interest him and that he can handle; he needs co-curricular activities that provide wholesome involvement; he needs, as do all young people, firm but compassionate supervision.

Drug abuse is, in the final analysis, just one of several possible symptoms of or responses to emotional problems. Therefore all of the various aspects of health education, services, and the school environment which help support mental health as discussed in Chapter 9 become in effect vital segments of the drug prevention program even though drugs per se may not be mentioned.

CURRICULAR CONSIDERATIONS

The success of health education with respect to any instructional area is usually dependent on (1) administrative factors, (2) curriculum emphasis,

[8] For a thoroughly developed hypothesis explaining drug use and abuse see Gary Fisher, and Irma Strantz, "An Ecosystems Approach to the Study of Dangerous Drug Use and Abuse with Special Reference to the Marijuana Issue," *American Journal of Public Health*, Vol. 62, No. 10 (October 1972), pp. 1407–1414.

and (3) modes of instruction or presentation. Although there is considerable difference of opinion among health educators regarding all these aspects as applied to drug education the following points appear to be widely supported.

Administrative Factors

As emphasized by Bland and Shibuga, "One of the first considerations in placing drug education in the school curriculum is that it be incorporated into the existing curriculum structure of the school." As they explain, "it is impractical to expect time to be allocated to separate courses on drugs, or for any other health-related subjects, however important they may be." [9] And drug education is, of course, very important, but so are several other health topics; therefore, it should get no more and no less than its fair share of time and resources. As implied earlier, the specific goal of minimizing the risk of the development of drug dependency among adolescents is probably best pursued within a general unit on personality or mental health. In a similar manner, considerable material that contributes to drug education is often presented in other units on consumer health or household safety, for example. The effectiveness of instruction within all areas may be enhanced when these opportunities for integration and correlation are properly utilized.

Within drug education, as in other sensitive areas, the general attitude, the training, and general instructional approach of the teachers involved are crucial. Here the characteristics of honesty, credibility, and ability to relate on a personal level to the students are paramount. These qualities are naturally associated with teachers who sincerely desire to provide young people with the learning experiences they need to make independent decisions as compared with the too common practice of seeking to manipulate behavior in narrowly defined ways. As one educator clearly describes:

The goal of "keeping kids off of dope" has been so zealously pursued that the question of the means has been somewhat ignored, often intentionally. Honesty and objectivity have become subservient to expediency. We have become so convinced of the nobility of our objectives that we easily rationalize our deceit and dishonesty.[10]

In addition to the fundamental need for honesty, the teacher needs a thorough subject-matter background; however, perhaps the most important aspect of this background is the knowledge of the personality dynamics of adolescents and of human beings. In general such items as

[9] Hester Beth Bland and Ruth R. Shibuga, "Drug Education and the Curriculum," *Journal of School Health*, Volume XLII, No. 6 (June 1972), p. 326.

[10] Gere Fulton, "Drug Abuse Education—Tell It Like It Is," *School Health Review*, Vol. 3, No. 4 (July–August 1972), p. 33.

emotional needs, peer status, alienation, and the dynamics of interpersonal relationships are of particular importance to drug education as they are to many other health topics. A good basic knowledge of the pharmacology of commonly used drugs is also important; however, the level of competency required in this area is well within the grasp of any teacher with a firm commitment to health education. Although this knowledge is basic to drug education, the main thrust of the curriculum should be largely directed elsewhere.

Curriculum Emphasis

Within the general realm of drug education, as in other health topics, the content presented to the learner can be divided into two categories. First there is the material needed for current ongoing needs. For example, the elementary child has an immediate need to know about the poison potential of the family medicine cabinet, and the adolescent needs to know about the effects of alcohol, since its use is common to his age group. Included in the second category are "prerequisite learnings." These involve material the child needs to prepare him for participation in more sophisticated classroom learning experiences at a later grade level. The whole issue of drug abuse control is, in one sense, a complex social issue which an eleventh- or twelfth-grade student might profitably investigate at quite a mature level, provided he had learned the basic concepts of the drug problem during his earlier school years.

ELEMENTARY LEVEL. The elementary years represent a golden opportunity for drug education that is frequently missed. Too often both teacher and parents see no reason to provide drug education for children who for the most part have few drug problems. Then when problems actually appear in junior high they are ready for a frantic game of "catch-up-ball." The fifth-grade child, for instance, is mature enough to understand the general hazards of drug abuse; he knows what peer pressure and parental conflicts are, but he is not likely to be overwhelmed by them; adult opinions, values, and impressions carry more weight than will be the case two or three years later. In short, he is ready intellectually and emotionally to develop values and understandings that he needs in preparation for the hazards and pressures of later grade levels.

Both the primary and the upper elementary years provide an ideal time for the development of sound personal values related to their health in general. Children are capable of learning at an early age that their health is a precious resource that requires judgment and care for its preservation. If the study of the normal structure and function of the human body is handled properly, children will develop an appreciation of its complexity and capabilities that will tend to deter many types of abuse. An appreciation of the importance of a healthy personality and a rudimentary understanding of the factors that determine its development may also affect health behavior in many beneficial ways. Although instruction in these areas does not constitute drug-abuse education per se, it is important to the development of sensible behavior toward drugs.

SECONDARY LEVEL. Somewhat in contrast to the lower grades the need for drug-abuse education at the secondary level has been recognized for several years. Therefore the major subtopics within this area of study generally receive their first intensive coverage at the junior high level. Unfortunately there is a tendency to underestimate the breadth of student needs and concentrate too single-mindedly on the personal behavior of the student. The narrowness of this approach leads to repetition and boredom, which in the long run is self-defeating insofar as behavior change, intellectual understanding, or any other worthwhile educational goals are concerned. Although specific suggestions for content will be presented later in the form of concepts, the following broad topical areas are typical of those that deserve attention at the secondary level.

1. *Motivations for use.* Including the more plausible theories concerning the various social, emotional, and physical needs related to drug use and abuse.
2. *Common pattern of use.* Including what groups within our diverse society tend to use particular drugs and the extent and apparent purpose for this use.
3. *Consequences of various patterns of drug use.* Although detrimental consequences should be covered, innocuous or beneficial results should not be ignored.
4. *Common approaches to prevention and control of drug-related problems.* Here a "social issues" approach is needed to investigate legal, medical, and public health measures that warrant emphasis and support.
5. *Nature and effects of common drugs or common drug categories.* Including subjective effects and effect on bodily functions and structure; although commonly overemphasized, this material still merits appropriate consideration in a well-balanced program.
6. *Self-concept—feelings about oneself—and feelings about others.* Although more properly a part of the general study of mental health, this area is mentioned here because of its vital relationship to levels of personal susceptibility to drug dependency.

A factor that is equal in importance to the proper selection of content to include in the drug education curriculum is the development of a proper editorial slant or tone of its general presentation. Heretofore most drug information was presented to the learner almost solely in terms of its value for guiding his personal decisions concerning drugs. We feel that this intense focus on personal behavior is counterproductive because it overlooks each citizen's obligation and general desire to help others through personal and community efforts and at the same time tends to create a backlash and resistance to its original purpose of changing personal behavior. Kenneth Clarke advocates an approach designed to deal with these problems when he states:

> Those who direct formal classroom experiences involving drugs may find themselves more effective if instead of trying to influence personal decisions for behavior they use the approach of "helping others" make decisions. There is a distinct difference in relevancy potential. In emotionally charged content areas, the learner often refuses to accept concepts as personally relevant. But there also is the wonderful utilizable phenomenon among youth called "idealism," in which they are concerned about the welfare of others. By relating concepts and principles to one's increased ability to understand others and *their* problems, the threat of "he's talking at me" is avoided, and the positive carry-over elements are reinforced.[11]

Note Clarke's explanation for use of the "helping others" approach; it not only encourages young people to help one another but also "the threat of 'he's talking at me' is avoided," and it thus becomes perhaps the best way to reach the learner for his own personal needs.

This general approach also provides implications for the selection of learning activities. Such specific techniques as role playing and other forms of dramatizations are particularly appropriate, as peer conversations can be depicted or later analyzed in the classroom where adult guidance is available. Situations wherein older students can prepare and make presentations to young students are also very appropriate.[12] Various forms of value clarification techniques are also very useful in this sensitive curriculum area. Such adult-centered activities as films, resource speakers, and lecture discussions also can be used to good effect in conveying needed pharmacological information. When this type of content is not allowed to dominate the drug education unit, its appropriate presentation can be very effective.

Suggested Concepts
The concepts suggested in this chapter include those that we feel are vital to school programs of drug education. Because of the more widespread use of alcohol and its special tradition as a legally acceptable psychoactive substance, it is not included here but is treated separately in Chapters 15 and 16. Also there may be other unintentional omissions in terms of local needs which should, in the final analysis, serve as the ultimate criterion for content selection. For purposes of clarity and conciseness in communication with adults the concepts are expressed in their mature form as they

[11] Kenneth S. Clarke, "The Relevance Perspective in Drug Education," *School Health Review*, Vol. 3, No. 2 (March–April 1972), p. 5.

[12] For an excellent account of student-mediated instruction see "Students Concerned with Public Health," *School Health Review*, Vol. 3, No. 4 (September–October 1972), pp. 39–42.

hopefully might be understood by the student upon completion of the total K–12 program. At the lower grade levels their translation into terminology and situations appropriate to the learners involved by formulation of behavior objectives constitutes an important part of the instructional process.

1. *The use of psychoactive substances for medicinal, social, and religious reasons has persisted throughout the history of mankind.* Alcohol, marijuana, the opiates, and various other drugs have been used for thousands of years; the consequences of this use have ranged from the highly beneficial, through the innocuous, to the deeply tragic.

2. *Virtually all persons are drug users to some degree, and the distinction between use and abuse is often difficult to ascertain.* Alcohol and prescription and over-the-counter drugs are often abused in actions that are legal; whereas many instances of illegal use are nonabusive in any real sense, the use of alcohol or a strong antihistamine might be helpful or innocuous in one's home but abusive when used during work.

3. *The drug-related attitudes and practices of individuals and cultural groups vary greatly because of a wide variety of factors.* Religious doctrines, family traditions, the norms of various formal and informal groups, situational factors within various occupations, and various individual constitutional or personality factors, may all exert important effects on permanent patterns of use, nonuse, or abuse.

4. *The physiological and psychological effects of drugs vary greatly, depending on a wide variety of factors.* Most drugs produce relatively predictable pharmacological effects as stimulants, depressants, or hallucinogens; however, these effects may be modified by a variety of personal and situational factors.

5. *When properly used most drugs are beneficial to mankind.* Drugs are valuable in the relief of pain and suffering and have been instrumental in increasing life expectancy.

6. *Drug abuse occurs when an individual's use of a drug produces effects which markedly impair his functioning or expose him to unnecessary risks.* This pattern may take the form of drug dependency and repeated intoxication, the use of drugs in inappropriate situations as when driving or performing complex vocational tasks, the spending of more money than one can afford on drugs, or some combination of these and other patterns of self-inimical abuse.

7. *The abuse of drugs constitutes a major social problem with wide-ranging effects.* The millions of persons heavily dependent on such drugs as heroin, alcohol, and the barbiturates represent a tremendous loss of human resources; the crimes, accidents, and family disruption associated with drug problems bring hardship and expense to both the close associates of drug abusers and to society in general.

8. *A strong and healthy personality appears to constitute the single most important factor in individual levels of resistance to drug abuse.* Individuals whose early needs for physical necessities, security, and affection

tend to develop styles of behavior based on facing and coping rather than escaping from problems and responsibilities.

9. *The control of drug abuse is a difficult and constant task.* Local, state, and federal agencies are attacking the problem in various ways. International control of narcotics requires great effort by many countries.

10. *Treatment and rehabilitation of serious drug dependence is difficult, expensive, and time consuming.* Federal, state, and community facilities are currently inadequate. Many problems and controversies exist concerning medical treatment and rehabilitation techniques.

REFERENCES

Bland, Hester Beth, and Rugh R. Shibuga. "Drug Education and the Curriculum," *Journal of School Health*, Vol. XLII, No. 6 (June 1972).

Clarke, Kenneth. "The Relevance Perspective in Drug Education," *School Health Review*, Vol. 3, No. 2 (March–April 1972), pp. 5–7.

deLone, Richard H. "The Ups and Downs of Drug-Abuse Education," *Saturday Review of Education* (November 11, 1972).

Fisher, Gary, and Irma Strantz. "An Ecosystems Approach to the Study of Dangerous Drug Use and Abuse with Special Reference to the Marijuana Issue," *American Journal of Public Health*, Vol. 62, No. 10 (October 1972), pp. 1407–1414.

Fulton, Gere B. "Drug Abuse Education—Tell It Like It Is," *School Health Review*, Vol. 3, No. 4 (July–August 1972), pp. 33–37.

Johnson, Kit G. "Survey of Adolescent Drug Use I—Sex and Grade Distribution," *American Journal of Public Health*, Vol. 61, No. 12 (December 1971), pp. 2418–2431.

————, et al. "Survey of Adolescent Drug Use II Social and Environmental Factors," *American Journal of Public Health*, Vol. 62, No. 2 (February 1972), pp. 164–166.

Kaplan, John. *Marijuana—The New Prohibition*. New York: Pocket Books, 1971.

Keniston, Kenneth. "Heads and Seekers: Drugs on Campus, Counter-Cultures and American Society," *The American Scholar*, XXXVIII, No. 1 (Winter 1968–69), United Chapter of Phi Beta Kappa, 1968.

Levengood, Robert, et al. "Heroin Addiction in the Suburbs—An Epidemiologic Study," *American Journal of Public Health*, Vol. 63, No. 3 (March 1973), pp. 209–214.

Matchett, William Foster. "Who Uses Drugs? A Study in a Suburban Public High School," *The Journal of School Health*, Vol. XLI, No. 2 (February 1971).

Mayright, Gerald F. "Considerations in the Development of the School Drug Policy," *Journal of School Health*, Vol. XLII, No. 8 (October 1972), pp. 435–440.

Nickerson, Carl J. "An Examination of Five Difficult Issues Related to School Drug Problems," *Journal of School Health*, Vol. XLII, No. 8 (October 1972), pp. 441–445.

Richardson, Donald W., et al. "Attitudes of Fifth Grade Students to Illicit Psychoactive Drugs," *Journal of School Health*, Vol. XLII, No. 7 (September 1972), pp. 389–391.
Weitman, Morris et al. "Survey of Adolescent Drug III. Correlations Among Use of Drugs," *American Journal of Public Health*, Vol. 62, No. 2 (February 1972), pp. 166–170.

14 ■ DRUG EDUCATION II: APPLICATIONS

The sensitive and controversial nature of drug use and abuse as an area of study makes it necessary for the teacher to use special care in the selection and application of teaching techniques. The moral connotations which are often attached to this topic in various subtle and at times not so subtle ways have tended to discourage any public discussion of the different issues in anything other than biased or emotionalized tones. This highly subjective approach has tended to permeate many school health programs and school health materials. The National Coordinating Council for Drug Education, for example, recently conducted a thorough review of drug education films and found that about 80 per cent contained factual errors.[1] In practical terms this means that most children the health teacher may encounter, particularly at the secondary level, will have already been subjected to considerable drug-related information of a biased, preachy, abstinence-oriented nature. Consequently, techniques and material that reflect these outmoded approaches generally "turn off" the learner in short order.

ELEMENTARY LEVEL. As is the case with other health topics, teacher-centered presentations in the forms of discussions and audiovisual materials are generally effective at the elementary level. The children tend to be oriented toward adults and they have for the most part not yet had to endure excessive adult moralizing. Although projects, dramatizations, role playing, and other high-involvement techniques are generally preferred, the simpler discussion-centered approaches are also quite valuable and to a certain degree necessary. The general openness and vulnerability of elemen-

[1] Richard H. deLone, "The Ups and Downs of Drug-Abuse Education," *Saturday Review of Education* (November 11, 1972), p. 28.

tary school children dictate a special responsibility for the teacher. It represents a prime time to lay a sound foundation both in understanding and in attitudes for the later development of a mature conceptualizing of the drug phenomenon; it is also very easy to emphasize the traditional prejudices and clichés that tend to immunize students to any serious consideration of the subject.

In addition to straightforward drug information, educational experiences that help the pupil develop a valid self-concept and constructive ways of dealing with problems and frustrations constitute a vital element in the prevention of drug abuse. This is, of course, education for mental health, and the techniques for this area are generally oriented toward the affective domain as discussed in Chapter 7.

THE SECONDARY LEVEL. Education for personality development is also of obvious importance at the secondary level as perhaps the primary means to prevent drug abuse. Techniques for this area were discussed in Chapter 10.

Some drug-related content is complex and scientific in nature, such as the review of research studies on drug effects, for instance; these lend themselves to teacher-centered presentations and the use of visual aids. However, the most important concepts in this area are primarily psychosocial in nature, such as those pertaining to life-styles, peer pressure, and social policies and thus lend themselves to student-mediated learning activities. Students of high school age by and large get their real meaningful education about drugs from their peers. The only way that health teachers can hope to exert significant influence on this "lay-referral system" is to give it a chance to flourish in the classroom through use of small-group discussions, role playing, value clarification techniques, and similar techniques with heavy student involvement.

PRACTICAL APPLICATIONS [2]

The following examples represent an effort to show how the recommendations for drug education presented earlier might be applied to specific school situations.

I. BOTTLED TROUBLE

Respect for medicine does not come naturally to most children. They accept with trust whatever their mother, school nurse, or family physician administers; this is the way it should be. An understanding of what a medicine looks like and what it does can be easily learned if the effort is made at home and in school. However, the concept that medicines can be dangerous when used improperly is more difficult to develop because most

---

[2] The teaching examples that appear in this section were originally written for the first edition by Randolph E. Edwards of Southern Connecticut State College.

children have been fortunate enough to avoid direct experience with this problem.

Concept

Drug abuse occurs when an individual's use of a drug produces effects which markedly impair his functioning or expose him to unnecessary risks.

Pupils

Suggested for first and second grades.

Techniques

Storytelling, role playing, and dramatizations.

This lesson begins with the teacher reading a story to the class. Narrative which illustrates health content may be obtained from a variety of sources (as discussed on pages 163–165). This particular one was composed by the teacher herself.

I. TIMMY AND THE PINK CANDY

One bright sunny afternoon last week six-year-old Timmy Hanson was on his way home from the Elmwood Elementary School, where he was a member of Miss Phillips' first-grade class. He was walking with his two best friends, Fred Block and Jay Arnold. They were discussing play plans for the remainder of the afternoon and decided to do some exploring in the large patch of woods behind Timmy's house.

As they approached Ferry Lane, where Timmy would leave his friends to go home, Timmy spotted a small round bottle with a bright red top. "Hey, look at this you guys," cried Timmy as he picked up his new discovery for closer examination. "It's full of candy, pink-colored candy!" exclaimed Jay. Taking off the bottle top and sniffing, Timmy noticed that the candy had no special odor. "Let's try some," said Fred as he reached for the bottle. But Timmy had a better idea; he suggested they take their new-found treasure into the woods when they went exploring. The three boys agreed on this and hurried home to change into play clothes and have a quick snack.

Upon meeting at Timmy's house about thirty minutes later, they hurried excitedly into the woods and began to follow one of the several trails. After going a short way Jay suggested that they climb up on a big flat-topped rock and use it as a lookout post. As they sat on the rock, Timmy pulled the bottle of pink tablets from his pocket and popped one into his mouth. He passed the bottle to his friends, who also took tablets and chewed them cautiously. Fred and Jay made faces and agreed that the candy tablets did not taste very good. Timmy liked the taste and continued to eat many tablets before finally putting the bottle in his pocket and leading his playmates deeper into the woods.

Timmy did not eat much dinner that evening. His stomach felt odd and he had a headache. Strangely, though, he did not want to go to bed. His mom and dad noticed that he was rather restless, even nervous. Going to bed appeared to be out of the question. He complained that his mouth felt dry, and his body appeared warm and sweaty.

As the evening wore on, Timmy's parents became more worried. Timmy seemed excited and full of energy. He could not sit still and could not stop talking.

They had never seen their son act this way before. Upon questioning, Timmy told of finding the bottle of pink candy and how he ate many of them while playing with Fred and Jay. His father asked if he still had the bottle and Timmy said, "Yes! It's in my pants pocket." One look at the label on the bottle that Timmy showed them and his parents knew that they must call their doctor immediately.

When Timmy's dad read the label to Dr. Bradford—"One tablet one-half hour before each meal"—the doctor almost shouted into the telephone, "Get that boy to the hospital immediately." (The doctor suspected the pills were an amphetamine, prescribed in this case for diet control.) Timmy's mother wrapped him in his bathrobe and slippers and his dad sped them all to the hospital in the family car. Dr. Bradford met them at the emergency entrance and quickly took Timmy into a special room. His parents went into the waiting room, where they stayed until hearing from the doctor. Timmy's mother immediately telephoned the parents of Fred Block and Jay Arnold to tell them what had happened. Their parents were quite surprised to hear about Timmy being sick and in the hospital. They reported that Fred and Jay were well and sound asleep. They were relieved to learn that their sons had swallowed only one pink pill.

Timmy's mom and dad were very worried. They could not understand why their son had eaten strange pills without first asking them. The more they thought about it, the more they realized that perhaps it had not been strongly impressed upon Timmy that children should not eat strange foods and candies, whether they are found or offered by someone. They also wondered if this subject had ever been discussed in his first-grade class at school. (When this unhappy situation was over, they were sure to sit down with Timmy and talk about eating strange foods, particularly away from home.)

After what seemed to be a very long wait, Dr. Bradford came out to report that Timmy was out of danger and was going to be all right. He had been given some special medicine to counteract the amphetamines that he had taken. Such pills can make anyone very sick, children in particular, when too many are eaten or swallowed at any one time. Timmy stayed in the hospital overnight so that the doctors and nurses could maintain a constant check on him. He was a sick little boy, and very lucky that his mother, father, and Dr. Bradford had been there to help.

STORY LESSON POSSIBILITIES

Storytelling can be effective as a teaching technique with young children in several different ways.

1. *Complete story flow.* Timmy's story is first told in its entirety. Following this the teacher may *emphasize* or *dramatize* particular situations or pertinent points. In this story several examples might be

A. Timmy's decision to eat some of the pink candies.
B. Timmy's failure to tell his parents about eating the strange candies.
C. Dr. Bradford's reaction to the description of the bottle's contents.
D. Discussion and thoughts of the reactions of Timmy's parents as expressed in the hospital waiting room.
E. Dr. Bradford's explanation of Timmy's treatment and need to stay in the hospital.

Pupil questions, commentary on personal experiences, and discussion, will naturally follow and should be encouraged and utilized.

2. *Problem-situation approach.* This storytelling technique calls upon the teacher to stop and emphasize pertinent points, ask significant ques-

tions, and pose meaningful problems. Teacher questions and/or problems might include the following:

A. What should Timmy have done with the bottle? (A natural and logical solution is desired, not an arbitrary decision to show it to his parents immediately. Childish curiosity should be accounted for and understood by the class. The teacher may note with interest the varied answers.)

B. Was eating the pink candies an intelligent thing to do? Why? Was it a natural thing for curious boys to do?

C. Why did Timmy not tell his parents at dinner what he had done? Did he forget? Did he think it unimportant? Was he afraid of being punished? (This is a logical time to stress the importance of children reporting to their parents or teachers any strange feelings of dizziness or sickness following the ingestion of any substance; this is particularly vital if a strange substance has been swallowed.)

D. Why was Dr. Bradford so alarmed? (This is an opportune time to explain the doctor's role in prescribing medicine.)

E. How had Timmy been treated at the hospital? Has anyone in class ever been to the hospital for this purpose?

F. Why was Timmy a lucky boy? What do you think Timmy will learn from this experience? What will you do if you find a bottle of strange-looking candy?

Regardless of the storytelling technique used, the teacher should strive for pupil comprehension of the story's "message." In Timmy's story there are several points that refer significantly to the original concept. These should be clearly illustrated along with other related factors that are important to pupil health and safety awareness. Simplicity and clarity are essential storytelling attributes.

STORY FOLLOW-UP

The story has been presented and discussed and the pupils are interested and eager to learn more. To maintain this favorable teaching–learning atmosphere the teacher will want to follow up with an interesting and effective activity, one that is practical and preferably related to the home and familiar surroundings. Two suggested activities follow:

1. *Discovering potential trouble areas in the home.* With the assistance of their parents a selected group is instructed to examine the home medicine chest. Pupils may discuss the use or uses that are made of the various medicines, drugs, pills, and so on, with their parents and bring a general list to school. Children should be made aware of the type of container, dispensing top, and any obvious markings and warnings. Medicines that require a doctor's prescription should show the pharmacist's label with specific directions.

2. *Discovering potential trouble areas in the school.* It may be advisable to have several pupils visit the school nurse in her quarters and follow

the same procedure as that described in the home. Home and school are the two familiar areas where young children feel secure, and these learning experiences will have practical implications for them.

A combination of role playing and dramatizations could be used as a means of sharing the information gleaned from the home or the visit with the nurse. One possibility would be to have pupils represent themselves as various forms of medicine found in the home medicine chest. This calls for forming working groups to participate in the varied phases of this class project. One group of pupils reports on its experience of checking the home medicine chest. This group should develop a short story or narrative report that emphasizes personal thoughts, observations, and ideas related to the subject. Another group does the art and construction work. This involves the construction of paper and cardboard medicine bottles and pill boxes. (Light corrugated cardboard is excellent for shaping bottles and small boxes.) These will be covered with paper, colored, and labeled in large letters. This type of activity is enthusiastically endorsed by most youngsters of this age. The teacher may assist a third group in creating a dramatic presentation procedure. A large paper or cardboard medicine chest or bottle is constructed with a separation in the middle. This should stand or be held erect in front of the class. Each reporting pupil steps through the middle slit with his labeled bottle or pill box in hand to make his verbal presentation and then moves over to one side. Each pupil may role-play a particular medicine or drug and verbally dramatize his little story. Some pupils, however, may prefer to report in a factual manner.

Following this culminating class project the teacher may choose to sum up the important points through use of a short discussion and question–answer session.

II. FLYING HIGH

The desire to be accepted is very strong in young people. Many social aspects of drug abuse seem to exemplify the role of friends and friendship groups, particularly where glue sniffing is involved. It seems to follow that when the motive of imitative behavior is to attain status, various antisocial acts or acts which may involve personal harm may be expected.

Concept
The drug-related attitudes and practices of individuals and cultural groups vary greatly, depending on a wide variety of factors.

Pupils
Fifth and sixth grades.

Techniques
Class discussion culminated with sociodrama.

A class discussion on glue sniffing would be best introduced with some references to specific events or cases that would convey real meaning to the pupils. Appropriate lead-ins would include newspaper clippings, magazine aritcles, or references to recent television shows or assembly programs covering this topic. Occasionally some dramatic occurrence within the immediate neighborhood or community provides an ideal teaching opportunity for the alert and flexible teacher. Regardless of the specific means used to generate interest and involvement, the teacher should guide the class through a systematic coverage of the essential points. The information and ideas found in the following paragraphs should prove generally useful in stimulating and guiding such a discussion.

GENERAL DISCUSSION POINTS

Young glue sniffers are usually introduced to the habit by one of their own crowd. Is this because they have the wrong friends? Glue-sniffing parties are popular, because there is a strong desire to be accepted by glue-sniffing companions. Is this kind of popularity desirable? Is this situation potentially dangerous?

As with any beginning drug experimenter, the extent and length of involvement are always unpredictable. Youngsters should be aware of the many potentialities. Sniffing can lead to antisocial acts or acts that may cause personal harm. There are countless stories of youngsters going berserk—stabbing family members, driving with extreme recklessness, and so on.

A tendency toward self-destruction is often veiled by a dreamlike exaggeration of a sense of power. An example of this is one case in which a boy fell from a roof and suffered severe injuries while attempting to fly. In another case a young sniffer attempted to fight an onrushing train and barely escaped with his life. Although these acts of violence and self-destruction are the exception rather than the rule, it must be understood that such potential is always present.

Other antisocial acts that have been attributed to sniffing include truancy, burglary, disorderly conduct, running away from home, drinking, and curfew violation.

The possibility of arrest is ever present for the youngster who commits various antisocial acts as a result of sniffing glue. Laws prohibiting glue sniffing have been passed in several states. The possibility of arrest is worthy of serious contemplation by the young person inclined to sniff glue.

The available data suggest that glue sniffing is a reflection of susceptibility to social pressure. Many sniffers have a low opinion of themselves and find it difficult to communicate with others. They tend to be passive, anxious, withdrawn, and disorganized and tend to have a weak personality which may break down under stress.[3]

Glue sniffing should not be considered as an isolated event. It usually involves the family and community and is symptomatic of underlying emotional disturbances. It is not the use per se which is important, but the factors that cause the youngster to engage in this practice. This fact, which may well apply to the majority of youthful drug abusers, merits special emphasis.

[3] Charles Winick and Jacob Goldstein, *The Glue Sniffing Problem* (New York: American Social Health Association, n.d.), p. 15.

SPECIFIC TEACHING HINTS

A teacher would be wise to emphasize the *dangers to health* rather than the "badness" of the glue-sniffing practice. Emotional and negative teaching may serve only to "turn youngsters off" and destroy good intentions, regardless of factual validity. Because self-destructive impulses play a major role in glue sniffing, an emotional appeal dramatizing the dangers to health may attract the attention of those few potential sniffers whose self-destructive impulses are particularly strong.[4]

Provide the pupils with an opportunity to analyze and discuss all types of acceptable behavior and contrast them with the antisocial varieties that are exhibited by the glue sniffers.

Depending on the time allottment for this topic the teacher will want to provide a variety of learning and fact-finding opportunities for his class. Aside from class discussion, personal guidance, and factual contribution, the teacher may wish to consider the following areas for student research:

1. School and community libraries.
2. Physicians.
3. Federal Bureau of Narcotics and Dangerous Drugs, local division.
4. Youth agencies.
5. Public health department.
6. Police department.

Student research, whether individual or in committee, should be well planned. Specific aspects of the problem should be investigated. Teacher guidance with reference materials is essential. Articles in the current popular periodicals can be good sources of information and often include a bibliography, a potential source of further information. Teachers should also consider the possibility of hearing knowledgeable speakers from the community, or possibly from within the school system. Informal presentations are best. Provide an opportunity for class questions and discussion with the guest.

Students from higher grade levels, appearing either as individuals or panel discussion participants, can often function very effectively as speakers. This approach is being used with increasing effectiveness as educators discover that our youth readily identify with the problems and experiences of one of their own kind in the use of dangerous drugs and other questionable substances.[5] The teacher should plan the presentation with this youngster and understand his approach to the problem and what his message will be. The teacher may wish him to touch on or emphasize certain points. He could explain how he got started on glue, particularly if "friends" introduced sniffing to him. He could discuss "following the crowd" as he experienced it. This could conceivably be the most significant and successful teaching technique used during this unit of study.

[4] Ibid., p. 17.

[5] For a good description of this technique as applied to smoking see Lorraine J. Henke, "Student-to-Student Teaching About Tobacco Smoking," *School Health Review*, Vol. 4, No. 1, Jan.–Feb. 1973, pp. 17–18.

SOCIODRAMAS

Now that the class has discussed the basic aspects of glue sniffing, the teacher may decide that a creative dramatic effort would be an interesting culminating activity. He introduces the idea to his pupils, explaining that they are going to participate in a series of sociodramas and that basically this involves the spontaneous acting out of situations by two or more persons who show the emotional reactions of the people in the situation as they perceive them. Students are to play these various roles using their imagination and newly acquired knowledge. There is no script, no formal rehearsing, and no memorizing of lines. (See pages 143–144.)

Problem Situations. A number of varied problem situations involving glue-sniffing activities must be posed. Total class involvement is called for. Typically realistic situations include the following:

1. Four youngsters are meeting in Billy's garage to sniff glue. Jim brings along one of his classmates to acquaint him with his pals and show him how to sniff. (Portraying negative and positive reactions would be valuable here. Pupils should see both sides of the issue and make their own judgment.) This could be two short sociodramas showing opposite reactions, or Jim could bring two friends at the same time and they could disagree on their choice of joining the sniff club, and state their reasons.

2. An older student from a secondary school attempts to entice an elementary school pupil to sniff glue. If talking and coaxing prove worthless, the older youngster may threaten physical harm. (This again points up the danger of questionable companions. In this case a much older person is involved.)

3. Brothers Tommy and Timmy are trying to sniff glue in the back yard. Mother (or Dad) happens to find them and asks for an explanation. Caught in the act, the boys describe their attempts at glue sniffing for the first time. Two possibilities are

   a. Parents are completely uninformed about glue sniffing. They find someone who is familiar with this activity (doctor, nurse, public health department, police, neighbor) to explain the dangers involved to the entire family.
   b. Parents are knowledgeable. They discuss the situation with their sons. Is punishment justified in this case? Where did Tommy and Timmy learn about sniffing, and from whom?

4. A group of youngsters are members of a glue-sniffing club. They have been using glue as well as sniffing from open gas tanks of automobiles. What are some of the significant physical reactions that can result? Such reactions can be described and portrayed with surprising realism by pupils who understand what is involved. This is particularly true in classes where one or more youngsters have at one time sniffed glue. When possible, take advantage of willingness to share personal experiences. This type of realism can create an indelible impression.

5. Two ex-glue sniffers are sitting and discussing their experiences. Pertinent thoughts could include

a. How they got started.
b. How they sniffed.
c. When and where they sniffed.
d. Immediate reactions, mental and physical.
e. How they stopped (who discovered them and what, if any, punishment they received).
f. Advice for other youngsters.

III. GOING TO POT?

Marijuana is perhaps the most controversial drug used in our society. The advocates for its legalization or decriminalization point to an impressive body of research which identifies marijuana as producing generally mild psychoactive effects with no threat of physical dependency. Opponents maintain that the widespread use of any intoxicant, whether it be mild or strong, fear that our present problems with alcohol will only be compounded if the controls on marijuana are controlled or compromised. These complex and emotional issues have been further complicated by a tendency for the sides to divide along old versus young, or establishment versus antiestablishment lines wherein the arguments tend to degenerate into a "our-drug-is-better-than-your-drug" affair. This issue will seldom be settled to everyone's satisfaction by any classroom group; however, its examination can serve as a lead-in or focal point for a useful study of many other drug-related issues.

Concept

The physiological and psychological effects of drugs vary greatly, depending on a wide variety of factors.

Pupils

Eighth and ninth grades.

Technique

Brainstorming, with variations.

Brainstorming as a teaching technique is extremely useful for getting students to express their real feelings concerning specific issues. It can be used to develop interest early in a unit of study, or as in this example, to stimulate free expression of facts and opinions once the class has gained some familiarity with the specific problems. The research, individual study, and group discussion of our hypothetical ninth-grade class have resulted in the formulation of five major questions.

1. Why is marijuana popular among many teen-agers?
2. What are the actual physiological and psychological effects of smoking marijuana?
3. Is smoking marijuana a stepping-stone to the abuse of more dangerous drugs?

4. Should the use of marijuana be legalized?

5. What does smoking marijuana mean to me now and in the future?

ESTABLISHING THE RULES

Because there are five problems to be dealt with, the class will be divided into five groups, each with one student to record ideas as they are presented. If the ideas come too fast, it may be necessary to use two recorders, with each one jotting down alternate ideas. With five topics being discussed, students will want to choose the group dealing with their topic of interest. This will undoubtedly ensure greater individual participation.

Negative statements are taboo. Group members are instructed to offer any ideas that come to mind; "free-wheeling with wild ideas" is to be encouraged. Quantity rather than quality is the main concern here. Criticism of an idea is not allowed during the session.

Instructions should be given clearly, with emphasis on quantity and combination of ideas. The problem or problems under consideration must be introduced, and the students must be primed and stimulated with a variety of approaches. Quick thinking and rapid-fire contributions are the essence of the activity.

This brainstorming session might well begin with the teacher discussing the total marijuana problem in something like the following:

> We all know that pot is popular among many young people. You know that it is probably being smoked by some of your friends right here in this school. Marijuana is a highly controversial drug and there is much misinformation concerning it. Even many of the experts disagree on a number of important points. Do you feel that it is worthwhile to learn some of the accurate facts, to understand just what pot can and can't do to and for those persons using it? What are your thoughts as to the desired role that pot might play in the life of your friends and associates?

Following this introduction the class is asked to begin their brainstorming. Beginning sessions should not last too long; eight to twelve minutes is ample time.

BRAINSTORMING THE QUESTIONS

Student ideas and comments will vary according to type of community, economic status, familiarity, and experience with marijuana. Where multiple groups are functioning there may be a lessening of inhibitions, because the teacher can sit in on only one group at a time. With the entire class working on a single problem a student may feel inhibited simply by the presence of all classmates and the teacher. Some students will want to "see how it goes" before making a contribution.

The following ideas and comments advanced by these students are indicative of early teen-age awareness of the marijuana problem.

Problem I. Why is marijuana popular among many teen-agers?
- You can buy it almost anywhere.
- It's easy to hide.

- It makes you feel great.
- It's not addicting.
- Alcohol is a lot more dangerous.
- It means getting together with the crowd.

Problem II. What are the physiological and psychological effects of smoking pot?
- Eyes get red.
- Smoker laughs and giggles.
- Some users talk loudly and a lot.
- Mouth may become dry.
- Some become nauseated and vomit.
- Smoker feels good mentally, as if "floating on air."
- Smoker is very moody and changes mood easily.
- Smoker loses judgment.
- Some feel very excited.

Problem III. Is smoking pot a stepping-stone to the abuse of more dangerous drugs?
- Not too often.
- It happens to just a few teen-agers.
- Addicts-to-be would have gotten around to heroin anyway.
- Most heroin addicts have used alcohol prior to pot or heroin.
- If you use one drug it's easier to use another.

Problem IV. Should the possession and use of marijuana be legalized?
- Legalization would eliminate illegal traffic.
- If it's not too dangerous, why not?
- Legalization would add another questionable drug to a growing list.
- The stronger hashish might become popular, and the effects could be very dangerous.
- Legalization would increase use.
- If legalized it would probably come under laws similar to those for alcohol.

Problem V. What does smoking pot mean to me now and in the future?
- It sounds like fun.
- I could be arrested.
- I don't believe it would hurt me.
- It's part of growing up.
- It sure would shock my parents.
- It's not really a big deal.

EVALUATING THE IDEAS

When the stipulated time is up, all brainstorming activity ceases and evaluation of ideas takes place. The most common method is general class discussion. In this case each group summarizes and decides on the best ideas for class consideration. It is here that the teacher's knowledge and discussion leadership become so important. This final discussion and summary should endeavor to leave the students with the following:

1. A clearer understanding of the specific factors that motivate drug use.
2. Some accurate and pertinent facts concerning the various effects of marijuana.
3. Increased appreciation of the importance of the factors that surround the drug-using situation (who's in the group, location, emotional tone before use, etc.).
4. Some general knowledge of the phenomena of drug dependency, particularly the personality factors that increase susceptibility.

The newly gained knowledge and broader perspective resulting from this activity should enable the students to evaluate their responsibilities better and make intelligent decisions. Brainstorming should be lively, and it can be unfair. The temporary protection from criticism that is provided encourages students to think creatively and speak rapidly. The resulting enthusiasm and involvement that this technique usually generates may then be channeled into a deeper and more critical examination of the various issues.

Another effective and interesting technique for summarizing and evaluating the ideas presented could have each group decide which ideas and observations are the most important and meaningful to them. If some forty ideas per group have been advanced, condense the list down to eight or ten. Each group will retain its final selections, then pass the longer original list on to the next group for its appraisal and subsequent condensation. The result is a composite of significant thoughts and ideas that should become an integral part of each student's notebook. The more meaningful ideas may also be portrayed to the class through use of an impromptu debate. Two students are selected to present one pertinent fact and/or point of view. This can be extemporaneous or quickly prepared, perhaps overnight. To be particularly effective this dialogue should be unrehearsed, and the two students should take their cues from each other. Youngsters with diverse attitudes and opinions who are willing to air them in open forum will add markedly to a creative learning situation. Other students in the listening audience will be constantly evaluating their own thoughts and beliefs.

IV. BE SMART—PLAY IT SAFE

Many drugs are extremely valuable to modern medicine. They are used in various ways for the relief of pain and suffering. A number of these sedative and pain-relieving drugs may be purchased over the counter or by a doctor's prescription. They can be beneficial if used with caution and an awareness of their potential to cause dependency. It is important to remember that *any* drug may be poisonous if misused.

Concept
When properly used most drugs are beneficial to mankind.

Pupils

Seventh, eighth, and ninth grades. Depth of involvement will depend on previous background, age, and grade level.

Techniques

Committee research, varied panel reports, spontaneous acting, colloquium.

The initiation of a committee work assignment in the typical eighth-grade class would logically take place on the second or third day of a unit on drugs after the class had been provided with the opportunity to develop some general orientation to the topic. Particularly interesting films or resource speakers are effective ways of developing the necessary enthusiasm for this rather demanding task. Following this, the teacher may proceed directly by listing a number of subtopics or study areas on the chalkboard (or have them already mimeographed and ready to hand out). The class should then be divided into committees for purposes of investigating and reporting on these areas. Insofar as possible students should be allowed to select the committee of their choice. Some committees may choose to cover two closely related areas and they should be allowed this option if the teacher feels the committee members are capable enough.

STUDY AREAS

Each study area is presented, together with a series of questions or directives which serve to define the scope of the area and guide the work of the student committee. These may call for concise answers or for broad, open-ended discussions. Regardless of their specific form, they should effectively guide the committee to the important points. Three examples of these study outlines follow:

    I. *The Nature of Drugs*
       A. Check several authoritative definitions as found in standard dictionaries, medical dictionaries, and related textbooks.
       B. What are the common drug categories? Provide several examples from each.
       C. What are the main drug sources (e.g., plants, laboratory culturing, synthesis, and so forth)?
       D. Describe how the body functions as a chemical factory (e.g., hormones, enzymes, and so forth).
       E. What are the basic uses of drugs?
    II. *Prescription Drugs*
       A. What are the criteria for placing a drug in the prescription category (e.g., usually powerful, potentially dangerous, and so on).
       B. How do the laws governing prescription drugs apply to the physician, the pharmacist, the dentist, and the patient?
       C. What information is required by law to be placed on the label of prescription drugs (e.g., name of patient, name of doctor, directions, and so on)?

    D. Investigate the education and training of pharmacists.

    E. What are the basic uses of drugs?

  III. *Central Nervous System Drugs*

    A. For each class of drugs that affect the central nervous system provide:

      1. A standard definition.

      2. A list of common examples.

      3. A description of the basic effects.

      4. A description of important medical uses.

      (Provide this information for narcotics, barbiturates, stimulants, hallucinogens, and tranquilizers.)

    B. Which of the central nervous system drugs are commonly abused? How serious is the problem for each drug? What general groups of people seem most prone to abuse drugs?

    C. What are the apparent reasons for drug abuse (e.g., lack of self-confidence, discouragement about the future, emotional problems, and so forth)?

    D. What kinds of problems result from drug abuse for the individual, the family, and the community?

    E. What is done to prevent and control drug abuse by law enforcement authorities, medical personnel, educators, reformed abusers, religious workers, and others?

Other major topics might include over-the-counter drugs, the advertising of drugs, and drug research and development. Similar groups of guiding questions could be formed for the use of the student committee assigned to each topic. If students of low academic ability are involved, the questions should be broken down into a greater number of simpler and more specific questions. Conversely, bright, enthusiastic student groups may need little more than a clear verbal description of the scope of their topic.

INFORMATION GATHERING

The manner in which the committee members gather the information needed to gain a reasonable degree of mastery over their topic will vary considerably according to specific situations. However, visits to local pharmacies, interviews with nurses and doctors, where practical, and surveys of the contents of home medicine chests are common supplements to the usual library sources. Generally a minimum of one week will be required to carry out these activities. In many situations a longer period of time will be needed, particularly where the health class itself meets only once or twice a week.

REPORTING TECHNIQUES

There are several interesting and effective techniques which may be used by the committees as a means of sharing their information with the other members of the class. These should be described to the class early in the unit to facilitate the planning of the reporting phase. The teacher should be ready both to help individual committees with the standard techniques and to provide encouragement to those groups who chose to improvise or create novel ways of conveying the gathered information. Some of the more promising alternatives will be described here.

Question the Experts. Each committee forms a list of significant questions pertaining to their issues. Copies are handed to class members so that they may quiz the committee members who will be sitting in panel fashion in front of the class. Any panel member may receive the question, and any of his associates may feel free to contribute additional information. Student panel members, realizing their responsibility, will usually study the questions and be prepared to respond in a knowledgeable fashion. The teacher, of course, should be alert to the need to correct inaccuracies. However, as far as possible, this is an activity by and for the students, and they should be allowed to run the show. Sample questions might include the following:

- Are all drugs sold on prescription?
- Name one law pertaining to dangerous drugs that your state, city, or community has passed.
- Is a drug different from a medicine?
- What are the "wonder drugs"? Why are they so named?
- What are the basic characteristics of the central nervous system drugs?
- Once a drug is cleared for sale in the United States by the F.D.A., can it ever be taken off the market?

Take a Stand. Each committee member makes a short list of important statements. They should be brief, factual, and to the point. It is also necessary that several statements must be false or questionable. A moderator is then selected, preferably a capable youngster from another committee rather than the teacher. Committee members, in turn, will field a statement from the moderator and take a stand on its validity. Sample statements might include the following:

- Federal narcotic laws are enforced by the Bureau of Narcotics, U.S. Department of the Treasury. (Having researched the subject of protecting society this committee is aware that the appropriate agency is the Bureau of Narcotics and Dangerous Drugs [BNADD] under the aegis of the Department of Justice.)
- A good way to study is to take a pep pill. (This can be a debatable issue. Many students may feel certain occasions merit artificial assistance.)
- The pharmacist will be glad to diagnose your ailment and prescribe the correct medicine.
- Vaccines are drugs that come from animals.
- Misuse of aspirin can lead to trouble.

A valuable feature of this technique is that when the student takes a stand, he must be able to defend his opinions. Whenever personal experience can be utilized, it should be employed with conviction. Disagreeing committee members should be heard, and there should be a reasonable amount of participation from the main body of the class.

Act a Role. One of the committees has expressed a desire to depict important facts resulting from its research efforts through some form of dramatization. The members may work singly, in combination, or in small groups as they plan their presentation. Acting may be a monologue, pantomime, or short skit. Any costume, stage props, and so on, that can be used will add to effectiveness and realism. Acting portrayals could include the following.

- A sick patient reads aloud from a label on a real bottle of pills or medicine and wonders about some of this information.
- A pharmacist behind the counter explains to an annoyed lady why he cannot sell her a drug without a doctor's signed prescription.
- A mother is examining her bathroom medicine chest and attempts to clean out old and partially used bottles of drugs and medicines. Labels are peeling off two bottles currently in use and transparent tape is applied. (A running commentary is apropos here as she examines all bottles and containers.)
- A customer explains to a pharmacist about his aches and pains and wants to know what he should take. He eventually decides to prescribe for himself and buys some drugs. A physician who happens to be listening nearby shakes his head and makes several comments after the customer leaves.
- A girl is thinking about taking pep pills while studying for a test. Her "conscience" answers as she wonders out loud. (Her conscience is out of sight behind a desk or screen.)
- Three of four teen-agers are sitting around discussing "blowing some pot or popping a pill." There is some "big talk" from these inexperienced drug users. The conversation swings around to getting caught, being kicked out of school, and the possible consequences of a police record.

The possibilities for spontaneous acting are numerous. Impromptu speaking and acting encourage creativity. Youngsters will appreciate the opportunity and challenge to use their imagination and creative ability. The class audience will benefit as it seeks to interpret the meaning of the presentations. Experience has shown that the teacher may be amazed at what his students have learned, can appreciate, and can produce interpretatively.

Form a Panel. The standard symposium is a very traditional yet very effective way for a committee to present its findings to the class (see pages 160–161). It also lends itself to some interesting variations when suitable resources are available. One example of these that has particular application to large classes involves the participation of two panel groups. One panel should be composed of interested and intelligent class members who are likely to ask appropriate questions and make relevant comments; the other panel should be made up of resource persons selected for their knowledge as well as interest and concern. Possible choices for this panel may include the following:

1. School or local physician.
2. School nurse.
3. Faculty member in the areas of science, chemistry, health and physical education, or home economics.
4. Parent.
5. Drug manufacturer.
6. Law enforcement officer.
7. Former drug abuser (preferably a young person).

A representative from each of the preceding would probably be too large a group for the classroom. Therefore, the teacher should talk with prospective guest panelists, define objectives, and then select the most appropriate group possible.

Students should select the members of their panel, and this panel should be seated with the guest panel before the class. Student panelists should be armed with pertinent questions and issues for discussion. Resource panel members serve in this situation as consultants and contribute their opinions and knowledge on various aspects of the subject. A competent student moderator may guide the panel discussion and encourage the class audience to participate whenever it desires.

This technique puts the students on an equal footing with the experts and stimulates attention and participation. Students are prone to ask objective questions in the hope of receiving direct answers in return. Discussion with and among the resource persons may well serve to clarify questionable issues. Selecting experts who can communicate with teenagers and understand their concerns will assure the success of this stimulating activity.

V. THE CONSEQUENCES

With modern society experiencing extreme difficulty in coping with drug abuse, high school seniors should be well aware of the major health and social problems involved. Although the major focus of these problems may shift from one population group to another, or from one drug to another, the basic principles remain largely unchanged.

Concept
The abuse of drugs constitutes a major social problem with wide-ranging effects.

Pupils
High school seniors.

Techniques
Projective techniques and variations.

By the time today's youngsters become high school seniors they are reasonably familiar with many aspects of the complex drug-abuse problem. Prominent among the reasons for this are the following:

1. Inclusion of drug-abuse education in school curriculums.
2. Increased emphasis in the entertainment media, particularly television and movies.
3. Greater coverage in the news media.
4. Growing abuse of drugs in the suburban and smaller urban areas.
5. Social patterns and habits of today's youth which involve various forms of drug abuse as a natural circumstance.

TAKING A LOOK

High school seniors typically look upon themselves as a rather sophisticated group. They may give little thought to personal health and social problems that can result from the indiscriminate use of drugs. After all, who thinks about negative future possibilities when partying on Saturday night or "blowing a stick" (smoking marijuana) quietly by oneself?

Although high school seniors may admit that they have their "hang-ups" concerning drugs, they do not appreciate being preached to on the subject. However, they are often curious and intelligent enough to realize that it is to their advantage to view the drug-abuse problem as one that could affect them. These positive qualities can be utilized with a proper teaching approach. Following a particularly lively discussion, the hypothetical teacher in this example made two suggestions as follows:

1. The class should develop a list of drug-related health and social problems and/or issues that may affect them now and in the future.
2. These problems and issues should be discussed through a series of informal and spontaneous *projective techniques* with all students participating.

Through use of the projective technique students will be encouraged to discuss some of their personal and social problems, opinions, and ideas. This technique can be valuable in assisting students to evaluate their attitudes and beliefs and in aiding them in solving problems of personal and social adjustment.

PROBLEMS AND ISSUES

Some of the major problems that might be listed are as follows:

- Possibility of arrest, including a jail term and police record.
- Interference with academic work, with reduced chance of graduation and college placement.
- Disruption of relationships with peers and friends with differing patterns of use or nonuse.
- Disruption of family relationships with parents and other members.
- Possibility of death or permanent damage.

• Disruption of personality development resulting from long-term preoccupation with drugs and the neglect of other goals.

As these and similar items are proposed and briefly discussed they are left on the chalkboard for reference during the projective phase of the lesson.

PICTORIAL TECHNIQUE

Pictures related to any of the problems and issues are shown to the students, who are to compose extemporaneously a story to fit each picture, reveal what has led up to the event shown, describe what is currently happening, relate how the characters feel, and predict or state the outcome. Picture examples might include the following:

1. A teen-ager sitting at a lunch counter, head buried in his arms, has "nodded out" after gulping down several pills and a cup of tea. A policeman standing at his elbow is trying to rouse him.
2. A boy and girl meeting after dark in a deserted parking lot. The girl is buying her "kicks" from a teen-age pusher.
3. A boy and his girl are at a swinging party. Several friends are offering them marijuana.
4. High school senior in a serious discussion with his guidance counselor; the discussion seems focused on academic records and both parties look distressed.

Imagination and creativity should blossom with this technique. Students will have an opportunity to express their feelings in their own ways.

VARIATIONS

1. Students may bring in their own pictures as selected from magazine advertisements and other similar sources; the projections themselves should be unrehearsed presentations by other class members.

2. If there is sufficient artistic talent and enthusiasm, these students might be encouraged to draw or sketch their own picture or scene. Others should then be called upon to describe their interpretations.

3. A truly creative twist could be accomplished by having one or more willing students set up their own scene with a camera. This can be one picture or a series of pictures designed to offer a variety of opportunities for extemporaneous interpretations.

4. A class member could briefly describe a conflict situation or an unfinished story or plot; several of his classmates could then finish the story as they see it within a specified time. This may be effectively followed by questions from the class as to why each narrator chose a particular approach or made certain statements.

5. It would be a fine experience for the students if the teacher could procure a top-notch sociologist, psychologist, or psychiatrist for a guest appearance. Ideally, this expert would sit in on a session of the projective-technique activities and contribute his professional evaluations. It would

be advisable to stage a number of shortened demonstrations in order to cover a variety of student experiences and attitudes. The guest expert should be a person who understands today's teen-agers and can communicate with them.

GENERAL HINTS

The projections that students describe can often be dealt with on two levels. In the first instance the student is developing a narrative based on his basic knowledge of the factors involved and his impression of what the teacher and/or his classmates want him to say. This sort of response, although somewhat superficial, is the more common one and is useful as a means of examining and discussing student views of specific topics. However, a second possibility exists. Student reports are occasionally dominated by strong emotional needs to see certain aspects of a situation or block out others. If this should result in bizarre interpretations, the teacher should realize his or her limitations and generally not attempt any sophisticated analysis of the report. If the student involved shows other unusual symptoms, a referral to school guidance personnel might be advisable.

It should be noted that the projective technique can easily wander off target and become meaningless play. In order to keep specific goals in sight, the pictures or narratives must be of reasonably high caliber and directed along a central theme.

VI. A DISTINGUISHED VISITOR

The legal approaches to prevention and control of drug abuse constitute some of the more intriguing aspects of the entire drug problem. Both the international smuggler and the small-town, back-street pusher recognize law enforcement as the bane to profit and illicit commercial expansion. Prevention and control also include federal, state, and local legislation regarding importing, manufacturing, distributing, purchasing, and possession of drugs of all types, both legal and illegal.

Concept
The control of drug abuse is a difficult and constant task.

Pupils
Senior high school.

Technique
Resource speakers.

The various types of persons that make effective resource speakers for drug education may be divided into two basic categories. The first group includes all those whose specialized training and job experience has provided them with special expertise in the drug areas. Many psychiatrists, pharmacologists, and specially trained law enforcement personnel are found in this category. The second group is composed of reformed drug abusers who gain their special knowledge by personally experiencing

drug-related problems and in many cases by participants in self-help programs designed to help other abusers live drug-free lives. Each of these
kinds of speakers has his advantages and limitations, and the effectiveness
of persons within each group will vary greatly depending on the personal
qualities of the individual.

VISITING EXPERTS

One commonly used source of speakers in the expert category is the
district offices of the Federal Bureau of Narcotics and Dangerous Drugs.
Offices of this agency are located in every section of the United States.
Speaker representatives from this agency are knowledgeable in the legal
aspects of the drug problem. After gaining an authentic picture of what is
involved in controlling narcotics and dangerous drugs, students can direct
their concentration in areas of interest and choice. Other potential sources
of speakers are the following:

- Customs office
- Post office
- F.B.I.
- Border patrol
- Coast Guard
- Police, state and local
- Shipping and transportation companies

All of the preceding could render a specific contribution. If possible,
one or several of these experts should follow the FBNDD agent. The invita-
tion and speaking arrangements could be a part of the study assignment
for various students in their particular area of interest.

REFORMED ABUSERS

The reformed abuser can bring a high degree of realism and candid-
ness to a class discussion on drugs. When this alternative is selected it is
vital to obtain the very best person possible. He must not be too much
older than the students in the class. The age association and identification
factors are strengthened if the age differential is minimal. The teacher
must be as prudent in his selection as possible. Unless the teacher happens to know of the right person, he may wish to try several rehabilitation
centers, usually located in or near large cities, such as the following:

- Synanon
- Narcotics Anonymous
- Halfway House
- Teen Challenge
- Daytop Village
- Encounter
- SODAT (Service to Overcome Drug Abuse Among Teen-agers)

Based on the self-help, informal-group theory, these nonprofit organizations provide assistance for the addict and youthful drug abuser

through counseling, education, and vocational and cultural training. Development of the individual personality is a major objective.

Many of these and other similar organizations have organized speaker bureaus from which a school district may obtain an ex-narcotics addict and/or youthful drug abuser. In this situation the teacher should state the type of person he is seeking and the characteristics of the audience. For someone to come in and simply recount his experiences with marijuana is not sufficient. He must be able to relate to his younger audience, to recognize their curiosity, uncertainty, and need for answers. He should understand that many students will look upon him with curiosity and awe, and some with adulation.

Thus, it is important, if not imperative, that the teacher take the time and effort first to meet the guest speaker and brief him on his role. Invitations, acceptances, and a general briefing by telephone or letter are not recommended. The teacher should show his speaker the problems and questions that his class has raised. Explain that for many of these students this is probably the first time they have even met an ex-addict, marijuana smoker, or whatever the case may be. The need for an honest impression based on truth as the speaker knows it should also be stressed.

The students, of course, should have the opportunity to ask questions and promote informal discussion with their guest. He in turn may be briefed to ask for questions and opinions from his audience. This special activity should not be hurried. An interesting follow-up activity is student discussion of their reactions. This may occur immediately after the guest's departure. However, it may be more fruitful to have a summary discussion the next day, after everyone has had an opportunity to digest what they have heard. The teacher might also ask what new thoughts and changes in philosophy have resulted from listening to one who has experienced drug abuse.

COMMON PITFALLS

It goes without saying that comprehensive drug-abuse education should have the sanction of the home and school system. If a creative instructor decides to expose his students to an admitted ex-user of harmful drugs, he should procure official permission. Similarly, all details pertinent to the visit should be clearly outlined beforehand. If these details are not handled properly, it is quite possible that someone will complain that children are being exposed to the evil influence of drug addicts and criminal characters. Even when the best precautions are taken, this may happen.

Upon learning of a teacher's idea for a guest speaker, administrators and other teachers may wish to build the affair into a large assembly presentation. The teacher should generally avoid this. His students have studied about marijuana; they know something about the problem and are ready for the guest speaker and his message. All-school assemblies have their place; however, outside speakers generally make a more lasting impact when they deal with smaller groups, where the opportunity for real communication is greater.

REFERENCES

Cornacchia, Harold J., David J. Bentel, and David E. Smith. *Drugs in the Classroom: A Conceptual Model for School Programs.* St. Louis: The C. V. Mosby Co., 1973.

Drug Abuse: Escape to Nowhere. Philadelphia: Smith, Kline, and French Laboratories in cooperation with the American Association for Health, Physical Education and Recreation, 1970.

"Students Concerned with Public Health." *School Health Review,* Vol. 3, No. 4 (September–October 1972), pp. 39–42.

Tucker, Karen. "Critical Thinking," *School Health Review,* Vol. 4, No. 1 (January–February 1973), p. 3.

15 ■ ALCOHOL EDUCATION I: FOUNDATIONS

The increased attention that drug problems of all types have received during the past few years have added new fuel to the traditional controversies which surround beverage alcohol, American society's most widely used and legally acceptable psychoactive substance. The modern tendency to view drug problems in broader perspective, with aspirin, alcohol, and heroin all located along the same continuum, has brought both new insights and new emotionalism to the study of American drinking practices. The relatively recent linking of alcohol with the defenders of established society as opposed to the advocates of the counterculture has added a new area of bias to a topic that sorely needs dispassionate and objective deliberation. This new debate, although involving different participants, has followed a pattern remarkably similar to the historical "wets versus drys" strife of prohibition days wherein polarized groups with moral and economic motives presented arguments of dubious scientific accuracy.

Recently the debate concerning alcohol has reached new levels of intensity because of the interjection of new issues such as the marijuana legalization controversy and similar aspects which have often carried sociopolitical overtones. Although this new and colorful aspect of the problem has attracted considerable public attention, it has provided little of value to thoughtful decision making. Marijuana supporters characterize alcohol as a serious destroyer of liver and brain tissue, a phenomenon that has not been observed in the moderate drinker, and the defenders of alcohol warn against the long-term consequence of using a drug of which we "know so little about" when in fact Americans are absorbing scores of additives and legal prescription drugs that we probably know less about than the "venerable weed."

312

This issue appears to be as lacking in relevance as it is in the exposure of accurate information. In their overwhelming concern with possible physical damage, both sides tend to overlook the fundamental danger associated with the habitual use of any psychoactive substance: "that is, developing a personality based on escaping rather than coping."[1] If the user of alcohol or any other psychoactive substance is concerned about possible detrimental effects he should look, not so much to his cells and tissues as to his habits and behavior. Such questions as "How am I spending my time? What are my goals? Who are my friends? What do I think about my life?" point more clearly to the real hazards associated with the use of any drug. Fortunately the large majority of alcohol users manage to avoid the twin behavioral problems of alcoholism and abusive episodes of intoxication such as those related to auto accidents and criminal acts. However, the substantial minority of drinkers that do encounter serious problems comprise a public health problem of massive proportions.

PUBLIC ATTITUDES

Perhaps the most serious inhibitors of the constructive action needed to solve alcohol-related problems are the confusion and ambivalences that surround the issues in this area. Throughout the history of the nation little consensus has existed, and this schism appears to exist both between different persons and within the personality of the individual himself. It is interesting to examine the possible factors that led to this state of affairs.

Wets Versus Drys

The term *alcohol* carries predominately negative connotations for most Americans. It often evokes thoughts of drunkenness, alcoholism, automobile accidents, family disruptions, or teen-age delinquencies. In the mass media, alcohol-related problems are given considerable, and at times disproportionate, attention. Except for the obviously biased and hedonistic appeals of the advertisers, the average citizen hears little that is good about alcohol, yet he continues to drink. A gradually increasing majority of Americans report that they use alcohol.[2] Although scientific investigations of the effects of alcohol on the living effectiveness of the moderate drinkers, as opposed to the abuser, are exceedingly scarce, the common statement that 90 per cent or more of the users are not adversely affected by their association with this beverage seems reasonable.[3] Recently, modest support has appeared for the point of view that alcohol enriches the life of many of its

[1] Dana L. Farnsworth, "Drug Use for Pleasure: A Complex Social Problem," *The Journal of School Health*, Vol. XLIII, No. 3 (March 1973), p. 158.
[2] Don Cahalan and Ira H. Cisin, "American Drinking Practices," *Quarterly Journal of Studies on Alcohol*, Vol. 29 (March 1968), pp. 130–151.
[3] Morris E. Chafetz, *Liquor: The Servant of Man* (Boston: Little, Brown, 1965).

users. Yet although millions of Americans have experienced no apparent harm and possibly even tangible benefits from their drinking, our average citizen has been aptly described as one who "drinks wet" but "thinks dry."

The Silent Majority

The basic reasons for the ambivalence that Americans generally manifest toward beverage alcohol are exceedingly complex. At the risk of considerable oversimplification, they can be summarized with the statement that a society with the same need for some readily available tension-reducing substance that virtually every present or past society has exhibited was subjected to one of the most enthusiastic and well-organized temperance movements in history. Several volumes have been written in an effort to record and interpret this significant historical phenomenon properly.[4] Although different versions conflict on many points, there is general agreement concerning the force and potency of the American temperance movement. Bacon describes the classical dry philosophy which emerged from this movement as the only well-defined position concerning beverage alcohol ever developed in the United States, and one which still exerts a strong influence on American thought. The "classical wet" philosophy was formulated mainly by those with an economic stake in the alcoholic-beverage industry and consisted of little more than irrational denials of the equally irrational "dry" position. The average person was understandably reluctant to endorse either of these extremes; consequently, he tended to give little serious thought to the matter. He then became part of the vast silent majority that Bacon terms the "unaligned avoiders."[5]

CURRENT SCHOOL PROGRAMS

Abstinence Orientation

In the years since the repeal of Prohibition there has been some erosion of the strength of the temperance philosophy throughout our larger society. However, in the smaller arena of the school, there has been little evidence of decline. Even though many of the original state laws of the nineteenth century mandating instruction on the "evil and deleterious" effects of tobacco and alcohol have been modified, there has been little change in the spirit of their implementation. The school's efforts have been for the most

[4] For thorough accounts of the temperance movement see Henry Welsh Lee, *How Dry We Were: Prohibition Revisited* (Englewood Cliffs, N.J.: Prentice-Hall, 1963), or Andrew Sinclair, *Prohibition: The Era of Excess* (Boston: Atlantic Monthly Press, 1967).

[5] Selden D. Bacon, "Education on Alcohol: A Background Statement," *Alcohol Education: Proceedings of a Conference*, U.S. Department of Health, Education, and Welfare, March 1966, p. 14.

part quite thoroughly abstinence oriented.[6] This emphasis on abstinence has generally resulted in a heavy preoccupation with the problems related to the use of alcohol and a consequent neglect of objective information concerning alcoholic beverages and the sociocultural aspects of their use. Little attention is generally given to the topic of moderate drinking. As one observer describes it, "The moderate drinker [is] allowed on stage only as an apprentice alcoholic or as a heedless tempter of his weaker brother."[7] This point of view leads to programs consisting largely of content focused on one single aspect of the student's life, namely, his basic choice to drink or abstain. They provide little information of value to the potential social drinker, who needs practical information if he is to avoid the hazards inherent in the use of alcohol.

Typical Patterns

A few health teachers no doubt still adhere to the "militant dry" position, particularly in sections of the country where this constitutes the majority position among the local populace. These teachers do not disguise their attempt to draw students into the ranks of the lifelong abstainers. But there are at least two other, more common patterns that produce the same results in a less forthright fashion. The holders of the first position pay lip service to the right of each individual student to make his own decision; they then proceed to place disproportionate, if not complete, emphasis on the problems associated with drinking. They say, "Make up your own mind, but remember that drinkers often jeopardize their marriages, kill people with guns and automobiles, become alcoholics and develop delirium tremens." This is often called the make-up-your-own-mind-but-don't drink approach.

A second common position is not really directed toward abstinence; however, it manages to move in that direction without active guidance. Teachers adopting this position are not opposed to moderate drinking per se, they simply wish to avoid the complexities and controversies involved in handling moderate drinking as a classroom topic. These sticky problems are effectively circumvented by dwelling exclusively on alcoholism, a safe topic upon which everyone can agree. Their approach is commonly termed *alcoholism education* rather than *alcohol education*.

Although these approaches differ somewhat in their expressed philosophy and ultimate goals, they are similar in the basic way they are perceived by the student. Directly or indirectly, someone is telling him that alcohol has nothing to offer except problems; that those who drink are exhibiting some sort of personal weakness, either in their inability to resist

---

[6] Hilma Unterberger and Lena DiCicco, "Alcohol Education Re-Evaluated," *National Association of Secondary School Principals Bulletin*, Vol. 52 (March 1968), p. 15.

[7] Joseph C. Furnas, *The Life and Times of the Late Demon Rum* (New York: Putnam, 1965), p. 344.

social pressure or to face up to their problems without some sort of chemical crutch; that those who drink realize no positive benefits and expose themselves to any number of hazards. It is not hard to imagine the student enduring all this, then taking a look at the world around him and wondering, "Why do so many people drink? Do they enjoy it? If so, why? Does alcohol serve any useful function? Does the pattern of use differ much among individual drinkers? Are there ways to minimize the risks associated with drinking?"

The student may speculate about these questions, but if he wants to search for answers, he will probably have to find his own sources of information. The odds are against such questions being effectively discussed in modern classrooms.

MOUNTING CRITICISM

In recent years many professionals working in fields related to the specific problem of alcoholism have grown increasingly dissatisfied with the irrational or apathetic attitude exhibited by the general public toward alcohol-related problems. They characterize this reaction as one that alternates between passive indifference and misguided emotionalism, with either response constituting a serious obstacle to the implementation of constructive programs. Moreover, school health educators with abstinence- or temperance-orientated teachings are often viewed as one of the main factors perpetuating these detrimental attitudes.

A Drinking Society

What is wrong with the educational efforts of those persons committed to a temperance philosophy? There are several points on which it might be criticized, but one disenchanted investigator [8] manages to sum up the main problem in two short sentences. "Their program is simple and vivid. The only trouble with it is that it does not take into account the fact that the majority of Americans drink." This point seems well taken, for within the United States few social phenomena have shown such a consistent and stable pattern as has the use of alcohol. Although the popularity of specific types of alcoholic beverages has varied from generation to generation, the average consumption in terms of absolute alcohol has remained virtually the same. Americans consumed 2.10 gallons of alcohol for each person aged fifteen years or over in 1850, 2.15 gallons in 1900, 2.04 gallons in 1950, and 2.07 gallons in 1960.[9] Recent data does tend to show a marked increase in

[8] Albert D. Ullman, *To Know the Difference* (New York: St. Martin's, 1969), p. 223.

[9] Raymond G. McCarthy, *Alcohol Education for Classroom and Community* (New York: McGraw-Hill, 1964), p. 133.

per capita consumption; however, it is too early to tell if the historic pattern of stability has been broken.

Although the per capita consumption is relatively easy to compute, it is considerably more difficult to determine who is drinking all this alcohol. The first serious attempt to assess the pattern of use with American society was made in 1947; at that time it was found that 65 per cent of a nationwide sample used alcohol.[10] More than twenty years later a similar study placed 68 per cent of our population in the user's category.[11] Once again a very consistent pattern is shown. A review of the subcategories within this latter study shows that the adult population can be roughly divided into three major groups of approximately equal size. These are abstainers; occasional drinkers, who drink less than once per week; and regular drinkers, who drink at least once per week.

The general pattern shown by objective studies of alcohol use is one of balance and consistency; however, it would be a gross exaggeration to say that the nature and extent of alcohol use in the United States have not varied. Within the broad and stable pattern of per capita consumption, there has been a historic decline in the consumption of distilled spirits and a corresponding rise in the consumption of beer and wine, and increases are apparent in the percentage of women and teen-agers that use alcohol. Although these trends merit attention for their specific implications, the overriding consideration is that we live in a society that accepts the moderate use of alcohol.

Youthful Imbibers

As is so often the case, the acceptance of alcohol within adult society is reflected in the prevailing attitudes and practices of young people. This effect, which is most visible among teen-agers, has stimulated considerable research. The work of Maddox and McCall [12] seems particularly valuable in this regard. They found that the large majority of young people used alcohol on at least one occasion before graduation from high school. Also, a small but significant majority reported using alcohol with some regularity during their high school years. Most of their subjects reported that they received their first drink in the home in the presence of approving adults. With regard to the motives for teen-age drinking, Maddox and McCall saw little evidence of rebellion against authority or peer persuasion as the prime motive. They felt that the evidence strongly supported the view that teenagers begin drinking as part of their normal efforts to assume adult roles.

10 J. W. Riley and C. F. Marden, "The Social Pattern of Alcoholic Drinking," *Quarterly Journal of Studies on Alcohol*, Vol. 8 (1947), pp. 265–278.

11 Cahalan and Cisin, op. cit., p. 136.

12 George L. Maddox and B. C. McCall, *Drinking Among Teenagers: A Social Interpretation of Alcohol Use by High School Students* (New Brunswick, N.J.: Rutgers Center of Alcohol Studies, 1964).

Although some "rebellious" drinking undoubtedly takes place, the need to strike out against adult authority appears to be a motive of relatively minor importance.

While the analysis of Maddox and McCall seems quite appropriate for the majority of American communities, where social drinking is generally accepted, a somewhat different situation appears to prevail in those areas of high adult abstinence. Here fewer teen-agers drink but relatively more drink without parental approval. This, of course, restricts the number of potential abusers, but there are higher rates of alcohol-related problems and more evidence of unwholesome drinking patterns reported for this smaller group.[13] In these communities peer influence appeared to be the immediate factor in motivating teen-agers toward use or abuse. It appears safe to assume that the urge to rebel against authority plays a larger role as a fundamental reason for youthful drinking in these instances. A cause-and-effect relationship between use of alcohol and antisocial behavior was not apparent, regardless of the cultural setting; however, alcohol abuse often seems to complicate and intensify destructive behavior prompted by other factors.

The widespread contact that many teen-agers have with beverage alcohol either as direct users or as persons indirectly involved in drinking situations lends a sense of urgency to the need for a sound program of alcohol education. A brief consideration of the properties of the substance itself serves to increase this concern.

A Self-prescribed Drug

For the sake of an interesting discussion, consider this hypothetical situation. Assume for a moment that beverage alcohol had just been developed by the pharmaceutical industry. What use would our society make of it? How would it be controlled? Although most pharmacologists would hold that alcohol does not offer anything to the physician that cannot be better accomplished with other substances, at least one, Dr. William Dock,[14] feels that it would play a useful role as a medical tool if it were advertised in the professional literature as vigorously as present-day drug discoveries. He describes the effects of alcohol in small doses as "a superb tranquilizer; in larger doses a good sedative; and in even larger doses, an effective anesthetic agent." And, one might add, it can be habit-forming and, if taken in overdose, lethal. The question of alcohol's medicinal value still remains unanswered; however, one thing seems clear, if it were discovered today, its sale as an over-the-counter drug would not be permitted. Many drugs with

---

[13] Gerald Globetti, "Social Adjustment of High School Students and Problem Drinking," *Journal of Alcohol Education*, Vol. 13, No. 2 (Fall 1967), pp. 21–39.

[14] William Dock, "The Clinical Value of Alcohol," in Salvatore Lucia (ed.), *Alcohol and Civilization* (New York: McGraw-Hill, 1963), pp. 75–86.

far milder effects and far less potential for harming the user have been restricted to use by prescription only.

Alcohol is not, of course, a recent discovery; the circumstances surrounding this event remain buried in the past. It predates both recorded history and, with the possible exception of the family, the development of the usual agencies and organizations that society normally uses to control potentially dangerous substances. It has become so much a part of mankind's culture that no major government has successfully prohibited its use. Few social phenomena have shown as consistent and stable a pattern as has the use of beverage alcohol. In many sections of the country it is almost as readily available and widely used as aspirin tablets. Consequently, efforts to control the abuse of alcohol by making it more difficult to obtain appear to be impractical and probably undesirable. The real answer appears to lie in providing the public with the knowledge and understanding necessary for intelligent and constructive behavior with respect to its use.

Minimal Influence

The provision for accurate and thorough information pertaining to the safe and constructive use of beverage alcohol is systematically avoided in the typical abstinence-oriented program. As is the case with any instructional program, it is difficult to determine just what the long-term effects of this bias on the behavior of the students really are. It is only fair to say that some reinforcement of commitments probably occurs among those whose home and/or religion influenced them to abstain.[15] Some students may be undecided on whether to use alcohol and others may be on the verge of alcohol abuse. In these cases, a reasonable presentation of the consequences might have a decisively favorable effect.[16] But for the most part the educational efforts of the school have had little apparent effect on the very things they seem designed to accomplish, namely, influencing students to abstain. As noted previously, American drinking patterns have remained remarkably stable for a century or more, whereas educational efforts both within the school and in the larger society have varied considerably in their intensity. There appears to be considerable truth in the statement "that values surrounding drinking and embedded in drinking patterns are primarily shaped by experiences in the family and in peer groups rather than by formal educational agencies." [17] Those who accept his assumption feel that it would be much more realistic to direct educa-

---

15 Bacon, op. cit., p. 12.

16 Godfrey Hochbaum, "How Can We Teach Adolescents About Smoking, Drinking, and Drug Abuse?" *Journal of Health, Physical Education and Recreation*, Vol. 36, No. 8 (October 1968), p. 38.

17 Edwin M. Lemert, "Alcohol, Values and Social Control," in David J. Pittman and Charles R. Snyder (eds.), *Society, Culture, and Drinking Patterns* (New York: Wiley, 1962), p. 563.

tional efforts at *helping the individual operate more intelligently within the framework of his basic choice to drink or abstain.*

Possible Harm

Although many authorities feel that present programs fail to meet the needs of the large majority of young people, others view the consequences as being much more serious. In their well-regarded text, *Alcoholism and Society*, Chafetz and Demone [18] came to this conclusion following a review of several cross-cultural studies. They felt that the results supported the view that, "Cultures which preach prohibition are likely to create unhealthy attitudes about drinking which contribute to alcoholism." [19] They draw particular attention to the extremely low rate of alcoholism among American Jews, who generally condone moderate drinking and place considerable value on the intelligent control of one's intake, as compared with the relatively high rate of alcoholism among Protestants, who violate the principles of their particular sect in order to drink. There seems to be some tendency among those who have been taught that all drinking is essentially evil to view excessive drinking as being little different from moderate drinking.

This point of view is consistent with studies which show that teen-age drinking taking place in communities where an abstinence philosophy prevails tend to be more abusive than that reported elsewhere.[20] Other preliminary research findings concerned with addictive drinking patterns also conform to this pattern. These show a disproportionate number of alcoholics among persons whose first drinking experience took place in circumstances typical of those who drink without family approval. This drinking specifically took place (1) at a later age, (2) in the company of nonfamily members, and (3) in a place other than the home or a public establishment.[21]

SOME POSITIVE ALTERNATIVES

It is easy to criticize, one might say, but what about some positive suggestions? Perhaps the most comprehensive and thoughtfully prepared recommendations have been put forth by the Cooperative Commission on the Study of Alcoholism.[22] Financed by a grant from the National Institute of

[18] Morris E. Chafetz and Harold W. Demone, Jr., *Alcoholism and Society* (New York: Oxford University Press, 1962).

[19] Ibid., p. 182.

[20] Gerald Globetti, "The Use of Beverage Alcohol by Youth in an Abstinence Setting," *Journal of School Health*, Vol. 39, No. 3 (March 1969), pp. 179–182.

[21] Albert D. Ullman, "First Drinking Experience as Related to Age and Sex," in David J. Pittman and Charles R. Snyder (eds.), *Society, Culture and Drinking Patterns* (New York: Wiley, 1962), p. 262.

[22] Cooperative Commission on the Study of Alcoholism, *Alcohol Problems: A Report to the Nation* (New York: Oxford University Press, 1967).

Mental Health, the commission was able to recruit a highly qualified panel of experts for an in-depth study of alcohol-related problems. Even though its study was focused on alcoholism and related problems, many of its recommendations merit consideration as guiding principles for any program of alcohol education. Those that seem particularly relevant are presented here, together with interpretive comments by the authors:

1. *"Reduce the emotionalism associated with alcoholic beverages."* [23] The tendency to portray alcohol as possessing highly positive or negative qualities should be discouraged. Its presence is not a guarantee that one's party will be a success, nor does its use inevitably lead to inappropriate or dangerous behavior. Less distinction should be made between drinkers and nondrinkers at social gatherings. Guests at social functions should not be pressured to drink. A "take it or leave it" attitude should prevail.

2. *"Clarify and emphasize the distinctions between acceptable drinking and unacceptable drinking."* [24] Although the traditional distinction between drinkers and nondrinkers should be minimized, the line between acceptable and unacceptable drinking patterns should be more clearly drawn. This recommendation takes into account one of the fundamental criticisms of an abstinence culture wherein the individual is strictly on his own once he moves into the ranks of the users. If any drinking is viewed as evil, whether it be one drink or twenty drinks, there is little guidance or motivation toward moderation.

3. *"Discourage drinking for its own sake and encourage the integration of drinking with other activities."* [25] If drunkenness is appropriate anywhere, then it is probably more appropriate in a barroom than at the dinner table or in a bowling alley. Drinking that takes place within the context of social and recreational activities tends to be controlled by built-in restraints. Laws that restrict drinking to such narrowly designated places as bars and taverns tend to encourage unhealthy drinking patterns.

4. *"Assist young people to adapt themselves realistically to a predominantly 'drinking' society."* [26] Reduce the legal drinking age to eighteen years, because the common standard of twenty-one years is largely unenforceable and encourages clandestine teen-age drinking under conditions lacking social restraints. Create situations wherein teen-agers may become acquainted with alcohol in adult-supervised activities. Provide meaningful and realistic instructions regarding alcohol both in the home and in the school. Emphasize objectivity and free discussion during this instruction.

It is impossible to capture the full force and meaning of this significant report in this brief overview. We perhaps do it an injustice by presenting some of its more controversial items somewhat out of context. It is only

[23] Ibid., p. 138.
[24] Ibid., p. 142.
[25] Ibid., p. 146.
[26] Ibid., p. 148

fair to say that in the full report very telling arguments are put forth for its specific recommendations. One point should be kept clearly in mind by those who attempt to interpret and evaluate its content. Its intent is to reduce alcohol-related problems; it was developed and written by men who were fully cognizant of the human misery that alcohol abuse can cause. Although its recommendations are quite liberal in effect, they are not designed to protect the average citizen's right to drink, but simply to encourage him to stop perpetuating a system that turns susceptible people into problem drinkers and alcoholics. Effective programs of school health education have much to contribute to this worthwhile goal.

A NEW ROLE FOR THE SCHOOL

The importance of alcoholism and other alcohol-related problems in American society is well known. Conservative estimates place the number of alcoholics somewhere between 6 and 9 million. This alone would constitute a significant public health problem even without consideration of such related problems as auto fatalities, crime, family disorganization, and economic loss. Decisions concerning appropriate individual and community actions in regard to alcohol often involve consideration of complex physiological, emotional, and social factors. The knowledge needed for this task requires a systematic educational program for its acquisition. Moreover, young people need opportunities to form attitudes and clarify values in educational environments which permit free discussion of all the issues. The school seems to be the only resource with the potential to meet such needs. For these reasons alcohol education merits attention as a priority area of content within school programs of health education.

Universal Need

Too often instruction on alcohol topics becomes too narrowly focused on the potential abuser. All students have important educational needs with respect to alcohol regardless of their present or future patterns of use or nonuse. The needs of regular users or potentially regular users are obvious. The infrequent drinker needs knowledge to offset his inexperience which may produce relatively higher degrees of risk during his occasional periods of use. Knowledge provides the abstainer with the basis for the development of constructive attitudes toward users with whom he comes in contact. Finally, a commonly overlooked factor is the need of all citizens for knowledge if they are to discharge intelligently their community responsibilities pertaining to the support of constructive legislation and programs for the prevention and control of alcohol abuse.

Realistic Content

Any comprehensive program of alcohol education must give due attention to the frequency and intensity of the problems related to alcohol. This may involve the presentation of material that will provide an emotional impact. However, the purpose of any such presentation must be to inform the student, not to threaten him. The use of content, materials, or activities designed primarily to produce fear or guilt reactions would have no place in any educational program, even if it did discourage alcohol abuse, which it does not. Speculation on the real effects of such experiences range from mere avoidance or rejection of the teacher's efforts, through the possible development of damaging conflicts with parental attitudes, to the possible encouragement of personal practices of alcohol abuse. A comprehensive program must also give due attention to the fact that millions of persons drink without apparent harm. The two-thirds or so of one's students who will no doubt seek to join these millions need useful information if they are to drink intelligently. The remaining potential abstainers need to examine their attitudes and practices so that they can learn to abstain without becoming unduly defensive about their own position or antagonistic toward users with whom they come in contact.

Once the health educator accepts the fact that a certain portion of his students are using or will someday use alcohol, that another portion will never use alcohol, and that his job is to provide educational experiences of value to both groups, then his position becomes more realistic, but also more complicated. Consider for a moment these different situations that often involve teen-age drinking:

- drinking an occasional beer or glass of wine at the family supper table
- experimenting by getting high at a teen-age party
- drinking at a bar or tavern
- drinking at a beer party where there are only boys (or only girls)
- having a mixed drink at a family gathering [27]

There is much that those students who are committed to the use of alcohol can learn about the advisability of drinking or not drinking in each of these specific situations. Most people would see nothing wrong in a sixteen-year-old having a glass of wine at the family dinner table, but what if one of his teen-age friends is present as a guest? Now the propriety of each minor's drinking is affected by the views of the guest's parents and, in many states, by legal factors. Suppose an abstinent girl discovers that her steady boyfriend occasionally drinks at family gatherings. Does this mean that the relationship should be dissolved? Probably not, but what if he also uses a borrowed driver's license to drink in taverns? How should she interpret this? The appropriate response for these situations would require a dispassionate consideration of much more information about the situations and persons involved. The forthright consideration of such

[27] U.S. Department of Health, Education, and Welfare, *Thinking About Drinking?*, Public Health Service Publication No. 1683, Washington, D.C., 1968, p. 6.

realistic situations in the classroom illustrates the type of experiences that an effective program should provide.

Implications for the Elementary School

Although the need for alcohol education is commonly accepted at the secondary level, it is even more commonly omitted in elementary school curricula. This is extremely unfortunate, for most children become aware of alcoholic beverages at an early age. This awareness comes to many as they observe the drinking habits of their parents. It is not unusual for parents who use alcohol to allow the children in the home to taste these beverages occasionally as a means of satisfying their curiosity. In a few homes children are permitted watered-down wine or some mild equivalent on a fairly regular basis. Even in the homes of abstaining parents, the ever-present television set brings information on alcohol to viewers of all ages.

Throughout all of this incidental exposure the information that children acquire is sometimes charged with emotion and sometimes quite matter of fact. Nevertheless, the child takes all this in and begins the process of forming concepts and values with regard to these significant phenomena. This process takes place for the most part in a relatively placid manner; to the average elementary school child, the issue of alcohol is largely a hypothetical one. Unlike the secondary school youth, the elementary school child is seldom exposed to situations which involve the temptation for alcohol abuse. Although he does not become very emotional about alcohol, he is interested in this substance and ready to learn. Unfortunately this learning generally takes place in a hit-and-miss fashion, with little effective guidance provided by teachers or parents. Most elementary schools fail to include the study of alcohol in their curricula, and parents often find that alcohol, like sex, is a topic that is difficult to discuss with their children.

It seems logical to assume that children should have access to accurate facts and mature guidance as they begin to form concepts concerning the use of alcohol. The School Health Education Study, whose curriculum framework is widely endorsed, offers specific recommendations for teaching this topic at the elementary level. Among the behavioral objectives it provides for their first progression level, which is normally comparable to the primary grades, two apply specifically to alcohol. These are as follows:

- *Is aware* that there are differences between alcoholic beverages and other beverages.
- *Realizes* there are differences in family practices and feelings about use of tobacco and of alcoholic beverages.[28]

[28] Reproduced by permission of Minnesota Mining and Manufacturing Company, publishers of *Health Education: A Conceptual Approach to Curriculum Design* and copyrighted 1967 by School Health Education Study, Inc.

These modest objectives seem very appropriate for the primary grades. They call for the acquisition of knowledge that is both useful to the young child and within his capacity to understand. For the second progression level, which is normally comparable to the upper elementary grades, two of the behavioral objectives that are particularly relevant to the topic of alcohol are the following:

- *Differentiates* among controls on purchase, possession, and use of substances that modify mood and behavior.
- *Illustrates* how, when, and where certain mood and behavior-modifying substances are used for dietary, ceremonial, social, pain relieving, and other reasons.[29]

Although some progression is evident when these are compared with the objectives for level I, these objectives also deal with things that are generally nontechnical and within the average child's realm of experience. Most elementary children become aware of the fact that minors are not allowed to purchase alcoholic beverages or consume them in public establishments. They know that for some people, special occasions call for the use of alcohol and that social drinking takes different forms among different groups. All in all, the objectives seem directed toward a basic familiarization with the various ways alcohol is commonly used in our society. The emphasis is on customs, preferences, restrictions, and so on; any consideration of the technical or pharmacological aspects should be restricted to very simple and basic points.

Implications for the Secondary Level

In contrast to the situation at the elementary level, health educators generally experience little difficulty in convincing parents, school boards, school administrators, and the like of the need for alcohol education at the secondary level. In most states, of course, its teaching in these schools is required by law. As implied earlier, the problem within junior high school and high school programs is not one of program acceptance but of program emphasis and effectiveness. Secondary students are generally ready to respond to a consideration of common alcohol problems with a surprising degree of maturity and effectiveness if given a suitable opportunity in the classroom. And as with most other areas of study the provision of this "suitable opportunity" is not an easy task; it is what teaching is all about.

Suggested Concepts

The following concepts are presented in an effort to express our views concerning the proper scope of a school program of alcohol education. They were developed following a review of several sources.[30] Each concept,

[29] Ibid., p. 86.
[30] Most helpful were *Health Concepts: Guides for Health Instruction*, American Association for Health, Physical Education and Recreation, 1967; *School Health Education Study*, op. cit.

in effect, describes an area of study which would require many specific learning experiences for its full development. They should, of course, be reviewed and modified to meet local needs if their incorporation into specific programs is contemplated.

Physical Aspects of Alcohol Use

1. *Beverage alcohol is a single, well-defined substance produced by the fermentation of grains and fruits; it is the only ingredient of alcoholic beverages which produces significant effects on the nervous system.* Although alcoholic beverages vary considerably in their taste, smell, and appearance, they all have intoxicating qualities. This intoxicating potential is almost entirely determined by the proportion of pure alcohol present in the beverage.

2. *The blood alcohol concentration of the user is determined largely by the amount ingested, the rate of ingestion, and the blood volume of the user.*[31] Among other factors the presence or absence of food in the stomach is also quite significant; exercise, perspiration, and excretion seem to have little or no effect.

3. *There is no evidence that beverage alcohol causes significant damage to the tissue of those who use it moderately; the nature of its relationship to the common medical problems of the abuser is largely unknown.* Even during heavy intoxication, blood alcohol concentration rarely exceeds 0.4 per cent, an amount considered too low to produce structural damage to the body. Many chronic alcoholics develop severe medical conditions; however, dietary deficiencies and general health neglect appear to be significant factors in their development.

Behavioral Effects of Alcohol Use

4. *Beverage alcohol functions principally as a depressant to the nervous system.* Although persons who have been drinking sometimes become more active, this occurs because they have become less concerned about their actions. Alcohol temporarily slows down most bodily activities and thus reduces one's sensory and motor efficiency.

5. *The specific chemical effects of beverage alcohol vary according to the blood alcohol concentration and range from an insignificant effect, through mild tranquilization, to heavy intoxication.* In small amounts alcohol produces a reduction in emotional tension which is accompanied by a slight reduction in motor and sensory efficiency; in larger amounts, alcohol functions as a sedative, narcotic, or anesthetic, depending on the concentration.

6. *The effects of a given blood alcohol concentration on the behavior of the individual vary considerably because of the influence of a wide variety of situational and personality factors.* Although the basic pharma-

[31] *Health Concepts: Guides for Health Instruction,* op. cit., p. 11.

cological effects are relatively predictable, the emotional tone and voluntary behavior of a drinking person are determined in large part by such things as basic personality type, recent experiences during the days or hours before imbibing, and the mood and actions of others present in the drinking situation.

Cultural Attitudes and Patterns of Use

7. *Individual attitudes and practices regarding beverage alcohol are affected by a wide variety of social and cultural factors.* The nature of one's home life in terms of religion, ethnic tradition, and parental attitudes; the public attitude of one's community; the norms of one's peer group; and the specific characteristics of one's personality—all affect one's concept of alcohol.

8. *Individual and group attitudes pertaining to beverage alcohol have important personal, social, and community consequences.* The effect of individual attitudes on practices is obvious; however, public opinion affects the conditions of individual use via the medium of formal and informal controls; by more subtle means, it affects emotional responses to alcohol in ways that may have positive or negative effects.

9. *The use of beverage alcohol is a relatively permanent and prominent feature of man's culture.* Alcoholic beverages have been used to a significant degree throughout American history despite the effort of many groups to reduce or eliminate their use; periodic studies of the percentage of users and the per capita consumption show an extremely consistent pattern.

10. *Individual patterns of alcohol use vary widely; however, the majority of those who drink use alcohol moderately.* Approximately one-third of the American population abstains; of those who drink, roughly 90 per cent do so moderately, whereas the remaining 10 per cent exhibit a drinking pattern that often leads to serious problems.

11. *Many persons use beverage alcohol intelligently for pleasure and enjoyment with no ill effects.* Although the many problems related to alcohol use are serious and widely publicized, the large majority of users avoid these problems through the exercise of mature judgment and control.

Alcohol Abuse

12. *The behavior of individuals during periods of alcohol abuse produces a variety of personal and social problems.* The presence of alcohol tends to increase the difficulties inherent in situations where there are physical hazards, as in operating an automobile or power machinery of any kind, and in situations where there is emotional stress, as in family arguments or personality conflicts.

13. *Alcoholism is a disease condition which renders an individual incapable of controlling his drinking and expose him to the consequences of frequent abuse.* Some persons lose control of their drinking because of

their personal susceptibility and the circumstances surrounding their use of alcohol. Although a relatively small proportion of drinkers are affected, alcoholism ranks as a leading health problem in terms of consequences and numbers of cases.

14. *The specific cause or causes of alcoholism are unknown; however, alcoholism often appears to result from the prolonged use of beverage alcohol as a means of reducing emotional tension.* Several theories have been advanced and investigated, yet there is still considerable disagreement on basic causes. Factors of personal susceptibility and stressful circumstances seem to be essential to the development of this disease.

15. *The problems related to the abuse of beverage alcohol require both individual and community efforts for their prevention, control, and amelioration.* Each individual is responsible for his personal behavior in alcohol-related matters and for the encouragement of responsible behavior among members of his own family. On the community level, alcohol-related problems have many detrimental effects and require intelligent support of programs and legislation directed toward their control.

16. *Alcoholism can be successfully treated, but the process frequently involves intensive social, psychological, and medical procedures.* Both the causes and consequences of alcoholism appear to involve a complex group of emotional, social, and psychological factors that interact in a unique way for each individual; the factors necessary to correct this condition are equally complex.

REFERENCES

Bacon, Selden D. "Education on Alcohol: A Background Statement," *Alcohol Education: Conference Proceedings.* Washington, D.C.: U.S. Department of Health, Education, and Welfare, (March 1966), pp. 7–15.

Berland, Theodore. "Should Children Be Taught to Drink," *Today's Health,* Vol. 47, No. 2 (February 1969), pp. 46–49.

Cahalan, Don, and Ira H. Cisin. "American Drinking Practices: Summary of Findings from a National Probability Sample," *Quarterly Journal of Studies on Alcohol,* Vol. 29 (March 1968), pp. 130–151.

———, and Robin Room. "Problem Drinking Among American Men Aged 21–59," *American Journal of Public Health,* Vol. 62, No. 11 (November 1972), pp. 1472–1482.

Chafetz, Morris E. *Liquor: The Servant of Man.* Boston: Little, Brown and Company, 1965.

Daniel, Ralph. "Alcohol Education vs. Alcoholism Education," *Journal of Alcohol Education,* Vol. 13, No. 1 (Spring 1967), pp. 44–45.

Demone, Harold W. "Implications from Research on Adolescent Drinking," *Alcohol Education: Conference Proceedings.* Washington, D.C.: U.S. Department of Health, Education, and Welfare (March 1966), pp. 16–19.

Farnsworth, Dana L. "Drug Use for Pleasure: A Complex Social Problem," *Journal of School Health*, Vol. XLIII, No. 3 (March 1973), pp. 153–158.

Fox, Vernelie. "Alcoholism In Adolescents," *Journal of School Health*, Vol. XLII, No. 1 (January 1973), pp. 32–35.

Globetti, Gerald. "Social Adjustment of High School Students and Problem Drinking," *Journal of Alcohol Education*, Vol. 13, No. 2 (Fall 1967), pp. 21–39.

Hanson, David J. "Social Norms and Drinking Behavior: Implication for Alcohol and Drug Education," *Journal of Alcohol and Drug Education*, Vol. 18, No. 2 (Winter 1973), pp. 18–24.

Keller, Mark. "Alcohol in Health and Disease: Some Historical Perspectives," *Annals of the New York Academy of Science*, Vol. 133 (1966), pp. 820–827.

Lucia, Salvatore P. (ed.). *Alcohol and Civilization*. New York: McGraw-Hill Book Company, 1963.

Maddox, George L., and B. C. McCall. *Drinking Among Teenagers: A Social Interpretation of Alcohol Use by High School Students*. New Brunswick, N.J.: Rutgers Center of Alcohol Studies, 1964.

Miles, Samuel A. (ed.). *Learning About Alcohol*. Washington, D.C.: American Association for Health, Physical Education and Recreation, 1974.

Pittman, David J., and Charles R. Snyder (eds.). *Society, Culture and Drinking Patterns*. New York: John Wiley & Sons, Inc., 1962.

Russell, Robert D. "A New Way of Thinking About Alcohol," *Journal of Alcohol Education*, Vol. 12, No. 3 (Winter 1966), pp. 25–28.

Stacey, Barrie, and John Davies. "Drinking Behavior in Childhood and Adolescence: An Evaluative Review," *Journal of Alcohol and Drug Education*, Vol. 17, No. 3 (Spring 1972), pp. 1–11.

Windham, Gerald O., James D. Preston, and Harold B. Armstrong. "The High School Student in Mississippi and Beverage Alcohol," *Journal of Alcohol Education*, Vol. B, No. 1 (Spring 1967), pp. 1–12.

16 ■ ALCOHOL EDUCATION II: APPLICATIONS

As discussed in the preceding chapter, the overwhelming task in alcohol education is the need to counteract or somehow neutralize the highly emotional bias that people of all ages commonly attach to the various issues within this topic. In homes where alcohol is used, parents often adopt a policy of evading any serious questions their children might have concerning this substance in a manner that resembles their treatment of sexual issues. Drinking, like sexual activity, is something that adults do after the children have been put to bed, or otherwise disposed of; therefore, these topics should not concern them, and a "conspiracy of silence" is imposed. In other homes, where the parents advocate abstinence, the child may be subjected to a heavily negative point of view which is equally damaging to his ability to give alcohol-related issues objective consideration. This admittedly oversimplified analysis does a disservice to the great many drinking and nondrinking parents who do manage to convey sensible, constructive attitudes to their children related to alcohol; however, most classes will include many students that have been handicapped in their ability to deal with this topic.

SELECTION OF TEACHING TECHNIQUES
The physical- and biological-related facts and principles pertinent to alcohol use and abuse may be covered quite readily by conventional techniques once any serious emotional obstacles to learning have been overcome. Textbooks, pamphlets, filmstrips, and sound films can be used to good advantage. Special caution is needed, however, in the selection of these materials. As is the case with any controversial areas, alcohol-related educational materials often reflect the bias that prevails within the general public.

330

The Elementary Level

Many useful facts and concepts regarding alcohol may be acquired by elementary school children as incidental or correlated instruction presented within the context of other health topics or other fields of study. A consideration of various beverages naturally arises in any study of nutrition, thus providing an opportunity to discuss the special features of those that contain alcohol. The study of history and literature frequently contains references to the use of alcohol and thus provides a natural occasion for its consideration. When alcohol education occurs in this manner, the particular techniques or learning activities are naturally determined by the requirements of the principal topic of study. The advantages of utilizing these situations merit special emphasis; the efficiency from the standpoint of saving time in a crowded curriculum is obvious, but beyond this lies the great benefit of normalizing an inherently emotional topic by dealing with it as it naturally occurs in common life situations.

When alcohol-related content is presented directly as an independent topic at the elementary level, considerable emphasis should be placed on techniques that provide for broad participation in class discussion. Children generally have many questions they wish to ask and many feelings and opinions they want to express regarding alcohol use. These needs may be provided for by the development of an open and trusting classroom climate, which is, of course, the very essence of good teaching in any sensitive area, and the use of an appropriate preliminary activity in the form of a good film, art project, role-playing situation, or other stimulating technique. The various value-clarifying activities tend to combine the elements of stimulation and free discussion within a single format and thus have particular application to this topic, especially at the upper elementary level.

Secondary Level

The guidelines for the selection of techniques for alcohol education at the secondary level are very similar to those for the elementary level. However, two closely related differences that merit important consideration are the secondary student's increasing ability to participate in learning activities without direct supervision by the teacher, and his increasing reliance on his peers as a source of guidance for his opinions and behavior. These factors place increased importance on value-clarification techniques, buzz sessions, and other activities that enable students to talk to other students in relatively free discussions. Secondary students of course have plenty of time to talk about beverage alcohol outside of class time but, without the responsible leadership and small but necessary measure of assistance that a good teacher can provide, these spontaneous discussions are more often than not unproductive and frequently harmful in the attitudes, misconceptions, and behavior patterns they encourage.

Once the students have had this opportunity to clarify their feelings regarding alcohol and are thus able to consider specific issues in a relatively mature and objective fashion, they will then be better prepared to study various alternatives for handling society's many alcohol-related problems. These include the prevention and treatment of alcoholism, the prevention of alcohol-related traffic accidents, and the role of alcohol as a contributing factor in many criminal acts and family conflicts. The specific issues and alternatives related to these issues are often complex, requiring a great deal of information gathering and dispassionate application of principles if they are to be properly considered. These often call for library work, good films, resource speakers, and small-group field trips and other types of community investigations. These rather conventional techniques designed basically for cognitive learning can work well once attitudes and emotions have been dealt with and interest aroused by techniques where student involvement is stressed.

PRACTICAL APPLICATIONS
In this section examples of workable techniques as related to six concepts will be presented. These examples are designed to illustrate a general tone or approach for this somewhat controversial topic as well as specific procedures for the presentation of content.

I. TO EACH HIS OWN
Things that are different interest children. Alcoholic beverages and issues involving alcoholic beverages are generally treated as something special in most homes, regardless of the particular pattern of use or nonuse that prevails. When children become perceptive enough to detect the "different" status of beer, wine, whiskey, and so on, it is time for them to acquire the information that will keep this difference in proper perspective. In this teaching example the simple medium of still pictures is used to convey rudimentary information and help children develop the proper kind of respect for alcohol and for the rights of other persons whose attitudes and practices may differ from their own.

Concept
Beverage alcohol is a single, well-defined substance produced by the fermentation of grains and fruits; it is the only ingredient of alcoholic beverages which produces significant effects on the nervous system.

Pupils
This example was designed for second-grade pupils of average socioeconomic and academic status; with slight modification it would be appropriate for grades K through 3.

Techniques
Still pictures combined with class discussion.

The correlation of alcohol content with other health topics can be a very effective procedure; however, particular care is needed to ensure that essential points are included and that coverage is accurate and complete. Nutrition units provide the opportunity to discuss beverages of all types. One common device used in teaching nutrition is to ask children to find pictures of common food groups in old magazines which may then be mounted as posters or used in notebooks. On successive days the children might be asked to collect examples of meat dishes, casseroles, vegetables, desserts, and so on, so that the special features of each might be discussed. The following are some special recommendations for handling alcoholic beverages within this context:

1. When the children are asked to search out pictures of commonly used beverages, emphasize the fact that they may select any type, whether the children feel it is nutritious or not. In a matter-of-fact way mention that, in addition to the milk and fruit juices that most children drink at mealtime, it is all right to bring in examples of soft drinks and things that children do not use often, such as coffee, tea, beer, or wine. Ask each child to bring in one example and to try to think of two important things he can tell about the beverage he selects.

2. Prior to the next class meeting secure a skeleton set of properly mounted pictures from a classroom picture file or elsewhere. Be sure to include the alcoholic and nonnutritious items that the children may not select. This will ensure that all types will be available for the next day's discussion.

3. On the following day provide paste, construction paper, and crayons so that the pictures may be mounted and labeled. Also a simple border may be drawn in to display better the content of the picture. When this task has been completed, bring the children together in a circular formation or into some other arrangement that will permit them to view one another's work. Have the children hold up their pictures for a few moments so that the others may see and so that each child may have the satisfaction of displaying his efforts. At this time the teacher should make mental notes on the best examples available for discussion. Once this is accomplished, ask the children to turn in their pictures.

4. Select one picture from each basic category for discussion; give first priority to those examples prepared by the children, but fill in the gaps with the preselected "back-up" material. Begin the discussion for each item by calling on the child who prepared it to point out two things of importance. The discussion points for milk and fruit juices are simple, obvious, and generally well emphasized. Some suggested points to bring out for other nonalcoholic items are the following:

a. Coffee and tea are not regularly used by children in most homes because they do not contain the food elements that milk can provide for the needs of growing children. They also sometimes interfere with sleep if taken near bedtime.

b. Carbonated beverages and other soft drinks are generally not used at meal times for the same reasons that apply to coffee and tea. Many families use them at picnics, parties, and on other occasions as treats. If they are used between meals it is well to rinse one's mouth to minimize the chance of tooth decay.

5. The discussion of alcoholic beverages should be generally directed toward the development of (a) a basic awareness of alcohol and the different forms of alcoholic beverages, and (b) recognition and acceptance of the different attitudes that different people have regarding alcohol. Some specific points follow.

a. Alcohol is made by allowing sugary or starchy substances to ferment.

b. Wine, beer, gin, whiskey, and so on, all have the same kind of alcohol in them, but some contain more than others.

c. Many adults enjoy drinking these beverages for their flavor, to stimulate their appetite, or to help them relax.

d. Because alcoholic beverages have little food value and because large amounts of these beverages can interfere with normal behavior, most parents do not allow children to use them. However, some parents let their children taste alcoholic drinks occasionally and a few let them use wine regularly with meals.

e. There are many different opinions concerning the use of alcoholic beverages. Some people use them regularly, some just on special occasions, and others are opposed to any use of alcohol.

This example was designed for the average community, which can usually be expected to contain sizable groups of abstinent families, infrequent users, and regular users. In these circumstances the actual contact of second-graders with alcohol will probably be limited to an occasional taste of their parents' drinks, and only a few pupils will have this much contact with alcohol. These pupils may volunteer information concerning these experiences, and if they do, it should be treated in a normal manner. If one is teaching in a "dry" area, or in a predominantly Italian community, where the children may be drinking watered-down wine, then changes in the tone and emphasis of the discussion would be indicated.

II. THE GOOD WITH THE BAD

The basic job of any educator is to help people develop accurate and comprehensive impressions of those things which are relevant. Few people deny the relevance of alcohol use as a social issue, but the task of conveying a valid impression of this many-faceted topic is a challenging one. The difference in the way people view alcohol is illustrated by an "anonymous" writer in the following spoof:

If, when you say whiskey, you mean that brew, the poison spirit, the bloody monster that defiles innocence, detrones reason, destroys the home and creates misery, poverty, yes, literally takes the bread from the mouths of little children—then I am certainly against it with all my heart.

But if when you say whiskey, you mean the oil of conversation, the philosophic wine, the ale consumed when good fellows get together, that puts a song in their hearts and laughter on their lips, the warm glow of contentment in their eyes—then, I am certainly in favor of it.[1]

Alcohol, of course, means both of these things; more commonly, it means something between these extremes, depending on how it is used. Children can begin to develop this broader view of alcohol use if they are provided with an opportunity to become acquainted with the many ways alcohol is used. In this example, magazine pictures are once again used to illustrate this general idea.

Concept
Many persons use alcohol intelligently for pleasure and enjoyment with no ill effects.

Pupils
This example was developed for use with fifth-grade pupils of average socioeconomic and academic status; however, it would be appropriate for most any classroom group from grades 4 through 6.

Technique
Bulletin-board displays.

This teaching example provides a description of how a bulletin-board display may be used to depict the various circumstances and consequences related to alcohol use and abuse. A typical display might be organized into four sections to show alcoholic beverages as an adjunct to sociability, a main ingredient of ceremonies, a contributing cause of auto accidents, and the focal point of alcoholism. Only situations with positive connotations would have to be displayed and discussed if the objectives were confined to the development of the preceding concept. However, inclusion of both negative and positive aspects provides an opportunity simultaneously to begin development of a concept of alcohol abuse and to forestall possible parental objections that might result if apparent benefits were discussed in isolation. As is the case with any health topic, specific procedures are affected by local conditions; the following recommendations should be generally useful:

1. The development of a classroom bulletin-board display can serve very well as the central activity of a unit on beverage alcohol at the elementary level; work on the display should get under way on the first day of the unit.

[1] *Notes on Alcohol Education for Teachers,* Bulletin 371 (Lansing, Mich.: Department of Education, 1967), p. 13.

2. At the end of the first day's session, which normally covers introductory material, ask the children each to bring two pictures involving the use of alcohol. These will have to come largely from old magazines, although newspapers and leaflets or pamphlets sometimes also serve as good sources. If possible, each pair of pictures should contain one example of acceptable use of alcohol and one of alcohol abuse or the consequences of abuse. Allow at least two days for this search and remind the class of his obligation on each intervening day. As the pictures are brought in, immediately sort them into categories corresponding with the bulletin-board divisions.

3. Start work on the display by organizing the class into groups corresponding with the bulletin-board choices. Allow as much freedom of choice as possible; occasionally, abstinent parents may object if their child is forced to work on an assignment which depicts alcohol in a favorable light. Once the subgroups have been formed, one or two pupils from each should be selected to work on an oral report based on the same theme as their portion of the display—alcoholism, ceremonial use, and so on. These children may begin on this task immediately, probably starting with a trip to the library. The remaining portion of each group should begin planning the layout of their display.

4. The specific mechanics of the bulletin-board construction will necessarily vary according to the resources available and the training and background of the individual teacher. Probably the simplest procedure involves pasting the pictures on individual pieces of construction paper with captions applied by use of stencils and felt-tipped pens. The construction paper may be cut to a size and shape that most effectively accommodates the picture and caption. As the work gets under way, circulate from group to group to assist the children with their plans. The following are some basic hints to keep in mind: [2]

    a. A good display should be *harmonious,* with appropriate combinations of objects, colors, lettering, and so on.
    b. Proper *contrast* is important if pictures, words, and so on, are to command attention.
    c. Direction or *emphasis* should be apparent; the eye should be guided to the central theme of the layout.
    d. An underlying *shape or pattern* is generally useful in organizing the picture and guiding the viewer's attention; "S" or "T" patterns are often used for this purpose.

Once the individual sections have started to take shape, some thought needs to be given to some method of tying the entire display together. This can usually be accomplished by deciding on a common style of lettering for the four section titles and using large letters for a major title for the total project.

[2] James W. Brown, Richard B. Lewis, and Fred F. Harcleroad, AV *Instruction: Media and Methods* (New York: McGraw-Hill, 1969), pp. 410–411.

5. During the health lesson following the completion of the display, the oral reports should be presented; these should be brief, factual, and delivered in conversational style. Also provide an opportunity for the leader of each display group to point out and describe the highlights of their section of the bulletin board. Although it is important that the pupils be allowed to participate freely in any discussions these activities may stimulate, it is also important that the teacher be alert to correct any misconceptions that may be apparent. This may be done directly or by guiding the children toward accurate information, as the situation dictates.

III. A LITTLE PERSPECTIVE

A review of the facts reveals that alcoholic beverages rank next to water and milk in terms of widespread use. The people of virtually every age and country have both sung the praises of wine, or its equivalent, as a civilizing influence and cursed it as a cause of human misery. Even as one delves into the specific aspects of use and abuse, remarkable similarities still prevail. The benefits to be gained from a cross-cultural and historical study of alcohol use extend far beyond the mere satisfaction of learning that other countries and ages also have, or have had, their share of troubles; often, promising approaches to our modern problems can be found and dangerous patterns identified and avoided. In this example suggestions for introducing eighth-grade students to this type of study are provided; the learning activity described calls for compiling a series of individual reports into a class "book."

Concept

The use of beverage alcohol is a relatively permanent and prominent feature of man's culture.

Students

This example was designed for eighth-graders of average socioeconomic and academic status; with appropriate modifications it could be used throughout grades 7 through 12.

Technique
Written reports.

Written reports are perhaps one of the oldest forms of learning activities; however, in this example they are supplemented with a rather unique innovation. The students are asked to copy their reports on ditto masters; these are then duplicated, collated, and stapled to form "books" which are then distributed to each class member. One principal advantage of this technique is the additional motivation that it provides for each class member to do his best work. This pressure may be held to an optimum level by use of a tight format that tends to standardize the appearance of the reports while leaving room for creative expression within the designated structure. The following are some specific recommendations that apply to most situations:

1. This activity should be started early in the teaching unit. After spending perhaps one class meeting on a general overview of the broad cultural significance of alcohol, the next meeting should be devoted to planning and initiating the assignment. After first providing a general overview, spell out some of the details as follows:

   a. Each report will be on the topic of drinking practices in either a particular country or a particular historical era.
   b. The length of the report will be limited to one printed or type-written page; the final draft is to be placed on a ditto master.
   c. Each paragraph of the report will cover a specific subtopic; these subtopics will be planned by the class.

As these directions are presented the students should be given an opportunity to suggest changes and alternatives. Some ambitious classes may not want to be limited to one page. Occasionally two or three preco-cious young typists may volunteer to type all the reports to provide a uniform appearance to the final product. The students may wish to estab-lish an editing committee to prepare a title page, introduction, table of contents, and so on. Teachers fortunate enough to receive such sugges-tions should be flexible enough to accept them.

2. The next step consists of planning the general scope and content of the reports with the class. When time is short this information is best issued as instructions, but class involvement will produce better motiva-tion and a better understanding of the assignment. In response to the question, "What historical periods should be represented in our book?" the brighter students should soon produce a standard breakdown, such as (a) Prehistoric, (b) Biblical, (c) Classical, (d) Medieval, (e) Renaissance, (f) Colonial, and (g) Modern. When asked about geographical representation, the typical class response will result in a roll call of the continents plus some special subclassifications such as Polynesia, England, the Arab countries, Israel, and so on. At this point solicit volunteers for the various historical periods and the representative countries. Once one country from each continent has been chosen, allow duplications—for example, Italy, France, and Sweden, for Europe; Japan, China, and India, for Asia.

3. The development of specifications for the internal organization of the individual reports also lends itself to teacher–student planning. Call for ideas but be ready to fill in the gaps with suggestions so that a com-prehensive set of subcategories may be selected. A typical group might include (a) the most common forms of beverages used; (b) the categories of people that drink—for example, men, women, the young, and so on; (c) the drinking circumstances—for example, with meals, celebrations, and so on; (d) the problems that may exist; (e) the legal and other controls that are used. The need to list the sources of one's information should also be established.

4. The students should be encouraged to review a wide variety of sources in their search for the specified information. Some school libraries may have books on the cultural aspects of alcohol use, but these will be the exception rather than the rule. Much of the information will have to

come from general texts on individual countries and historical periods. The *Reader's Guide to Periodic Literature* may list good magazine articles, and the always reliable encyclopedias will probably be one of the more valuable sources. Even a careful search will sometimes fail to provide a specific type of information for a particular country or era. This problem should be recognized and the students should be encouraged to compensate with an expansion of other sections of their report.

5. A ditto master should be issued to each student and some basic directions provided for its preparation. Legibility can be ensured by insisting that the reports be typed or printed with a ball-point pen. Show the students how errors can be corrected and caution them to remove the protective tissue before beginning. The teacher may have to do the necessary duplicating; however, student volunteers can usually be found to do the collating and stapling.

6. Once the "books" are ready for distribution, the teacher should review the contents carefully for major errors and misrepresentations. Some of these may need to be pointed out in class, and the teacher may ask each student to make changes on his copy. Following this, the complete project should be read and discussed to emphasize the salient facts and generalizations.

IV. BROTHER RAT TAKES A DRINK

The issue of alcohol tolerance or resistance to intoxication is one that provokes a great deal of confusion in the mind of the average citizen. Virtually anyone who has had any contact with alcohol use will commonly relate stories of "good old Joe" who can drink all night and not show it. Those who are truly knowledgeable in the ways of alcohol know that if Joe has really been drinking all night without showing it, then he probably has not tried to do anything more demanding than lift his glass to his mouth —a skill with which he is presumably quite familiar. A certain degree of physiological tolerance admittedly does exist; however, this effect is greatly exaggerated by a large portion of the public.

The relatively predictable effects of alcohol on individual levels of motor and sensory efficiency, as noted previously, can be effectively presented in conventional films, reading assignments, and discussion. But those fortunate enough to have access to the necessary equipment and supplies can illustrate this concept in dramatic fashion by use of laboratory animals.

Concept

The blood alcohol concentration of the user is determined largely by the amount ingested, the rate of ingestion, and the blood volume of the user.[3]

Students

This example is recommended specifically for ninth-grade students of average socioeconomic and academic status; with appropriate modifica-

[3] *Health Concepts: Guides for Health Instruction*, op. cit., p. 11.

tions, it could be used with most classroom groups throughout the secondary level.

Technique
Laboratory demonstration.

One of the main ingredients necessary for the proper implementation of teaching procedures involving this concept is a basic knowledge of the dynamics of alcohol concentration in the blood. Teachers who do not feel sure of themselves on this topic should undertake a good review of the facts and principles involved. The important part of this type of lesson comes during the discussion that follows the demonstration when the teacher must help the class interpret the significance of the events that were observed. The laboratory materials constitute a second major need; if these are not available as part of the health teacher's instructional equipment, they can often be borrowed from the school's science department. The specific directions that follow were adapted from the work of Leon A. Greenberg (Rutgers Center of Alcohol Studies) by Frances Todd: [4]

Purposes
1. To show the effects of various concentrations of alcohol on the postural reflex, righting reflex, and corneal reflex.
2. To show the relationship between the presence of protein food in the stomach and the effects of alcohol.

Materials
1. Six white rats, matched as nearly as possible in size, sex, age, heredity, and weight, and identified by ear notches or other means
2. Hypodermic syringe, 5 cc
3. Hypodermic needle, no. 19
4. Stomach tubes (at least 4)
5. Small beaker
6. Alcohol (30% solution)
7. Amino acid, such as glycine or glycocol (NH_2, CH_2 C 8H)
8. Forceps (to pin mouth of rat)
9. Gloves (to prevent injury in case of biting)
10. Cotton
11. Scales (to weigh rats)

Procedure
Inject the 30% solution into the peritoneal cavity of each of 6 rats which have had no food for 12 h. as follows:
Rat 1: 1 g alcohol per k of body weight
Rat 2: 2 g alcohol per k of body weight
Rat 3: 3 g alcohol per k of body weight
Rat 4: 4 g alcohol per k of body weight

[4] Frances Todd, *Teaching About Alcohol* (New York: McGraw-Hill, 1964), pp. 182–183.

Rat 5: 4 g alcohol per k of body weight, by tube
Rat 6: 4 cc glococol solution by tube, and 4 g alcohol per k of body weight

Observations to Be Recorded for Each Rat
1. Postural reflex: staggering
2. Righting reflex: ability to right the body
3. Corneal reflex: blinking eyes when an object nears

Even in this small sample, a direct relationship will probably be observed between the amount of alcohol injected and the effects on the animal's behavior. Note that the factor of time or rate of ingestion is not observed, because the administration of alcohol takes place instantaneously. The factor of food in the stomach, however, is demonstrated and may be discussed. It is interesting to note that food in the stomach and a slow rate of intake are similar in their effect, because both increase the time required for alcohol to get into the bloodstream.

V. WHAT DO YOU DO IF . . . ?

Whether we like it or not, teen-agers get into situations involving alcohol both within the home and outside in activities with their peer group. Either as participant or bystander they may find themselves called upon to make decisions based upon their knowledge of beverage alcohol and the circumstances surrounding its use. Very often their knowledge is small and the issue important, and occasionally crucial to their safety or welfare. Although teachers can do little to keep teen-agers out of these situations, they can do much to remedy the young person's lack of knowledge. In the following example sociodrama is used as a means of adding interest and a degree of realism to what would otherwise be a purely abstract discussion.

Concept

The problems related to the abuse of beverage alcohol require both individual and community efforts for their prevention, control, and amelioration.

Students

This example was designed for tenth-graders of average socioeconomic and academic status; with only slight modification it would be appropriate for all grades 10 through 12.

Technique

Sociodrama.

Because general suggestions concerning the actual mechanics of the sociodrama have been presented on pp. 143–144, only the specific roles and situations will be described here.[5]

[5] Adapted from situations originally described in *Thinking About Drinking*, op. cit., pp. 17–20.

SITUATION ONE: I'D RATHER NOT, I THINK

A sixteen-year-old girl is on her first date with an eighteen-year-old whom she very much admires. They go to a party where everyone seems to be drinking, including her date. Several persons urge her to try a highball. The cast includes.

> *Jill:* The girl, who has never drank and who is somewhat fearful of what the effects might be; she has never discussed this matter with her parents.
>
> *Chuck:* Her date, who has had a drink or two on several occasions in the past; he would like to see Jill drink with him; but it is not vitally important to him.
>
> *First Bystander:* He is nineteen, enjoys getting a little "high" at parties, and likes to see his companions in a similar condition.
>
> *Second Bystander:* She is also sixteen, this is her second occasion of drinking. She feels somewhat guilty about it and finds the presence of a nondrinker disturbing.

SITUATION TWO: LET'S HAVE A REAL BLAST!

A seventeen-year-old boy's parents allow him to have a can of beer with them now and then. He is planning a party for several of his friends and he is discussing the arrangements with his parents. The cast includes

> *Jake:* The boy who thinks that beer should be made available to the older kids he is inviting.
>
> *Jake's Mother:* She actually finds the idea somewhat appealing but generally relies on her husband's judgment in such matters.
>
> *Jake's Father:* He is not very enthusiastic about the idea and raises several practical questions concerning legal restrictions and the rights and attitudes of the guests' parents.

SITUATION THREE: WHO WANTS TO DRIVE?

A seventeen-year-old and his date have attended his brother's party given primarily for his college buddies. After several trips to the alcoholic punch bowl, he finds himself somewhat woozy when the time comes to drive his date home. The cast includes

> *Steve:* The boy who does not feel he should drive but wonders what the effect will be on his date's opinion of him if he confesses his lack of confidence.
>
> *Vickie:* She has stayed with nonalcoholic punch all evening and has not noticed Steve's gradually declining capabilities. She has not had her driver's license long and has some doubts about her own ability to drive at night on busy streets.

SITUATION FOUR: THE TROUBLE WITH FATHER

A mother and her teen-age boy and girl are just finishing breakfast on Monday morning during the early portion of summer vacation. Father has just left for work without any breakfast as he was quite severely "hung over" from his Sunday night drinking bout. This has been happening frequently enough to make Father miserable company on the weekends, a poor performer at work, and a threat to the stability of the family budget. Although the other members of the family have noticed the problem, they have not yet discussed it as a group; each one has been waiting for someone else to bring up the subject. The cast includes

Mother: She has had some bitter discussions with Father over the problem but is hesitant to involve the children in the matter. She does not drink and knows little about drinking problems. She believes that her husband will stop drinking once he realizes how much trouble he is causing.

Margie: She has recently graduated from high school and plans to enter college in the fall. She too does not drink but she knows enough about alcoholism and problem drinking to realize that the problem is not going to be solved easily.

Brian: He is seventeen and has just finished studying about alcohol in his health class this year. He knows some textbook solutions but has trouble focusing on the practical aspects of the problem.

In these, as with most other sociodramas, the direction they take will often be unpredictable. The teacher should attempt to anticipate the possible alternatives and be prepared to guide the class toward a reasonable consensus on each situation. However, the teacher should remember that value judgments are involved in all these situations; few courses of action are the best or the worst. The teacher's most valuable device during the follow-up discussions will be that of returning the question to the group. Although the conclusions that may result are significant, the examining process that takes place should be even more valuable as a learning device.

As a final note of caution, the teacher should remember that many humorous situations will arise during these activities, and although most will contribute to a good learning environment, the teacher should be alert to situations where humor is inappropriate. This is particularly true of discussions dealing with drinking problems among parents. This topic is not humorous to the occasional student who may be living in such a situation.

VI. THE CLERICS STATE THEIR CASE

Alcohol abuse has traditionally been viewed as a moral question by a significant portion of the public. Regardless of the validity of this viewpoint, its wide acceptance has served to involve religious leaders in the search for solutions to alcohol-related problems. In the name of prevention, religious leaders have also taken an interest in the broader aspects of alcohol use. Although the modern trend is to attribute most of the blame to social and cultural factors outside the individual's control, the church in all its forms is broadening its role and retaining an interest in many human problems that are not generally considered moral or religious. The net result of all this is that religious leaders are generally conversant with most issues concerned with alcohol and often have occasion to deal with them in a practical way in programs of religious education or in counseling families with alcohol problems. Health educators are often surprised to discover that these qualities enable them to communicate with teen-agers in a truly educational way. In this example four of these gentlemen deal with modern issues through use of the traditional format of the panel discussion:

Concept
Individual and group attitudes pertaining to beverage alcohol have important personal, social, and community consequences.

Students
This example was specifically designed for use with twelfth-grade students with socioeconomic and academic statuses somewhat above average; however, it is generally recommended for grades 9 through 12.

Technique
Panel discussion.

The specific procedures involved in the organization and presentation of a panel discussion are more dependent on local conditions than are most other teaching techniques. The availability of good resource persons varies greatly from community to community. The most desirable combination of panelists is affected in this example by the religious pattern of the populace. Perhaps most important, administrative considerations differ in terms of possibilities for the flexible scheduling of large group meetings by pooling sections and other such devices. These basic factors will be discussed as they apply to various combinations of circumstances.

1. The attempts should be made to secure a broad and diverse representation of religious leaders as panelists. An ideal arrangement for an urban, and somewhat cosmopolitan, community might consist of a Catholic priest, a Protestant minister with a somewhat "permissive" stance on alcohol, a Protestant minister with an "abstinent" orientation, and a rabbi. In communities with a more homogeneous makeup, only two or three of these groups might need to be represented. If a large Jewish population were present, then perhaps representation from more than one Jewish subgroup might be appropriate. A good topic for such a panel would be "Acceptable and Unacceptable Drinking Practices." The basic task of the panel would be to react to questions dealing with specific examples of alcohol use.

2. The preparation of students for this activity is particularly important. Therefore a panel of this type is best scheduled for a day toward the end of study on alcohol. The basic effects of alcohol on the nervous system should be reviewed beforehand; basic misconceptions should be corrected; and some general views on acceptable versus unacceptable drinking behavior should be discussed.

3. One of the key factors in securing good panelists and making good use of them lies in arranging for their broad and effective exposure. It is often difficult for any professional person to forsake his more pressing responsibilities to appear before a small number of students; this often necessitates some special arrangements on the part of the teacher. There are several possible arrangements, each with advantages and disadvantages.

   a. *Presenting the panel to a single classroom group.* If the panelists accept this arrangement, it makes for ideal student impact and involvement. However, other sections meeting simultaneously are not served, and spontaneity will suffer if the panel is repeated a number of times throughout the school day.
   b. *Pooling of sections into large group meetings.* If facilities are available this serves all the students. However, the problem of securing an all-day commitment and preserving spontaneity still remains.
   c. *Videotaping a classroom or large group presentation for closed-circuit replay.* This is a good arrangement for those schools possessing the necessary equipment.
   d. *Arranging a modified assembly-hour program limited to the grade level involved in the study of alcohol.* This enables the panel discussion to be presented at one time to all the students that will benefit most. The main disadvantage is the disruption of the school day.
   e. *Staging a full-assembly program.* Unless the program is truly outstanding, this procedure is probably not worth the trouble. Any impact on the students will be temporary unless there are adequate preparatory and follow-up activities; these are not often possible to arrange on a school-wide basis.

4. Regardless of the scheduling pattern used, it is well to ask the students to submit written questions prior to the actual panel presentation. These should be reviewed so that a group of the most representative and the most constructively provocative ones can be worked into the discussion. A certain amount of time should also be allowed for additional student questions following the formal portion of the program.

5. One-shot presentations by outside experts generally raise more questions than they answer, particularly those dealing with opinions and value judgments. Therefore, small group follow-up discussions with effective leadership are a necessary part of any such program. If possible, these should take place immediately; however, it is usually more practical to meet this need in the next regular class session. A buzz group format (pp. 162–163) works well in this situation.

REFERENCES

McCarthy, Raymond G. (revised by John J. Pasciutti). *Facts About Alcohol.* Chicago: Science Research Associates, 1967.

Todd, Frances. *Teaching About Alcohol.* New York: McGraw-Hill Book Company, 1965.

U.S. Department of Health, Education, and Welfare. *Thinking About Drinking.* Public Health Service Publication No. 1683, Washington, D.C., 1968.

Unterberger, Hilma, and Lena DiCicco. "Alcohol Education Re-evaluated," *The Bulletin of the National Association of Secondary School Principals,* Vol. 52, No. 326 (March 1968), pp. 15–29.

17 DISEASE AND ENVIRONMENT I: FOUNDATIONS

Throughout mankind's existence, disease has always been its ultimate enemy. Other traditional antagonists such as famine, warfare, and accidental death are threats that may or may not occur. Yet disease always remains ready to attack the individual at any stage of his development. Even the relatively germ-free environment of the womb provides no sanctuary from the virus of rubella or the spirochete of syphilis, which occasionally snuff out young lives before they really begin. In many of our urban slums and rural "poverty pockets," the infant is still exposed to enteritis and diphtheria even though these infections are virtually 100 per cent preventable with adequate medical supervision. No child is immune from nature's cruel genetic tricks, such as PKU or cystic fibrosis, which may handicap him from birth. All persons must run the gauntlet of rheumatic fever, diabetes, and leukemia during both childhood and adulthood, and if these hazards are successfully avoided, they become candidates for the various forms of arteriosclerotic disease and cancer that pose a constant threat during the later years of life.

This rather grim description of disease is not presented to provoke a sense of alarm or hopelessness, for neither of these emotions are appropriate in the light of the progress that has been made in combating diseases of all categories. Within this century, mortality rates for most of the communicable diseases have been reduced to a fraction of their former size, with a consequent twenty-year increase in the average American lifespan. Improved medical technology has held the rate for apoplexy (stroke) steady in spite of the growing proportion of elderly persons in our national population, and this very increase in the average age of our citizens has hidden the substantial progress that has been made in the treatment of cancer and heart disease. In 1937 the treatment of cancer saved one out of

347

every five patients; however, this ratio has since been improved to one in three.[1] Meanwhile the development of intensive-care units for cardiac patients has vastly increased the heart-attack victim's chances of survival, and improvements in rehabilitative techniques are gradually improving the prospects for years of normal life after the attack.

A Fair Appraisal

Health progress has been very aptly described as "a periodic redefining of the unacceptable," [2] and this description appears to be exceedingly accurate as it applies to man's efforts to combat disease. Tuberculosis was a leading killer at the turn of the century, but its heavy toll has since been reduced to 5,500 or so annual deaths. This represents tremendous medical progress, yet these 5,500 deaths are totally unacceptable at a time when virtually all deaths from tuberculosis can be prevented by early detection and treatment. Deaths from uterine cancer have been reduced by half over the past thirty years, yet practically all the 12,000 deaths that do occur are needless. As health professionals become more efficient at reducing deaths from certain types of disease, the few remaining victims become relatively more tragic by comparison. Everyone has to die from something, but not from whooping cough at eleven months, not from tetanus at twelve years, uterine cancer at forty, heart disease at forty-five, or lung cancer at fifty.

Thus far we have discussed disease only within the narrow framework of mortality. Many of the generalizations that have been made also apply to the problems of disease-caused disability. Tremendous strides have been made in the battle against rheumatic heart disease, yet the relatively few young people who are still disabled represent a tragic and needless waste of human resources. Hundreds of young women are sterilized by untreated gonorrhea, and thousands of essentially young men find that life is not quite the same after a coronary attack even if recovery is almost complete. An unnecessary disability that occurs early in life is often more tragic than a normal and expected disease that terminates a long and full life.

Needed Action

One of the more disturbing aspects of man's struggle against disease is the great difficulty we seem to have in applying newly developed technology to practical situations. Medical technology has developed to the point that one out of every two cancer patients can be cured, yet we apply this technology to only one out of three. Many factors that are significantly related to heart disease have been identified. We know that persons who control their weight, avoid heavy cigarette smoking, and exercise appropriately can

---

[1] *Progress Against Cancer* 1970, Washington, D.C.: U.S. Department of Health, Education, and Welfare, 1970, p. 2.

[2] George James, "Emerging Trends in Public Health and Possible Reactions," *Public Health Reports*, Vol. 80, No. 7 (July 1965), p. 580.

minimize their risk of heart disease, but we are not very clever at encouraging people to take these measures. Nature is a tough adversary; we will probably never develop solutions for all our disease problems. This is understandable, but our failure to apply the knowledge we have is becoming increasingly inexcusable. Therein lies the health educator's greatest challenge.

OLD REMEDIES. A good deal of the problem appears to result from the average citizen's tendency to apply historical solutions to modern problems. At the turn of the century, the greatest threats to health within the United States were other living things in the form of microbes. Although progress in the fight against these outside invaders has been little short of phenomenal, the average citizen's role has been passive. For the most part, he hired others to do his disease fighting for him. He paid a few additional tax dollars for the filtration and chlorination of his water supply, and thereby eliminated typhoid as a major threat. He paid a few more cents for pasteurized milk or tuberculin-tested cows and greatly reduced the spread of tuberculosis. He sat by and waited for the scientific community to develop effective vaccines for tetanus, diphtheria, and whooping cough or, at the most, lent financial support to this work. He supported the medical profession with his dollars and confidence and it responded with well-trained professionals armed with sulfa drugs, penicillin, and improved obstetrical techniques.

Meanwhile the very same economic progress and improved technology that provided the basis for the fight against communicable disease was also having an effect on the living habits of the average citizen. He was able to buy good foods that were often rich in fats and cholesterol. He was freed from much of the burden of hard physical labor. The automobile, with its trail of carbon monoxide, solved many of his transportation problems. His safer but less convenient cigar, pipe, or "chaw" gave way to the pack-a-day cigarette habit. When it became apparent that cardiovascular disease and cancer had become the major threats to his health, he responded again with dollars for research and improved technology, that is, with the same basic behavior that he had exhibited during the successful struggle against communicable disease.

The American citizen has demonstrated his willingness to pour millions of dollars into the fight against chronic disease in several ways: his federal tax dollars support the research work of the National Institutes of Health; his charitable donations go to the American Heart Association; his Social Security payments support the Medicare program; and an increasing proportion of his paycheck is devoted to medical and hospital bills or to various insurance programs which cover these expenses.

BITTER PRESCRIPTIONS. Simply stated, this impressive financial outlay facilitates greatly improved care to the individual once he develops any of the common chronic diseases. However, it does not provide what he really desires, namely, a ready cure or convenient means of prevention. Our hypothetical citizen wants the scientists to present him with a pill, a vaccine, or something to add to his water supply that will alleviate each serious health problem. But instead of these convenient solutions, he is provided with admonitions to give up pleasurable habits, to seek out hard physical exercise, and to go to the doctor for expensive and sometimes unpleasant examinations when he is not sick. He would much rather have a pill or a simple injection, but these do not seem to be in the offing as solutions to our modern disease problems.

These comments, of course, somewhat overstate the case. All of our modern disease problems are not caused by chronic disease; venereal disease is certainly a major health problem. One of the old solutions may someday be found in the form of a vaccine for some or all forms of cancer. But for the most part, we are now in a new situation in which the enemy comes not from without, but from within our bodies. In the words of George James, Dean of New York's Mount Sinai School of Medicine, "Man is rapidly becoming the cause of his own major reasons for death and disability through various errors of either omission or commission." [3] Man eats too much saturated fat, smokes too many cigarettes, exercises too little, subjects himself to too much nervous strain. The venereal disease victim will not seek prompt treatment; he will not reveal his sexual contacts and the physician he eventually sees may refuse to report his case.

Even at the tissue level, it is man's cells that run wild to produce malignancy, man's antibodies that apparently produce the disabilities of arthritis and asthma, and man's gene's that produce hemophilia and to a large extent diabetes. Thus the new enemy to health is man himself, who practices self-destruction either through overt action or through the inner functioning of his physiological processes, and he is proving to be a tougher animal to control than the microbe.

THE ROLE OF THE SCHOOL

The well-designed and effectively administered school that is becoming increasingly prevalent in modern-day America combats disease in several important ways. Some of these are obvious, such as mass screening for active tuberculosis; others are less apparent, such as using properly designed drinking fountains that keep the fount head clear of the exhaust water. Beyond providing direct and immediate disease-controlling procedures, the school's greatest potential is found in the health education phase of the school program. But before considering this aspect of the health program in detail, a brief review of school health services and the protection of the school environment should prove useful.

[3] George James, as quoted in *Human Potential in a Dynamic Environment* (Proceeding of the Airlie House Conference), School Health Education Study, Washington, D.C., 1968, p. 1.

Environmental Considerations

Many features of the modern school plant that seem directed toward the improvement of general comfort or the aesthetic qualities of the school also serve to minimize the spread of communicable disease. An efficient heating and ventilation system serves to break up heavy concentrations of airborne germs; the proper control of temperature and humidity helps maintain the protective qualities of the mucous membrane of the nose and throat; modern sweeping and cleaning procedures reduce the exposure to spore forms of microorganisms found in dust particles; generous policies concerning sick leave reduce the chances of contact with teachers with communicable diseases; requirements that teachers show proof each year of their freedom from tuberculosis and that cafeteria workers be free of dangerous infections provide further protection of the school environment; the provision of adequate classroom space helps prevent pupil-to-pupil transfer of infection. Although dramatic benefits do not result from any single one of these procedures, their combined effect makes the school a generally safer environment in terms of communicable disease than the average home and neighborhood. Public health departments attest to this fact by encouraging the schools to remain open during occasional epidemics of influenza and streptococcal infections.

School Health Services

Unlike the environmental controls, which are for the most part focused on the communicable disease problem, school health services deal with chronic disease as well as communicable disease. Cumulative health records provide a means of keeping track of children with heart defects, diabetes, severe asthma, or epilepsy as they move from grade to grade or otherwise come into contact with new teachers. This enables teachers to be systematically informed about children requiring special attention because of their health status. Alert and responsible teachers, school nurses, or other school personnel can provide the parent with needed stimulus and support in securing thorough treatment and care for children with chronic defects.

In the area of communicable disease control, the school often cooperates with public health personnel to provide tuberculin screening and in some cases free immunizations. Also, accurately kept health records often allow school personnel to alert parents whose children lack the needed protection that a good immunization program can provide. Another important service is the identification and isolation of children who are ill when they arrive at school or become ill during the course of the day. Prompt removal from the classroom benefits both the ill child and his classmates whose risk of exposure is thereby reduced. The school usually stands ready to contact family physicians or an ambulance service in those emergencies where this action is justified.

Education and Disease Control

The benefits that result from an effective educational program dealing with disease are less tangible than those related to environment or services; however, they are probably far more important in terms of long-term results. A young girl who learns the fundamentals of weight control and develops an appreciation for a slender figure may reduce her chances of heart disease forty years later. The boy who grasps the basic concepts concerning the role of microorganisms in the cause and transmission of disease during the fifth or sixth grade may be ready to acquire needed information concerning venereal disease during his junior high and senior high school years. The remaining portion of this chapter will be devoted to the task of organizing and implementing this educational program.

DISEASE-RELATED INTEREST PATTERNS OF CHILDREN AND ADOLESCENTS

Elementary Level

Most developmental psychologists feel that children of elementary school age (seven to twelve years) possess a tremendous curiosity about their environment. For many children of these ages this interest is probably greater than at any other stage. The preschool child typically is preoccupied with his social status within the family and the adolescent is commonly overwhelmed with his problems of heterosexual adjustment. Meanwhile, the fourth-grader is busily catching tadpoles, collecting rocks or leaves, and bringing home toads and snakes; and these activities are only slightly less popular among girls than among boys at these ages.

These young botanists and zoologists do not have any immediate plans for going into horticulture, nor are they attempting to cure any of their health problems with toad skins or snake oil; they simply want to learn more about their natural environment. This natural interest can be used to lead children into a study of many important topics that may not appear too practical at the moment but that will pay big dividends at later grade levels. To understand disease, one must first understand the normal structure and functioning of the body; many health textbook series properly place heavy emphasis on anatomy and physiology in their fourth- or fifth-grade texts. Adults in our society may have occasion to deal with complex antigen-antibody reactions such as immunizations and allergy reactions and with autoimmune conditions such as arthritis, tissue compatability, Rh factors, and so on. The elementary-level child should not be expected to master the concept of the antibody response, but he can learn a great deal about cells of all types whether they be found in human tissue or in single microorganisms. This background will facilitate his acquiring knowledge about the production and function of antibodies during his secondary school health classes.

Secondary Level

If one is permitted to overgeneralize concerning the changing pattern of interests exhibited by the typical secondary school youth as he matures, it can be described quite simply. He begins as a seventh-grader with a high degree of interest in physical objects he can observe directly. During his junior high school years he becomes increasingly interested in abstract qualities that apply to him personally, such as courage, popularity, intelligence, and so on. During his senior high years a good deal of youthful idealism emerges in the form of concern for selected social issues. Although there are many individual exceptions and it does tend to ignore some important sex differences, content and learning activities selected in accordance with this scheme will generally meet the least amount of resistance for any given group of secondary school students.

THE JUNIOR HIGH LEVEL. When this general pattern is translated into specific plans for teaching concepts on disease and environment, it becomes very logical to emphasize biological content in the seventh and eighth grades. Examples of topics in this area include disease agents, immunization, and the basic characteristics of cancer and heart disease. These topics will capture the interest of junior high students if good learning activities are used, such as experiences involving microprojective techniques, simple experiments with bacterial cultures, and attractive films for use when it is not practical to use other materials. Some health educators will say that eighth-graders cannot become interested in cancer or heart disease because these conditions do not pose an immediate threat to them; however, any good biology teacher knows that such children can become interested in normal cells and normal hearts and that abnormal conditions are even more fascinating. The biology teacher generally approaches the child with specimens, test tubes, and microscopes; too often the health teacher makes his approach with words about future consequences. Frequently the methods of science education are not appropriate for teaching health, but when they are, they should be adopted with little hesitancy.

As junior high students move further into adolescence and become more aware of the implications of their approaching adult role, particularly the sexual aspects of this role, they become increasingly self-conscious. Matters of personal appearance, body image, and overall personality characteristics become increasingly important to them. This enables them to become interested in many topics of long-range value because they are immediately useful. For example, exercise becomes important because it offers the possibility of controlling weight and toning up the body. Weight control itself has obvious implications for personal appearance and considerable knowledge is needed to achieve lasting success in a weight reduction program. It becomes sensible for students to consider the prospects of stained teeth and a steady drain on one's finances before becoming too fully committed to the cigarette habit. It becomes foolish to miss a big dance or basketball game because of a heavy cold that could have been avoided. If the health educator uses these motivational "hooks" tactfully, without presenting these considerations too forcefully, then he can provide young people with the opportunity to develop living habits with far more important benefits than the seemingly trivial aspects that were originally used to attract their interest.

THE SENIOR HIGH LEVEL. As the adolescent moves along into the last year or two of senior high school, he becomes increasingly attracted to social and political issues. He may not be too enthusiastic over the specific legal or governmental aspects, but he is quite capable of becoming heavily involved with the basic issue itself. The commonly offered American Problems course for twelfth-graders often finds students delving into such topics as civil rights, capital punishment, and honesty in government. In a similar way, the health teacher can stir up excitement concerning aid and water pollution, community programs for venereal-disease control, and the proper role of the government in the control of the cigarette industry. Many of these topics provide fascinating combinations of scientific complexities, economic considerations, and value judgments.

CURRICULAR CONSIDERATIONS

As is the case with other areas of health content, the specific topics or sub-areas that are included in the study of disease may vary considerably according to the organization of the particular curriculum. Combining the study of chronic and communicable disease and environmental protection into a single content area, as implied in the chapter title, is a logical and widely accepted pattern; however, other combinations exist which may better serve the needs of specific school situations. Many issues in disease control and protection of the environment involve consideration of community action in the form of the enactment of legal controls, the support of health agencies of various types, the sponsoring of tax-supported research programs, and other similar activities. Thus much of what might be taught in a unit on community health may be included within the context of man, disease, and environment.

It is also necessary to properly coordinate the study of disease as a health topic with the science curriculum. Human anatomy and physiology, heredity, nutrition, microorganisms, and parasitic and symbiotic relationships are examples of topics either directly or closely related to the study of disease which commonly appears in science units. Because there seldom seems to be enough time available for health education, it is important to avoid wasteful duplication. A careful review of the science and health curriculums will often reveal opportunities for scheduling topics to supplement each other. This is particularly true at the elementary level, where closely related topics, such as microorganisms and communicable disease, for example, may be combined into one well-integrated unit.

Student Needs and Disease Content

LIVING HABITS. Elementary school children can begin to develop valid concepts of disease prevention while learning to practice needed hygienic routines at school. These include covering one's face when sneezing or coughing, washing one's hands before meals and after trips to the toilet, avoiding the use of other children's drinking straws and candy bars, reporting illness promptly to one's teacher, and other related procedures. These practices would belong in any well-managed classroom even if health education were not part of the curriculum; however, when basic information about communicable diseases is given at the time that these practices are taught or reviewed, then a mutual reinforcement can result. The disease concepts help support the practices and the practices add a realistic touch to the concepts. It should be emphasized that any long-term educational benefits require planned instruction. It is a gross misnomer to train elementary children in a few hygiene routines and call that a program of health education. This is comparable to helping children to keep track of their milk money as their sole exposure to arithmetic.

The student's adolescent years provide the teacher of any important subject with a prime opportunity. These are the years in which the individual forms concepts and attitudes which can serve important needs throughout his lifetime. Very often relatively permanent behavior patterns regarding diet, exercise, cigarette smoking, and to a lesser extent, medical care are either formed or consolidated during one's years as a teen-ager. Although these patterns often have important effects on the overall quality of one's life and on longevity, they are often adopted rather passively on the basis of trivial considerations. An effective program of health education can help young people examine facts and alternatives regarding important habits while it is still relatively easy to change them. This examining process is valuable in itself, regardless of the apparent quality of the choices that result. A high school girl may examine the health hazards incurred as a result of cigarette smoking but may still feel that the social advantages outweigh the health liabilities. However, if she has learned to examine new courses of action before adopting them, she may make a more favorable decision on a later occasion when she finds herself tempted to rely on barbiturates and amphetamines during her college years.

VENEREAL DISEASE. The problem of venereal disease is somewhat distinct from other disease problems within school populations because of the serious consequences of untreated cases and the inherent problems in its control. Although a review of objective evidence concerning increases in teen-age sexual activity does not support the exaggerated estimates of many alarmists, the trend does seem to be relentlessly upward.

One consideration which adds a sense of urgency to the problem of the venereal diseases is their insidious nature. The remission of symptoms in the third stage of syphilis may lead one to believe that he or she is free from the infection at the time of greatest danger. The characteristic mildness of the symptoms of gonorrhea in the female may cause treatment to be delayed until the fallopian tubes have been irreversibly damaged. At the very least, a missed case of syphilis may yield positive results years later in a premarital blood test, a rather inconvenient situation at best.

The more effective units on venereal disease have content that is largely biologically, rather than morally, oriented. This approach places first priority on the encouragement of those exposed to seek treatment. This is a much more realistic goal than attempting to minimize exposure by reducing sexual activity through use of fear-provoking or moralizing techniques. The importance of treatment should be stressed in a relatively unemotional but realistic way while at the same time providing accurate information on the symptoms and the procedures for obtaining treatment. However, a positive appeal to one particular area of ethical conduct has proved to have considerable merit; this involves the responsibility to protect others from the dangers of undetected cases by such practices as encouraging one's companions to seek treatment following possible exposure, and cooperating fully with any case-finding efforts of public health personnel.

COMMUNITY ACTION. Secondary school students are only a few short years away from adult responsibilities, among which is the task of supporting needed legislation and programs designed to ameliorate health problems that require community approaches. These group efforts are not needed merely to serve some vaguely defined "common good" but, rather, to provide clean air for individual citizens to breathe, to provide fluoridated water (and consequently reduce family dental bills), and to regain unpolluted streams and lakes (and thereby protect citizens from an outbreak of hepatitis). To an increasing degree community action is needed to solve problems related to disease and environment. School health education could do much more than it now does to prepare citizens for this task.

One of the more frustrating aspects of work in the community health field is the unacceptable gap between the things that should be done and the things that are actually put into practice. This "performance gap" seems to result from the difficulties involved in the time-consuming task of overcoming public inertia and overriding vested interests to institute action needed for the overall benefit of the community. It is these problems in community matters that have particular importance to disease problems, especially those involving improvement of the environment. There is little the individual can do on his own to keep radioactive strontium out of his milk or to put fluoride into his drinking water. However, if the individual citizens understand something of the practical aspects of generating support for public measures, then they are capable of taking appropriate supportive or leadership roles in community efforts to achieve these goals. Students need to understand the potential power of a well-organized delegation to the appropriate board or agency of one's local government, or the force a letter from a large church group can exert on one's congressional representative.

Community issues can be studied quite profitably in the classroom, provided the essential facts are examined and that a free-inquiry approach is encouraged. If a student's attention is directed toward the hard realities of cost as well as toward the potential benefits, then he will have an opportunity to prepare himself for future decisions as a tax-paying citizen. Too often the financial aspects are ignored as students develop strong cases in favor of every measure designed to promote health then systematically oppose most of these very same measures as soon as they leave school and assume tax burdens. Certainly some sort of balance is needed between these extremes. If students have an opportunity to examine the negative as well as the positive factors in the classroom, they will not be shocked later on when confronted by the real situation.

Suggested Concepts

The concepts presented here were formulated on the basis of a review of several sources.[4] This list, like any similar one, should be carefully reviewed in the light of local needs before any part of it is incorporated into lesson plans or curriculum guides.

Nature of Disease

1. *Communicable diseases are characterized by the excessive growth of various types of microorganisms within the body.* The human body commonly harbors numerous types of microorganisms; many of these are either helpful or harmless to bodily functions, but others cause damage when their number becomes excessive. Many factors can upset the normal balance between the body and its microorganisms.

2. *Chronic diseases are persistent conditions involving bodily malfunctions which typically result from a wide variety of factors.* A few diseases such as tuberculosis are both infectious and chronic; however, most chronic diseases result from a variety of factors other than microorganisms, for example, those related to environmental or hereditary phenomena, or general living habits.

3. *Disease causes various types of disability ranging from mild and temporary to severe and permanent.* The significant aspect of a disease is the threat it poses to one's life or functional capacity. This factor varies greatly both between and within various disease categories.

4. *Disease represents a marked disequilibrium in bodily processes resulting from some form of direct stress or reaction to stress.* The stress

[4] Most helpful were *Health Concepts: Guides for Health Instruction* (Washington, D.C.: National Education Association, 1967); and School Health Education Study, *Health Education: A Conceptual Approach to Curriculum Design* (St. Paul, Minn.: 3M Education Press, 1967).

may be the result of microbes, a blood clot, a disorderly growth of cells, or an inappropriate reaction of the body's own defense system, as in allergy conditions.

Etiology of Disease

5. *Individual susceptibility to certain diseases may be directly or indirectly affected by a wide variety of characteristics such as age, sex, race, ethnic background, or occupational status.* Certain infections that threaten life during infancy present little danger to the mature person; hereditary conditions such as sickle cell anemia are typical of those that show racial or ethnic patterns; heart disease commonly affects men at an earlier age than it does females.

6. *The severity of a particular occurrence of communicable disease depends basically on the effectiveness of one's resistance to the agents involved.* Often the resistive forces of the body destroy harmful microorganisms or hold their number to manageable limits, thus preventing any disease symptoms; in other cases, the harmful effects are so minimal that the disease condition is not recognized. However, when resistance is ineffective, serious illness and death may result.

7. *Detrimental living habits that contribute to the development of chronic disease often begin early in the life of the individual.* Many behavior patterns such as cigarette smoking, overeating, and avoidance of exercise are established before and during early adolescence; these habits often contribute to disease conditions that become manifest during middle age or the declining years.

8. *Communicable diseases are transmitted from one person or organism to another by a typical series of events which may be analyzed and predicted.* Some diseases are transmitted directly from one person to another, whereas others require a vehicle such as water or an intermediate host such as the mosquito; knowledge of the specific mode of transmission of a given disease enables selection of the most efficient means of controlling it.

9. *Disease represents a marked disequilibrium in bodily processes resulting from some form of direct stress or reaction to stress.* The stress may be the result of microbes, a blood clot, a disorderly growth of cells, or an inappropriate reaction of the body's own defense system, as in allergy conditions.

Individual Measures of Control

10. *Effective treatment methods exist for most forms of disease which can reduce the severity and permanence of disease-related disabilities.* Many diseases can be completely cured by proper treatment; others can be minimized or controlled for long periods of time. Even those conditions that are inevitably progressive can be moderated by supportive therapy.

11. *The occurrence of most diseases can be delayed, minimized, or prevented completely by intelligent health practices.* Some diseases can be prevented entirely by immunizations, and others can often be avoided by maintaining one's general resistance on a high level; many forms of chronic disease can be delayed by proper living habits and minimized by early diagnosis and prompt treatment.

12. *The natural defenses of the body represent the most important single category of factors that prevent or minimize disease.* Specific defenses, such as those resulting from antibodies, or outside aids, such as drug therapy, are highly useful; however, the natural defenses of the body provide a measure of protection against virtually all potential disease conditions.

Community Approaches to Control

13. *Because individual disease conditions vary greatly in their potential for producing death and disability, mankind commonly establishes priorities in efforts to develop techniques of prevention and treatment.* The basic destructiveness of various diseases, together with such factors as the proportion of the population susceptible, the age group typically attacked, the specific nature of the symptoms, and other such factors, affects the importance commonly attached to various diseases.

14. *Research has provided, and continues to provide, findings that are highly effective in the prevention and treatment of various diseases.* The process of scientific inquiry has been a key factor in the great progress that has been made against communicable disease and is currently serving a similar function in the fight against chronic disease.

15. *Effective disease-prevention and control measures often require organized community efforts for their development and implementation.* Modern research requires personnel and facilities, environmental control requires regional agreements and legal enforcement, the training of health professionals requires complex programs; these and other important aspects of disease control necessitate an organized community approach.

16. *Various social, emotional, and economic factors commonly influence the degree to which modern technology is used in combating disease.* The appropriate application of modern knowledge concerning disease often involves changes in behavior or monetary expenses that the individual is unwilling to tolerate; this problem is often further complicated by an unawareness of the implications involved.

REFERENCES

Anderson, Gaylord, Margaret G. Arnstein, and Mary R. Lester. *Communicable Disease Control*, 4th ed. New York: Macmillan Publishing Co., Inc., 1962.

Brown, James D., and Donald B. Stone. "Doomsday Prophets, Humanists, and Responsible Educators," *School Health Review*, Vol. 3, No. 4 (July–August 1972), pp. 19–22.

Control of Communicable Diseases in Man, 11th ed. New York: American Public Health Association, 1970.

Diehl, Harold S. *Tobacco and Your Health*. New York: McGraw-Hill Book Company, 1969.

Health and Disease. New York: Time, Incorporated, 1965.

Hilleboe, Herman E., and W. L. Larimore Granville. *Preventive Medicine*. Philadelphia: W. S. Saunders Company, 1965.

James, George. "Emerging Trends in Public Health and Possible Reactions," *Public Health Reports*, Vol. 80, No. 7 (July 1965), pp. 579–587.

Kilbourne, Edwin D., and Wilson G. Smillie. *Human Ecology and Public Health*. New York: Macmillan Publishing Co., Inc., 1969.

Kohuth, Barbara J., and Boyd T. March. "Environment in Education: A Pragmatic Look," *Educational Leadership*, Vol. 30, No. 7 (April 1973), pp. 656–658.

Smoking and Health: Report of the Public Health Service. Washington: U.S. Department of Health, Education, and Welfare, 1964.

Smolensky, Jack, and Franklin B. Harr. *Principles of Community Health*. Philadelphia: W. B. Saunders Company, 1972.

Wheatley, George M., and Grace T. Hallock. *Health Observation of School Children*, 3rd ed. New York: McGraw-Hill Book Company, 1965.

Wilson, Charles C. (ed.). *School Health Services*. Washington, D.C.: National Education Association and the American Medical Association, 1964.

DISEASE AND
■ ENVIRONMENT II:
APPLICATIONS

The specific techniques that are appropriate for use with disease-oriented content vary according to the scope of this area as defined in the particular curriculum involved. Many of the concepts pertaining to disease etiology and the related implications for personal practices lend themselves to laboratory type methods; if community health topics are included, then field trips, resource speakers, and committee-type investigative activities become very useful; specialized topics such as venereal disease and cigarette smoking often require such socially oriented approaches as role playing and value-clarification activities for their most effective presentation. Although the general guidelines for matching technique to content and objectives within the general topic of disease are similar to those for other health topics, the following considerations have proved to be generally useful.

SELECTION OF TECHNIQUES

Elementary Level
A large portion of the content included in teaching units on disease for young children is based on the biological rather than the behavioral sciences. As applied to communicable diseases, instructional time is most properly spent developing the basic concepts of disease agents, modes of transmission, and basic methods of prevention. These constitute the real educational task. Although objectives related to attitudes and practices are also important, these are commonly presented as part of a training process outside the context of normal classroom routines. These attitudes and practices are most likely to endure when they are supported with a good

understanding of the fundamentals of disease transmission, so once again the priority educational tasks appear to lie in the biological realm.

GENERAL TOPICS. Probably the two most useful techniques for this content area are classroom experiments and demonstrations. These activities can provide the vitality and enrichment necessary to good learning at this level. College and secondary school students can often benefit from discussing and theorizing about basic issues in disease, but the elementary school child needs real experiences such as seeing bacteria colonies growing in a culture plate and tars condense from the smoke of a cigarette. These are traditional methods, but when handled with a modern twist they can suddenly become quite creative. An open-ended approach provides the key to this transformation. When this principle is applied, experiments lose their cookbook quality and become methods of discovery. In a similar fashion, the demonstration no longer is used to prove something we already know, but to provide a challenge to youthful powers of interpretation and application.

Although most of class time could be profitably devoted to laboratory-oriented activities, this is often impossible because of limitations in equipment, materials, and more importantly, teaching time for preparation and organizational tasks involved. Fortunately, many good films are available which can add realism to the study of disease without making excessive demands on teaching time. Films represent a necessary and acceptable compromise when laboratory activities are not practical; however, they can also bring information to the children that would not otherwise be available. Pathological organisms cannot be put into the elementary classroom for observation, nor can disease-transmitting insects or animals, but films, pictures, and diagrams can portray their activities effectively.

CIGARETTE SMOKING. One important exception to the biological orientation in the study of disease at the elementary level should be noted. Study of the common factors that motivate young children toward the use of cigarettes is useful. Social and emotional pressures often lead the child into a lifelong habit that greatly increases his risk of disease. It is important that the child learn about the physiological hazards related to this habit; however, this alone is not enough. If he is to preserve his freedom of choice, he must gain some understanding of the specific ways that peer pressure, the normal desire for adult status, and other such factors move people into the cigarette habit in a somewhat insidious way. The proper handling of this type of content requires the use of such student-centered techniques as buzz sessions, problem stories, and sociodramas. For this reason, many curriculum guides call for the grouping of smoking with alcohol and drug abuse in a unit on stimulants and depressants. Although such a grouping is admittedly logical, smoking will be discussed here within the context of disease because of the predominantly biological nature of its detrimental effects. It does not cause the behavioral problems and personality damage commonly associated with alcohol and drug abuse.

Secondary Level

Biologically oriented topics should be presented by laboratory-type techniques involving actual materials or such facsimiles of materials as realistic films for maximum impact; however, charts, still pictures, and other less dramatic methods are also effective. Those subtopics dealing with problems related to personal or community behavior that commonly involve value judgments should generally be presented through the use of student-centered techniques. A student-conducted survey to determine the extent of cigarette smoking within the student body, a student panel on the under-reporting of venereal-disease cases by family physicians, and a debate on the relative advantages of government-sponsored versus privately sponsored cancer research are examples of possible ways to get students involved in topics that require value judgments. The teacher's role in these activities is to help students find pertinent facts and then to provide opportunities for the open discussion of the issues involved.

In most situations the student-centered techniques will prove most useful at the senior high level and the laboratory- and materials-centered activities that involve stronger teacher guidance will work out best with junior high students. This is only a matter of emphasis, not an inflexible rule.

PRACTICAL APPLICATIONS

In this section, examples of workable techniques and general approaches to the teaching of content related to eight specific concepts will be presented. Both the elementary and secondary levels will be included in these illustrations.

I. FULL DISCLOSURE—THE BEST POLICY

In terms of morbidity, or prevalence at any one point in time, dental disease ranks first among school-age children as well as among most other age groups. Although much is still unknown about the process of tooth decay, the basic cause appears to be similar to that of so many other disease conditions, namely, the action of harmful microorganisms. Lactobacilli and other acid-forming bacteria take up residence in the mouth, ingest carbohydrates, and excrete acid that dissolves the enamel of the teeth to produce dental caries. At least two characteristics of this process give it an insidious quality that tends to work against well-motivated dental care. First is the time factor; it normally takes weeks of neglect to produce significant damage and months or years before painful conditions develop. Second, this process is largely invisible. The infectious bacteria cannot be seen, so the individual remains unaware of their activities until serious damage has occurred. In this example, disclosure tablets are used to reveal immediately the presence of acid on the surface of the teeth.

Concept

The occurrence of most diseases can be delayed, minimized, or prevented completely by intelligent health practices.

Pupils

Developed for second-graders of average academic ability and socioeconomic status; also recommended for grades three and four.

Technique

Experiment involving the use of dental disclosure tablets.

From the standpoint of decay prevention, it would be ideal if children would brush their teeth thoroughly following every meal or snack. Although this is generally not practical, an acceptable alternative is available in the form of a rinsing of the mouth after lunch and each in-between-meal snack involving sugary or starchy foods. Anything that can encourage children to substitute fresh fruits or vegetables for candy and cookies is also very helpful. Apples or carrots, for instance, do not produce sticky deposits on the teeth and actually provide some mechanical cleaning action because of their rough texture. There are several ways to demonstrate these facts to elementary school pupils. Here is one possibility for use with a class that is already familiar with disclosure tablets.[1]

1. Soon after class starts in the morning, select four students who have previously demonstrated good teeth-brushing ability and ask them to brush their teeth thoroughly using any standard dentifrice. Use this opportunity to review proper brushing techniques for the total class.

2. After the teeth have been thoroughly brushed, ask each demonstrator to rinse his or her mouth to remove as much of the dentifrice as possible. Direct each subject to eat something sweet and sticky such as a cookie.

3. Immediately atfer the cookies have been eaten, tell the first child to brush his teeth using the same dentifrice, the second to rinse his mouth thoroughly with water, the third to eat an apple, and the fourth to do nothing. The class should then resume its normal schedule of activities for the next two to three hours.

4. Shortly before lunch, ask each of the four children to chew a disclosure tablet for a few moments; after they have swallowed or spit out the residue, ask the class to observe their teeth. Discuss the differences that are observed.

In most cases, the child who did nothing after eating the cookie will be found to have large reddish areas on his teeth indicating the presence of acid resulting from bacterial activity. The teeth of the child who brushed thoroughly should be quite white by comparison and the teeth of the remaining two children will normally show an intermediate condition. Be prepared to discuss unexpected results, as some children develop acid

---

[1] These procedures are based on a similar example presented in Leslie W. Irwin et al., *Health in Elementary Schools* (St. Louis, Mo.: Mosby, 1966), pp. 269–270.

plaques (bacterial deposits) more quickly than others for various reasons. The amount of saliva produced or the general acidity or alkalinity of the mouth can produce these differences. If the tablets have been used during previous class activities, it may be possible to select children with approximately equal plaquing tendencies for the experiment. If the class has not had previous experience with this material, the four subjects should each chew a tablet before their initial brushing as the first step in the experiment. This will provide a chance to familiarize the class with the purpose of the tablets and allow the teacher to gain some idea of the plaquing tendencies of the subjects for a better interpretation of the results.

II. THE TOO, TOO COMMON COLD

Any reasonable efforts that can be made to avoid the common cold are exceedingly worthwhile. Although this affliction is not as dramatic in its effects as many others, it rivals more widely feared conditions in its ability to reduce the overall satisfaction we receive from life. Each year it disables us for a few days and denies us the activities, accomplishments, and feeling of well-being associated with good health. Occasionally, when it allies itself with pneumonia and influenza, a much more serious threat to our health results; in this role the common cold becomes more than a nuisance.

In one sense, however, the cold serves as a valuable ally to the health educator for its acts as a concrete, believable condition to avoid. It might be unreasonable to encourage young people to make substantial modifications of their living habits to avoid such diseases as pneumonia, mononucleosis, or spinal meningitis. These conditions occur with relative infrequency (and usually to someone else) but everyone knows the unpleasantness of a cold. But while we are combating this very real, if minor threat, with good nutrition, adequate sleep and rest, and avoidance of undue exposure, we are also minimizing our chances of contracting more serious conditions. Also, these measures yield benefits extending far beyond the increasing of one's resistance to infections. As teachers, we can teach children that proper foods and adequate rest will lessen the severity and frequency of their colds and do so with a clear conscience; by stretching the facts ever so little, we can add fresh air and exercise to these preventive measures and be well on the way to a program for total health. In the following example, children plan and construct posters to illustrate these desirable practices:

Concept

Communicable diseases are transmitted from one person or organism to another by a typical series of events which may be analyzed and predicted.

Pupils

Developed for third-graders of average to below-average academic and socioeconomic status: also recommended for grades 4 and 5.

Technique

Art project involving poster painting.

The use of various types of art projects as learning activities is generally a surefire means of eliciting the interest and enthusiasm of elementary school pupils. Because pupils are going to enjoy the assignment regardless of the specific details, the teacher's challenge lies in leading the children toward relevant and meaningful outcomes. There is a time and place in the curriculum to practice art for art's sake, but in this instance the focus is on health knowledge and attitudes. Here are some specific recommendations that apply to the typical situation:

1. Begin this activity toward the end of a unit on disease prevention or, if initiated early, delay the actual poster construction until the end of the unit. If the children are to work with the proper degree of independence and still be effective, they must first gain some idea of the important concepts to be illustrated in their posters.

2. In order to achieve diversity and comprehensiveness in the posters, organize the class into small working groups of four to eight pupils and select a theme or topic for each group. This places the children working on similar posters in close proximity to one another, thus enabling them to share ideas and avoid duplications. Because this project bears on disease transmission, one logical basis of organization would be the various steps of this process:

a. *Reservoir of infection.* Cold germs live in the bodies of persons who already have colds; these people should stay home. If they do not, stay away from them if you can.

b. *Escape and transmission.* The germs must escape from the reservoir and travel to someone else if the cold is to spread. They do this by riding in little droplets of fluid that are given off when the sick person coughs, sneezes, or exhales. The little droplets ride on air currents. Handkerchiefs, tissues, sufficient space and ventilation, and so on, are needed.

c. *Overcoming the resistance of the host.* The germs must overcome the resistance of the new person if the disease is to be effectively transmitted. Resistance can be strengthened by proper nutrition and rest.

In small classes, one group may be assigned for each area. Normally these areas should be broken down further, such as by having one group work on nutrition and another on rest in the resistance area.

3. The simplest materials to use in this project are construction paper and colored crayons. However, poster board and poster paint produce more satisfying results. Provide the children with some basic tips on poster composition. Brown and his associates suggest that posters should be

- Aimed at one main purpose.
- Forceful and clear in treatment (don't leave the viewer in doubt about the message).
- Colorful (vivid, bold colors draw attention and focus it on the topic).
- Large enough to be easily seen.
- Concerned with the topic that is currently being studied by the class.[2]

If possible, illustrate these points by using pupil-constructed or commercial posters as examples.

4. Arrange for the proper display of the posters once they are completed. In some rooms there will be enough bulletin-board space for this purpose. If appropriate, some of the better ones may be displayed about the school on hallway bulletin boards and in similar locations. Another useful procedure is the so-called clothesline art show, in which a cord or length of heavy twine is strung along one side of the room and the posters attached with clothes pins.

5. After the posters have been displayed for a week or two, they should be removed and the better ones saved to serve as examples for future classes. Some teachers may prefer to save all the posters in a loose-leaf book for future use.

III. FRIENDS AND ENEMIES

Man shares his environment with many organisms that are normally invisible to him because of their small size. Within this category, bacteria are among his most important neighbors. Although the advent of modern drugs and immunizations have removed many bacterial infections as significant problems, a few, such as strep throats, staph infections, meningitis, and gonorrhea still cause trouble. Meanwhile many of our recently subdued enemies, such as typhoid, pertussis, and tetanus, stand ready to make a comeback once we let our guard down. But while these pathogenic types of bacteria get our attention, other forms quietly perform useful functions. Several varieties participate in the constant task of transforming organic wastes into useful nitrates as part of the vital nitrogen cycle; others contribute to the production of cheese and other dairy products; and still others establish themselves in man's large intestines, breaking down cellulose and synthesizing vitamins for his use.

To the elementary-level child seeing is believing, and a learning activity that enables children to observe bacteria can greatly improve their understanding of these important organisms. Learning activities involving the microscope can meet this need; however, these instruments are often not available to the elementary school teacher. A very acceptable alternative is the culturing of bacteria in colonies large enough to be seen without artificial aid. Here are some specific ways to accomplish this.

Concept

Communicable diseases are characterized by the excessive growth of various types of microorganisms within the body.

[2] James W. Brown, Richard B. Lewis, and Fred Harcleroad, AV *Instruction: Media and Methods* (New York: McGraw-Hill, 1969), pp. 175–176.

Pupils

Developed for fifth-graders with average academic and socioeconomic status; also recommended for grades 4 and 6.

Technique

Experiment involving bacterial cultures.

In a broad sense, the culturing of bacteria goes on in every classroom every day and in many other places as well; so there is really nothing too mysterious about manipulating a few of the factors in this process in order to observe it more directly. These manipulations can range from the extremely simple to the extremely complex according to the resources available and the requirements of particular situations. Here are some workable procedures:

1. Begin any culturing experiments early in the unit involving the study of bacteria. It usually takes about three days to grow observable cultures, although sometimes much more time is required because of the specific conditions. However, provide a general introduction or overview before initiating the experiment so that the children have a basic understanding of what they are trying to learn. This can be accomplished with a good film or reading assignment followed by a class discussion. While waiting for results, a more detailed study of bacteria and other microorganisms can proceed.

2. One of the simplest and most practical methods of culturing bacteria is described by Irwin, Cornacchia, and Staton.

To show the growth of germs, boil some small, peeled potatoes until firm and place one in each of four sterile pint jars with lids. Maintain one jar as a control but contaminate the potatoes in the other three jars by (a) rubbing with dirty hands, (b) rubbing with hands after washing with soap and water, and (c) rubbing with tissue after blowing nose. Put lids on all jars, label, and place in a warm but visible location. Observe daily the growth of bacteria and compare with the control potato.[3]

Except for the intentional contamination as described, be careful to avoid further exposure of the potatoes, particularly excessive handling or exposure to the air. Also, be sure the "warm but visible location" is protected from direct sunlight.

3. Those teachers who are blessed with a reasonably generous budget and a little foresight can substitute more elaborate materials by purchasing Petri dishes already prepared with nutrient agar from appropriate supply houses. Or if they wish to conduct more extensive experiment at minimal cost, they can prepare their own Petri dishes according to directions provided by Wailes, using a household pressure cooker:

Wash the Petri dishes with detergent and allow them to dry. Then place the covers in position and sterilize the covered dishes in the oven by heating at a

[3] Leslie W. Irwin et al., op. cit., p. 273

temperature of 400° F. for about one hour. Remove the dishes and set them aside to cool keeping the covers in place.

Buy prepared dehydrated nutrient agar from a supply house. Mix with water according to the directions on the label. Heat, stirring constantly, until the mixture comes to a boil. Pour into a Pyrex flask that will fit into your pressure cooker and plug the mouth of the flask loosely with absorbent cotton. Place the flask in the pressure cooker and add water to the pressure cooker to provide steam for at least 30 minutes. Close the pressure cooker and cook at 15 pounds of pressure for 15 to 20 minutes. Allow the pressure cooker to cool; then open and remove the flask. Allow the flask to cool slightly but not enough for the agar to gel.

Carefully lift one side of the cover of each sterile Petri dish and pour enough of the nutrient agar into it to form a layer about ¼ inch thick over the bottom. Quickly close the cover and allow the dishes to cool and the agar to gel.[4]

Wailes recommends an experiment involving a control dish that is kept covered at all times and four experimental conditions that involve (1) exposing a dish to the air for half an hour, (2) touching a dish with the fingers of thoroughly washed hands, (3) touching a dish with unwashed finger tips, and (4) having a child comb his hair over a dish. The five covered (including the control) are then placed in a warm, dark place for three days, after which the results may be recorded and discussed.

6. Although the risk of children becoming infected during these experiments is slight, it can occur if precautions are not taken. Therefore, once the lids are replaced on the jars or Petri dishes, *do not let the children come into contact with the culture mediums* by touching or sniffing or in any other way. Keep the lids in place throughout the experiment, and when it is completed dispose of the contents in an incinerator. If Petri dishes were used and their reuse is planned, then:

First flood the surface of each dish with Lysol, or a 5 per cent solution of cresol. Let the solution stand for about half an hour and pour off. Empty the dishes into a newspaper, and burn it in an incinerator. Do not touch the cultures. Wash dishes in a strong detergent as a further safeguard.[5]

7. Many different facts and understandings can result from experiments involving the culturing of bacteria. Some of these are illustrated directly by the results, whereas others can arise from discussions and readings. Some specific things that may be learned are

a. The need for a "control" in any experiment and the specific purpose it serves.
b. The constant presence of bacteria in almost all places.
c. The general characteristics of bacteria as microscopic, nongreen plants found in a variety of sizes and shapes.
d. The ways to kill bacteria (heat, pressure, direct sunlight, disinfectants, and so on).

[4] James R. Wailes, *Living Things* (Darien, Conn.: Teachers Publishing Corporation, 1968), p. 23.
[5] Ibid.

e. The conditions required for optimum growth, including darkness, moisture, and warmth (as inside one's body, among other places).

f. The fact that the majority of bacteria are either harmless or beneficial to man.

g. The fact that some bacteria cause disease.

h. The ways to prevent undue exposure to bacteria.

IV. A ONE-WAY STREET

As adults we often complain that children are shortsighted, that they conduct themselves with little thought of future consequences. The behavior patterns that many children adopt which eventually produce detrimental health effects provide one of the more aggravating examples of this general characteristic of youth. In spite of our admonitions they seem determined to embark on a regular pattern of late hours, ear-shattering music, french fries, and cigarette smoking. But are they really so oblivious to the future? We also find the typical child agitating for the privileges of his older siblings, mimicking the actions of some glamorous adult entertainer or sports figure, and dreaming about his future career and accomplishments in very specific ways. Young people do seem capable of reacting to future consequences when they are confronted with them in a concrete or realistic manner. The present example deals with cigarette smoking. With no time machines yet available, an interview project was selected to provide sixth-graders with some perspective on this questionable habit by bringing them into meaningful dialogues with other age groups.

Concept

Detrimental living habits that contribute to the development of chronic disease often begin early in the life of the individual.

Pupils

Developed for sixth-grade co-ed classes with average academic and socioeconomic status; also recommended, with modifications, for grades 7 through 12.

Technique

Interview project.

The interview project described here takes on many of the aspects of a survey, in that information is obtained from many persons; however, unlike the survey, no attempt is made to select the subjects or interviewees in a systematic manner. The following are some specific recommendations for a typical situation:

1. Begin the project early in the unit on cigarette smoking so that the project report will be presented to the class before the end of study on this topic. The line of discussion leading to the assignment might go something like this.

a. Many children begin smoking when they are quite young.
b. The longer one smokes, the more difficult it is to quit.
c. Therefore it is a good idea to take a good look at this habit before deciding if it is for you.
d. One way to do this is to ask those who have already faced this issue what they think of cigarette smoking.

This, of course, is only an example, there are many other good approaches. Regardless of the variation used, try to avoid a negative or condemning attitude toward this topic. Even sixth-graders know, in a general way, that cigarettes are a health hazard, so a "hard-sell" approach is not needed.

2. Help the class plan the project in terms of (a) who they are going to interview and (b) specifically what they are going to ask. Because sixth-graders will not have regular access to persons outside their own home, it would be well to ask the total class to participate in the gathering of the information by interviewing one of their parents and any older brothers or sisters that may be in their households. The interviews should be guided by a set of prepared questions selected by the class. Typical questions might be the following:

a. Do you believe that cigarettes are harmful to health?
b. Do you think that someone can smoke now and then without picking up the habit?
c. Do you think that cigarettes can help people relax?
d. Do you think that cigarettes can help young people socially?
e. Does smoking cause you any particular problems (if you smoke)?
f. What do you think about elementary pupils that smoke?

3. Once the list of questions is decided upon, ask each member of the class to copy it down. Ask the pupils to conduct the interviews in private if possible and to record the responses for each person on a separate piece of paper. Each response sheet should also include the interviewee's sex, age, and his smoking status, if he chooses to reveal it. Emphasize the necessity for legible handwriting in recording the answers.

4. Ask the class to set a definite deadline for the completion of all the interviews and remind the children daily of this obligation until the appointed time arrives. When all or almost all of the response sheets are in, divide them into three groups for interviewees of junior high school age, of senior high school age, and of adult age. If enough persons of college or young-adult age were interviewed, a separate category should be formed for them; otherwise, they may be grouped with the parents in the adult category. Form three (or four) committees, each consisting of two or three of the more capable members of the class. Ask each committee to review the response sheets for its category and prepare a brief report of its findings. The time required for this task will necessarily vary according to how many response sheets were returned; thirty minutes should be sufficient in most cases.

5. When the committees have finished their work, call the class together to hear the reports and discuss the findings. When possible summarize the answers for each age group on each question. This information may be conveniently displayed on the blackboard in a simple grid, with vertical lines to designate age categories and horizontal ones to form rows for all, or the more important, questions (see the following).

	JUNIOR HIGH	SENIOR HIGH	ADULT
1. Are they harmful to health?	Only if you smoke too many.	Yes, but not for several years.	Yes, they are very harmful.
2. Are they always habit forming?	Not for everyone, only heavy smokers.	Sooner or later you get the habit.	Yes, and it's very hard to stop.
3. Do they help you socially?	Yes, with some groups you have to smoke.	Depends on what people you're interested in.	No, they're often a handicap.

6. The best strategy for handling the final discussion will vary according to the nature of the results. The most obvious information to extract is the identification of relationships between age and opinion. Such trends as "the older the smoker, the more the health concern" or "the older the smoker, the stronger the habit" will be commonly found. Be alert for prominent minority opinion differences between boys and girls, or between groups one suspects to be smokers and nonsmokers. Once again, avoid obviously biased interpretations against cigarette smoking. Under anything resembling normal circumstances, the honest facts will make their own point far more effectively than any "teacher manipulation" of the results. At the very least, the results will show differences between adult opinion and student opinion, but with just a little good fortune, these sixth-grade investigators will uncover a trend toward smoking disenchantment starting in junior high and growing stronger with increasing age.

V. TEACHING THE "NOW" GENERATION TO PREVENT HEART DISEASE

It is usually not difficult to get junior high school students interested in the study of heart disease. As is the case with wars, plagues, and earthquakes, people of all ages can develop at least a morbid interest in something that kills thousands of persons. This somewhat questionable source of motivation can be used to lead teen-agers toward a reasonably good understanding of the mechanics and causes of a coronary thrombosis. But a problem arises immediately when someone suggests that they do something about it, that they disrupt their life-style, ever so slightly, to delay something that is not going to happen for thirty or forty years. This attitude is unfortunate but understandable; adults too are notoriously poor at taking steps to forestall misfortunes that may occur at some indefinite time in the future. It is probably impossible, and undesirable as well, to convince people that they should take all possible steps to avoid heart disease; however, it is both possible and desirable to guide people toward behavior patterns that yield immediate benefits as well as some protection for the future. This general principle is applied in the present example, wherein eighth-graders embark on "health habit projects" to see if they can find any short-term advantages to habits designed to minimize the risk of future heart disease.

Concept

The occurrence of most diseases can be delayed, minimized, or prevented by intelligent health practices.

Students

This example was designed for use with an eighth-grade co-ed class with average socioeconomic and above-average academic status; with suitable modifications, it could be used throughout the junior high grades with advanced students and with all groups at the senior high level.

Technique

The health habit project.

The "health-habit project" is simply a voluntary outside assignment wherein a student adopts an improved health practice for a specified period of time. On completion of the project the student reports on his subjective reaction to the new practice and also on any objective improvement in his health status that may have occurred. This type of assignment may be used independently by simply soliciting volunteers at an opportune time during the course of a particular teaching unit. However, in the present example, the projects serve as a follow-up activity to a symposium. The following procedures should work well with a typical eighth-grade class.

1. As part of a unit on chronic disease or heart disease, secure student volunteers to conduct a symposium (see pages 160–161) on the factors related to heart disease. Ask them to emphasize finding and reporting on health procedures that apparently help prevent or delay the onset of heart trouble. Also charge them with the responsibility of identifying from among these practices those that they feel will also improve the individual's health in the near future.

2. If the student reporting group is reasonably competent and has had access to good sources of information, it will probably include all or most of the following recommendations in its report:

a. Avoid cigarette smoking.
b. Practice weight control.
c. Limit the intake of fats to 20 per cent of one's caloric requirements.

d. Limit saturated fats to 50 per cent of one's total fat intake.
e. Engage in regular physical exercise.
f. Avoid excessive emotional stress.
g. Obtain early treatment for diabetes.
h. Obtain early treatment for high blood pressure.
i. Have regular medical examinations appropriate to one's age.
j. Give special attention to preventive measures if one's family has a history of heart disease.

3. Ask the reporting group to conclude its discussion with recommendations of practices that may provide early rewards. Suggestions may include such items as avoiding cigarettes, reducing body weight, reducing the intake of fats, and exercising properly as practices within this special category. At this point the class should be given an opportunity to discuss these items so as to identify and evaluate the possible short-term benefits. Class members may suggest clean teeth, improved figure or physique, better complexion, and improved recreational skills as worthwhile fringe benefits. If possible, the teacher should lead the class toward a common acceptance of and some enthusiasm for these particular health habits.

4. At the conclusion of the symposium, solicit volunteers for participation in a number of four-week projects of their particular interest. Some students may wish to embark upon a weight-reduction program (with parental or medical supervision), or campaign to reduce fat intake in hopes of securing some improvement in complexion or reduction in body weight. Others may be interested in adding more exercise to their routine.

5. In some teaching situations students can be motivated to volunteer for such projects out of pure interest and the prospects of self-improvement; however, many teachers prefer to provide added incentives in the form of extra credit or the opportunity to meet a standard term-project assignment through this activity.

6. Ask each volunteer to submit a brief one-page outline of his or her program. Review these carefully to ensure their general safety and workability. Once the students have started their programs, provide informal encouragement by occasionally asking them about their progress. Set aside five or ten minutes of class time per week to hear brief oral progress reports from the volunteers and require a complete oral report from each of the participants at the end of the designated project period. If three or more reports are involved, a symposium format may be used in their presentation. This will provide for the more effective discussion of any common experiences or generalizations.

7. The content of the reports will vary widely according to the characteristics of the reporters and the nature of the project. Generally the report will be more valuable if the participants are advised ahead of time to include information pertaining to their degree of success in sticking to their program, the factors that helped or hindered their efforts, any positive benefits they experienced, and whether or not they plan to continue their program.

VI. LET'S VISIT THE WATER FACTORY

To the average citizen water is a natural right, something that is always present in the environment and available to every one. For the added convenience of having water immediately at hand in his home, the average citizen is willing to pay a small fee so that the community can set up a simple delivery system. But few things in our modern world are simple. More and more, water is becoming a manufactured product. Few cities are so fortunate as to be able to pump untreated water into their systems. The water being used must usually undergo a complex series of processes which must be carried out with considerable precision if the "water factory" is to deliver a safe and palatable product. In the following example, ninth-grade students gain some realization of the elaborate equipment and trained personnel that a modern water-treatment plant requires by an on-the-scene visit.

Concept

Effective disease prevention and control measures often require organized efforts for their development and implementation.

Students

This example was designed for use with a ninth-grade co-ed group of average socioeconomic and academic status; with suitable modifications it could be used throughout grades 7 through 12.

Technique

Small-group field trip.

In the ideal field trip we would probably find the entire class transported to the facility involved and organized into small tour groups, each with a competent guide. This, of course, is seldom practical in the average teaching situation. However, the small-group field trip can provide a very practical and acceptable alternative which retains many of the advantages of the conventional field trip. Because the small-group trip is described in some detail on pages 166–167, the suggestions here will deal primarily with the handling of the specific subject matter involved.

1. Encourage the investigating team of students to become as knowledgeable about water-treatment procedures as possible through the study of library sources. Help the group organize the information-gathering process into logical tasks for assignment to individual members. A team of four might charge individual members with responsibility for gathering data on (a) the basic water supply, including where it is obtained, its initial state when received, and its adequacy in terms of future needs; (b) the treatment process, including purposes of various chemical additives, the type of filtration, and the control of purity and palatability; (c) storage and delivery, including the function of local tanks and reservoirs, the need for mains, laterals, and so on; and (d) items of special interest. This fourth assignment should go to a student with access to a camera who could then make a photographic record of the trip. If the school or the

student committee is affluent enough to afford the film, 35-mm slides provide the ideal way to embellish the report. However, good black-and-white prints are inexpensive and can be viewed by the class through use of an opaque projector.

2. Impress the individual investigators with the importance of developing a reasonable degree of expertise regarding their phases of the project. Each participant should develop a specific list of questions to ask or points to look for. A partial list of questions that a student might develop for the area of water treatment would include the following:

    a. Do any specific disease organisms pose a particular threat to this specific source of water?
    b. What particular tests are most useful in determining the purity of the water supply?
    c. Upon what principles are these tests based?
    d. How often are they performed?
    e. What measures are taken to ensure the destruction of pathogenic organisms?

An alert student that begins his tour with this sort of checklist might return with some interesting information on, for example, infectious hepatitis, membrane filter techniques for determining the presence of coliforms, and the need for free chlorine residuals. Although these terms may seem difficult for ninth-graders, the important ideas associated with them are basically simple. Students who grapple with these technicalities will develop a fuller appreciation of the many factors involved in protecting a community water supply.

3. During the actual tour the student responsible for reporting on a particular area of the operation should be alert to the need for photographs with which to illustrate this report. He should point out particularly good picture possibilities to the photographer of the group.

4. As soon as possible after the visit the student committee should present its report in the format described for the symposium (pp. 160–161). The general discussion following the individual reports should provide the teacher with the opportunity to guide the attention of the class toward some important subconcepts, such as the following:

    a. The demand for water is increasing much faster than the population.
    b. Water must be reused if modern needs are to be met.
    c. Polluted water can be treated to make it potable, but the process is expensive.
    d. Water with an unpleasant taste and odor is not always dangerous; water with a pleasant taste and odor is not always safe.
    e. A safe and abundant supply of water is essential to the economic growth of a community.

6. Although this project as described can be used as the sole means of direct contact with the community during the study of environmental

health, an extremely rewarding (and demanding) alternative consists of organizing the total class into investigating teams, with each assigned to a separate aspect of the total topic. This would result in concurrent visits to such facilities as sewage treatment plants, air-pollution monitoring stations, slaughterhouses, and canneries; visits might also be made to those agencies dealing with noise abatement and rat control. The relevance and practicality of visits to specific facilities vary from community to community, but the guidelines for providing leadership and encouragement to the students remain much the same.

VII. GANG UP AND HELP YOUR BUDDY FIGHT V.D.

Venereal disease would probably not exist in the United States as a significant public health problem were it not for the shameful and guilty connotations that the general public persistently attaches to it. Community efforts to encourage sexual morality and eradicate venereal disease are both exceedingly worthy causes; however, experience has shown they do not work well together. If one chooses to view a given instance of sexual intercourse as immoral, then the fact that venereal disease is or is not transmitted in the process should not thereby increase or decrease the degree of sexual immorality involved. However, by uniting a moral problem with a disease problem, society has created a number of serious obstacles to the effective control of venereal disease. The treatment of common forms of venereal disease with suitable antibiotics is virtually 100 per cent effective, is free or inexpensive, and is less embarrassing than most persons realize. In this example the tenth-graders of a large urban high school hear these facts from a public health officer.

Concept

Various social, emotional, and economic factors commonly influence the degree to which modern technology is used in combating disease.

Students

This example was designed for use in an urban setting with a tenth-grade co-ed class ranking below average in socioeconomic and academic status; with suitable modifications it could be used throughout grades 9 through 12 in most all types of school situations.

Technique

Resource speaker.

The problems associated with obtaining good resource speakers are often so difficult that many health teachers eventually ask, "Why bother?" Although this point of view is perhaps justified with respect to some topical areas, it is generally unwarranted when dealing with venereal disease in metropolitan settings. Teachers in these situations will often find their local health departments ready to send knowledgeable persons into the schools to discuss all aspects of venereal disease. Public health workers with responsibilities in this field realize the importance of reaching the public, and they properly identify teen-agers as members of a priority group for their educational endeavors. Many teachers provide a worthwhile experience for their classes by simply phoning the disease-control section of the health department and requesting a speaker; however, much greater value can be gained from such a visit if a few additional measures are taken. The following are some specific recommendations.

1. If at all practical, arrange for the speaker to appear before groups no larger than regular sections of twenty to thirty students. Those students who may have occasion to seek treatment of a local public health facility need an opportunity to develop confidence in the person associated with the program. This will occur much more readily in a small-group setting than in an assembly-hall type of presentation.

2. Schedule the resource speaker's visit late enough in the unit of study covering venereal disease that the students have a reasonable degree of knowledge on the topic. The speaker's time should not be spent in covering the same basic material that is found in most health texts. The nature of venereal-disease transmission, the symptoms, the possible consequences of untreated cases, and other such material should have been covered at the junior high level and reviewed again in depth before the arrival of the speaker.

3. Venereal-disease education at the senior high level should provide students with the opportunities to realize the importance of (a) seeking legitimate medical treatment if they have any reason to suspect that they have been exposed to venereal disease, (b) cooperating with physicians or case workers in finding others who may be infected, and (c) supporting community efforts in the form of laws and services that are needed to combat venereal disease. Ideally, this type of content would be covered in a general way prior to the speaker's visit, thus allowing his presentation to focus on the specific aspects of the local programs.

4. As soon as the date and time of the visit have been established, provide the prospective speaker with a clear indication of the content that has been covered in class. Offer suggestions as to what aspects he should cover in his report. Be sure to inform him of any films or the topic of venereal disease that the students have recently viewed. This serves to inform him further on the background of the students and prevents any duplication in the event he plans to use films in his presentation.

5. During the class meeting immediately preceding the visit, distribute 3- by 5-inch cards and ask each student to write one question that he would like the visitor to answer. After all such cards have been collected, review them carefully and select about eight of the more relevant questions that are most representative of the total group of cards. Present these to the speaker promptly on his arrival for possible incorporation into his presentation if he so desires. Also encourage him to allow time for additional student questions within his presentation for each group. A group that has been well prepared for a resource person may ask such questions as the following:

a. Is it better for persons who think they have venereal disease to go to their family doctor or to a public health clinic?

    b. If someone goes to a public health clinic for venereal-disease treatment, will his parents be told?

    c. Why should persons with venereal disease tell investigators the names of all their friends if they only had sex with one person?

    d. What will happen to me if one of my friends gives my name to a venereal-disease case worker?

    e. What do you do to those suspects that refuse to be examined or that refuse treatment?

6. In the class meeting following the resource speaker's presentation, allow at least part of the class period for follow-up discussion. This process can be facilitated by some careful note taking during the presentation of points that merit reemphasis or that did not seem to get through to the class at the time. This procedure is particularly valuable if more than one section is involved. Often the content covered by the speaker necessarily varies from class to class because of the nature of student questions, shortened periods, and other such factors.

7. Use every intellectually honest opportunity to emphasize (a) the importance of treatment for all those exposed, (b) the availability of treatment, and (c) the practical necessity of cooperation with venereal-disease case workers.

VIII. YOUR FAVORITE CHARITY

A rather ancient joke that makes its appearance now and then in any one of several variations goes something like this: A somewhat charitable judge extends to a condemned criminal the privilege of selecting his own means of death; the criminal immediately chooses "old age" as his selected form. Few persons spend much of their time contemplating their preferred form of death. They probably feel that there are much more pleasant ways to occupy one's time and that, at any rate, they have little choice in the matter. But if certain aspects of human behavior are observed closely, it is apparent that people establish definite priorities in regard to their fear, respect, and concern for various death-dealing and disabling diseases. In many instances these priorities seem to represent reasonable choices based upon important values; in other cases these largely implicit choices seem ill advised. People can devote only a limited amount of their time, money, and other resources toward the prevention of disease and the pursuit of health before the process becomes self-defeating; therefore, it becomes worthwhile to examine priorities. In the following example, twelfth-graders seek to accomplish this by investigating the degree of financial support that their community extends to various voluntary health organizations. This provides a very realistic measure of the puplic's concern over various health problems.

Concept

Because individual disease conditions vary greatly in their potential for producing death and disability, mankind commonly establishes priorities in efforts to develop techniques of prevention and treatment.

Students

The present example was designed for twelfth-grade co-ed students of average socioeconomic and academic status; with only slight modification it could be used with most any senior high school classroom group.

Technique
Interview project.

The number of voluntary health agencies and their degree of activity vary a good deal from community to community. The manner in which funds are obtained also varies, with some agencies relying heavily on United Fund drives and others concentrating on individual collection campaigns. The practice of selling memberships and operating along the lines of a regular professional organization is another alternative. Students will need guidance in their efforts to analyze these factors both as they affect the selection of agencies to investigate and the interpretation of any information that they eventually obtain. Many of the general procedures for the symposium (pp. 160–161) apply to this teaching example; the following specific recommendations are also appropriate for most situations:

1. Although large numbers of students could be used in this project, particularly in metropolitan areas with many active agencies, four to six students are sufficient to carry out the basic assignment. Because these students will be, to a certain extent, representing the school to the community, it is well to select the committee members from among the more mature and responsible student volunteers.

2. The student investigators' first task is to compile a list of voluntary health agencies that are active in their locality. In many larger communities health councils or health and welfare councils maintain offices that can make this information available. In smaller communities the local public health department can advise students on the presence of the local offices of the major voluntary health agencies. The use of either of these sources as starting points will usually make unnecessary a tedious search of the phonebook in an effort to run down the dozens of possibilities.

3. The students should next select five to ten agencies for inclusion in their study. The older and better-established agencies that have had a chance to get their local fund-raising activities well organized generally provide a better basis for comparison. In view of the concept being studied, it is best to restrict the choice to those agencies that are more clearly identified with a single disease or a closely related group of diseases.

4. After the selections have been made, the students should organize themselves into interview teams of perhaps two students each and phone for appointments with the personnel of the agencies to be visited. Prior to the visit the student interviewers should become acquainted with the nature and importance of the disease condition the agency seeks to combat. Also the questions to be asked should be planned carefully in advance. Some of the main points to cover for each agency would be the following:

a. The amount of money collected locally during the past year and the scope of the geographical area in which the collections took place.
b. The basic methods used to collect funds—for example, neighborhood campaigns, mailed requests, appeals at work, and so on.
c. Particular factors that made local fund raising easy or difficult as compared with the drives of competing agencies in the area.
d. Total figures for state and national fund raising or the address of state or national offices that could provide this information.

5. Once the interviews have been completed, the student committee should meet and pool all the information gathered as it prepares a symposium-style report. The committee's basic task is to develop some carefully formed hypotheses or inferences in regard to public concern for the various disease conditions included in its study. In addition to the basic amount of money raised by the various agencies, committee members must consider the nature of the fund-raising campaign so as to make some judgment on the degree to which this figure reflects genuine public concern as opposed to efficient methods of solicitation. The following are some questions that the report might profitably consider.

a. Does the potential for causing death seem to be the main factor in the determination of public concern for a particular disease or are other factors, such as its disabling qualities, equally or more important?
b. How important does the prevalence of a disease seem to be in comparison with its severity as a factor affecting public concern?
c. Does the public show more concern for diseases that primarily attack children rather than older persons?
d. Does the public seem to be more sympathetic toward diseases that are purely organic in their causes and symptomology as opposed to conditions with psychiatric or psychosomatic connotations?
e. Does the locality in which the survey was conducted show the same pattern of financial support as that found on the state or national levels? If not, why not?

It will be impossible for answers to these questions to be determined in an absolute sense; therefore, the teacher should point out the need for considerable caution in drawing conclusions. However, in their efforts to bring information to bear on these issues, students will gain a much better idea of the degree of public willingness to support various disease conditions and find out a good deal about the activities and importance of the agencies themselves.

REFERENCES

Anderson, Hans O., and Paul G. Koutnik. *Toward More Effective Science Instruction in Secondary Education.* New York: Macmillan Publishing Co., Inc., 1972.

Cox, Mary Jane. "Environmental Awareness Projects for Children," *School Health Review*, Vol. 3, No. 4 (July–August 1972), pp. 19–22.

Henke, Lorraine J. "Student-to-Student Teaching About Tobacco Smoking," *School Health Review*, Vol. 4, No. 1 (January–February 1973), pp. 17–18.

Jones, Herbert, Dorothy Nowack, and Jean Heindel. "Which Methodology for Venereal Disease Education?", *School Health Review*, Vol. 3, No. 2 (March–April 1972), pp. 8–9.

Morholt, Evelyn, Paul F. Brandwein, and Alexander Joseph. *A Sourcebook for the Biological Sciences.* New York: Harcourt, Brace & World, Inc., 1966.

Schwartz, William F. *Teacher's Handbook on Venereal Disease Education.* Washington, D.C.: American Association for Health, Physical Education and Recreation, 1965.

Troyer, Donald L., Maurice G. Kellogg, and Hans O. Anderson. *Sourcebook for Biological Sciences.* New York: Macmillan Publishing Co., Inc., 1972.

Wailes, James R. *Living Things.* Darien, Conn.: Teachers Publishing Corporation, 1968.

PART

V

Creative Evaluation and Professional Growth

Pursue, keep up with, circle round and round your life, as a dog does his master's chaise. Do what you love. Know your own bone; gnaw at it, bury it, unearth it, and gnaw it still.

THOREAU

19. TEACHER-STUDENT ■ EVALUATION AND PROFESSIONAL GROWTH

When teachers teach, they want some assurance that their students are learning. This is the purpose of evaluation. Evaluation, when used correctly, is a way of determining how successful the teacher is, how the information has affected the students, and, in general, how relevant the information is to the class.

In this chapter we shall examine the usual methods of teacher evaluation and offer some suggestions for evaluating creative products and thinking. A final section will deal with professional growth, which is necessary if the teacher is to be as effective as possible both now and in the future.

Subjective Evaluation

Evaluation can be either "informal" or "formal"; effective teachers generally use a combination of both methods. More "informal" ways that do not necessarily include objective measurements are teacher observations, questionnaires, interviews, teacher and student diaries, and other student autobiographical records.

TEACHER OBSERVATIONS. The technique of teacher observation has been described in detail in Chapter 2. An effective teacher must be sensitive to an individual's personal idiosyncrasies and learn to distinguish the student's "intended" impressions from his more typical personality that manifests itself in sometimes subtle mannerisms. Sensitivity training can do much to enhance this characteristic in an instructor. Otherwise, increased efforts on the teacher's part to recognize the students as growing individuals with needs can fulfill this necessary requirement.

QUESTIONNAIRES. A questionnaire is a means of taking inventory of an aspect of personality. Unlike achievement and aptitude tests, which are considered objective, it is a subjective tool. Therefore, it must not be utilized as a measurement of a student's ability in health. It can be used to determine whether the instructor has covered relevant material in which the students were interested, how the students reacted to various ideas or techniques, how the students feel about themselves, and so on.

Because lower elementary children do not have sufficient background experiences in many areas of health, and because they do not communicate well at a nonverbal level, the use of questionnaires is limited at this age. In higher grades it would be used sparingly, to prevent overexposure. If given too frequently, the questionnaire's responses become less and less honest.

INTERVIEWS. Many teachers often feel a need for discussing particular students with another person who is knowledgeable about that student. Of foremost importance is the student himself. Ironically enough, teachers often do not go to the student himself for information which can often be obtained merely by asking him. Discovering areas of student concern and interest and discovering student feelings about class involvement, health knowledge, and other topics can facilitate a subjective evaluation.

Teachers can also add their opinions and estimates of a student's abilities and interests. These must be weighed carefully, but can add to the fund of information about an individual. A teacher can discover patterns in the way a student's health attitudes have grown and changed, and whether his habits and health practices have been influenced by the health classes.

Interviews with parents are more common at the elementary and junior high levels than at the high school level and above. Parents have more influence over a child and know more about his specific life patterns when he is younger. As a child matures, he is often to be found more out of the home than in, and few parents honestly know in what specific activities their high school child is involved most of the day.

Parents of younger children can provide clues about health practices at home and can be helpful in enabling the teacher discover whether practices stressed in school are carried out in the home. This not only helps in student evaluation but also aids the conscientious teacher in determining his effectiveness.

DIARIES AND OTHER AUTOBIOGRAPHICAL RECORDS. Students at upper levels (junior high through college) are quite capable of recording their feelings about themselves in diaries or assignments on such topics as "I want (do not want) to smoke marijuana because . . ." "I feel (do not feel) good about being me because . . ." and "Marriage frightens (does not frighten) me because . . . ." A diary can be used by students to record impressions of the material presented to them in class each day or week. If they were stimulated, provoked, bored, confused, they can indicate this and briefly state why.

A perceptive instructor can use such records to estimate an individual's development in various areas of health. Sometimes the instructor will discover the misconceptions and/or lack of background a class has in specific areas. When this occurs, he might find himself changing overall class objectives in order to compensate for the students' lack of exposure to a particular area or topic.

Measurement

When a student knows he is going to be evaluated, he often automatically thinks of tests. This word-association process is not unreasonable, for tests are currently the most popular way to measure what a student knows about a subject. Fortunately, few teachers rely on tests alone when evaluating a student, but even when tests are used, they can be poorly constructed and lack objective results.

Good test construction requires a careful analysis of the original class objectives. It would be unfair to judge a student on information or skills the instructor did not present in the context of the class. If the objectives have been carefully selected, they should include skills, behaviors, and knowledge as listed in the three domains discussed in Chapter 3. A knowledge of these cognitive, affective, and action domains is a wise investment in any future teacher's time, and this knowledge would be valuable background for the following paragraphs.

Norris Sanders,[1] using the *Taxonomy of Educational Objectives*[2] as a basis, did an excellent job of classifying questions into the categories designated by Bloom and his colleagues. These categories include memory, translation, interpretation, application, analysis, synthesis, and evaluation. Sanders realized that each category necessitated a different kind of thinking, and it follows that a complete, objective evaluation should give the students an opportunity to organize their thinking into each category of thought. The categories of thought are sequential and cumulative. Each area has unique characteristics, and the higher categories include some element of each of the lower ones. (See Sanders' model shown in Figure 19–1.)

A creative teacher can find many keys to good test construction by a careful consideration of Sanders' book. A summary of these seven areas follows.

QUESTIONS DESIGNED FOR MORE THAN MEMORY

The objective of the book is to describe a practical plan to ensure a varied intellectual atmosphere in the classroom. The approach is through a

[1] Norris M. Sanders, *Classroom Questions, What Kinds?* (New York: Harper & Row, 1966).

[2] Benjamin S. Bloom (ed.), *Taxonomy of Educational Objectives* (New York: Longmans, 1956).

systematic consideration of questions that require students *to use ideas rather than simply remember them.* Bloom's *Taxonomy* is used as a basis. Sanders replaced Bloom's term "knowledge" with the term "memory"; holding that "memory" better described the mental activity and was parallel with the names of the other categories. Sanders also divided "comprehension" into two of its component parts: "translation" and "interpretation." He considered each as a separate classification (see Figure 19–1).

Sanders stated that memory questions dominate education. Using Bloom's *Taxonomy* as a guide, however, helps the teacher to be more sensitive to the opportunities for many kinds of questions.

The *Taxonomy* may also be used in evaluating instructional material and educational objectives. Sanders submitted three hypotheses:

1. Students who have more practice with intellectual skills will develop them to a greater degree than those who have less practice.
2. After a teacher studies the *Taxonomy*, he is likely to offer his students a greater variety of intellectual experiences than he did before.
3. A greater emphasis on the teaching of intellectual skills, other than at the memory level, will not decrease the amount of knowledge the student retains.[3]

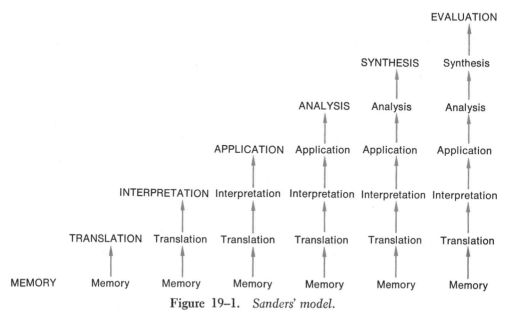

Figure 19–1. *Sanders' model.*

Source: *Norris M. Sanders,* Classroom Questions: What Kinds? *New York: Harper & Row, Publishers, Inc. 1966. Copyright (c) 1966 by Norris M. Sanders. Reprinted by permission of Harper & Row, Publishers, Inc.*

[3] Sanders, op. cit.

Sanders pointed out that teachers sometimes do not agree on the category into which questions should be classified. In fact, different students may answer the same questions from different levels of cognitive behavior; for example, one student may correctly state (recall) that gonorrhea is the most common type of venereal disease in the United States because he read the answer in a textbook. This is memory. Another student may have *analyzed* the available data on the various types of venereal disease and concluded another answer.

All levels of the *Taxonomy* can be used with any age group. (For evidence tending to support this hypothesis see the study by Clegg, Farley, and Curran.[4]) Sanders felt that it should also be used with slow learners. Perhaps some students who have difficulty with memory questions may have greater success at other levels.

Memory

This chapter emphasizes the need to distinguish between important and less important ideas. It defines a memory question as one that asks the student to *recognize* or *recall* information presented to him earlier. It states that the memory category is indispensable on all levels of thinking. Questions involving definitions, generalizations, and values are usually more desirable than the mere recall of isolated bits of information.

Translation

Translation means nothing more than asking a student to identify one part of a communication at a time and to express it in a new form. When a student is asked to explain something in his own words, he must *translate*.

Another form of translation occurs when a student is asked to explain a picture or a drawing, or vice versa. A student might also be asked to select from a group of passages those that express the same idea. The use of a sociodrama, where students are asked to act out a specific event is another form of translation.

Interpretation

The essential characteristic of interpretation is that the student *relates* or *discovers a relationship* between two ideas. The emphasis is that the student discovers or uses relationships on a relatively simple or common-sense level. The difference between a commonsense use of relationships and a more sophisticated understanding serves as one distinction between the interpretation and analysis categories.

Interpretation questions have two other characteristics: they tell the

[4] Ambrose A. Clegg, George Farley, and Robert Curran, "Training Teachers to Analyze the Cognitive Level of Classroom Questions," Research Report No. 1, Applied Research Training Program, School of Education, University of Massachusetts, Amherst, Massachusetts, June 1967.

student explicitly what to do and they have one or only a few logical answers and therefore are objective.

There are six kinds of relationships found in interpretations: comparative; implication; inductive generalization; value, skill, or definition; quantitative, or numerical, relationship; and cause and effect. Each is described below.

COMPARATIVE. Students are asked whether two or more ideas are the same or different. For example, "Is the incidence of auto deaths the same in Florida as it is in Massachusetts?" or "Which of the five communities listed below have similar birth rates?" (This deals with the degree of similarity.) or "Compare the types of health care in the U.S. and Sweden." (This assumes that the students have studied these two.) The process of comparison is rather simple because it does not require much mental power. If such questions are missed, it is more likely because the student does not remember the facts.

IMPLICATION. An implication is an idea that follows inevitably from specific evidence. The thought process in finding an implication is deduction, although in the interpretation category students need not be aware of the thought process. The possibilities for questions relating to implications are almost unlimited.

INDUCTIVE GENERALIZATION FROM SUPPORTING EVIDENCE. A scholar draws an inductive conclusion when he observes that many members of a class of things have a common characteristic and then concludes that all members of a class must have the same characteristic. The difference between an implication and a generalization is that the former is beyond serious doubt, whereas the latter can never be accepted as certain. Full use of the induction falls within the analysis category rather than in the interpretation category, because inductive thinking requires a certain amount of formal training.

A question of this subcategory that might be used is: "From your text, cite evidence that drug use was known to ancient man."

VALUE, SKILL, OR DEFINITION. Students are asked either to recognize or to develop an example of a value, skill, or definition. It should be kept in mind that the student, when working with a value, is not called on to make a judgment regarding the goodness of that value. Such action on the student's part is related more to the evaluation category.

QUANTITATIVE. Students are asked to use statistical information to draw conclusions. Usually the arithmetic involved is not difficult, as the real purpose of such questions is to stimulate the student to draw conclusions.

CAUSE AND EFFECT. The relationship between cause and effect is simple to comprehend. Sanders points out, however, that usually the cause of something may be considered from several perspectives. For example, one might ask, "What was the cause of the accident?" Several correct answers may be given, such as—a flat tire caused the accident, or a child ran in front of the car causing the accident, or the driver fell asleep at the wheel causing the accident.

INTERPRETATION QUESTIONS BASED ON THE FORMAT OF THE QUESTION. Such questions fall into the category of finding analogies, irrelevant items, or scrambled outline. For example:

1. The engineer is to the locomotive as the _____ is to the airplane. (analogy)
2. Which date does not fit? 1812, 1824, 1914, 1941 (irrelevant item)
3. Which statement about milk production is out of order?
   a. Cows in pasture.
   b. Farmer milks.
   c. Children drinking milk.
   d. Milkman delivering milk.

Application

Application is the ability to use ideas, principles, and generalizations in new situations. The application category is designed to give students practice in the transfer of training. Application questions have three characteristics:

1. They have problem-solving power.
2. They deal with the whole of ideas and skills rather than their parts.
3. They include a minimum of directions, as the student is expected to know what to do.

Sometimes application questions may partially violate one of their characteristics or principles because it is difficult to produce lifelike problems in the classroom.

Application questions give practice in independent use of knowledge and in skills. They always deal with ideas that have been studied previously. The difference between interpretation and application questions lies in the fact that with the former the student is asked to demonstrate the use of some abstractions, whereas in the latter he is expected to put the appropriate abstraction to use. A sample question might be: "Tell me how the U.S. and Russia are different."

Analysis

Analysis is the ability to break down material into its parts by using the formal rules of logic. The distinctive feature of analysis is that it requires solution of problems in the light of *conscious knowledge of the parts and process of reasoning*. The student must be conscious of the intellectual process he is performing and know the rules for reaching a valid and true conclusion. Among other things, the student must have knowledge of the methodology of the discipline and training in formal logic.

There are four possible approaches to the parts and processes of reasoning: induction, fallacies, deduction, and semantics.

Induction involves reasoning from the specific to the general. Real induction requires generalization based on observation of only some of the members of a class. As such, an inductive conclusion never can be considered true beyond a doubt.

Fallacies are the common mistakes made in reasoning such as faulty premises, unwarranted conclusions, etc.

Deduction is the process of applying a generalization to a specific instance, thereby reaching a conclusion. The most common forms of deduction are the immediate inference, the syllogism, and the dilemma. (Sanders attempted to develop analysis questions related to deduction for social studies classes but was unable to locate enough good examples to use with the students.)

Semantics is related to the correct use and definition of words. Both parties in a conversation should be using key terms in the same manner.

Sanders stated that students should not be asked analysis questions until they have had some instruction in the reasoning process. He felt that analysis questions are one of the most important kinds, but require much planning and experimentation on the part of the teacher. He suggested, however, that analysis questions related to induction may be used with elementary school students, as examples of inductive reasoning are common in elementary textbooks.

Synthesis

Synthesis is the process of drawing elements from many sources to form a unified structure not clearly perceived before. The product is created by the individual. One characteristic of synthesis questions is that they allow the student *great freedom in seeking a solution.* The student is encouraged to use information and thought processes he may know about from any part of his life experience. *Synthesis calls for divergent thinking.*

A second characteristic is that the solution requires a product. The product may take the form of a unique communication, a plan, or a set of abstract relations.

Most important in developing synthesis questions is a classroom atmosphere that encourages divergent thinking. The teacher and the class should respect unusual questions and answers. A teacher with a well-organized pattern of subject matter and carefully formulated lesson plans must resist the temptation to brush aside student ideas that do not fit easily into his plans. *Insecure teachers often stifle creative thinking and questioning because they interpret this as a threat to their position of authority.*

Evaluation

Evaluation is the process of making a judgment about the value of an idea, a solution, a method, etc., using criteria developed by the individual, himself. Evaluation requires two steps:

1. Setting up appropriate standards or values.
2. Determining how closely the idea or subject meets these standards or values.

Questions that specify the values for making a judgment should be classified as interpretation questions. It is important to remember that evaluation questions deal with values, and *not facts or opinions*.

Evaluation is always somewhat subjective in one of two ways. Either the standard cannot be proved to be correct, or the idea to be judged cannot be proved to violate the standard.

Evaluation is among the most difficult of mental activities because there is no absolute assurance that the product represents truth. This does not mean, however, that we should avoid making value judgments. Rather, we should employ all available techniques in attempting to obtain the highest possible reliability.

PLANNING FOR QUESTIONING

A reasonable rule of thumb for an academic course is that *a minimum of one-third of the time allotted to questioning in both instruction and evaluation of learning should be devoted to levels above memory.*

A teacher needs a deep mastery of the subject in order to ask questions above memory. For example, if a teacher knows only one example to illustrate a principle, he must revert to the memory level for evaluation because he must use the same example again. A teacher who knows two or more examples can use one for instruction and the others for interpretation or application.

Textbooks create a major problem for teachers concerned with composing good questions. Most textbook authors are too specific in dissecting, integrating, and providing visual images. Consequently, the textbook offers little opportunity for any mental activity except remembering. Sanders has suggested, therefore, that in order to encourage thinking, the teacher must present subject matter from sources other than the conventional textbook. Such sources of information would include contrary accounts, different interpretations, additional evidence, different line of reasoning, a different example, or more recent and accurate materials. Providing the class with additional information allows the teacher to ask many provocative questions. For example, if contrary information was given, the teacher could ask, "What conclusions might be drawn using this information?"

The teacher should remember that information can be presented in different ways. It is the responsibility of the teacher to determine the method that will best illustrate his point. For example, he may develop the abortion question by first showing pictures of various methods of abortion, by providing accounts of women who have had (or are considering) an abortion—both pro and con—or by having the class read about abortion. To determine which method will be best, the teacher must consider the ability and motivation of the students, the time available, and the objectives of the course.

Short-answer questions (true-false, completion, matching, multiple-choice) can lead to thinking in all areas except synthesis and evaluation. The short-answer question does not guarantee that there is only one correct answer, although in most instances this seems to be the case. Discussion questions are obviously needed if we wish to explore all categories of the taxonomy.

ALTERNATIVES TO THE GRADING GAME

There are, in fact, a number of alternatives to the traditional teacher-oriented grading system that is used by the majority of teachers today. Kirschenbaum, Simon, and Napier, in their book *Wad-Ja-Get?*,[5] suggest a number of alternatives including:

Written evaluations. Here the teacher (and sometimes the student) provides written evaluations of student performance. Here the form may provide space for the teacher to comment on student "strengths," "weaknesses," etc.

Self-evaluation. Here the student evaluates his own progress and growth, either in writing or in a conference with the teacher.

The contract system. Individual contracts, calling for different types of activities, are provided each student. After the student has had a chance to determine which grade (which often determines amount of work to be done) he wishes to contract for, he then returns the contract to the teacher. An example of one type of contract, based on a unit of work, is shown in Figure 19–2.

PERSONAL AND PROFESSIONAL GROWTH

It seems appropriate to include a discussion on personal and professional growth in the same chapter with evaluation. In many ways they are closely related. For one, every act, such as evaluation, which requires the teacher to venture into a new area of inquiry helps to advance one's personal and/or professional growth. The art of thorough planning for evaluation certainly requires the teacher to review, interpret, and construct evaluative instru-

[5] Howard Kirschenbaum, et al., *Wad-Ja Get?* (New York, N.Y.: Hart Publishing Co., Inc., 1971).

VENEREAL DISEASE UNIT—CONTRACT FOR GRADE

Each student has the opportunity to determine his own grade for the venereal disease education unit. After carefully reading the following, each student "contracts" the grade he desires to earn and agrees to complete all phases of the chosen grade. The requirements for each grade are listed below.

GRADE "A"
1. Review two magazine articles about venereal diseases.
2. Report on three venereal diseases other than syphilis and gonorrhea.
3. Report on the incidence of VD in Indiana and other parts of the United States.
4. Answer the questions to the Schwartz VD test.
5. Take the McHugh test at the end of the unit and get 80% of questions correct.

GRADE "B"
1. Review one magazine article about venereal diseases.
2. Report on three venereal diseases other than syphilis and gonorrhea.
3. Report on the incidence of VD in Indiana and other parts of United States.
4. Answer the questions to the Schwartz VD test.
5. Take the McHugh test at the end of the unit and get 70% of questions correct.

GRADE "C"
1. Review one magazine article about venereal diseases.
2. Report on three venereal diseases other than syphilis and gonorrhea.
3. Report on the incidence of venereal diseases in Indiana.
4. Answer the questions to the Schwartz VD test.
5. Take the McHugh test at the end of the unit and get 60% of questions correct.

GRADE "D"
1. Review one magazine article about venereal diseases.
2. Report on one venereal disease other than syphilis or gonorrhea.
3. Answer the questions to the Schwartz VD test.
4. Take the McHugh test at the end of the unit and get 50% of questions correct.

Additional Information
- For the magazine articles reviewed, state the main theme of the article, main points mentioned, author's conclusion, and your reaction. Secure form from teacher.
- For reporting on venereal diseases other than the main two, state the etiology, mode of transmission, symptoms, treatment, and prognosis. Secure form from teacher.
- Secure from the teacher question forms on Indiana and U.S. venereal disease incidence. Complete all questions.
- Get the Schwartz VD test from teacher and answer questions out of class.

GRADE CONTRACT

Date_____ Period_____

I, _____ do hereby agree to be responsible for my own grade and work during the venereal disease unit. I understand that I must correctly perform and complete all phases of the work for the grade I chose to earn. The teacher has agreed to give class time for library work and for lecture and discussion about venereal diseases. On May 21 I will turn in to the teacher the completed forms secured earlier. Also on May 21, I will complete the requirements for the grade by taking the McHugh VD knowledge test. I understand that I may renegotiate my grade.

I wish to contract for the grade _____.

Signed _____

Figure 19–2. *Example of a contract for grade.*

Source: *William Yarber, "Contract-for-Grade in a Venereal Disease Unit,"* School Health Review *(March–April 1972), p. 28.*

ments which will not only help the student to learn, but will also benefit the teacher's own self-evaluation.

This leads to a second link between evaluation and growth. The teacher should never view student evaluation solely as a method of determining grades. It should also be looked upon as a form of self-evaluation, for how well the teacher's students do on a particular evaluative instrument reflects how successful the teacher has been in teaching and/or in construction of that evaluative instrument. The poor teacher rarely uses this information to his advantage; the good teacher spends time in analyzing the results. The following are examples of questions that might be asked: What questions were missed constantly? In what subject areas did the students do poorly? How can instruction be improved in these areas?

Why Teachers Must Continue to Grow

Someone once said that the human mind is like a parachute in that it is useless until open. This applies to teachers, who must be open to all ideas. This is imperative if one is sincere in his desire to stay in tune with modern education.

Because of the knowledge and technological explosion, one must have competence in the specialized field(s) he plans to teach. The teacher not only must be thoroughly conversant with his subject matter but also must be aware of the teaching devices that are available to help him present his subject in a variety of ways.

It is imperative today that health teachers also have a facility in areas germane to health education. They must have insights into motivation, individual differences, group influences, the effects of the social and physical milieu, ecology, anthropology, and so on. This, it is hoped, will lead to an interdisciplinary approach to teaching and understanding in health education.

Some factors that will facilitate personal and professional growth are

1. Becoming involved in professional organizations and in-service educational programs.
2. Keeping abreast of current information in professional and related books and periodicals.
3. Contributing to the profession through active participation, writing, research, and experimentation.
4. Continuing with one's education through classes, travel, reading, and in-depth discussions.
5. Continuing development of creative materials and procedures for teaching.
6. Allowing for teacher-course evaluation by students at various intervals during the year.

PROGRAMS. To keep abreast of new ideas, the health teacher will find that participating in professional organizations through membership and attendance will help to facilitate an exchange of new and innovative ideas. Not only do these organizations provide an exchange of ideas but they also help new teachers in their professional preparation, set standards for the profession, present research, and help in the securing of jobs.

Some of the organizations that the health teacher may wish to investigate for possible membership are the following:

American Association for Health, Physical Education, and Recreation, Department of the National Education Association, 1201 16th Street, N.W., Washington, D.C. 20036.
American Association of Sex Educators and Counselors, 815–15th Street, N.W., Washington, D.C. 20005.
American Public Health Association, 1740 Broadway, New York, N.Y. 10019.
American School Health Association, Kent, Ohio 44240.
American College Health Association, University Health Center, 5513 Merrich Drive, Coral Gables, Fla. 33146.
The American National Council for Health Education of the Public, 800 Second Avenue, New York, N.Y. 10017.
National Education Association, 1201 16th Street, N.W., Washington, D.C. 20036.

To learn more about what these organizations have to offer, one can consult some of the more recent journals, bulletins, or handbooks that are published periodically.

In addition to the six national organizations listed, most states have local chapters and state teachers' associations that hold conferences, meetings, and special-problems meetings from time to time. Membership in these organizations provides the teacher with numerous pamphlets, books, and periodicals which discuss a wide range of topics.

In-service educational programs allow the teacher to participate in a varied number of activities relating to current teaching techniques, updating of knowledge in specialized areas, and new instructional materials and aids, as well as the construction of objectives, opportunity for insights into problem areas, and so on. The subjects generally covered in in-service programs are endless.

Most in-service programs are offered through local, county, or state educational systems and through teacher educational institutions. They are offered to any teacher who is currently teaching in the designated system. The type of in-service program offered depends on the sponsor, the type of program and subject being discussed, and the resources available to the planners.

One type of in-service program is the *teacher institute*, which is usually planned by a school system to promote professional growth. Another type is the *teacher workshop*, in which small groups are formed to discuss teaching techniques, curriculum improvement, and so on. Many school districts hold workshops a few days before the opening of school or a few days at the end of the year. *Teacher clinics* also offer teachers an opportunity to observe teaching demonstrations of new techniques. *Class visitations* are similar to the clinics in that teachers may observe their colleagues or teachers in another system. This may be done by merely visiting another school in the community or by traveling to another town or state.

The various media of *films, television,* and *tapes* are also becoming a popular method of transmitting knowledge and techniques from one group of teachers to another. In areas that have educational television, in-service credit is given to teachers viewing programs designed for professional advancement.

Even in cases where participation is not required for the system's in-service programs, teachers should take every advantage of them. Of course not all of these programs will prove to be worthwhile; every teacher has suffered through at least one. However, just the exposure to other teachers participating in them can often compensate for a poorly constructed program.

KEEPING ABREAST OF CURRENT INFORMATION IN PROFESSIONAL AND RELATED BOOKS AND PERIODICALS. To keep abreast of current information seems an almost impossible task, but few teachers can disagree with the statement by Wiles that "A strong professional library is a basic element of a good in-service training program." [6] Nevertheless, some teachers use over and over as their main sources of information a few old books left over from their college days. Such teachers say, "There is not enough time for reading," or, "When I need a book, I can get it from the school library," or, "Reading is too expensive a habit."

A personal library of books, periodicals, and nonprofessional magazines is a valuable and worthwhile part of a teacher's repertoire of information. When a book is owned, it is always available and is able to be used without the inconvenience of having to go to a library. The professional library should contain not only the standard books and periodicals within one's own field, but also a healthy assortment of works from related disciplines, such as education, sociology, psychology, curriculum planning, and history.

Following is a list of a number of professional books and periodicals within the profession as well as a few from related areas. This list should not be considered complete, but it offers a good start.

GENERAL

Anderson, C L. *School Health Practice*, 5th ed. St. Louis, Mo.: The C. V. Mosby Co., 1972.

Fodor, John T., and Gus T. Dalis. *Health Instruction: Theory and Application*. Philadelphia: Lea & Febiger, 1971.

Grout, Ruth E. *Health Teaching in Schools*, 5th ed. Philadelphia: W. B. Saunders Company, 1968.

Haag, Jessie Helen. *School Health Program*, 3rd ed. Philadelphia: Lea & Febiger, 1972.

Nemir, Alma. *The School Health Program*, 3rd ed. Philadelphia: W. B. Saunders Company, 1970.

Oberteuffer, Delbert, et al. *School Health Education*, 5th ed. New York: Harper & Row, Publishers, Inc., 1972.

Turner, Clair C., et al. *School Health and Health Education*, 5th ed. St. Louis, Mo.: The C. V. Mosby Co., 1970.

ELEMENTARY/SECONDARY

Hafen, Brent Q. *Health for the Secondary Teacher*. Dubuque, Iowa: William C. Brown Company, Publishers, 1971.

Mayshark, Cyrus, and Roy A. Foster. *Health Education in Secondary Schools*. St. Louis: The C. V. Mosby Co., 1972.

Willgoose, Carl. *Health Teaching in Secondary Schools*. Philadelphia: W. B. Saunders Company, 1972.

――――. *Health Education in the Elementary School*, 4th ed. Philadelphia: W. B. Saunders Company, 1974.

[6] Kimball Wiles, *Supervision for Better Schools: The Role of the Official Leader in Program Development*, 2nd ed. (Englewood Cliffs, N.J.: Prentice-Hall, 1955), pp. 262–263.

PROFESSIONAL JOURNALS AND PERIODICALS
American Journal of Public Health and the Nation's Health
International Journal of Health Education
Journal of the American College Health Association
Journal of Health and Social Behavior
Journal of Health, Physical Education and Recreation
Journal of School Health
Journal of Social Health
Research Quarterly
School Health Review
Today's Health

RELATED JOURNALS AND PERIODICALS
Consumer Reports
Education
The Education Digest
The Elementary School Journal
The Instructor
The Journal of Creative Behavior
Journal of Education
Journal of Educational Psychology
Journal of Educational Sociology
Medical Aspects of Human Sexuality
National Education Association Journal
The National Elementary Principal
Psychology Today
School and Society
Science
Science Digest
Sexual Behavior
Social Education
Sociology of Education
UNESCO Courier

If it is beyond the means of the individual instructor to purchase a number of these books and subscribe to two or three of the journals, the teacher can encourage the school library or other faculty to maintain an up-to-date library of books and periodicals. Then some sort of exchange program can be arranged between teachers so that all can benefit from the materials.

CONTRIBUTING TO THE PROFESSION THROUGH ACTIVE PARTICIPATION, WRITING, RESEARCH, AND EXPERIMENTATION. Professional contributions are a most beneficial and rewarding experience. After one has conducted original research and/or experimentation, with significant results, he may want to make an additional contribution to the profession by submitting the results to a journal, such as the *New York State Journal of Health*,

Physical Education, and Recreation, California School Health, the *Journal of Health, Physical Education, and Recreation, Journal of School Health,* or the *School Health Review.*

Writing and participation in one or more conferences or workshops takes more than mere wishing. One must be well read, capable of communicating effectively, willing to work beyond the normal school hours, and dedicated to the principle that knowledge is to be shared. Many teachers guard their ideas and techniques closely. They do this for various reasons, one of which is that they feel that a successful new technique sets them apart from the other teachers. If others shared the "secret," this particular individual would be no different. Fortunately, however, most educators feel that offering ideas and research results to others leads to the betterment of the whole profession.

Basic sources of research that should be periodically consulted by every teacher include the following:

Encyclopedia of Educational Research. Robert L. Edel (ed.). New York: Macmillan Publishing Co., Inc., 1969.

Handbook of Research on Teaching. R. M. W. Travers (ed.). Skokie, Ill.: Rand McNally & Co., 1973.

Health, Physical Education, and Recreation Microcard Bulletin. School of HPER, University of Oregon. Eugene, Ore.: University of Oregon (semi-annually).

Journal of Education Research. Madison, Wis.: Dembar Publications, Inc. (monthly).

NEA Research Bulletin. American Educational Research Association. Washington, D.C.: National Education Association (bi-monthly).

Research Quarterly. American Association of Health, Physical Education, and Recreation. Washington, D.C.: The Association.

Review of Educational Research. American Educational Research Association, Washington, D.C.: National Education Association (bi-monthly).

CONTINUING WITH ONE'S EDUCATION. Continuing education is one area of personal and professional growth not yet discussed. It can include graduate study, reading, travel, and participation in educational programs outside of the school context. Graduate study will be covered more extensively here, for it is the best method of strenghtening one's knowledge in a specialized field.

Although the present situation looks bleak, as indicated by the data on certification requirements in Chapter 1, it is hoped that the future will see an increased emphasis on strengthening teacher certification requirements in health education. The School Health Division of the AAHPER held a national conference on teacher preparation in health education. Its recommendation was that teachers of health in the secondary schools have a major in health education, with the minimal preparation being at least a health education minor.[7]

With the complex task that has resulted from the explosion of knowledge, these recommendations seem necessary indeed. Enforcing this has come the requirement of several states that a master's degree or its equivalent in semester hours of college credit, plus a certain number of years of teaching experience, be necessary to obtain a permanent certificate.

In view of the recommendations for teacher preparation in health education and the requirements of certain states, many students, as well as teachers, are contemplating graduate study. For those who are considering graduate work in health education, the question may be, "Where do they offer an advanced degree in health education?" Other questions asked by students are, "Am I qualified to go on to graduate school?" and, "How can I finance my education?"

INSTITUTIONS OFFERING AN ADVANCED DEGREE IN HEALTH EDUCATION. In 1967, fifty-eight institutions offered a separate undergraduate degree in health education, fifty-seven colleges and universities offered a master's degree, and twenty-seven institutions offered work toward a doctorate degree.[8] These schools range from the University of Oregon to the University of Northern Colorado to the University of Maryland. Students who are interested in pursuing graduate work in health education should write the School Health Division of the American Association of Health, Physical Education and Recreation and/or consult a member of the faculty of an institution that has a health education department.

ADMISSION REQUIREMENTS. Generally speaking, the trend among graduate schools within the last few years has been toward more flexible admission requirements. This has been based on a number of things. One of these has shown that not all students with good academic records in undergraduate school will make good in graduate school. It should also be remembered that some graduate schools make a distinction between admission to graduate school and admission to a program leading to a graduate degree. Requirements for the latter are often more strict than for the first.

Admission requirements for a graduate school or division usually include one or more of the following.

1. An undergraduate cumulative grade-point average which equals a C + average or better. Some schools will not accept a student with an average below a B. Some are interested in the grade average in

---

[7] National Conference Steering Committee, "Recommended Standards and Guidelines: Teacher Preparation in Health Education," *Journal of Health, Physical Education, and Recreation* (February 1969), pp. 32–38.

[8] *Institutions Offering Programs of Specialization in Health Education* (Washington, D.C.: School Health Education Study, December, 1967), 33 pp.

one's major only. Others are interested in the undergraduate's class standing, or average for last two years.

2. A bachelor's degree or the equivalent for many college or university of recognized standing.

3. One or more official transcripts of all previous college work.

4. Two or more letters of recommendation from persons in your field of specialization.

5. A qualifying examination either for all applicants or for those applicants with marginal undergraduate records. An institution may administer its own qualifying examination or give a standardized test, in which case the applicant may be able to take the test at a local institution. Two of the most frequently used tests are the Graduate Record Examination (GRE) and the Miller Analogies Test (MAT). Information and addresses of test centers for the GRE can be obtained from the Educational Testing Service, 20 Nassau Street, Princeton, N.J. 08540; or Box 27896, Los Angeles, Calif. Information concerning the MAT can be obtained from the Psychological Corporation, 304 East 45th Street, New York, N.Y. 10017.

FINANCING AN EDUCATION. It costs a lot of money to go to school today. Not only is tuition high, varying from $300 to $600 per semester at certain state colleges and universities, but one must also calculate the loss of income for those years he is not employed in his profession. Then the cost becomes staggering.

Many people who are actively teaching choose to continue their education on a part-time basis. Colleges and universities are more and more becoming aware of this need and are planning their graduate course listings with an eye to meeting the needs of the part-time student. Generally they accomplish this by offering necessary courses in the late afternoons and early evenings and on weekends. They also offer a wider range of classes during the summer. Some institutions do have specific residence requirements, requirements for full-time study and uninterrupted study, and time limits within which all degree requirements must be completed. Students should check carefully the specifiic requirements for the institution they are planning to attend.

Alternatives to part-time study are saving enough money to finance one's education or applying for fellowships and/or traineeships available at the majority of institutions. These include the following:

National Defense Education Act fellowships, which provide for three years of support based on student needs and the amount of money available at that particular institution.

Teaching fellowships, available in many departments. Instructional and other duties are required and recipients are usually restricted in the number of credits they may carry in one semester.

Research fellowships, also available in many departments. Duties and stipends vary.

Graduate assistantships, available in the instructional and research programs of various departments. Duties vary according to the needs of individual departments.

Research assistantships, available in various departments to qualified graduate students. Stipends vary with the type of work and the amount of time involved.

Residence-hall assistantships, available in most institutions and requiring residence-hall duties with men or women undergraduates. Such assistantships provide varying amounts of room, board, and remuneration.

Many institutions also offer interest-free, short-term loans through their office of financial aid.

All students should take the time to search out information concerning financial aid, fellowships, and traineeships that are available at the institutions of their choice as well as student loan information from their home state and banks.

CONTINUING DEVELOPMENT OF CREATIVE MATERIALS AND PROCEDURES FOR TEACHING

There is a beautiful quote from *Winnie-the-Pooh* by A. A. Milne:

Here is Edward Bear, coming downstairs now, bump, bump, bump, on the back of his head, behind Christopher Robin. It is, as far as he knows, the only way of coming downstairs, but sometimes he feels that there really is another way, if only he could stop bumping for a moment and think of it.

In the area of teaching, we sometimes continue to bump, bump, bump along, never stopping to consider the possibilities for change. But we must, from time to time, think about what we are doing. Also, more often than not, we let our materials get old, along with our teaching. Some excellent journals to consider reading in the area of educational change are:

Free School: The Journal of Change in Education
Radical Teacher
Red Pencil
Summerhill Bulletin
The Futurist
The Horripilator
The Red Pencil Bulletin

The Teacher Paper
Toolkit

TEACHER-COURSE EVALUATION. One form of personal evaluation is to check to see if students have been able to meet stated behavioral objectives. If they have not, then the teacher should be asking the question "Why not?" Some possible answers may include:

- Were the stated objectives too difficult to meet?
- Was in-class work at fault?
- Was the teacher at fault?
- Were the teaching materials and resources used at fault?

Another method of teacher-course evaluation is having students evaluate the teacher and the course at some specified time during the year (usually at the end of a term). Here the teacher gets direct feedback on how he has been teaching. Certainly, it is also hoped that the teacher creates an atmosphere in which the student feels free to comment on the class throughout the entire year.

SUMMARY

The educational scene is rapidly changing. Many teachers who have been professionally involved in elementary/secondary schools have seen the number of report cards dwindle to as few as two per year. College teachers are experimenting with student self-evaluation in many courses. The function of evaluation in the classroom is criticized, justified, and criticized again at every level. Many educators believe that evaluation should benefit the pupil; all too often it is used (sometimes too effectively) solely to aid the teacher.

There will always be subjectivity applied to every form of health evaluation. That is why a teacher must utilize every possible tool at his disposal in order to judge a student. If a teacher is truly interested in the growth of his students, he must attempt to understand their viewpoints, value their opinions, and evaluate their abilities in health with utmost objectivity, using every tool available.

Not only must a teacher remain a student of current evaluation methods, but he must also continue to develop himself. Almost any activity that keeps one abreast of the current scene can be considered a valuable addition to one's life-style. Students are quick to see whether their instructors keep abreast of new thoughts and trends. To remain static is a sure way of losing not only the respect of one's students and colleagues but also the support of that part of the self which needs a continual renewal.

REFERENCES

Ahmann, J. S., et al. *Evaluating Elementary School Pupils.* Boston: Allyn & Bacon, Inc., 1960.

————, and Marvin D. Glock. *Evaluating Pupil Growth*, 2nd ed. Boston: Allyn & Bacon, Inc., 1963.

Bloom, Benjamin I. (ed.). *Taxonomy of Educational Objectives.* New York: Longmans, Green & Company, 1956.

Burton, William, et al. *Education for Effective Thinking.* New York: Appleton-Century-Crofts, 1960.

Curtis, Paul Ramsey. "Testing in Tomorrow's Schools," *Educational Leadership*, Vol. 17 (May 1960).

Daly, William C. "Test Scores: Fragment of a Picture," *Elementary School Journal*, Vol. 60 (October 1959).

Educational Testing Service. *Making the Classroom Test: A Guide for Teachers.* Princeton, N.J.: Educational Testing Service, 1961.

Ennis, Robert. "A Concept of Critical Thinking," *Harvard Educational Review* (Winter 1962), pp. 81–111.

Holt, John. *How Children Fail.* New York: Dell Publishing Co., Inc., 1964.

Johnson, James W. *Logic and Rhetoric.* New York: Macmillan Publishing Co., Inc., 1962.

Karmel, Louis. *Measurement and Evaluation in the Schools.* New York: Macmillan Publishing Co., Inc., 1970.

Kirschenbaum, Howard, et al. *Wad-Ja-Get?* New York: Hart Publishing Co., Inc., 1971.

Little, Wilson, and W. Edgar Moore. *Applied Logic.* Boston: Houghton Mifflin Company, 1955.

Morgan, H. Gerthon. "What Is Effective Evaluation," *NEA Journal*, Vol. 48 (November 1959).

Nelson, Clarence. *Measurement and Evaluation in the Classroom.* New York: Macmillan Publishing Co., Inc., 1970.

Sanders, Norris M. *Classroom Questions.* New York: Harper & Row, Publishers, Inc., 1966.

Solleder, Mariani K. "Evaluation in the Cognitive Domain," *The Journal of School Health* (January 1972), pp. 16–20.

Taylor, Ralph W., et al. *Proceedings, 1959 Invitational Conference on Testing Problems.* Princeton, N.J.: Educational Testing Service, 1960.

Torrance, E. Paul. *Education and the Creative Potential.* Minneapolis: University of Minnesota Press, 1963.

Vincent, Raymond J. "Selected Instructional and Behavioral Objectives for a Tenth Grade Drug Education Program," *The Journal of School Health* (June 1971), pp. 310–313.

SOURCES OF
INFORMATION IN SEX
EDUCATION

The following references in sex education are by no means meant to be complete or comprehensive. New references are published continually, and it is impossible to keep abreast of them.

No reference material should be used in a classroom situation without careful review or preview.

References on venereal disease have been omitted because it is felt that this subject should be treated as part of communicable-disease education.

No attempt has been made to list articles in professional journals and magazines because of the overwhelming number involved.

BOOKS

AGES FIVE TO NINE

Andry, Andrew C., and Steven Schepp. *How Babies Are Made*. New York: Time-Life Books, 1968.

Butterfield, Frances W. *From Little Acorns*. New York: Emerson Books, Inc., 1964.

Clarkson, E. Margaret. *Growing Up* Grand Rapids, Mich.: Wm. B. Eerdmans Publishing Co., 1962.

———. *Susie's Babies*. Grand Rapids, Mich.: Wm. B. Eerdmans Publishing Co., 1960.

De Schweinitz, Karl. *Growing Up*, 4th ed. New York: Macmillan Publishing Co., Inc., 1965.

Gardner, Richard. *The Boys' and Girls' Book About Divorce*. New York: Science House, Inc., 1972.

Johnson, Dorothy. *All About Babies*. Grand Rapids, Mich.: Zondervan, 1962.

Levine, Milton J., and Jean H. Seligmann. *A Baby Is Born*, rev. ed. New York: Golden Press, 1962.

———. *The Wonder of Life*. New York: Garden Press, 1964.

Meilach, Dona Z. *A Doctor Talks to 5- to 8-Year-Olds*. Chicago: Milex Products, 1966.

Odenwald, Robert P. *How You Were Born*. New York: P. J. Kenedy and Sons, 1963.

Orenstein, Irvine. *Where Do Babies Come From?* New York: Pyramid Books, 1962.

Power, Jules. *How Life Begins*. New York: Simon & Schuster, Inc., 1965.

AGES NINE TO TWELVE

Gordon, Sol. *Ten Heavy Facts About Sex*. Syracuse, N.Y.: Ed-U-Press, 1971.

Gottlieb, Bernhardt. *What a Boy Should Know About Sex*. Indianapolis, Ind.: The Bobbs-Merrill Co., Inc., 1961.

———. *What a Girl Should Know About Sex*. Indianapolis, Ind.: The Bobbs-Merrill Co., Inc., 1961.

Gruenberg, Benjamin C., and M. Sidonie. *The Wonderful Story of You*. Garden City, N.Y.: Doubleday & Company, Inc., 1960.

Hofstein, Sadie. *The Human Story: Facts on Birth, Growth and Reproduction*. Glenview, Ill.: Scott, Foresman and Company, 1967.

Johnson, Eric W. *Love and Sex in Plain Language*. Philadelphia: J. B. Lippincott Co., 1965.

Lerner, Marguerite. *Who Do You Think You Are?* Englewood Cliffs, N.J.: Prentice-Hall, Inc., 1963.

Lerrigo, Marion O., and M. A. Cassidy, M.D. *A Doctor Talks to 9 to 12 Year Olds*. Chicago: Budlong Press, 1964.

Levine, Milton I., and Jean H. Seligmann. *The Wonder of Life—How We Are Born and How We Grow Up*, rev. ed. New York: Golden Press, 1964.

Power, Jules. *How Life Begins*. New York: Simon & Schuster, Inc., 1965.

Wilson, Charles, and Elizabeth Wilson. *Growing Up*. Indianapolis, Ind.: The Bobbs-Merrill Co., Inc., 1966.

AGES THIRTEEN TO FIFTEEN

Bauer, W. W. *Moving into Manhood*. Garden City, N.Y.: Doubleday & Company, Inc., 1964.

Davis, Maxine. *Sex and the Adolescent*. New York: Permabooks, 1960.

Duvall, E. M. *Love and the Facts of Life*. New York: Association Press, 1967.

———, and G. R. Duvall. *Sense and Nonsense About Sex*. Toronto, Ont.: Welch Co., 1962.

Gottlieb, B. S., M.D. *What a Boy Should Know About Sex*. Indianapolis, Ind.: The Bobbs-Merrill Co., Inc., 1960.

———. *What a Girl Should Know About Sex*. Indianapolis, Ind.: The Bobbs-Merrill Co., Inc., 1961.

Growing Up and Liking It. Miltown, N.J.: Personal Products Co., 1964.

Johnson, Eric W. *Love and Sex in Plain Language*. Philadelphia: J. B. Lippincott Co., 1965.

———. *Sex: Telling It Straight*. Philadelphia: Bantam Books, Inc., 1971.

Kirkendall, Lester, and Wesley Adams. *The Students' Guide to Marriage and Family Life Literature*. Dubuque, Iowa: William C. Brown, Inc., 1971.

Levine, Milton, M.D., and Jean H. Seligmann. *The Wonder of Life*, rev. ed. New York: Golden Press, 1962.

Lorand, Rhoda. *Love, Sex, and the Teenager*. New York: Macmillan Publishing Co., Inc., 1965.

Wilson, Charles, and Elizabeth Wilson. *Human Growth and Reproduction*. Indianapolis, Ind.: The Bobbs-Merrill Co., Inc., 1966.

World of a Girl. Philadelphia: Scott Paper Co., 1965.

SIXTEEN TO YOUNG ADULTS

Bauer, W. W. *Moving Into Manhood*. Garden City, N.Y.: Doubleday & Company, Inc., 1963.

———. *Way to Womanhood*. Garden City, N.Y.: Doubleday & Company, Inc., 1965.

Boll, Eleanor S. *The Man That You Marry*. Philadelphia: Macrae Smith Co. 1963.

Botwin, Carol. *Sex and the Teenage Girl*. New York: Lancer Books, 1972.

Call, Alice L. *Toward Adulthood*. Philadelphia: J. B. Lippincott Co., 1964.

De Schweinitz, Karl. *Growing Up*, 4th ed. New York: Macmillan Publishing Co., Inc., 1965.

Duvall, Evelyn M. *Love and the Facts of Life*. New York: Association Press, 1963.

———. *Why Wait Till Marriage?* New York: Association Press, 1965.

———. *The Art of Dating*. New York: Association Press, 1967.

———, and Reuben Hill. *When You Marry*. New York: Association Press, 1962.

Farber, Seymour M., M.D., and Roger H. L. Wilson, M.D. (eds.) *Teenage Marriage and Divorce*. Berkeley, Calif.: Diablo Press, 1968.

———. *Sex Education and the Teen-ager*. Berkeley, Calif.: Diablo Press, 1968.

Glassberg, Bert Y., M.D., *Teen-Age Sex Counselor*. Woodbury, N.Y.: Barron's Educational Series, 1965.

Hettlinger, Richard F. *Living With Sex—The Student's Dilemma*. New York: The Seabury Press, 1966.

Julian, Cloyd, and Elizabeth N. Jackson. *Modern Sex Education*. New York: Holt, Rinehart and Winston, Inc., 1967.

Krich, Aron. *Facts of Love and Marriage for Young People*. New York: Dell Publishing Co., Inc., 1960.

Levinsohn, Florance, and G. Lombard Kelly, M.D. *What Teenagers Want to Know*. Chicago: Budlong Press, 1962.

Miller, Benjamin, et al. *Masculinity and Femininity*. Boston: Houghton Mifflin Company, 1971.

Sakol, Jeanne. *What About Teen-Age Marriage?* New York: Julian Messner, 1961.

Saltman, Ed. *Teen Love, Teen Marriage*. New York: Grosset & Dunlap, Inc., 1966.

Sugarman, Daniel A., and Rolaine Hochstein. *The Seventeen Guide to Knowing Yourself*. New York: Macmillan Publishing Co., 1967.

Thomas, John L. *Looking Toward Marriage*. Notre Dame, Ind.: Fides Publishers, Inc., 1964.

Wood, A. *The Seventeen Book of Answers to What Your Parents Don't Talk About*. New York: David McKay Co., Inc., 1972.

SELECTED REFERENCE BOOKS FOR ADULTS, CURRICULUM PLANNERS, AND TEACHERS

American Institute of Biological Sciences. *Reproduction, Growth, and Development*. New York: McGraw-Hill Book Company, 1963.

Anderson, W. J. *How to Understand Sex*. Minneapolis: T. S. Denison & Co., 1966.

Beigel, H. G. (ed.). *Advances in Sex Research*. New York: Harper & Row, Publishers, Inc., 1963.

Bonaparte, Marie. *Female Sexuality*. New York: Grove Press, 1953.

Bromley, Dorothy, and Florence Britten. *Youth and Sex*. New York: Harper & Row, Publishers, Inc., 1938.

———. *Release from Sexual Tensions*. New York: Random House, 1960.

———. *Manual of Contraceptive Practice*. Baltimore: The Williams and Wilkins Co., 1964.

Caprio, F. S., et al. *Sex Education Library*. New York: Health Publications, 1964.

Comfort, Alex. *The Joy of Sex*. New York: Crown Publishers, Inc., 1972.

Crawley, L. Q., et al. *Reproduction, Sex, and Preparation for Marriage*. Englewood Cliffs, N.J.: Prentice-Hall, Inc., 1964.

Davis, Maxine. *Sex and the Adolescent*. New York: Permabooks, 1960.

Denton, W. *Family Problems*. Philadelphia: Westminster Press, 1971.

Duvall, Sylvanus and Evelyn. *Sex Ways in Fact and Faith*. New York: Association Press, 1961.

Duvall, Evelyn. *Love and the Facts of Life*. New York: Association Press, 1963.

———. *Family Development*. Philadelphia: J.B. Lippincott Co., 1962.

Eckert, Ralph G. *Sex Attitudes in the Home*. New York: Popular Library, 1963.

Eichenlaub, J. E. *The Marriage Art*. New York: Dell Publishing Co., Inc., 1961.

Ellis, A. *If This Be Sexual Heresy*. New York: Lyle Stuart, 1963.

———. *Sex and the Single Man*. New York: Lyle Stuart, 1963.

———. *Sex Without Guilt*. New York: Hillman Periodicals, 1959.

———. *The American Sexual Tragedy*. New York: Lyle Stuart, 1962.

———. *The Folklore of Sex*. New York: Grove Press, 1961.

Filas, Francis L. *Sex Education in the Family*. Englewood Cliffs, N.J.: Prentice-Hall, Inc., 1966.

Flanagan, Geraldine. *The First Nine Months of Life*. New York: Simon & Schuster, Inc., 1962.

Frank, L. K. *The Conduct of Sex*. New York: Grove Press, 1963.

Frankfort, Ellen. *Vaginal Politics*. Chicago: Quadrangle Books, Inc., 1972.

Gavin, Arthur. *Circle of Sex*. New Hyde Park, N.Y.: University Books, Inc., 1966.

Glassberg, Bert Y., M.D. *Teen-Age Sex Counselor*. New York: Barron's Educational Series, 1965.

Gottlieb, Bernhardt. *What a Boy Should Know About Sex*. Indianapolis, Ind.: The Bobbs-Merrill Co., Inc., 1960.

————. *What a Girl Should Know About Sex*. Indianapolis, Ind.: The Bobbs-Merrill Co., Inc., 1961.

Green, G. *Sex and the College Girl*. New York: Dial Press, 1964.

Greeley, Andrew M. *Strangers in the House*. New York: Sheed and Ward, 1961.

Group for the Advancement of Psychiatry. *Sex and the College Student*. New York: Mental Health Materials Center, 1965.

Grunwald, Henry A. *Sex in America*. New York: Bantam Books, Inc., 1964.

Guttmacher, Alan. *Pregnancy and Birth*. New York: Signet Key, 1964.

————, et al. *Planning Your Family*. New York: Macmillan Publishing Co., Inc., 1963.

Hernton, Calvin C. *Sex and Racism in America*. New York: Grove Press, Inc., 1965.

Heron, A. (ed.). *Toward a Quaker View of Sex*, rev. ed. New York: Friends Bookstore, 1964.

Hilu, Virginia (ed.). *Sex Education and the Schools*. New York: Harper & Row, Publishers, Inc., 1967.

Katchadourian, Herant A., and Donald T. Lunde. *Fundamentals of Human Sexuality*. New York: Holt, Rinehart and Winston, Inc., 1972.

Kirkendall, Lester A. *Sex and Our Society*. Public Affairs Committee, 1964.

————. *Helping Children Understand Sex*. Chicago: Science Research Associates, 1957.

————. *Pre-Marital Intercourse and Interpersonal Relations*. New York: Julian Press, Inc., 1961.

————. *Sex Education as Human Relations*. Sweet Springs, Mo.: Inor Publishing Co., 1950.

Lloyd, C. W. *Human Reproduction and Sexual Behavior*. Philadelphia: Lea & Febiger, 1964.

Masters, W. H., and Virginia E. Johnson. *Human Sexual Response*. Boston: Little, Brown and Company, 1966.

Maternity Center Association. *A Baby Is Born*. New York: Grosset & Dunlap, Inc., 1964.

McCary, James Leslie. *Human Sexuality*. New York: D. Van Nostrand Co., Inc., 1973.

Miller, Claire G. *What Boys Want to Know About Girls*. New York: Grosset & Dunlap, Inc., 1962.

Packard, Vance. *The Sexual Wilderness*. New York: David McKay Co., Inc., 1968.

Pike, James A. *Teen-agers and Sex*. Englewood Cliffs, N.J.: Prentice-Hall, Inc., 1965.

Ridenour, Nina E., and Isabel Johnson. *Some Special Problems of Children Aged Two to Five*. Child Study Association, 1966.

Rimmer, Robert H. *The Harrad Experiment*. New York: Bantam Books, Inc., 1966.

Sex Education and the New Morality—A Search for a Meaningful Social Ethic. New York: Distributed by the Columbia University Press, 1967.

Spock, Benjamin, and Marion O. Lerrigo. *Caring for Your Disabled Child.* New York: Macmillan Publishing Co., Inc., 1965.

Stekel, Wilhelm. *Auto-Erotism.* New York: Washington Square Press, Inc., 1967.

Stone, Abraham, and Norman E. Himes. *Planned Parenthood: A Practical Guide to Birth Control Methods,* rev. ed. New York: Macmillan Publishing Co., Inc., 1965.

Thomas, John L. *Looking Toward Marriage.* Notre Dame, Ind.: Fides Publishers, Inc., 1964.

Unger, Arthur, and Carmel Berman. *What Girls Want to Know About Boys.* New York: Grosset & Dunlap, Inc., 1962.

Williamson, Robert C. *Marriage and Family Relations.* New York: John Wiley & Sons, Inc., 1966.

Womble, Dale L. *Foundations for Marriage and Family Relations.* New York: Macmillan Publishing Co., Inc., 1966.

PHILOSOPHY AND VALUES

Andreas, Carol. *Sex and Caste in America.* Englewood Cliffs, N.J.: Prentice-Hall, Inc., 1971.

Benjamin, H., and R. E. L. Masters. *Prostitution and Morality.* New York: Julian Press, 1964.

The British Council of Churches. *Sex and Morality.* London: SCM Press Ltd., 1966.

Brown, Joe David (ed.). *Sex in the '60's.* New York: Time-Life Books, 1968.

Havermann, Ernest. *Men, Women, and Marriage.* Garden City, N.Y.: Doubleday & Company, Inc., 1962.

Hefner, Hugh M. *The Playboy Philosophy.* Chicago: HMH Publishing Co., Inc., 1962–64.

Kirkendall, Lester. *Premarital Intercourse and Interpersonal Relations.* New York: Julian Press, Inc., 1961.

Linner, Birgitta. *Sex and Society in Sweden.* New York: Pantheon Books, 1967.

Reiss, Ira L. *Premarital Sexual Standards in America.* New York: The Free Press, 1960.

Sex Education and the New Morality—A Search for a Meaningful Social Ethic. New York: Columbia University Press, 1966.

Udry, J. Richard. *The Social Context of Marriage.* Philadelphia: J. B. Lippincott Co., 1966.

Wilson, John. *Logic and Sexual Morality.* Baltimore: Penguin Books, 1965.

SEXUAL ABERRATIONS

Bieber, I., et al. *Homosexuality: A Psychoanalytic Study.* New York: Basic Books, 1962.

Ellis, A., and R. Brancale. *The Psychology of Sex Offenders.* Springfield, Ill.: Charles C Thomas, Publisher, 1956.

———, and E. Sagarin. *Nymphomania.* New York: Gilbert Press, 1964.

Masters, R. E. L. *Patterns of Incest.* New York: Julian Press, 1963.

PREMARITAL SEX

Kirkendall, Lester A. *Premarital Intercourse and Interpersonal Relations.* New York: Julian Press, 1961.

McCary, James Leslie. *What I Would Tell My Daughter About Premarital Sex.* New York: Sexology Corporation, 1966.

Reiss, Ira L. *Premarital Sexual Standards in America.* New York: The Free Press, 1960.

SEXUAL REVOLUTION

Reiss, Ira L. et al. *The Sexual Renaissance in America.* Worcester, Mass.: Hefferman Press, 1966.

Schur, Edwin M. *The Family and the Sexual Revolution.* Bloomington, Ind.: Indiana University Press, 1964.

INFORMATION FOR CURRICULUM PLANNING IN FAMILY LIFE AND SEX EDUCATION AT THE ELEMENTARY SCHOOL LEVEL

American Association for Health, Physical Education, and Recreation. *Sex Education: Resource Unit for Grades 5, 6, or 7.* Washington, D.C.: The Association, 1967.

American School Health Association. *Growth Patterns and Sex Education: A Suggested Program Kindergarten Through Grade Twelve,* Vol. XXXVII, No. 5a (May 1967).

———. *Growth Patterns and Sex Education: An Updated Bibliography,* 1972.

Baruch, Dorothy W. *New Ways in Sex Education.* New York: Bantam Books, Inc., 1962.

Boys' Clubs of America. *Need and Interest Study of 11–12–13 Year Old Boys' Club Members.* New York: Boys' Clubs of America, 1963.

California State Department of Education. *Family Life Education Bibliography of Selected Books, Pamphlets, Curriculum Guides and Materials Since 1960.* California State Department of Education, Bureau of Home-making Education, 721 Capitol Mall, Room 407, Sacramento, Calif. 95810.

Chanter, Albert G. *Sex Education in the Primary School.* London: Macmillan and Co., Ltd., 1966.

Clark, LeMon, and Isadore Rubin (eds.). *150 Sex Questions and Answers.* New York: Health Publications, 1960.

Contra Costa County Schools. *Reference List of Resource Materials in Child Development and Family Life for Classroom Use in Elementary School.* Contra Costa County Schools; 75 Santa Barbara; Pleasant Hill, Calif. 94523.

Curriculum Guides for Family Life and Sex Education: An Annotated Bibliography. Eugene, Oregon: E. C. Brown Foundation/Center for Family Studies, 1972.

Family Life Education Program. *Sex Education Guide for Teachers.* Flint, Mich.: Flint Community Schools, 1967.

Hilu, Virginia (ed.). *Sex Education and the Schools.* New York: Harper & Row, Publishers, Inc., 1967.

Hook, Andrew J. *Sex Education Curriculum*. Aurora, Ill.: Aurora Public Schools, 1966.

Kilander, H. Frederick. *Sex Education in the Schools: A Study of Objectives, Content, Methods, Materials and Evaluation*. New York: Macmillan Publishing Co., Inc., 1969.

Linner, B. *Sex and Society in Sweden*. New York: Pantheon Books, 1967.

Manley, Helen. *A Curriculum Guide in Sex Education*. St. Louis, Mo.: State Publishing Co., 1964.

National Board of the YWCA. *YWCA: Sex Morality Teaching Kit*. New York: YMCA, 1965.

Reading Materials on Aspects of Sex Education for Parents and Children. Washington, D.C.: U.S. Department of Health, Education, and Welfare, Welfare Administration Children's Bureau, n.d.

Schmieding, Alfred. *Sex in Children and Youth: A Guide for Christian Parents, Teachers and Counselors*. St. Louis: Concordia Publishing House, 1957.

Schulz, Ester D., and Sally R. Williams. *Family Life and Sex Education: Curriculum and Instruction*. New York: Harcourt, Brace & World, Inc., 1969.

Southard, Helen. *Sex Before 20*. New York: E. P. Dutton & Co., Inc., 1967.

Stokes, W. "Sex Education of Children," in H. G. Biegel (ed.), *Advances in Sex Research*. New York: Harper & Row, Publishers, Inc., 1963.

Swift, Dr. Edith Hale. *Step by Step in Sex Education*. London: Macmillan and Co., Ltd., 1958.

INFORMATION FOR CURRICULUM PLANNING IN FAMILY LIFE AND SEX EDUCATION AT THE SECONDARY LEVEL

Anaheim Union High School District. *Family Life and Sex Education Course Outline Grades Seven Through Twelve*. Sally R. Williams, Coordinator; Anaheim, Calif.

District of Columbia Public Schools. *Health and Family Life Education Curriculum—Senior High School*. Washington, D.C.

District of Columbia Public Schools. *Health and Family Life Education Curriculum—Junior High School*. Washington, D.C.

Jefferson City Public Schools. *Curriculum Guide for Family Living Education*. Jefferson City, Mo.

Kilander, H. Frederick. *Sex Education in the Schools: A Study of Objectives, Content, Methods, Materials and Evaluation*. New York: Macmillan Publishing Co., Inc., 1969.

Laycock, S. R. *Family Living and Sex Education*. Toronto: Baxter Publishing Co., 1967.

Missouri Public Schools. *Family Relations for High School Seniors*. Kansas City, Mo.

Marin County Health Department. *Family Life Bibliography*. Marin County Health Department, Health Education Division, 920 Grand Ave., San Rafael, Calif. 94901.

Rubin, Isadore, and Lester Kirkendall. *Sex in the Adolescent Years: New Directions in Guiding and Teaching Youth*. New York: Association Press, 1968.

San Diego City Schools. *Guide for Social Health Education*. San Diego, Calif.

————. *Social Hygiene Education Program.* San Diego, Calif.
————. *San Diego Sex Education Program.* San Diego, Calif.
Schulz, Ester D., and Sally R. Williams. *Family Life and Sex Education: Curriculum and Instruction.* New York: Harcourt, Brace & World, Inc., 1969.
Willke, Dr., and Mrs. J. C. Willke. *Sex Education, the How-To for Teachers.* Ohio: Hiltz Pub., Co., 1970.

RESOURCE AGENCIES IN THE UNITED STATES
Each organization listed below offers information in family life and sex education. Send for a brochure describing their policy and program interests and for lists of publications and materials.

American Academy of Pediatrics, 1801 Hinman Ave., Evanston, Ill. 60204.
American Association of Marriage, and Family Counselors, 102651 Croydon Circle, Dallas, Texas 75230.
American Association for Health, Physical Education and Recreation, 1201 Sixteenth St., N.W., Washington, D.C. 20036.
American Home Economics Association, 1600 20th St., N.W., Washington, D.C. 20009.
American Institute of Family Relations, 5287 Sunset Boulevard, Los Angeles, Calif. 90027.
American Medical Association, 535 North Dearborn Street, Chicago, Ill. 60610.
American School Health Association, Kent, Ohio 44240.
American Social Health Association, Dir. Family Life Education, 1740 Broadway, New York, N.Y. 10019.
Association for the Study of Abortion, Inc., 120 West 57th St., New York, N.Y. 10019.
Children's Bureau: U.S. Department of Health, Education, and Welfare, Washington, D.C. 20201.
Child Study Association of America, 9 E. 89th St., New York, N.Y. 10028.
Community Sex Information and Education Service, Inc., P.O. Box 2858, Grand Central Station, New York, N.Y. 10017.
Family Life Bureau, United States of Catholic Conference, 1312 Massachusetts Ave., N.W., Washington, D.C. 20005.
Family Life Publications, Inc., Box 6725, Durham, N.C. 27702.
Family Service Association of America, 44 E. 23rd St., New York, N.Y. 10010.
Institute for Rational Living, Inc., 45 E. 65th St., New York, N.Y. 10021.
Institute for Sex Research, Inc., University of Indiana, Bloomington, Ind. 47401.
Maternity Center Association, 48 E. 92nd St., New York, N.Y. 10017.
National Council on Family Relations, 1219 University Ave., S.E., Minneapolis, Minn., 55414.
Planned Parenthood Federation of America, 515 Madison Ave., New York, N.Y. 10022.
Sex Information and Education Council of the U.S. (SIECUS), 1855 Broadway, New York, N.Y. 10023.
The National Sex and Drug Forums, 330 Ellis St., San Francisco, Calif. 94102.

FILM SOURCES

E. C. Brown Trust Foundation, 3170 S.W. 87th Ave., Portland, Ore. 97225. Inquire about special films on human and animal beginnings and human growth, fertilization, and birth.

Minnesota Council on Family Relations, 1219 University Ave., S.E., Minneapolis, Minn. 55414. *Family Life Literature and Films* (1967).

Planned Parenthood—World Population, 515 Madison Ave., New York, N.Y. 10022. *Guide to Films* (1968).

Selected Films on Child Life, rev. 1965. Booklet compiled by Inez D. Lohr. Children's Bureau Publication No. 376. Order from Superintendent of Documents, U.S. Government Printing Office, Washington, D.C. 20402. This booklet gives a brief description of 480 films about children, from infancy through adolescence.

U.S. Department of Health Education, and Welfare. Order from Superintendent of Documents. U.S. Government Printing Office, Washington, D.C. 20402. *Selected Mental Health Films* (1967).

FILMS

As Boys Grow; black and white; 17 minutes. Emphasis on changes that take place in the primary and secondary sexual characteristics in adolescent boys and girls. Junior High School. Medical Arts Production, P.O. Box 4042, Stockton, Calif. 95204.

A Concept of Family Life Education; color; 18 minutes. Designed to stimulate positive attitudes about sex in the development of personality, self-image, and the establishment of interpersonal relationships at an early age. High School. Ortho Pharmaceutical Corporation, Raritan, N.J. 08869.

Biography of the Unborn; black and white; 16 minutes. Film shows the development of the egg, embryo, and fetus by means of diagrams and premature human specimens. High School. Encyclopedia Britannica Films, 1150 Wilmetts Blvd., Chicago, Ill. 60019.

Boy to Man; color; 16 minutes. Shows developmental changes of boys from obvious physical growth to complete glandular changes and sexual maturation. Churchill Films, 662 North Robertson Blvd., Los Angeles, Calif. 40069.

Generation to Generation; color; 30 minutes. Film depicts the story of the coming of a baby into a family; animation shows the unfolding of life. Functioning of organs of human reproduction and the menstrual cycle, conception and development of the fetus, intrauterine nourishment, and elimination of waste by placenta. Animation shows the process of labor and birth. High School. McGraw-Hill Text Films, 1221 Avenue of the Americas, New York, N.Y. 10009.

Girl to Woman; color; 18 minutes. Shows the stages of the female maturation process, the variations in body structure, and the comparative differences in growth rate of boys of comparable age. Junior High. Churchill Films, 662 North Robertson Blvd., Los Angeles, Calif. 90069.

Human Beginnings; color; 22 minutes. Portrays what a group of young children believe about the origin of human life as expressed in their own drawings. Following this, a teacher answers questions and one of the children explains how his parents prepared him for the coming of a new baby into the family. Good discussion film. For grades 5 to 7. Seminar Films, 480 Lexington Ave., New York, N.Y. 10017.

Human Growth; color; 20 minutes. Class views and discusses animated film which traces process of reproduction. For grades 6 to 9. E. C. Brown Trust, 3170 S.W. 87th Ave., Portland, Ore. 97225.

Human Heredity; color; 18 minutes. Presents through animation and live action the facts about sex determination, sex role, multiple births, human heredity, and the influences affecting individual behavior and attitudes. E. C. Brown Trust, 3170 S.W. 87th Ave., Portland, Ore. 97225.

Human Reproduction; color; 23 minutes. Revision of the former "Human Reproduction" film produced in 1948. The reproductive process from conception to birth is presented by drawings and animation. Junior and Senior High School. McGraw-Hill; also American Medical Association, Medical Film Library, 535 North Dearborn St., Chicago, Ill. 60610.

It's Wonderful Being a Girl; color; 20 minutes. Tells story of menstruation and offers guides to good health, grooming, and poise. Junior High School. Personal Products Corporation, Milltown, N.J. 08850.

Miracle of Reproduction; black and white; 15 minutes. Explains the human reproductive process by comparison with plant and animal life, using animated drawings for illustrations. For Elementary and Junior High School. Sid Davis Productions, 3826 Cochran Ave., Los Angeles, Calif. 90008.

Molly Grows Up; black and white; 15 minutes. School nurse explains menstruation at school; both parents share in Molly's growing up. For girls 9 to 16 years of age. Personal Products Corporation; Milltown, N.J. 08850.

Phoebe—Story of Premarital Pregnancy; black and white; 20 minutes. Deals with the mental and emotional reactions of Phoebe, a teen-ager, when she discovers that she is pregnant. High School. McGraw-Hill Text Films, 1221 Avenue of the Americas, New York, N.Y. 10009.

Planned Families; color; 20 minutes. Through animation and film imagery, the functions of the male and female reproductive organs, how a baby is conceived, and how it develops are illustrated. The film presents birth control as a means of bringing children into the world by choice instead of by chance. Allend' or Productions, 3449 Cahuengo Blvd., West Hollywood, Calif. 90068.

Reproduction in Animals; color; 11 minutes. Fundamental principles of reproduction in animals described with emphasis on each parent's function. For grades 5 to 7. Coronet Films, 65 East Southwater St., Chicago, Ill. 60601.

The Game; black and white; 28 minutes. Introduces the problems of relationships between young members of the opposite sex—covering both premarital sexual behavior and individual relationships between boy and girl. The theme of the film revolves around the sexual exploitation of a girl by a boy. Senior High School. McGraw-Hill Films, 1221 Avenue of the Americas, New York, N.Y. 10009.

The Story of Menstruation; color; 15 minutes. Use of animated diagrams to show the menstruation process. For grades 5 to 7. Association Films, Inc., 347 Madison Ave., New York, N.Y. 10010.

The Merry-Go-Round; black and white; 23 minutes. Presents the viewpoints on sex and sex behavior of three well-known personalities: columnist Ann Landers, psychotherapist Albert Ellis, and educator Mary Winspeer. McGraw-Hill Films, 1221 Avenue of the Americas, New York, N.Y. 10009.

World of a Girl; color; 20 minutes. Feelings and thoughts of the American girl in the process of growing up and living happily with menstruation. For grades 5 to 7. Scott Paper Co., Philadelphia, Penn. 19113.

Your Body During Adolescence; black and white; 10 minutes. Puberty, what it means and how it affects the body, is the theme of this film. Shows growth through the influences of the pituitary and sex glands; brings about the changes that turn a boy into a man and a girl into a woman. For grades 4 to 10. McGraw-Hill Text Films, 1221 Avenue of the Americas, New York, N.Y. 10009.

FILMSTRIPS

About Sex and Growing Up; color; sound. Four filmstrips running about 10 minutes each. Develops positive feelings and stimulates curiosity about puberty. Describes the emotional and physical changes experienced by boys and girls as they enter puberty. Junior and Senior High School. Cathedral Films, Inc., 2921 W. Alameda Ave., Burbank, Calif. 91505.

Developing Basic Values; color; sound. Set of four filmstrips with records which emphasize the development of moral and ethical values in everyday settings. For grades 5 to 7. Society for Visual Education, 1435 Diversey St., Chicago, Ill. 60614.

Family Relationships and Young Teens; color; sound. Set of four filmstrips with records emphasizing the importance of good family relations:
Learning to Understand Parents (46 frames).
Living with Brothers and Sisters (47 frames).
Helping at Home (41 frames).
Teenage Allowances (45 frames).
For grades 5 to 7. Society for Visual Education, 1435 Diversey St., Chicago, Ill. 60614.

Family Life and Sex Education; color; sound. The following sound filmstrips are for use in family life, home economics, and health and sex education courses:
Values for Teenagers: The Choice Is Yours
I Never Looked at It That Way Before
Sex: A Moral Dilemma for Teenagers
The Tuned Out Generation
And They Lived Happily Ever After?
Guidance Associates, P.O. Box 5, Pleasantville, N.Y. 10570. (Teachers' guide is available.)

How Babies Are Made; color; 34 slides. Created not just to help parents, but to strengthen the parent–child relationship by enabling the basic facts of sex education to be an experience shared by father, mother, and child together. Tells the story of reproduction with accuracy, simplicity, and beauty. For ages 3 to 10. Creative Scope, Inc., 509 Fifth Ave., New York, N.Y. 10017.

SOURCES OF
INFORMATION IN
DRUG EDUCATION

RESOURCE MATERIALS FOR STUDENTS

BOOKS

Curtis, Lindsay R. *Why Not Marijuana.* Evanston, Ill.: Signal Press.
——. *LSD—Trip or Trap.* Evanston, Ill.: Signal Press.
——. *Glue Sniffing.* Evanston, Ill.: Signal Press.
——. *Let's Talk About Drugs.* Evanston, Ill.: Signal Press.
——. *Let's Talk About Goof Balls and Pep Pills.* Evanston, Ill.: Signal Press.
Drugs: Facts on Their Use and Abuse. Glenview, Ill.: Scott, Foresman and Company, 1969.
Eyerly, Jeannette. *Escape From Nowhere.* Philadelphia: J. B. Lippincott Co., 1968.
Read, Donald A. *Drugs and People.* Boston: Allyn & Bacon, Inc., 1972. (Teachers' Manual.)

SELECTED REFERENCE BOOKS FOR TEACHERS, CURRICULUM PLANNERS, AND ADULTS

Abramson, H. *The Use of LSD in Psychotherapy and Alcoholism.* Indianapolis, Ind.: The Bobbs-Merrill Co., Inc. 1967.
Adriani, J. (ed.). *Narcotics and Narcotic Antagonists.* Springfield, Ill.: Charles C Thomas, Publisher, Inc., 1964.
Agnew, D. *Undercover Agent—Narcotics.* New York: McFadden-Bartell, 1959.
Alpert, R., and S. Cohen, *LSD.* New York: New American Library, 1967.
American Council on Alcohol Problems, Inc. *The Problem: Alcohol-Narcotics, Teacher's Handbook,* 1966; 119 Constitution Ave., N.E.; Washington, D.C., 20002.
Andrews, G., and S. Vinkenoog (ed.). *The Book of Grass—An Anthology of Indian Hemp.* New York: Grove Press, 1967.
Becker, H. S. *The Outsider.* New York: The Free Press, 1963.

Beckman, H. *Dilemmas in Drug Therapy*. Philadelphia: W. B. Saunders Company, 1967.

Bloomquist, E. R., M.D. *Marijuana*. Beverly Hills, Calif.: Glencoe Press, 1968.

———. *Marijuana: The Second Trip*. Beverly Hills, Calif.: Glencoe Press, 1971.

Blum, R., et al. *The Utopiates*. New York: Atherton Press, 1964.

———. *Society and Drugs*, Vols. I & II. San Francisco: Jossey-Bass, Inc., 1969.

Brecker, Edward M. (ed.). *Licit and Illicit Drugs*. New York: Consumers Union, 1972.

Brown, T. T. *The Enigma of Drug Addiction*. Springfield, Ill.: Charles C Thomas, Publisher, 1961.

Burack, Richard. *The Handbook of Prescription Drugs*. New York: Pantheon Books, 1967.

Caldwell, A. E. *Psychopharmaca—A Bibliography of Psychopharmaca, 1952–1967*. Washington, D.C.: U.S. Government Printing Office, 1958.

Cashman, J. *The LSD Story*. Greenwich, Conn.: Fawcett Publications, 1966.

Chein, I. *The Road to H*. New York: Basic Books, 1964.

Cohen, S. *The Beyond Within: The LSD Story*. New York: Atheneum, 1964.

Cohen, Sidney. *The Drug Dilemma*. New York: McGraw-Hill Book Company, 1969.

DeBold, R. C., and F. C. Leaf (eds.). *LSD, Man and Society*. Middletown, Conn.: Wesleyan University Press, 1967.

DeRopp, R. S. *Drugs and the Mind*. New York: Grove Press, 1961.

———. *The Master Game*. New York: Delta Books, 1968.

Ebin, D. (ed.). *The Drug Experience*. New York: Grove Press, 1961.

Efron, D. H. (ed.). *Ethnopharmacologic Search for Psychoactive Drugs*. Washington, D.C.: Department of Health, Education, and Welfare, 1967.

Finch, B. *Passport to Paradise . . . ?* New York: Philosophical Library, 1960.

Gale, W. C. *Why Not Legalize Narcotics?* San Diego, Calif.: Publisher's Export, 1967.

Girdano and Girdano. *Drugs*. Reading, Mass.: Addison-Wesley Publishing Co., 1973.

Goode, Erich. *Drugs in American Society*. New York: Alfred A. Knopf, Inc., 1972.

Goldstein, R. *One in Seven: Drugs on Campus*. New York: Walker and Co., 1966.

Gorodetzky, C. W., and S. T. Christian. *What You Should Know About Drugs*. New York: Harcourt Brace Jovanovich, 1970.

Grinspoon, Lester. *Marijuana Reconsidered*. Cambridge, Mass.: Harvard University Press, 1971.

Harms, E. *Drug Addiction in Youth*. Oxford, England: Pergamon Press, 1965.

Hollander, C. (ed.). *Background Papers on Student Drug Involvement*. Washington, D.C.: United States National Student Association, 1967.

Huxley, A. *The Doors of Perception*. New York: Harper & Row, Publishers, Inc., 1954.

James, W. *On Psychical Research*. New York: The Viking Press, Inc., 1960.

Johnson, G. *The Pill Conspiracy*. Los Angeles: Sherbourne Press, 1967.

Jones, Kenneth, et al. *Drugs and Alcohol*, 2nd ed. New York: Harper & Row, Publishers, Inc., 1973.

Kalant, O. J. *The Amphetamines*. Springfield, Ill.: Charles C Thomas, 1966.

Kluver, H. *Mescal and Mechanisms of Hallucinations*. Chicago: University of Chicago Press, 1966.

Kolb, L. *Drug Addiction*. Springfield, Ill.: Charles C Thomas, 1962.

Leary, T., et al. *The Psychedelic Reader*. New Hyde Park, N.Y.: University Books, 1965.

Lewin, L. *Phantastica Narcotic and Stimulating Drugs*. New York: E. P. Dutton & Co., Inc., 1964.

Lindesmith, A. R. *The Addict and the Law*. Bloomington, Ind.: Indiana University Press, 1965.

————. *Drug Addiction: Crime or Disease?* (Interim and Final Reports of the Joint Committee of the American Bar Association and the American Medical Association of Narcotic Drugs). Bloomington, Ind.: Indiana University Press, 1961.

————. *Opiate-Addiction*. Bloomington, Ind.: Principia Press, 1947.

Livingston, R. B. *Narcotic Drug Addiction Problems*. Washington, D.C.: Department of Health, Education, and Welfare, 1960.

Louria, D. *Nightmare Drugs*. New York: Pocket Books, Inc., 1966.

Margolis, Jack S., and R. Clorfine. *A Child's Garden of Grass*. New York: Pocket Books, Inc., 1970.

Masters, R. E. L., and J. Houston. *The Varieties of Psychedelic Experience*. New York: Holt, Rinehart and Winston, Inc., 1966.

Matheson, D. W., and M. A. Davison. *The Behavioral Effects of Drugs*. New York: Holt, Rinehart and Winston, Inc., 1972.

Maurer, D. W., and V. H. Vogel. *Narcotics and Narcotic Addiction*, 3rd ed. Springfield, Ill.: Charles C Thomas, Publisher, 1967.

Mills, J. *The Panic in Needle Park*. New York: Farrar, Straus and Giroux, Inc., 1966.

Modell, W., and A. Lansing. *Drugs*. New York: Time, 1967.

Murton, T. (ed.). *Law Enforcement and Dangerous Drug Abuse*. Berkeley, Calif.: Regents of the University of California, 1966.

O'Donnell, J. A. (ed.). *Narcotic Addiction*. New York: Harper & Row, Publishers, Inc., 1966.

Pollard, J. C., L. Uhr, and E. Stern. *Drugs and Phantasy, The Effects of LSD, Psilocybin and Sernyl on College Students*. Boston: Little, Brown and Company, 1965.

Ray, Oakley S. *Drugs, Society, and Human Behavior*. St. Louis, Mo.: The C. V. Mosby Co., 1972.

Rickles, William H., M.D. *Marijuana: A Selective Bibliography 1924/1970*. Los Angeles, Calif.: BRA Publications Office, UCLA Center for the Health Services, 1971.

Roseman, B. *The Peyote Story*. Hollywood, Calif.: Wilshire Book Co., 1966.

Rosevear, J. *Pot: A Handbook of Marihuana*. New York: University Books, 1967.

Smith, H. A. (ed.). *Proceedings of the Conference on Drug Abuse*. April 6, 1966, Continuation Center, University of Mississippi, 1966.

Smith, W., and E. Olson. *The Menace of Pep Pills*. Chicago: Camerarts Publishing, 1965.

Solomon, D. *LSD: The Consciousness-Expanding Drug.* New York: G. P. Putnam's Sons, 1966.

———. *The Marihuana Papers.* Indianapolis, Ind.: The Bobbs-Merrill Co., Inc. 1966.

Stafford, P., et al. *LSD: The Problem Solving Psychedelic.* New York: Award Books, 1967.

Tart, Charles. *On Being Stoned.* Palo Alto, Calif.: Science and Behavior Books, 1971.

Taylor, N. *Narcotics: Nature's Dangerous Gifts* (rev. ed. of *Flight from Reality*). New York: Dell Publishing Company, 1966.

Uhr, L., and J. G. Miller. *Drugs and Behavior.* New York: John Wiley & Sons, Inc., 1960.

Usdin, E., and D. H. Efron. *Psychotropic Drugs and Related Compounds.* Washington, D.C.: Department of Health, Education, and Welfare, 1967.

Wakefield, D. *The Addict.* Greenwich, Conn.: Fawcett Publications, 1963.

Wilner, D. M., and G. G. Kassebaum (eds.). *Narcotics.* New York: McGraw-Hill Book Company, 1965.

Wolstenholme, G. E. W., and J. Knight (eds.). *Hashish: Its Chemistry and Pharmacology.* Boston: Little, Brown and Co., 1965.

Young, R., and J. R. Hixson. *LSD on Campus.* New York: Dell Publishing, 1966.

INFORMATION FOR CURRICULUM PLANNING IN DRUG–ABUSE EDUCATION

Alcoholism (Information Kit). Riderwood, Md.: Media Materials, Inc., 1972.

Bruno, L. *State of Washington Elementary Health Education Guide to Better Health.* State Office of Public Instruction, Olympia, Washington (1966).

Christian, F. T. *Alcohol–Narcotics Education.* A Handbook for Teachers. State Department of Education, Tallahassee, Florida (1967).

College Drug Abuse Programs. Smith, Kline and French Laboratories, National Education Association, Washington, D.C. (1967).

Drug Abuse: A Primer for Parents. National Education Association, 1201 Sixteenth St., N.W., Washington, D.C. (1968).

Drug Dependence and Abuse: A Selected Bibliography. National Clearinghouse for Drug Abuse Information, Washington, D.C., 1971.

Drug Education: A Bibliography of Available Inexpensive Materials. Metuchen, N.J.: Scarecrow Press, 1972.

Drugs: Road to Nowhere. Drug Abuse Committee; State Department of Education, 182 Tremont St., Boston (1968).

Girdano and Girdano, *Drug Education: Content and Methods.* Reading, Mass.: Addison-Wesley Publishing Co., 1972.

Hansen, C. F. "Health and Family Life Education, Junior High Schools," *Curriculum Resource Bulletin for Jr. High Schools.* Washington, D.C. (1964).

———. "A One-Year Course for Grade Eight Pupils," *Curriculum Resource Bulletin for Jr. High Schools.* Washington, D.C. (1962).

Health Curriculum Materials for Grades 4, 5, 6, Strand II, Sociological Health Problems, Alcohol-Drugs-Smoking, The University of the State of New York/The State Education Department, New York (1967).

Kitzinger, A., and P. J. Hill. *Drug Abuse—A Source Book and Guide for Teachers.* California State Department of Education; California (1967).

Levy, M. R. (ed.). *Drug Abuse—A Reference for Teachers,* New Jersey State Department of Education (1967).

McComb, P. (ed.). *A Guide for Instruction in Health and Safety, Grades 7–12.* State of Minnesota, Department of Education, Minnesota (1965).

National Coordinating Council on Drug Abuse Education and Information. *Directory.* The Council, P.O. Box 19400, Washington, D.C. (1969).

Narcotic and Dangerous Drug Abuse—Resource for Teachers. Joseph S. Langan, Supervisor of Health Education; Los Angeles City Schools, Los Angeles, Calif. (1967).

Narcotics Education Program. Sidney B. Birnback; H. K. Simon Co., Hastings-on-Hudson, N.Y. Teachers' Manual and Student Guide (1967).

Parris, W. A. *Drugs, Marihuana and LSD.* Department of Health, Physical Education, Athletics and Safety, Washington, D.C. (1967).

School Health Education Study. *Health Education—A Conceptual Approach to Curriculum Design.* Minnesota Mining and Manufacturing Company, St. Paul, Minn. (1967).

Spinazzola, A. *Drug Abuse—A Health Teacher's Manual.* East Brunswick High School, East Brunswick, N.J.

Supplementary Information for Teachers on the Use, Misuse, and Abuse of Drugs. The University of the State of New York/The State Education Department, Curriculum Development Center, Albany, N.Y. (1967).

Teaching About Drugs. Kent, Ohio, American School Health Association, n.d.

PAMPHLETS

American Association of Health, Physical Education, and Recreation, Department of National Education Association, 1201 Sixteenth Street, N.W., Washington, D.C. 20036.
> *Drug Abuse: A Primer for Parents*

American Social Health Association, 1740 Broadway, New York, N.Y. 10019.
> *The Life Cycle of the Narcotic Addict and of Addiction*
> *Drug Abuse: A Call for Action*
> *The Underground Bird*
> *The Use of Drugs by Jazz Musicians*
> *A Guide to Some Drugs Which Are Subject to Abuse*

Food and Drug Administration; U.S. Department of Health, Education, and Welfare, U.S. Government Printing Office, Washington, D.C. 20402.
> *How Safe Are Drugs?* (No. 44)
> *The Use and Misuse of Drugs* (No. 46)

Bureau of Narcotics; U.S. Treasury Department; Washington, D.C. 20226.
> *Living Death—The Truth About Drug Addiction*
> *The Federal Narcotics Laws*

Superintendent of Documents; U.S. Government Printing Office; Washington, D.C. 20402.

> *LSD: Some Questions and Answers*
> *Marihuana: Some Questions and Answers*
> *Narcotics: Some Questions and Answers*
> *Task Force Report: Narcotics and Drug Abuse*
> *Prevention and Control of Narcotic Addiction*
> *Traffic in Opium and Other Dangerous Drugs*

U.S. Bureau of Narcotics and Dangerous Drugs, Washington, D.C.

> *Terms & Symptoms of Drug Abuse Law Enforcement*

FILMS ON DRUG—ABUSE EDUCATION [1]

Since there is a difference of opinion on the effectiveness of the various films listed, this listing does not constitute an endorsement of any film by the National Coordinating Council. In fact, the Council recommends that anyone planning on using any film on drug abuse should obtain a print and review it prior to its intended use. The names and addresses of the producers and/or distributors are included in this listing to provide a source of information on rental and purchases. In conjunction with the film list we wish to call your attention to other film reviews that are available. One such review of films on drug-abuse education appears in the *School Health Education Study Teacher–Student Resources.* A copy of this publication may be obtained from the 3M Company, Visual Products Division, 3M Center, St. Paul, Minn., 55101. A second review of films appears in a series of articles by David O. Weber, Film Consultant, in the August and September, 1968, issues of *California Health.* A third annotated list of films appears in *Drug Abuse: Escape to Nowhere—A Guide for Educators,* published by Smith, Kline & French Laboratories in cooperation with the American Association for Health, Physical Education, and Recreation, a department of the National Education Association.

Bennies and Goofballs (National Medical Audiovisual Center, Chamblee, Ga. 30005). A special report by the Food and Drug Administration on abuse of amphetamines and barbiturates. (20 minutes)

Beyond LSD (Film Associates, 11559 Santa Monica Boulevard, Los Angeles, Calif. 90025). Describes the communication gap between two generations—teen-agers and young adults on one hand and the generation of those over thirty. The teenagers' use of LSD and other drugs is only one of the symptoms of this communication gap. In this film, a group of parents seek help in order to understand their relationships with their teenagers. (25 minutes)

Drug Addiction (Encyclopaedia Britannica Films, 38 West 32nd Street, New York, New York 10017). A film provided by the Encyclopaedia Britannica Educational Corporation. New York City. (22 minutes)

---

[1] Reprinted by permission of National Coordinating Council on Drug Abuse Education and Information, P.O. Box 19400, Washington, D.C. 20036.

Drugs and the Nervous System (Churchill Films, 662 North Robertson Boulevard, Los Angeles, Calif. 90069). The film explains how drugs affect many different parts of the body by working indirectly on the nervous system. It is designed to reach children at an age before many of them, it is hoped, have begun to experiment with drugs. (18 minutes)

False Friends (Sound Services, Limited, 269 Kingston Road, Merton Park, London, S.W. 19, England). Drug dependence is the subject of this color cartoon produced for WHO in London by G. Bucklandsmith of Interfilm in association with the Film Producer's Guild. The story is told in words and pictures. (10 minutes)

Fight or Flight (International Association of Chiefs of Police, 1319 18th Street, N.W., Washington, D.C. 20036). Film produced by IACP in cooperation with the federal Bureau of Narcotics on the uses of marijuana, LSD and "pills." (16 minutes)

Hide and Seek (Center for Mass Communication of Columbia University Press, 440 West 110th Street, New York, New York 10025). This is a boy's personal story of his life as an addict.

Hooked (Churchill Films, 662 N. Robertson Boulevard, Los Angeles, Calif. 90059). This is a description of the experience of drug addiction told in the words of young (age 18–25) former addicts. They talk about what impelled them to become addicted, how it affected their relationship with others and their perception of themselves and how they regard the experience in retrospect. (20 minutes)

LSD (Audiovisual Branch, United States Navy, Pentagon, Washington, D.C. 20350). A lecture-type film developed by the Surgeon General's Office, U.S. Navy. (28 minutes)

LSD-25 (Professional Arts, Inc., P.O. Box 8484, Universal City, Calif. 91608). *LSD-25* is a documentary designed to convey the facts about LSD to the growing audiences concerned about the drug scene and its impact upon youth. (27 minutes)

LSD: Insight or Insanity (Bailey Films, 6509 De Longpre Avenue, Hollywood, Calif. 90028). This film documents the dangers in the unsupervised use of LSD, explains what medical science knows of the physiologic actions of LSD and counteracts a few of the erroneous claims made for the use of LSD. (26 minutes)

LSD Trip—or Trap! (Sid Davis Productions, 2429 Ocean Boulevard, Santa Monica, Calif. 90405). Two teen-age boys, Bob and Chuck, both 17, have many interests in common and enjoy each other's company. When another boy, Frank, tries to introduce them to LSD, they disagree. While Chuck lets himself be persuaded to join Frank's acidheads, Bob decides to find out the truth about the notorious drug for himself. What he learns is disturbing to him and he realizes that he must warn his friend, who by now is firmly ensconced with Frank's crowd and already has taken several "trips." Bob puts his findings and feelings in a letter but on his way to mail it, Bob comes upon a grisly accident. Chuck has had a shattering recurrence of the LSD effects while driving, lost control of his car and rammed head-on into another car. Chuck is dead. (26 minutes)

Marijuana (Bailey Films, 6509 De Longpre Avenue, Hollywood, Calif. 90028). A pot party is interrupted by police . . . screaming, testing teenagers are caught and they speak out. A teenager idol (Sonny Bono) provokes the teenagers to think for themselves. (34 minutes)

Mind Benders (National Medical Audiovisual Center, Chamblee, Ga. 30005). Mind benders explores the potential therapeutic uses and the known hazards of LSD and other hallucinogens as well as some of the motivations of abusers. Medical authorities and users of the drugs appear in the FDA documentary. (26 minutes)

Narcotics: A Challenge to Teachers (The Narcotic Educational Foundation of America, 5055 Sunset Boulevard, Los Angeles, Calif. 90027). Narrated by Lowell Thomas, film provides basic information about narcotics and other drugs of abuse. The film challenges educators to combat student drug abuse by presenting young people with the facts about drug experimentation. (24 minutes)

Narcotics: Pit of Despair (Film Distributors International, 2223 S. Olive, Los Angeles, Calif. 90007). Designed to teach youngsters the perils of narcotics addiction. It shows how inexperienced young people are led to seek refuge in tobacco, alcohol, barbiturates. Then malignant companions, masquerading as true friends, introduce marijuana and opiates. (25 minutes)

Narcotics—The Inside Story (Charles Cahill and Associates, Inc., P.O. Box 3220, Hollywood, Calif. 90028). This film is designed to acquaint junior and senior high school students with the positive applications of narcotics and drugs when administered by doctors for medical purposes. The inside story is that experimenting with drugs and narcotics can seriously—even permanently—upset the central nervous system. (12 minutes)

Narcotics—Why Not? (Charles Cahill and Associates, Inc., P.O. Box 3220, Hollywood, Calif. 90028). Sixteen male and female residents of the California Rehabilitation Center relate how they were introduced to pills, glue, marijuana, and heroin—what it was like—and the hopes they hold for the future. (15 minutes)

Seduction of the Innocent (Sid Davis Productions, 2429 Ocean Park Boulevard, Santa Monica, Calif. 90405). A short film dealing with an ever-increasing menace to our youth. It is a story of two young people, a boy and a girl, who through a need to belong and a desire to go along with the group and its youthful zest to try something new, begin a one-way journey to self-destruction. (10 minutes)

The Addicted (Association Films, Inc., 600 Grand Avenue, Ridgefield, N.J. 07657). A film in two parts on drug addiction. (50 minutes)

The Agents of Drug Abuse (Penelope Films, Inc., 1440 Clay Street, San Francisco, Calif. 94109). A review of all drugs of abuse, discussing levels of abuse, effects, legal consequences and penalties pertaining to the various agents of drug abuse. (38 minutes)

The Dangerous Drugs (The Narcotic Educational Foundation of America, 5055 Sunset Boulevard, Los Angeles, Calif. 90027). This film portrays the dangers from abuse of amphetamine and barbiturate drugs—accidents, physical dependence, ruined health, even death. A candid account by a female abuser underscores the points made in the preceding vignettes. The potential relationship of heroin abuse and abuse of non-narcotic drugs is noted. (22 minutes)

The Losers (Carousel Films, Inc., 1501 Broadway, New York, N.Y. 10036). Produced and originally presented by WCBS-TV, New York, examines the prevalence of experimentation and the habitual use of chemical and drugs among youngsters from 12–21 years old. (31 minutes)

The Riddle (Public Affairs, Office of Economic Opportunity, 1200 19th Street, N.W., Washington, D.C. 20506). The camera follows actual glue-sniffers, cough medicine drinkers, and heroin addicts into the alleys, tenements and physicians' offices where their candid comments and bewildered responses clearly show the hopelessness of their lives. By contrast, an account of a youth who resists the drug abuse crowd to land a job strikes a hopeful note. (28 minutes)

The Seekers (State of New York Narcotic Addiction Control Commission, Albany, N.Y. 12203). A half-hour documentary on drug abuse prepared by the New York State Narcotic Addiction Control Commission. (30 minutes)

Trip to Where (Produced by DuArt Films Labs, 145 West 55th Street, New York, New York 10019; available from Naval District, Washington, D.C., Building 200, Navy Yard Annex, U.S. Navy, Washington, D.C. 20390). Film presents dangers of use and abuse of three basic groups of drugs: amphetamines, barbiturates and hallucinogens—including marijuana and emphasizing LSD. Points out psychological and physical effects, especially in relation to potentially dangerous effects on individual performance in critical operations. (49 minutes)

Way Out (Valley Forge Films, Inc., Chester Springs, Pa. 19425). A theatrical trip into the world of drug addiction. The principal roles are played by eight real life addicts who have kicked the heroin habit. (105 minutes)

AUDIO-VISUAL PROGRAMS

DCA Educational Products. Two sets of colored transparencies developed in consultation with the Food and Drug Administration by DCA Educational Products, Inc., 4865 Stenton Ave., Philadelphia, Pa. 19144. The first set consists of 22 units on, "How Safe Are Our Drugs," and the second series, 20 units on, "The Use and Misuse of Drugs." Complete transparency set also available.

Lockheed Missiles and Space Company. A 15-hour course of instruction aimed at junior and senior high school students entitled, "Drug Decision," consisting of a three-hour movie-animation segment produced by Warner Brothers; 300-page student response and decision manual; five-hour teacher preparation and data file. Price on request from Lockheed Information Systems, Box 504, Sunnyvale, Calif. 94088.

Raytheon Learning Systems Company. Set of ten filmstrips on drugs, each with record, teachers guide, and pad of 50 score sheets for student participation. Series covers: "Barbiturates and Amphetamines," "Marijuana," "LSD," 'Narcotics," and "Teenagers and Drugs." Complete drug set available from Raytheon Learning Systems Company, 475 South Dean Street, Englewood, N.J. 07631.

School Health Education Study (3M Company). A unified and comprehensive health education program developed by the School Health Education

Study, 1507 M Street, N.R., Room 800, Washington, D.C. 20005 and marketed by 3M Company, Box 3100, 3M Center, St. Paul, Minn. 55101. Set of four books in four grade levels from kindergarten through 12th grades, plus teacher-student resource on, "Use of Substances That Modify Mood and Behavior," from 3M Education Press, Box 3344, St. Paul, Minn. 55101. Four sets of color transparencies, each containing 20 visuals for Level 1 (Kindergarten through 3rd grades); four sets for Level 2 (4th through 6th grades); five sets for Level 3 (7th through 9th grades), and six sets for Level 4 (10th through 12th grades).

Texas Alcohol Narcotics Education, Inc. Film strip with 33⅓ rpm record and booklet on each of five subjects: "Alcohol: Fun or Folly"; "Smoking . . . or Health"; "Glue Sniffing: Big Trouble in a Tube"; "LSD: Trip or Trap," and "Why Not Marijuana." Authored by Lindsay R. Curtis, M.D., for the Texas Alcohol Narcotics Education, Inc., 2814 Oak Lawn Avenue, Dallas, Tex. 75219.

ADDITIONAL SOURCES

The following agencies are excellent sources of continuing, up-to-date information on drugs and drug abuse.

BUREAU OF NARCOTICS
UNITED STATES TREASURY DEPARTMENT
WASHINGTON, D.C.

DISTRICT OFFICES

DISTRICT	TERRITORY	HEADQUARTERS
1	Maine, New Hampshire, Vermont, Rhode Island, Massachusetts and Connecticut	1425 Post Office and Courthouse Building Boston, Massachusetts 02109
2	New York State and the Newark District of New Jersey	90 Church Street, Suite 605 New York, New York 10007
3	Pennsylvania, Delaware and Camden District of New Jersey	605 U.S. Custom House Philadelphia, Pennsylvania 19106
4	Maryland, District of Columbia, North Carolina, Virginia and West Virginia	103 South Gay Street Room 301 Baltimore, Maryland 21202
5	Georgia, Florida, Alabama, South Carolina and Tennessee	1056 Federal Office Building Atlanta, Georgia 30303
6	Michigan, Kentucky and Ohio	602 Federal Building Detroit, Michigan 48226
7	Illinois, Indiana and Wisconsin	1836 U.S. Courthouse and Federal Office Building Chicago, Illinois 60604
8	Texas, Louisiana and Mississippi	1114 Commerce Street Dallas, Texas 75202
9	Missouri, Kansas, Arkansas and Oklahoma	1502 Federal Office Building Kansas City, Missouri 64106
10	Minnesota, Iowa, Nebraska, North Dakota and South Dakota	402 Federal Building Minneapolis, Minnesota 55401
11	Colorado, Utah, Wyoming and New Mexico	106 U.S. Custom House Denver, Colorado 80202
12	California, Nevada and Arizona	450 Golden Gate Avenue San Francisco, California 94102
13	Washington, Oregon, Idaho, Montana, Alaska and Hawaii	311 U.S. Courthouse Seattle, Washington 98104

BUREAU OF DRUG ABUSE CONTROL
FOOD & DRUG ADMINISTRATION
CRYSTAL PLAZA BUILDING No. 6
2121 JEFFERSON DAVIS HIGHWAY
ARLINGTON, VIRGINIA 22202

Atlanta Field Office
1831 Peachtree Road, N.E.
Atlanta, Georgia 30309
404–526-3111
  Resident Offices:
  Columbia, South Carolina
  Jackson, Mississippi
  Miami, Florida
  Nashville, Tennessee

Baltimore Field Office
401 Water Street
Baltimore, Maryland 21202
301–962-4800
  Resident Offices:
  Greensboro, North Carolina
  Washington, D.C.

Boston Field Office
John F. Kennedy Federal Building
Room E-311
Boston, Massachusetts 02203
617–223-6666
  Resident Office:
  Hartford, Connecticut

Chicago Field Office
Engineering Building, Suite 1700
205 West Wacker Drive
Chicago, Illinois 60606
312–828-5850
  Resident Offices:
  Cincinnati, Ohio
  Cleveland, Ohio
  Detroit, Michigan
  Indianapolis, Indiana

Dallas Field Office
1114 Commerce Street
Dallas, Texas 75202
214–749-3631

  Resident Offices:
  Albuquerque, New Mexico
  New Orleans, Louisiana
  San Antonio, Texas

Denver Field Office
New Custom House
721 19th Street
Denver, Colorado 80202
303–297-4291
  Resident Office:
  Salt Lake City, Utah

Kansas City Field Office
U.S. Courthouse, Room 225
811 Grand Avenue
Kansas City, Missouri 64106
816–374-5604
  Resident Offices:
  Minneapolis, Minnesota
  St. Louis, Missouri

Los Angeles Field Office
Petroleum Building
714 West Olympic Boulevard
Suite 1010
Los Angeles, California 90015
213–688-2650
  Resident Offices:
  San Diego, California
  San Francisco, California
  Seattle, Washington

New York Field Office
201 Varick Street
Room 1051-A
New York, New York 10014
212–620-3334
  Resident Offices:
  Buffalo, New York
  Philadelphia, Pennsylvania
  Pittsburgh, Pennsylvania

NATIONAL INSTITUTE OF MENTAL HEALTH
BARLOW BUILDING, CHEVY CHASE, MD. 20015

Region I, Boston, Mass.
John F. Kennedy Federal Building
Boston, Mass. 02203
617–223-6824
　Connecticut, Maine, Massachusetts,
　New Hampshire, Rhode Island,
　Vermont

Region II, New York, N.Y.
Room 1200, 42 Broadway
New York, N.Y. 10004
212–264-2567
　Delaware, New Jersey, New York,
　Pennsylvania

Region III, Charlottesville, Va.
200 Seventh Street NE.
Charlottesville, Va. 22901
703–296-5171, Extension 278/253/420
　District of Columbia, Kentucky,
　Maryland, Puerto Rico, North
　Carolina, Virgin Islands, Virginia,
　West Virginia

Region IV, Atlanta, Ga.
Room 404, 50 Seventh Street NE.
Atlanta, Ga. 30323
404–526-5231
　Alabama, Florida, Georgia, Mississippi,
　South Carolina, Tennessee

Region V, Chicago, Ill.
Room 712, New Post Office Building
433 West Van Buren Street
Chicago, Ill. 60607

312–828-5228
　Illinois, Indiana, Michigan, Ohio,
　Wisconsin

Region VI, Kansas City, Mo.
601 East 12th Street
Kansas City, Mo. 64106
816–374-3791
　Iowa, Kansas, Minnesota, Missouri,
　Nebraska, North Dakota, South Dakota

Region VII, Dallas, Tex.
1114 Commerce Street
Dallas, Tex. 75202
214–749-3426
　Arkansas, Louisiana, New Mexico,
　Oklahoma, Texas

Region VIII, Denver, Colo.
Room 9017, Federal Office Building
19th and Stout Streets
Denver, Colo. 80202
303–297-3177
　Colorado, Idaho, Montana, Utah,
　Wyoming

Region IX, San Francisco, Calif.
Federal Office Building
50 Fulton Street
San Francisco, Calif. 94102
415–556-2215
　Alaska, Arizona, California, Guam,
　Hawaii, Nevada, Oregon, Washington,
　American Samoa, Wake Island

Index